YHWH Is There

YHWH Is There

Ezekiel's Temple Vision as a Type

Drew N. Grumbles

WIPF & STOCK · Eugene, Oregon

YHWH IS THERE
Ezekiel's Temple Vision as a Type

Copyright © 2021 Drew N. Grumbles. All rights reserved. Except for brief quotations in critical publications or reviews, no part of this book may be reproduced in any manner without prior written permission from the publisher. Write: Permissions, Wipf and Stock Publishers, 199 W. 8th Ave., Suite 3, Eugene, OR 97401.

Wipf & Stock
An Imprint of Wipf and Stock Publishers
199 W. 8th Ave., Suite 3
Eugene, OR 97401

www.wipfandstock.com

PAPERBACK ISBN: 978-1-6667-0805-9
HARDCOVER ISBN: 978-1-6667-0806-6
EBOOK ISBN: 978-1-6667-0807-3

08/03/21

Scripture quotations marked NASB are taken from the New American Standard Bible, copyright © The Lockman Foundation 1960, 1962, 1963, 1968, 1971, 1972, 1973, 1975, 1977, 1988, 1995. Used by permission.

Scripture quotations marked NIV are taken from the Holy Bible, New International Version®, NIV®, copyright © 1973, 1978, 1984, 2011 by Biblica, Inc®. Used by permission. All rights reserved worldwide.

Scripture quotations marked ESV are taken from The Holy Bible, English Standard Version®, copyright © 2001 by Crossway Bibles, a publishing ministry of Good News Publishers. Used by permission. All rights reserved.

Unless otherwise noted, quotations from the Masoretic Text are taken from the *Biblia Hebraica Stuttgartensia*.

Unless otherwise noted, quotations from the Greek New Testament are taken from the Nestle-Aland Greek New Testament, 28th edition.

Unless otherwise noted, quotations from the Septuagint are taken from *Rahlfs's Septuaginta*.

To Helen, Owen, and Clara,
for all your love and encouragement.

Psalm 128:3–4

O Christ, He is the fountain,
The deep, sweet well of love!
The streams on earth I've tasted,
More deep I'll drink above:
There to an ocean fullness
His mercy doth expand,
And glory, glory dwelleth
In Immanuel's land.

—ANNE ROSS COUSIN,
"THE SANDS OF TIME ARE SINKING"

Contents

Abbreviations | ix
Introduction | xi

1. Ezekiel's Temple, Typology, and Thesis | 1
    Introduction | 1
    Views on the Temple in Ezekiel 40–48 | 1
    The Method of Typology | 15
    Three Additional Criteria in the Old Testament | 23
    Summary: Old Testament Criteria for Types | 33
    Thesis: Ezekiel 40–48 as Typology | 34

2. Evidence for a Type in Ezekiel's Temple Vision, Part I | 38
    Introduction | 38
    The Context of the Book of Ezekiel | 39
    Summary | 53

3. Evidence for a Type in Ezekiel's Temple Vision, Part II | 54
    Ezekiel 40:1–4 | 54
    Ezekiel 43:1–12 | 69
    Ezekiel 47:1–12 | 88
    Ezekiel 48:35 | 99
    Conclusion | 108

4. Evidence for a Type in Ezekiel's Temple Vision, Part III | 110
    Introduction | 110
    The Temple Building | 111
    Leadership in the New Society | 133
    Legislation: Furniture, Sacrifices, and Land | 155
    Conclusion: Legislation, Sacrifices, Land | 174

5. Ezekiel's Temple Vision in the New Testament | 176
    Introduction | 176
    The Gospel of John: Ezekiel's Temple Is a Type of Jesus | 178
    Revelation 21–22: Ezekiel's Temple Is a Type of the New Heavens and New Earth | 200
    Conclusion: Ezekiel 40–48 Typology in the New Testament | 231

6. Summary and Conclusion | 234
    Summary | 234
    Implications of the Study | 235
    Future Research | 238
    Conclusion | 240

Bibliography | 243

Abbreviations

Reference Works

ABD — *Anchor Bible Dictionary*, edited by David N. Freedman (New York: Doubleday, 1992)

BDB — *Hebrew-Aramaic and English Lexicon of the Old Testament*, edited by Francis Brown, S. R. Driver, and Charles Briggs (London: Oxford University Press, 1979)

DEJ — *Dictionary of Early Judaism*, edited by John J. Collins and Daniel Harlow (Grand Rapids: Eerdmans, 2010)

DJG — *Dictionary of Jesus and the Gospels*, edited by Joel B. Green, Jeannine K. Brown, and Nicholas Perrin (Downers Grove, IL: IVP Academic, 2013)

DOTP — *Dictionary of the Old Testament: Prophets*, edited by Mark Boda and J. Gordon McConville (Downers Grove, IL: Intervarsity, 2012)

DTIB — *Dictionary for the Theological Interpretation of the Bible*, edited by Kevin J. Vanhoozer (Grand Rapids: Baker, 2005)

GKC — *Gesenius's Hebrew Grammar*, by Wilhelm Gesenius, edited by E. Kautzsche and A. E. Cowley, translated by G. W. Collins (Oxford: Clarendon, 1910)

HAL — *Hebräisches und Aramäisches Lexikon Zum Alten Testament*, by Ludwig Koehler and Walter Baumgartner, edited by B. Hartmann, P. Reymond, and J. J. Stamm (Leiden: Brill, 1974)

HALOT	*The Hebrew and Aramaic Lexicon of the Old Testament*, by Ludwig Koehler and Walter Baumgartner, revised by Walter Baumgartner and Johann Jakob Stamm, translated and edited under the supervision of M. E. J. Richardson, vol. 3 (Leiden: Brill, 1996)
Louw-Nida	*Louw-Nida Greek-English Lexicon of the New Testament Based on Semantic Domains*, edited by J. P. Louw and E. A. Nida, 2nd ed (New York: United Bible Societies, 1989)
NDBT	*New Dictionary of Biblical Theology*, edited by T. Desmond Alexander et al. (Downers Grove, IL: IVP Academic, 2000)
TDNT	*Theological Dictionary of the New Testament*, edited by Gerhard Kittel and Gerhard Friedrich, vol. 8 (Grand Rapids: Eerdmans, 1979)
TWOT	*Theological Wordbook of the Old Testament*, edited by R. Laird Harris, Gleason L. Archer, and Bruce K. Waltke, vol. 1 (Chicago: Moody, 1980)

Bible Versions

CSB	Christian Standard Bible
HCSB	Holman Christian Standard Bible
ESV	English Standard Version
KJV	King James Version
LXX	The Septuagint, the Greek Translation of the OT
MT	Masoretic Text of the Hebrew Bible
NASB	New American Standard Bible
NET	New English Translation
NIV	New International Version
NRSV	New Revised Standard Version
NT	The New Testament of the Christian Scriptures
OT	The Old Testament of the Christian Scriptures
RSV	Revised Standard Version

Introduction

THE BOOK OF EZEKIEL is a notoriously difficult book to interpret. Evidence for the claim extends to ages long past. One rabbi wrote a story of a child who discovered the meaning of the word חַשְׁמַל in Ezek 1:27. As soon as the insight came to the boy, fire came out of the word on the page and burned him up.[1] Moreover, Jerome told of how the Jews would not let men study the book until they turned thirty years old, seeing as the book was "involved in so great obscurity . . ."[2] Interpreters find even greater difficulty with the final section, Ezekiel's temple vision in Ezek 40–48. Again, the challenge is not new. Rabbi Hananiah ben Hezekiah made it his mission to harmonize Ezekiel's legislation with Mosaic *torah*. He found a solution, but only after burning three hundred barrels of oil in nighttime study.[3] Even the canon of Scripture itself attests to the difficulty of interpretation and application. After all, when the Israelites returned from exile, they did not construct the new temple Ezekiel envisioned, and the older priests wept at the relative lack of glory in the second temple (Ezra 3:12). The Chronicler also neglected to mention Ezekiel's vision. In addition, the postexilic prophetic texts are completely silent regarding the matter. The writer of Haggai lamented that the glory of YHWH was absent in the temple (Hag 2:9), yet did not propose the enactment of Ezekiel's prophecy as the solution. As Greenberg says, "Wherever Ezekiel's program can be checked against subsequent events it proves to have had no effect. The return and resettlement of post-exilic times had nothing in common with Ezekiel's vision . . ."[4] Perhaps there was already

---

1. *B. Hag.* 13a, cited in Duguid, *Ezekiel*, 17.
2. Jerome, *Ep. Ad Paulinam* 8, cited in Duguid, *Ezekiel*, 17.
3. *B. Shabb.* 13b, cited in Duguid, *Ezekiel*, 18.
4. Greenberg, "Ezekiel's Program of Restoration," 208.

an understanding, even after the regathering under Cyrus, that Israel was not to build this temple physically.

As time passed, some began to interpret the vision in a more spiritual sense. The Qumran community provides evidence of this, as they interpreted Ezek 40–48 as a description of the heavenly temple. The members of the Qumran community did not see Ezek 40–48 as the true temple they should build on earth.[5] Instead, they had their own temple plan in the *Temple Scroll* (11QT), with similarities and differences to Ezekiel's temple.[6] Beyond the *Temple Scroll*, the *Songs of Sabbath Sacrifice* (4Q400–407) uses terminology from Ezek 40–48 to describe a heavenly temple.[7] Soon after, the New Testament (NT) authors also treated the vision in a more spiritual sense, making allusions to the text in the Gospel of John, regarding fulfillment in Jesus Christ,[8] and the book of Revelation, describing the new heavens and new earth.[9]

How, then, should one interpret Ezek 40–48? Is this text describing a physical building intended for construction, or is this intended to be symbolic in some sense? If the latter, how does the interpreter properly relate Ezekiel's vision to the fuller revelation of the NT? The question also relates to the larger issue of the relevance of the Old Testament (OT) today, a question recently raised in a book claiming that understanding and use of the OT is dying.[10] One of the main diseases, according to the author, is the problem of relating the OT and NT.[11] As Gunneweg states, "Indeed, it would be no exaggeration to understand the hermeneutical problem of the Old Testament as *the* problem of Christian theology . . . No more fundamental question can be posed in all theology . . ."[12] This study aims to work for a cure to the disease by at least treating one cause, the difficulty of relating Ezek 40–48 to the NT.

---

5. Martinez, "L'interprétation de la Torah," 441–52.
6. Vermes, *Dead Sea Scrolls*, 191–220.
7. Vermes, *Dead Sea Scrolls*, 329–39. For discussion see Davila, "Macrocosmic Temple," 1–19. The *Florilegium* also speaks of the temple as a "sanctuary of men," indicating their conception of a non-physical temple (4Q174; Vermes, *Dead Sea Scrolls*, 525).
8. Peterson, *John's Use of Ezekiel*, 187–200.
9. Block, *Ezekiel 25–48*, 502–3.
10. Strawn, *Old Testament Is Dying*.
11. Strawn, *Old Testament Is Dying*, 14.
12. Quoted in Strawn, *Old Testament Is Dying*, xxiii.

Ezekiel 40–48 and Biblical Theology

The difficulty in interpretation may explain why many scholars bypass, or at least give little treatment to, the text of Ezek 40–48 when constructing a biblical theology. Perhaps many agree with José Luis Sicre, who calls the legal material in Ezek 40–48 "aburridísimo."[13] Scholars have not extensively pursued the question of Ezekiel's temple vision and its connection to the larger canon, whether in works of OT theology in general, or volumes specifically about temple theology. This section will examine Old Testament theology and temple theology works by looking at the state of biblical theology scholarship thematically.

Three themes in OT theology lend themselves to a study of Ezek 40–48, but such discussion is notably lacking. First, numerous scholars examine the concept of covenant in OT theology. Though some of these authors mention the new "covenant of peace" described in Ezek 34–37, they do not connect it very extensively with Ezek 40–48.[14] Moreover, although scholars also explain the importance of the temple in regards to covenant, they barely discuss Ezekiel's temple.[15] Second, canonical biblical theology, popularized by Childs, largely ignores this section.[16] The canon contains links between Ezek 40–48 and the NT, yet discussions of the temple in canonical theologies provide little mention of Ezek 40–48.[17] Third, numerous works of Old Testament theology show how the temple plays an important role. Yet even where scholars deem the temple significant, Ezekiel's temple vision is almost entirely neglected.[18]

---

13. Sicre, *Introducción Al Profetismo Bíblico*, 293. Author's translation, "extremely boring."

14. Kaiser, *Toward an Old Testament Theology*, 237–44; Dumbrell, *Covenant and Creation*, 185–90; Nicholson, *God and His People*, 92, 108; Gentry and Wellum, *Kingdom Through Covenant*, 470–81.

15. Eichrodt, *Theology of the Old Testament*; Kaiser, *Toward an Old Testament Theology*, 243–44; Dumbrell, *Covenant and Creation*, 188–89; Gentry and Wellum, *Kingdom Through Covenant*, 481.

16. Childs, *Old Testament Theology*.

17. Childs, *Old Testament Theology*, 165; House, *Old Testament Theology*, 340–45; Hamilton, *Salvation through Judgment*, loc. 4892–95; Dempster, *Dominion and Dynasty*, 171–72; Rendtorff, *Canonical Hebrew Bible*, 257–59.

18. The closest "temple-centered OT theology," aside from Beale's work, is Alexander, *From Eden to the New Jerusalem*. See the comments on Alexander's work below. Other works deal with the temple, such as Sweeney, *Tanak*, 338–40; Merrill, *Everlasting Dominion*, 545–46; Goldingay, *Old Testament Theology*, 1:398–401.

A salutary development in scholarship concerns the theological importance of the temple in the OT.[19] Yet this advance in discussion regarding the theology of the temple adds relatively little to the treatment of Ezek 40–48. As with OT theology in general, one can also group scholarship on temple theology thematically. First, several scholars argue for the importance of the theme of God's presence in the OT. Terrien writes on the presence of God, but does not examine Ezek 40–48 in his work.[20] Likewise, in a newer work, Lister argues that the presence of God provides a unifying theme for the canon, yet he subsumes his discussion of the temple under the rubric of the Davidic covenant and discussion of the Messiah.[21] Andiñach writes an OT theology sympathetic to a liberation theology perspective with the theological theme of "el Dios que está" ("the God who is there"). Even so, he only dedicates a very small portion to Ezek 40–48.[22] Thus, even in studies of the presence of God, scholars downplay Ezekiel's temple vision.

Another related theme addressed in scholarship concerns the importance of God's dwelling places in the OT, including but not limited to the temple. One method examines divine dwelling places in comparison to Ancient Near Eastern (ANE) ideology to discover its OT theological importance.[23] Scholars therefore explore the ANE conception of temples in terms of cosmic mountain ideology. In these works, if Ezekiel's temple is mentioned at all, it is in general terms alongside the other dwelling places of God.[24] Other writers explore temple theology in general throughout the OT. In an article in 1972, Clowney shows how Ezekiel's

---

19. See the works cited in this section, as well as the dictionary entries in McKelvey, "Temple," 806–11; Meyers, "Temple, Jerusalem," 350–68; Jenson, "Temple," 767–75. Discussion of the theological importance of the temple took a new turn with the works of Clements, *God and Temple*; Clifford, *Cosmic Mountain*. Previously, discussion of the temple related largely to historical-critical questions of authorship, e.g., the difference between the Priestly and Deuteronomistic conceptions of the temple. For a historical overview, see Nicholson, *Pentateuch in the Twentieth Century*, 5–6.

20. Terrien, *Elusive Presence*.

21. Lister, *Presence of God*.

22. Andiñach, *Dios que Está*, 258–60.

23. Clements, *God and Temple*; Clifford, *Cosmic Mountain*; Levenson, *Sinai and Zion*; Levenson, "Temple and the World," 275–98; Hurowitz, *I Have Built You an Exalted House*; Day, *Temple and Worship in Biblical Israel*; Morales, *Tabernacle Pre-Figured*; Morales, *Cult and Cosmos*; Morales, *Who Shall Ascend?*.

24. However, Levenson's *Sinai and Zion* assumes a previous work that will be examined later, that is, Levenson, *Theology of Restoration*.

temple connects to the NT, but he spends little space examining the Ezekiel text itself and how it should be interpreted.[25] More recently, Hays presents an introductory-level book on the temple, but only devotes two pages to the interpretation of Ezek 40–48.[26] Additionally, Alexander and Gathercole provide a series of essays on the temple traced throughout the canon.[27] In this work, Taylor's essay focuses on the glory departing and returning. He briefly discusses interpretations of Ezek 40–48 and rightly suggests that Ezekiel ". . . freed Israel from the last vestige of a belief in the localized presence of God in a building in Jerusalem."[28] His treatment is helpful, but too brief. Likewise, in another work Alexander presents a theology of the OT centering on temple themes, and, even granting the brevity of his book, his treatment of Ezek 40–48 is insufficient.[29]

In contrast to these aforementioned studies, one study stands out. In *The Temple and the Church's Mission*, Beale writes a thorough work on the biblical theology of the temple, where he discusses Ezek 40–48 in depth.[30] While relying on much of the previous scholarship already mentioned in this study, Beale provides a lengthy chapter on the temple in Ezek 40–48 and its relationship to the NT.[31] Beale is a major dialogue partner for this study, and his view will be explained in later pages. The purpose here is simply to note that, aside from Beale, few have even attempted to bring Ezek 40–48 into their theology of the OT. This study argues that Ezek 40–48 should play an important role in a theology of the temple and, by extension, OT theology. The solution this study proposes is to see Ezek 40–48 as typology pointing forward to a greater fulfillment in the NT. In fact, Ezek 40–48 plays a pivotal role in the biblical theology of the temple, showing a transition point from viewing God's presence as dwelling in a physical building to dwelling among his people in a spiritual sense, without a building.

---

25. Clowney, "Final Temple," 156–89.
26. Hays, *Temple and the Tabernacle*, 180–82.
27. Alexander and Gathercole, *Heaven on Earth*.
28. Taylor, "Temple in Ezekiel," 70.
29. Alexander, *Eden to the New Jerusalem*, 57–59, 160–61.
30. Beale, *Temple and the Church's Mission*.
31. Beale, *Temple and the Church's Mission*, 335–64.

1

Ezekiel's Temple, Typology, and Thesis

Introduction

SINCE THIS WORK DISCUSSES the proper interpretation of Ezek 40–48, some history of interpretation of the passage is necessary. Historically, critical scholarship has focused on the background issues of the authorship and unity of the text. The present work does not discount those questions, but focuses on the theological interpretation of the received text. The first section, then, will outline the range of views on the meaning of the temple. Next, this chapter will examine the method of typology. Is typology a legitimate method in biblical studies? What are appropriate criteria for responsible typology? After this, the final section of this chapter will explain the argument of this work, that Ezekiel's temple should be interpreted typologically.

Views on the Temple in Ezekiel 40–48

The main burden of this study is to arrive at a proper interpretation of the temple vision in Ezek 40–48. According to Block, "[F]ew sections of the book [of Ezekiel] have yielded such a wide range of interpretations . . ."[1] This section will examine how recent scholarship has interpreted the temple vision.[2] To survey the landscape, one may consider two

---

1. Block, *Ezekiel 25–48*, 494.

2. Before the Reformation, Christian exegetes mostly interpreted the chapters allegorically. See Mein and Joyce, *After Ezekiel*. During the Reformation, John Calvin became a prominent leader in interpreting the text grammatically, historically, and

overarching categories of interpretation, the "physical temple" and "symbolic temple" views.[3] While not perfect, these labels helpfully summarize the basic viewpoints. The debate *in nuce* concerns whether or not the author of Ezekiel, in writing down the vision, intends for the structure described in Ezek 40–48 to be physically built. Jenson helpfully lays out the basic problem of interpretation. On one hand, the vision is so detailed that the interpreter is tempted to think of this as a literal temple that will be built. On the other hand, the vision contains "ideal or utopian features."[4] In addition to these two general categories, Beale has recently provided a unique third view.[5] While not arguing for a physically built structure, Beale also does not argue for mere symbolism. The following section will explain each perspective on the temple vision.

The Physical Temple View

Even within the "physical temple" view, a plethora of interpretations exist. A segment of scholars, mostly those known as dispensationalists, but also including a larger group of premillenialists, believe that Ezekiel's temple will be built in Jerusalem during a millennial age described in Rev 20. Other scholars such as Corrine Patton and Jacob Milgrom hold that this vision is intended to be a blueprint for a physical temple.[6]

Dispensationalist/Premillennial Interpretation

Premillennial or dispensationalist scholars often champion this vision as a temple plan or blueprint (תבנית). This view began to take hold among teachers and scholars in the early twentieth century. Though not necessarily espousing any eschatological interpretation, C. H. Toy presented a

---

christologically, although in reality the Reformers do not give this text as much attention as other portions of Scripture. See E. A. de Boer, *Calvin on the Visions of Ezekiel*.

3. Beale, *Temple and Church's Mission*, 335, provides four major views—first, a literal physical temple; second, an ideal heavenly temple that would never be physically built; third, a figurative vision of an ideal temple; fourth, a real heavenly temple that would be established on earth in non-structural form. I combine his second and third views under the rubric of "symbolic." His fourth view is his own, which will be presented in following pages.

4. Jenson, "Temple," *DOTP*, 772.

5. Beale, *Temple and Church's Mission*, 335–64.

6. Patton, "Ezekiel's Blueprint;" Milgrom, *Ezekiel's Hope*.

scholarly argument that coheres with a premillennial interpretation. Toy argued for a "face value" interpretation of the temple.[7] Among his reasons were the exact measurements, the detailed regulations, and the specific geographical descriptions. He stated that such instructions do not differ from those in the Pentateuch, Joshua, or other prophets. Toy described the tone of writing as "matter-of-fact and legislative."[8] He argued that most prophetic visions end with a moral exhortation, yet Ezekiel's vision is interrupted with the command to show the temple to Israel (Ezek 43:10–11; 44:5–9).[9] Hence, the vision is a command to build, not a moral lesson.

As a dispensationalist, H. A. Ironside also presented a literal interpretation even though he said, "We are not to take Ezekiel's vision too literally, but just as the vision of the heavenly Jerusalem [Rev 21] is very largely symbolic, so is the vision of the earthly Jerusalem given in these chapters."[10] Still, he claimed that architecturally every detail could be reproduced as if this were a blueprint for a physical structure.[11] He also held that the sacrifices of the temple would take place in the great tribulation, but not during the millennium.[12] One reason for such an interpretation is the description of Sabbath-keeping in Ezek 46. For Ironside, the observance of the Sabbath must mean that God would once again act in the "Jewish" dispensation.[13] Ironside concluded his discussion by saying that, when it comes to the river flowing from the temple, it would be "slavish adherence to literality" to think of it as an actual river.[14] Thus, while Ironside wished to let the symbolism speak for itself, his dispensationalist framework colored his interpretation. He could not conceive of these instructions being carried out apart from some event in the eschaton. Perhaps inconsistently, though, he left the door open for some images not to be interpreted woodenly.

Premillennial teaching on Ezek 40–48 continued with the publication of the *Ryrie Study Bible*.[15] The study Bible contains notes at the pertinent

7. Toy, "General Interpretation of Ezek. 40–48," xlv.
8. Toy, "General Interpretation of Ezek. 40–48," xlv.
9. Toy, "General Interpretation of Ezek. 40–48," xlvi.
10. Ironside, *Ezekiel*, 281.
11. Ironside, *Ezekiel*, 284.
12. Ironside, *Ezekiel*, 288–89.
13. Ironside, *Ezekiel*, 318.
14. Ironside, *Ezekiel*, 324.

15. Ryrie, ed., *Ryrie Study Bible*. Scofield, ed., *New Scofield Reference Bible*, also produced a study Bible from this perspective but provides only a few notes on Ezek 40–48.

verses that argue for a millennial temple. In fact, the heading of Ezek 40–48 says, "Prophecies Concerning Israel in the Millennial Kingdom."[16] One argument for the building of this temple is the amount of detail. If the text is symbolic, the amount of detail renders the vision meaningless.[17] Yet the instructions to build cannot be for the postexilic generation because ". . . it is inexplicable why Ezra, Nehemiah, or Haggai do not refer to it."[18] Therefore, the vision must refer to Israel when she is restored to her land, which would be "during Christ's millennial kingdom."[19] Ryrie claimed that the sacrifices in the temple are memorials of Christ.[20] Aside from these few notes, Ryrie gave few hermeneutical arguments for his interpretation.

Ralph H. Alexander provided another hermeneutical defense of the physical building interpretation.[21] First, he said that to interpret the temple symbolically or spiritually would open up the interpreter to complete subjectivity, in addition to abandoning the grammatical-historical hermeneutical method. This is especially the case since Ezekiel was told to write down specific details and relay them to the people.[22] Alexander also claimed that this vision could naturally be interpreted in a historical, chronological sequence. After the glory departed the temple (Ezek 8–11), God promised to restore Israel to the land and establish a shepherd over them (Ezek 34–37), but even then nations would attempt to destroy Israel (Ezek 38–39). Therefore, at this point God would establish his final kingdom and his glory would return forever (Ezek 40–48). Since holiness is one of the themes of the book, God's glory would not return until the people and land were completely cleansed in the last age.[23] Alexander also argued that the context and flow of Scripture in God's redemptive purpose would lead to a natural future fulfillment at the end of time. He gives the river as an example (Ezek 47), saying that the river that flowed through Eden would be fulfilled in Rev 22. Thus, there is reason to think that this river and temple will literally be part of that redemptive plan.

---

16. Ryrie, *Ryrie Study Bible*, 1289.
17. Ryrie, *Ryrie Study Bible*, 1289.
18. Ryrie, *Ryrie Study Bible*, 1289.
19. Ryrie, *Ryrie Study Bible*, 1289.
20. Ryrie, *Ryrie Study Bible*, 1299.
21. Alexander, "Ezekiel," 867–77.
22. Alexander, "Ezekiel," 868.
23. Alexander, "Ezekiel," 869.

Alexander also adds as a primary reason for physical fulfillment the distinction between the temple of Rev 21–22 and Ezek 40–48. Since Alexander also took Revelation "literally," the details need to harmonize. Since the two visions have significant differences, the harmonization must mean differing fulfillments. For example, Ezekiel, unlike John, described a sea (Ezek 47:15–20). Also, the OT prophet focused on many regulations for the temple, while Revelation does not. Additionally, in Ezekiel's city, the river flowed from the threshold of the temple instead of directly from the throne, as it does in Revelation.[24]

Next, Alexander answered the objection about the need for millennial sacrifices after the death of Christ. Alexander responded that God revealed himself to Ezekiel in the culture and perspective of his day. Since Ezekiel was a priest under the period of the Mosaic covenant, he could only be expected to describe the situation in that way. In the millennial kingdom Israel would be under the Mosaic covenant still (along with all the other covenants).[25] Ezekiel's vision would not preclude other forms of worship, but it would include these Mosaic forms. Hence, the temple would be needed as a place to offer sacrifices. What about the sacrifices in light of the finished work of Christ? Although Ezekiel's temple contained sin offerings, Alexander preferred to focus on the differences between Ezekiel and the Mosaic instructions. The important differences are that Ezekiel's instructions lack Yom Kippur, the ark of the covenant, and a high priest.[26] He believed these absences indicated Christ's presence in the millennium. Besides, the offerings were never meant to be efficacious in the first place and would not be so in the millennium.[27] These are some of the main arguments from a premillennial perspective.

---

24. Alexander, "Ezekiel," 870.
25. Alexander, "Ezekiel," 871.
26. Alexander, "Ezekiel," 873.
27. Alexander, "Ezekiel," 876 says, "The sacrificial system will be used as picture lessons to demonstrate the need for holiness in the consecration and purifying of the temple and the altar." Without specifying a timeframe, Scofield, *Scofield Reference Bible*, 890, also states, "Doubtless these offerings will be memorial, looking back to the cross, as the offerings under the old covenant were anticipatory, looking forward to the cross. In neither case have animal sacrifices power to put away sin (Heb. 10. 4; Rom. 3. 25)." Hullinger, "Millennial Sacrifices, Part 1," and Hullinger, "Millennial Sacrifices, Part 2," argues for the sacrifices as actually providing atonement for the people in the new temple (though he provides a unique definition of atonement). See further discussion in chapter four regarding the legislation of Ezek 40–48.

Other Scholars

A number of scholars interpret the vision as a prophet's desire for a future that was never realized. Some of them see no need to posit the unity of the canon, so they do not resort to the explanation that the temple will be built in a future millennium. They simply take the description as a blueprint, akin to descriptions like Exod 25–30 and 1 Kgs 6–7.[28] Normally this means building the temple at some point near the time the text was written, but Levenson held that the building will be constructed in the distant eschatological future.[29] The following describes a few of the arguments that scholars propose for the blueprint view.

Milgrom claimed a strong possibility that the prophet Ezekiel had in mind a physical manifestation. A major axiom of Milgrom's study is that the vision was based on the temple of Delphi built in the sixth century. As he said, "Thus, there is no point in seeking the origins of Ezekiel's sanctuary in the myths of Mount Sinai, the Garden of Eden, and Mount Zion. There is nothing miraculous about the structure. Even the prodigious dimensions of the perimeter wall (ca. 10 ft. high by 10 ft. thick) are feasible."[30] He also claimed, "Ezekiel's utopia of the equal subdivision of the land is pure fantasy . . . But the laws concerning the sanctuary, its personnel, and the *nasi* are viable and enforceable."[31] Unfortunately, Milgrom did not argue against alternate symbolic interpretations directly, nor provide much evidence for his view. The main point of his argument rests on the similarities of the vision with the Delphi temple.

Milgrom listed several similarities in the architecture of the Ezekiel and Delphi temples. First, the *temenos* (temple precinct) of each is built on the top of a southern slope and enclosed within a massive wall. Second, the temples are both built on raised platforms and have no inner wall. Third, a spring runs from under the temple. Fourth, priests washed at the spring near an altar at Delphi, while there is no laver by the altar in Ezekiel, implying washing in the river of Ezek 47. Fifth, the god speaks from the adytum (inner sanctuary) through a prophet(ess). Sixth, there

---

28. For the view that the blueprint reflects one archived from the first temple, see Cooke, *Ezekiel*, 425; Zimmerli, *Ezekiel 2*, 412; Talmon and Fishbane, "Structuring of Biblical Books," 139. For the view of a postexilic temple blueprint, see Greenberg, "Design and Themes," 182; Greenberg, *Ezekiel 1–20*, 15; Wevers, *Ezekiel*, 208.

29. Levenson, *Program of Restoration*, 33.

30. Milgrom, *Ezekiel's Hope*, 52.

31. Milgrom, *Ezekiel's Hope*, 60.

are no images in the temple. Seventh, the altar is the architectural center of the compound.[32] Milgrom also claimed the strong likelihood that the prophet Ezekiel would have been familiar with the culture and cult of Delphi. Thus, Ezekiel adopted this known structure to serve his theological purpose.[33]

Using a similar method as Milgrom, Ganzel and Holtz interpreted the temple as a structure that could be built.[34] In a brief footnote, they state, "After all, Ezekiel presents what appears to be a building plan."[35] The goal of their article was to show the similarities of Ezekiel's temple to Neo-Babylonian temples. The authors provided two main areas of similarities: the walls, gates, and courtyards; and the hierarchy of personnel. As to the first category, the three-part structure of courtyard, large room, and inner sanctuary resembles Neo-Babylonian structures, as would be expected of two cultures in Mesopotamia.[36] Importantly, the general layout of both temples arranges the space similarly to reflect increasing sanctity as one neared the altar.[37] For the second category, the hierarchy of personnel, Babylonian texts also discuss who may approach certain areas of the temple.[38] Moreover, Babylonian records also show strict regulations regarding the sanctity of priests, including their descent and ethical purity, an emphasis also present in Ezek 44.[39] In conclusion, Ganzel and Holtz showed that much of the architectural description does actually have a basis in reality, possibly indicating that the structure in Ezek 40–48 could be physically built.

One of the most sustained arguments for a physical structure is a dissertation on the subject by Corrine Patton.[40] First, like Milgrom and Ganzel and Holtz, Patton began by examining ANE temple building practices to show the importance of elements of the temple in Ezek 40–48. Next, she examined the temple in Qumran's *Temple Scroll* as an

---

32. Milgrom, *Ezekiel's Hope*, 45–49.

33. Milgrom, *Ezekiel's Hope*, 52.

34. Ganzel and Holtz, "Ezekiel's Temple in Babylonian Context," 211–26. The discussion in this article concerns whether or not the temple enforces strict standards of holiness, rather than whether or not this is to be physically built.

35. Ganzel and Holtz, "Ezekiel's Temple in Babylonian Context," 213.

36. Ganzel and Holtz, "Ezekiel's Temple in Babylonian Context," 219.

37. Ganzel and Holtz, "Ezekiel's Temple in Babylonian Context," 222.

38. Ganzel and Holtz, "Ezekiel's Temple in Babylonian Context," 223.

39. Ganzel and Holtz, "Ezekiel's Temple in Babylonian Context," 224.

40. Patton, "Ezekiel's Blueprint."

alternative temple to the one in Jerusalem, thus indicating that Ezek 40–48 also provided a legitimate alternative. Then, she explored the text of Ezek 40–48 to explain the differences between Ezekiel's and Solomon's temples. Her goal was "... to show that the variants represent a serious proposal for an alternative temple in the postexilic period."[41] Her evidence will be summarized here.

First, Patton examined archaeology and ANE literary texts to discover what temples in Mesopotamia looked like, including motifs and patterns held in common. She concluded that, even though there is a general pattern, specific temples have differences that demonstrate the ideology of the builders. Divergences reflect the theology of the builders.[42] In particular, she claimed that architectural emphases on separation and exclusivity, such as the deity residing in a small room, were not as prominent at Ezekiel's time. One finds these very emphases present in Ezek 40–48, however. As Patton states, "This supports [the] distinction that these concerns arise out of a remote and majestic royalty whose principles are then projected onto the deity ... [I]t was not Solomon's building that exploited these concepts to the full in ancient Israel. Rather Ezekiel employs imperial principles for his non-imperial state."[43] Next, by examining the *Temple Scroll*, she identified areas of what she termed fluidity in Israelite temple tradition. While there are many similarities, details such as the layout and number of courts are different.[44] The purpose of such examination is to show that different groups believed there could be legitimate versions of a temple that did not exactly replicate Solomon's temple. In the next chapters, Patton examined Ezekiel's vision in detail. She showed the differences in Ezek 40–48 from other ANE temples, the *Temple Scroll*, and Solomon's temple. The evidence demonstrates that Ezekiel adds some items and subtracts others. According to Patton, these changes "... derive their appointments from the principle of the need to separate the sacred and the profane."[45]

To conclude her argument, Patton wrote, "The primary purpose of the narrative of the temple plan is to relate the one true form of a

---

41. Patton, "Ezekiel's Blueprint," ii.
42. Patton, "Ezekiel's Blueprint," 26.
43. Patton, "Ezekiel's Blueprint," 60.
44. Patton, "Ezekiel's Blueprint," 140–41.
45. Patton, "Ezekiel's Blueprint," 160.

sanctuary that can house an eternally present God."[46] She appears to have argued that this is an actual blueprint. Elsewhere in the study she wrote, "The pericope ... although introduced as a vision, describes a temple so intricately detailed, that the reader is given the impression that the prophetic discourse relates the plan of some completed edifice or blueprint."[47] Also she says, "The discourse has a prescriptive force, and even though the vision finally evolves into a description of elements impossible for humans to recreate, the vision itself is concrete and functional."[48] Patton clarifies, though, that just because the vision is a blueprint does not mean the temple must be built, writing, "The temple not only did not have to be built, ... it should not be built."[49] Then she states, "The text is the *tabnit* for Ezekiel's community."[50] So, Patton's work claimed that this is a real temple and a real blueprint, despite the fact that it should not be built physically. Rather, the blueprint became "textualized" for theological reflection.[51]

The Symbolic Temple View

Many scholars also see this vision as one of an ideal or symbolic temple. In other words, the purpose of the vision is not for people to build a structure, but to communicate a message through symbols. For example, Niditch called the prophecy a symbolic representation of a sacred realm.[52] Similarly, Tuell described the vision as a verbal icon, a tangible description of a heavenly archetype.[53] Stevenson argued that the vision is "territorial rhetoric," a rhetorical tool for YHWH to claim the land of Israel as his own and declare his sovereignty.[54] Block used the term "ideational," stating that Ezekiel describes "... a spiritual reality in concrete terms, employing the familiar cultural idioms ..."[55] Carson called this passage

46. Patton, "Ezekiel's Blueprint," 187.
47. Patton, "Ezekiel's Blueprint," 143.
48. Patton, "Ezekiel's Blueprint," 143.
49. Patton, "Ezekiel's Blueprint," 187.
50. Patton, "Ezekiel's Blueprint," 188.
51. Patton, "Ezekiel's Blueprint," 189–90.
52. Niditch, "Visionary Context," 208–24.
53. Tuell, "Ezekiel 40–42 as a Verbal Icon," 649–64.
54. Stevenson, *Vision of Transformation*.
55. Block, *Ezekiel 25–48*, 505–6.

"prophetic-apocalyptic" and "eschatological."[56] This section, then, will demonstrate the different ways some explain Ezek 40–48 as symbolic. First, this section examines Niditch's view that Ezekiel's temple is related to a deity-enthronement pattern, then Tuell's view of Ezek 40–48 as an "icon," then the rhetorical analysis of Stevenson, followed by Carson's presentation of prophetic-apocalyptic, and, finally, Block's argument for an ideal temple.

Niditch argued for a symbolic interpretation that does not preclude the actual building of the temple.[57] Her views of Ezekiel as a "spirit medium" and Jewish mystic are questionable, as is her analogy to a Buddhist mandala (a sacred vision of the cosmos). Nevertheless, she was correct that a temple could be a microcosm of the cosmos.[58] Her claim was that Ezekiel did not intend to provide an architectural blueprint. The temple is symbolic, though not ". . . in a watery, nonvisceral sense."[59] The most helpful aspect of Niditch's analysis is her comparison of these chapters to ancient mythic patterns of the enthronement of a deity.[60] Rather than this text being a random appendix to the book, as many scholars treat it, she showed that this section clearly connects to Ezek 38–39. In ancient myths, such as the Babylonian *Enuma Elish* or the Canaanite story of Baal, (1) the god is challenged, (2) a battle takes place, (3) the god is victorious, (4) there is a procession, (5) the deity is enthroned, and (6) a feast is held. Ezek 38–39 describes the challenge, battle, victory, feast, and procession, while Ezek 40–48 shows the enthronement of the deity. Niditch's study helpfully provides parallels to the deity-enthronement pattern. Reading with attention to genre, Niditch claimed that Ezekiel's main purpose is to demonstrate that YHWH is on the throne.

Tuell proposed that Ezek 40–42 is a "verbal icon."[61] Tuell interpreted the vision as interconnected with the throne visions of Ezek 1; 8–11. The vision fulfills the promise of Ezek 11:16 that God would be a sanctuary "in small measure." Moreover, he claimed that the vision is a heavenly ascent

---

56. Carson, "Lord Is There," 49.
57. Niditch, "Visionary Context," 208–24.
58. See also Beale, *Temple and Church's Mission*, 29–80.
59. Niditch, "Visionary Context," 213.

60. Niditch, "Visionary Context," 220–23. Kutsko similarly compares Ezekiel to Mesopotamian concepts of the removal, repair, and return of divine images. Unfortunately, he rarely mentions Ezek 40–48. See Kutsko, *Between Heaven and Earth*, 148.

61. Tuell, "Verbal Icon," 649–64. Joyce also argues this view in Joyce, "Ezekiel 40–42."

narrative. Ezekiel is guided through a "real" structure, albeit the heavenly archetype and not something built on earth. Tuell showed that "heavenly pattern" language is found in Exodus, 1 Kgs 8, and ANE literature. He also provided biblical and extrabiblical sources (*Enoch*, Qumran) that speak of a heavenly ascent. The purpose of the vision is to be an "icon," a window into the heavenly reality, through which YHWH can be present in "small measure" (see Ezek 11:16). The earthly temple was gone, but the heavenly temple would remain forever. Ezekiel and the exiles could have access to that heavenly temple.[62]

Stevenson argued along different but complementary lines that the genre of these chapters is "territorial rhetoric."[63] The rhetorical purpose of this vision is to make a territorial claim. Territoriality concerns attempts to control a space and rhetoric is one way to control this space, that is, by writing about boundaries and rules of access. She writes, "The issue in Ezekiel 40–42 is not the correct building of structures, but the creation of spaces, and even more importantly, keeping these spaces separate."[64] Thus, her work focuses on the boundaries and access points throughout the temple. Violation of these boundaries led to the exile, but a proper flourishing in society will come as a result of respecting YHWH's kingship over his space. Therefore, Ezekiel does not describe a plan for a building to be constructed but instead seeks to define sacred space. The purpose of this territorial rhetoric is to issue a proclamation of who is king, since to make a territorial claim is to say that one is king over that territory. Stevenson puts it this way, "Kings build temples. YHWH built this temple. YHWH is king."[65] So Ezekiel does not receive a blueprint but a territorial claim, the vision of a temple built by King YHWH.

Stevenson provides thorough evidence, some of which includes the facts that vertical measurements are absent and that even some of the horizontal measurements are incomplete.[66] Stevenson left open the question of whether this is just a literary symbol, calling it ". . . incomprehensible that the Rhetor of this text could imagine a society without an

---

62. Strong, "Grounding Ezekiel's Heavenly Ascent," 192–211, attempts a rebuttal to Tuell's argument, arguing that the heavenly temple needs to have a counterpart in an earthly reality, and the vision was meant as an "archive" for the postexilic community to study.

63. Stevenson, *Vision of Transformation*, 11.

64. Stevenson, *Vision of Transformation*, 19.

65. Stevenson, *Vision of Transformation*, 116.

66. Stevenson, *Vision of Transformation*, 39.

actual temple as the symbolic center of the society."⁶⁷ At the same time, she acknowledged, "For twentieth century Christian readers, it is no great problem to read this text about a future temple as a literary symbol for the universal and transcendent presence of God. There is no need for an actual temple in Christian ideology."⁶⁸ Stevenson emphasized the rhetorical purpose of Ezekiel so that no physical temple is needed for the text to have meaning.

Carson called this passage "prophetic-apocalyptic."⁶⁹ Rightly, Carson noted the apocalyptic and eschatological features of the text. At the same time, Carson avoided the notion of mere symbolism that flattens out the old covenant tone of the passage. He wrote, "Ezekiel is given a vision of the coming messianic age, a vision that lies in the future of Ezekiel's time but grows out of the categories present to Ezekiel's time."⁷⁰ Carson based his interpretation partly on the final words in Ezek 48:35, "*YHWH Shammah*," indicating that the purpose of the vision is the return of the presence of God. He underscored this with an examination of the context of Ezek 1–39, showing the concern for the cleansing of sin and the return of YHWH's glory. He noted additionally that the rebuilt temple after exile did not measure up to the glory of Ezekiel's vision. Finally, Carson developed connections with Jesus as the temple and with Rev 21–22.⁷¹

Block in his commentary promoted a spiritual or symbolic view of the temple, calling the vision "ideational," a ". . . spiritual reality in concrete terms, employing the familiar cultural idioms . . . ."⁷² He also stated, "Ezekiel hereby lays the foundation for the Pauline spiritualization of the Temple."⁷³ Block provided ten "hermeneutical keys" to understanding Ezek 40–48.⁷⁴ This section will only mention a few of the most salient ones. One key is that Ezekiel tells the reader the genre when he describes what he sees in Ezek 40:2, מַרְאוֹת אֱלֹהִים ("divine visions," as Block translates the term). There are two other places where Ezekiel has divine visions, Ezek 1 and 8–11. Ezek 1 uses the same term as in Ezek

---

67. Stevenson, *Vision of Transformation*, 150–51.
68. Stevenson, *Vision of Transformation*, 150.
69. Carson, "Lord Is There," 49.
70. Carson, "Lord Is There," 49.
71. Carson, "Lord Is There," 60–62.
72. Block, *Ezekiel 25–48*, 505–6.
73. Block, *Ezekiel 25–48*, 506.
74. Block, *Ezekiel 25–48*, 494–506.

40 (מַרְאוֹת אֱלֹהִים). Another important detail is that Ezekiel provides a date for his vision in Ezek 1, linking it to Ezek 8 and Ezek 40.[75] In the first vision Ezekiel has difficulty putting the vision into words, based on the use of terms such as דְּמוּת ("likeness"), מַרְאֶה ("appearance"), and the preposition כ ("like"). Therefore, interpreters do not take this vision literally in the sense that they understand God's physical throne to actually be undergirded by living creatures with wheels. Instead, all of these images communicate a mosaic of the awesome glory of God on his throne, an image that is hardly expressible in words.

Ezek 8 is the second text where Ezekiel receives a vision from God. This vision begins differently, as the Spirit lifts Ezekiel up and brings him to Jerusalem in a vision. The particular location is named, yet this is distinctly called a vision. The Spirit does not take him to the physical Jerusalem to give him a prophecy, but instead Ezekiel goes to Jerusalem in the vision.[76] The prophet then states that this vision is like the first because the prophet sees the glory of God (Ezek 8:4).[77] As in the first vision, this one includes a date for the vision (Ezek 8:1). So, like Ezek 1 and Ezek 8, Ezek 40 identifies as a vision, the vision is about the glory of God, and the vision begins with a date formula.[78] These commonalities provide a key for interpreting the temple vision in the same way one interprets Ezek 1 and Ezek 8–11.

Another key Block provides is to consider the fantastic elements in the vision. For example, Ezekiel is taken to a "very high mountain" (Ezek 40:2). Though this could be a reference to Jerusalem, Jerusalem itself is

---

75. Much debate surrounds the dating of this vision, especially the meaning of the "thirtieth year." Along with others this study concludes that the date refers to the prophet's age when God called Ezekiel to his prophetic office. See Block, *Ezekiel 1–24*, 80–83.

76. Joyce, *Ezekiel*, 6, says, "There is no justification for regarding these references as evidence of physical journeys to Jerusalem from Babylonia . . ."

77. Beale, *Temple and the Church's Mission*, 337, contends that Ezek 8 is a glimpse of the "heavenly temple" because Ezekiel sees the ". . . heavenly dimension of the sanctuary dwelling in the midst of the physical temple." Although it is true that in Ezek 10 the glory of YHWH departs from the physical temple in symbolism reminiscent of Ezek 1, there is no indication in Ezek 8 that Ezekiel is seeing anything other than the physical temple in Jerusalem. Beale's argument would provide another link to Ezek 1 and Ezek 40, but the argument is not convincing.

78. Beale, *Temple and the Church's Mission*, 337, notes that the glory of God is an important part of each of these three visions. Joyce, *Ezekiel*, 97, also connects these three visions in this way.

only 2,500 feet above sea level.⁷⁹ Instead the mountain is reminiscent of Zion, the highest of all mountains (Isa 2:2; Mic 4:1). The mountain Ezek 40:2 describes cannot be the physical Jerusalem but must be a symbolic picture. The "very high mountain" also conjures comparisons with the mountain of Baal, Mount Zaphon, and Mount Olympus.⁸⁰ Ezekiel presents another fantastic element, the river flowing from the temple (Ezek 47:1–12). The river gets deeper the further down it goes and provides life and healing for everything in its vicinity, even providing life to the Dead Sea (Ezek 47:8). A clear connection exists between Eden (Gen 2:10–14) and cosmic symbolism.⁸¹ A few other fantastic elements in the temple-city's description occur as well, including the city being described in a perfect square, measurements in multiples of five, with twenty-five being the most common measurement, and, finally, the land apportionments ignoring geography and natural boundaries and instead being given in straight lines.⁸² So, according to Block's view, the vision describes what Duguid calls "theological geography."⁸³

G. K. Beale's "Real, Non-Structural Temple" View

G. K. Beale's presentation is distinct enough that it does not fit in a literal or symbolic category. Beale argued that the prophet sees a real, end-time heavenly temple in non-structural form.⁸⁴ He showed how the vision is not a description of a physical building to be constructed in Jerusalem, hence it is a non-structural temple, but also not merely a symbol, so the temple is real in some sense.

In his work Beale gave ANE background for the temple and examined the concept of temple through the OT and NT. Unlike other temple theologies, though, he wrote extensively on Ezek 40–48. In the work he presents several reasons why the temple is non-structural. First, the "very high mountain" must be symbolic geography, for Jerusalem is not very

---

79. Block, *Ezekiel 25–48*, 501 fn. 23.

80. Block, *Ezekiel 25–48*, 501.

81. Fishbane, *Biblical Interpretation*, 370, calls the temple the "axial point" between heaven and earth with the river as the "font of blessing." Odell, *Ezekiel*, 497, prefers to think of this as ". . . a perfect merging of the two realms . . . , a merging of mythic and historic space . . ."

82. Also Ellison, *Ezekiel*, 139.

83. Duguid, *Ezekiel*, 471–72.

84. Beale, *Temple and the Church's Mission*, 335–64.

Ezekiel's Temple, Typology, and Thesis

high and the new city would not fit on it. Second, the introductory vision formula is the same as Ezek 1 and Ezek 8, and those visions were of heavenly realities.

Beale also presents several reasons why the temple is eschatological. First, the vision connects to Ezek 11 and Ezek 37, both of which contain eschatological covenant promises that YHWH would be a "sanctuary" to his people. Also, Ezek 37:27 says God's dwelling place will be "over" them, showing God's spiritual presence over the entire land. Beale then exegeted Ezek 40–48 to argue how it points to a non-structural end-time temple. He equated the city to the temple because the whole city is filled with God's presence (Ezek 48:35), and because the temple is the same size as ancient Jerusalem. Other features require a symbolic understanding. The fertile waters of Ezek 47 allude to Eden and point to the "expansion" of paradise. Moreover, the vision describes perfect squares, multiples of five, and lack of vertical measurements. Beale then claimed that Rev 21 fulfills Ezekiel's temple, saying that in Rev 21:22 a physical structure is denied, but the "true temple" is not. In fact, Ezekiel anticipates the "true temple" of the expanding presence of God.[85] Here, Beale listed a number of similarities between Rev 21–22 and Ezek 40–48. In conclusion, Beale claimed that, though a physical temple would not be built, the fulfillment of Ezekiel's temple would come down in "non-structural" form at the end of time.[86]

The Method of Typology

Introduction

If, as Strawn claims, it is true that the Old Testament (OT) is dying (in terms of its use and understanding), what are the causes? Strawn lists several deadly diseases leading to the OT's decline in health, but one of the main illnesses is the problem of how to relate the OT to the New Testament (NT).[87] Many scholars have sought for a remedy, that is, an appropriate way to read the OT and NT together. In diagnosing the matter, Strawn is concerned that part of the problem lies in suggestions that, as he says, "The Old Testament *somehow needs or requires* a New Testament

---

85. Beale, *Temple and the Church's Mission*, 348.
86. Similarly, see Clowney, "Final Temple," 156–89.
87. Strawn, *Old Testament Is Dying*, 14.

text alongside it . . ."[88] Recently, typology has regained popularity as a method of reading the Scripture as a unified whole. Even in the study of typology, though, one faces this very problem of the OT seeming to require the NT to find a type. Though a significant number of scholars now see validity in typology, many descriptions of typology incorrectly assume that the NT sheds light on types that could never have been seen before in the OT. For example, Gentry and Wellum provide a standard definition using this unneeded assumption, saying,

> Typology as a *New Testament hermeneutical endeavor* is the study of the Old Testament salvation historical realities or 'types' (persons, events, institutions) which God has specifically designed to correspond to, and predictively prefigure, their intensified antitypical fulfillment aspects (inaugurated and consummated) in New Testament salvation history.[89]

For Gentry and Wellum, typology by definition derives from NT interpretation in its methodology. Likewise, Beale's definition of typology contains five essential characteristics, one of which is "retrospection."[90] Moo, though he rightfully states that typology is prospective, essentially comes to the same conclusion, saying, "[The] prospective nature of specific Old Testament incidents could often be recognized only retrospectively."[91]

One reason so many scholars inappropriately view typology as retrospective is that they see typology as a hermeneutical strategy, rather than a species of divine revelation, a subtle but important difference.[92] When scholars use typology as a hermeneutical strategy or exegetical method, they seek to determine the steps in that approach. This leads to questions like, "How did the apostles interpret OT texts? Were they accurate or inaccurate interpreters? Can that interpretive method be used by anyone who is not an apostle?" When scholars see typology as divine revelation, however, they should instead focus on what textual clues would indicate the presence of typology. Granted, the reader still has to determine if a text is typological or not, but this determination comes from the original text, rather than later interpreters, even when those

---

88. Strawn, *Old Testament Is Dying*, 224.
89. Gentry and Wellum, *Kingdom Through Covenant*, 103 (Emphasis mine).
90. Beale, *Handbook*, 14.
91. Moo, "Problem of Sensus Plenior," 197.
92. Caneday, "Biblical Theology for the Church," 96–98.

interpreters are the apostles.⁹³ In other words, typology exists because the divine Author, through the human author, placed the type within the text originally, not because the interpreter reads backwards and sees a text typologically (again, even if the interpreter is Paul).⁹⁴ Typology should be a textual strategy rather than a reading strategy. Very few, though, have sought to answer the question of how to determine a type within the OT text itself.⁹⁵ Therefore, this section seeks to provide criteria for textual evidence of types within the OT. This "textual typology" enables readers to better identify types, including those beyond the ones explicitly mentioned under the τυπος word group in the NT. The criteria also provide controls that keep the reader from allegorizing wildly.

As to Ezek 40–48, no scholar in the modern period appears to use typology to interpret the passage.⁹⁶ Perhaps this is because typology is often seen as a NT endeavor and NT authors never explicitly quote Ezek 40–48. Certainly, scholars note intertextual allusions to the text, but this does not lead to understanding the text as typological. Thus, an appropriate understanding of typology as being inherent in the OT text is important for understanding Ezek 40–48 as typological.

Prefiguration School of Typology

The modern study of typology began with Semler, who coined the term as a pejorative reference to those he believed made too much of types in Scripture.⁹⁷ In 1853, likely reflecting on the thinking of those like Semler, Fairbairn wrote, "The typology of Scripture has been one of the most neglected departments of theological science. It has never altogether escaped from the region of doubt and uncertainty; and some still regard it

---

93. Carson, "Mystery and Fulfillment," 433–34. Carson calls the notion of mystery and fulfillment "typology with teeth . . . , [an] unveiling of material that is actually there in the text (even if it was long hidden) . . ."

94. Sequeira and Emadi, "Nature of Typology," 11–34. One of the criteria for typology that Sequeira and Emadi hold to is that it is "authorially-intended." See also Provan, *Right Reading of Scripture*, 107, who claims that Jesus and the apostles read the OT literally, i.e., according to its communicative intention.

95. Ninow, *Indicators of Typology*, seeks to do so in tracing the Exodus theme throughout the OT, but ends up using Davidson's definitions, which are in fact based on the NT.

96. Fairbairn, *Ezekiel*, presents a typological interpretation, but his work does not specify criteria used by modern scholars.

97. Semler, *Versuch*.

as a field incapable, from its very nature, of being satisfactorily explored, or cultivated to as to yield any sure and appreciable results."[98] The statement shows that, in using the typological method, Fairbairn was in the minority during his time.

However, typology experienced a renaissance in 1939 through the publication of Goppelt's *Typos*.[99] Goppelt argued that the NT itself promotes typology as the way to connect the Old and New Testaments. He defined typology as rooted in history—historical events, persons, and institutions—and normally containing a "heightening" antitype (*Steigerung*).[100] The method continued to develop under scholars like von Rad and Eichrodt, and then matured even further after them.[101] In the past several decades, the study of typology has taken many directions.[102] What Carson stated regarding biblical theology applies equally to typology today, when he noted, "In short, the history of 'biblical theology' is extraordinarily diverse. Everyone does that which is right in his or her own eyes, and calls it biblical theology."[103] The following section will discuss the method used in this study, the prefiguration school of typology.[104]

---

98. Fairbairn, *Typology of Scripture*, 1–39, provides a more in-depth historical overview from the church fathers to the mid-nineteenth century, showing how few writers developed a system of typology.

99. Goppelt, *Typos*; Goppelt, "Τυπος, Κτλ.," *TDNT*, 246–59.

100. Goppelt, *Typos*, 17–18.

101. Von Rad, "Typological Interpretation," 174–92; Eichrodt, "Typological Exegesis," 224–45. Their detractors include Baumgärtel, "Hermeneutical Problem," 143–44; Barr, *Old and New*, 103–48; Barr, "Allegory and Typology," 11–15.

102. In reaction to opposition to typology, scholars who further developed the method include Lampe, "Reasonableness of Typology;" Woollcombe, "Biblical Origins and Patristic Development of Typology;" Foulkes, *Acts of God*; France, *Jesus and the Old Testament*.

103. Carson, "Systematic and Biblical Theology," 91.

104. The other major school is called the correspondence school. Its major proponents are von Rad, "Typological Interpretation," and Baker, *Two Testaments, One Bible*. See also Baker, "Typology and the Old Testament," 137–57. The distinction in the family tree of typology between the prefiguration and correspondence schools is helpfully provided by Ribbens, "Typology of Types," 81–95. Ribbens also provides an excellent historical overview. A more recent method gaining traction among scholars is known as figural reading or theological interpretation of Scripture. See Treier, "Typology," 823–27; Seitz, *Figured Out*; Seitz, *Character of Christian Scripture*; Frei, *Eclipse of Biblical Narrative*, 6–9. The method is inherently retrospective (Hays, *Reading Backwards*, 12). As Sequiera and Emadi, "Typology," 26, put it, "Typology and figural reading must be distinguished, for though these approaches bear some superficial similarities, they operate from different hermeneutical standpoints."

The title for the prefiguration school hails from the claim that the OT text inherently prefigures events or persons in the NT.[105] In other words, typology is not merely an analogy on the part of the reader, but actually inheres in the biblical text. Fairbairn claims, "It must not be *any* character, action, or institution occurring in Old Testament Scripture, but such only as had their ordination of God, and were designed by Him to foreshadow and prepare for the better things of the Gospel."[106] The prefiguration school states that a type must be divinely preordained, illuminate Christ, and have a superior NT antitype. The term prefiguration comes from this aspect of being "divinely preordained." As far as "illuminating Christ," these proponents indicate that typology must be christologically significant. The purpose of typology is to point forward to the person and/or work of Christ.[107] Minor details of a text, such as the five roofed colonnades in John 5:2, cannot typologically fulfill anything in the OT, because they do not sufficiently illuminate Christ.[108] Finally, the notion of a superior NT antitype, what Goppelt calls *Steigerung*, states that the NT fulfillment must be a greater fulfillment than its type.

Davidson further develops and even adds to these criteria that are well accepted by those in the "prefiguration school." He claims that a type must have five structures—historical, eschatological, christological-soteriological, ecclesiological, and prophetic.[109] Davidson bases these criteria completely on a NT study of the word group τυπος. First, he says, the type must be a historical event, person, or institution in the OT. The Scriptures themselves set forth both the type and the antitype as rooted in historical realities. By "historical structure," scholars mean that typology

---

105. The major proponents of prefiguration, in addition to Goppelt, *Typos*, are Fairbairn, *Typology*; Richard M. Davidson, *Typology in Scripture*.

106. Fairbairn, *Typology*, 46.

107. In contrast to contemporary Jewish typology, Goppelt, *Typos*, 200, writes, "In the NT, typology is the means regularly employed to relate the present to redemptive history in the past. What this means in essence is that the messianic fulfillment has come of the provisional redemptive events that are recorded in the OT . . . The results of typological exegesis are primarily statements about NT salvation . . ."

108. Eichrodt, "Typological Exegesis," 244, argues, "A genuine type can never be concerned with mere external similarities in non-essential points, but deals with an essential correspondence of central Old Testament facts of history with fundamental characteristics of the New Testament salvation." So also Beale, *Handbook*, 22, who says typology is not found in minute details but in the central theological message of the literary unit.

109. Davidson, *Typology in Scripture*, 397–405.

takes a redemptive-historical approach.[110] The historicity of the type distinguishes the method in a major way from allegory. Symbols cannot be types, so the statement "Your cheeks are like halves of a pomegranate ..." (Songs 4:3) is sometimes interpreted allegorically, but it is not typological. In contrast, the writer of Heb 8–9 bases his argument of typology on the historical reality of the tabernacle and Levitical priesthood.[111] Sometimes, however, even seemingly minor historical details are types, as long as these details are connected to a major salvation-historical reality.[112] For example, the burning of the animals' bodies outside the camp is significant because of the redemptive-historical importance of the sacrificial system (Heb 13:11–13).[113] Importantly, types are not only historical persons, such as Melchizedek, but can refer to events, such as the exodus, or institutions, such as the priesthood or temple. In addition, historical realities can be either comparisons (Noah and baptism in 1 Pet 3) or contrasts (Adam and Christ in Rom 5).[114]

Second, types are eschatological. Here the concept of *Steigerung* plays an important role. The eschatological criterion means that the antitype must be a heightened form of, or greater than, the type.[115] In Heb 11:8–10, the author commends Abraham for his faith, since Abraham understood that the "land of promise," i.e., Canaan, was a type pointing forward to "... the city that has foundations, whose designer and builder is God." The antitype of the city of God is a heightened version of the land. Likewise, in Heb 4 the "rest," entering the promised land led by Joshua, points forward to a greater Sabbath rest in the presence of God (Heb 4:8–11). Additionally, Paul in 1 Cor 10 connects the wilderness wanderings of Israel to the church, calling the latter "... [those] upon whom the end of the ages has come" (1 Cor 10:11). Davidson also notes

---

110. Levoratti, *Comentario Bíblico Latinoamericano*, 240. For a survey of different modern approaches to biblical theology, see Lockett and Klink III, *Understanding Biblical Theology*.

111. Davidson, *Typology in Scripture*, 346.

112. Davidson, *Typology in Scripture*, 398.

113. Davidson, *Typology in Scripture*, 346.

114. Davidson, *Typology in Scripture*, 398. Likewise, Eichrodt, "Typological Exegesis," 225.

115. Contra Provan, *Right Reading of Scripture*, 99, who argues that escalation implies "... that God's dealings with Israel in the OT are any less real, or any less important in themselves, than his dealings with the Church in the NT." In response, escalation does not imply lesser reality or importance in themselves. Because OT events are real and important in themselves, they point forward to an even greater antitype.

three aspects of eschatological fulfillment. First, typology may show how Christ's coming *inaugurates* the eschaton. Second, typology may show how Christ's return will *consummate* the eschaton. Third, typology may show that the church lives currently in the *tension* of "already" and "not yet." The eschatological fulfillment in the antitype could refer to just one or multiple aspects of eschatology.[116]

Third, types are christological-soteriological, that is, they center on Jesus Christ and his saving work. As Fairbairn puts it, "There must be a resemblance in form or spirit to what answers to it under the Gospel . . ."[117] This criterion highlights another major difference with allegory, which often focuses on minor details tangentially related to the NT. Even so, Christ is not always directly mentioned or pointed to in a type. Sometimes the type refers to an aspect of the new covenant that Christ inaugurated, such as baptism in 1 Pet 3.[118] Hence, the label includes not merely Christology but soteriology. The soteriological aspect of the label refers to the important events, persons, and institutions related to Jesus.[119] The purpose of Christ's coming was to save sinners (1 Tim 1:15), so major events relating to Jesus's life, such as the ministry of John the Baptist, fulfill OT types (Matt 11:14). However, not every detail of Jesus's life has a type in the OT.

Fourth, types are ecclesiological. Davidson states, "[This] includes three aspects: individual worshipers, the corporate community, and/or the sacraments of the church."[120] As an example, he mentions 1 Cor 10 as a text where all three aspects are used. The congregation is involved (1 Cor 10:6, 11), sacraments are involved (1 Cor 10:2–4), and the individual must personally decide whether to obey or not (1 Cor 10:5–10). He also cites as an example Rom 5, which names "the many" (Rom 5:15). However, of the five structures Davidson uses, this one is the least convincing. The use of "the many" is so vague in Rom 5 as to make it difficult to see it as an important typological structure. Rom 5 emphasizes the contrast of Adam and Christ, whereas the ecclesiological aspect of "many" is far less important. In short, "the many" is hardly an ecclesiological marker. If it were so, essentially every NT text would be ecclesiological. Additionally,

---

116. Davidson, *Typology in Scripture*, 399.
117. Fairbairn, *Typology*, 46.
118. Davidson, *Typology in Scripture*, 399.
119. Davidson, *Typology in Scripture*, 400.
120. Davidson, *Typology in Scripture*, 400.

including "individual worshipers" in an ecclesiological structure begs the question, for any text has to speak about at least one individual. The term "ecclesiological" should instead refer to a particular religious community, not merely an individual. Davidson himself points out that Heb 9 speaks of the conscience of an individual (Heb 9:9).[121] If so, how can the text technically be considered ecclesiological? A final problem is that some types refer directly to Christ and only indirectly to his salvation of a covenant community. For example, Melchizedek is a type of the priest-king Jesus (Heb 7).[122] Nowhere in Heb 7 does the writer discuss any ecclesiological aspect, but he focuses simply on the person and work of Jesus. Thus, although some types can be ecclesiological, not all are directly so.

Fifth, types are prophetic. Davidson includes three aspects of the prophetic structure.[123] The first aspect he calls "advance-presentation or pre-figuration." The type presents the NT reality beforehand in time, though still in form of "copies and shadows" (Heb 8:5). A second aspect is divine design, wherein the divine Author places these realities in the text as prefigurations. Third, Davidson says types have a "... *devoir-etre* ('must-needs-be') quality giving them the force of prospective-predictive foreshadowings of their NT fulfillments."[124] Type and antitype contain a necessary logical relationship, such that the antitype *must have* taken place as it did, based on a previous OT reality. The semantic meaning of τυπος hints at this aspect, since a type (*Nachbild*) is a mold or a stamp, such that the reality (*Vorbild*) is shaped by the mold already created.[125]

Considering all of this, Davidson provides his definition of typology,

> Typology as a hermeneutical endeavor on the part of the biblical writers may be viewed as the study of certain OT salvation-historical realities (persons, events, or institutions) which God has specifically designed to correspond to, and be prospective/predictive prefigurations of, their ineluctable (*devoir-etre*) and absolutely escalated eschatological fulfillment aspects (christological/ecclesiological/apocalyptic) in NT salvation history.[126]

---

121. Davidson, *Typology in Scripture*, 401.

122. Davidson does not technically consider Heb 7 a type because τυπος is not used in that passage.

123. Davidson, *Typology in Scripture*, 401.

124. Davidson, *Typology in Scripture*, 402.

125. Davidson, *Typology in Scripture*, 403.

126. Davidson, *Typology in Scripture*, 405–6.

This definition helpfully outlines the major emphases of the prefiguration school. This study sides with the aspect of the "prefiguration" school that claims types are divinely intended. Most of the criteria for prefiguration, barring the ecclesiological aspect, will be used in this study.[127] What prefiguration scholars have often neglected, though, is how to determine the type inherent within the OT text, as opposed to simply looking backwards from NT quotations. If the text at its origin is divinely intended to be a type, readers should be able to determine these types within the OT text.

Three Additional Criteria in the Old Testament

What, then, are some criteria by which one can discern typological features within the OT text itself? Here this study assumes some of the well-established criteria set forth by Davidson. There must be a historical referent (i.e., a real person such as Melchizedek), a prophetic indicator (i.e., an indication that a fulfillment is coming in the future), and an eschatological *Steigerung* (i.e., an indication that this fulfillment is greater than what is currently described).[128] In addition, normally, but not necessarily always, types are christological-soteriological.[129] Beyond this, this study proposes three more criteria when looking at an OT text, these being ambiguity, epochal events or persons, and OT development.

Ambiguity

A first additional criterion is ambiguity or dissonance. Here the interpreter looks for signs of ambiguity such that the text does not present an event, person, or institution in a completely straightforward manner.[130] The text may present a truth without a full explanation, or perhaps

---

127. For a previous study applying Davidson's criteria to the exodus type, see Ninow, *Indicators of Typology*.

128. Davidson, *Typology in Scripture*, 416. As seen earlier, contra Davidson, the claim for an ecclesiological characteristic in every type is not convincing.

129. Not all types are christological-soteriological. Many of them are better understood as *tropological*, giving moral exhortations, although even these exhortations are given to the new covenant people of God. Ribbens, "Typology of Types," 91, claims that tropological types are the most common of all. See Rom 6:17; 1 Cor 10:6; Phil 3:17; 2 Thess 3:9; 1 Tim 4:12; Tit 2:7; 1 Pet 5:3.

130. Beale, *Handbook*, 19, also argues for looking at clues in the text, but takes the

multiple facts appear in a dissonant manner. These dissonant facts do not seem to cohere and may even appear contradictory. In this case, a surface-level reading of the text does not suffice. Hence the initial reading of the text may not appear to have typological meaning, much like an initial survey of a crime scene may not yield any appropriate conclusions. However, later biblical writers investigate the text closely. In many cases the texts are investigated for thousands of years. These later writers then infer from the text truths that go deeper than the obvious, surface-level reading. So, the later biblical writers read the OT text this way not because they necessarily had special apostolic insight, but simply because they read the text more closely than we might today, not to mention that they were much closer to the original writer's cultural milieu.

The Melchizedek type furnishes a good example. The writer of the Pentateuch mentions Melchizedek only once, in Gen 14. On the surface of the text, Melchizedek does not seem to be too important of a figure. What makes Melchizedek any different from someone like Abimelech in Gen 20–21, who actually receives more attention in the book, in terms of space? The reader may look for several clues. Perhaps one clue is that Melchizedek brings out bread and wine. But, contrary to allegorical interpreters who would liken this to the church's Eucharist, this event is not a clue of Melchizedek's importance. The priest also blesses Abraham, but such an action is not out of the ordinary for a priest (see Num 6). Abraham also tithes to Melchizedek, but this could, on the surface, simply highlight Abraham's trust in God, not render a deep theological clue relating to Melchizedek in particular. Initially, the only obvious authorial highlight of Melchizedek's importance is his title, "priest of the Most High God," which begs for more explanation. Still, on an initial reading of Gen 14, to one who has never read Ps 110 or Hebrews, Melchizedek does not appear to be all that significant. He seems to be just another minor figure in the story, much like Abimelech.

Later biblical authors, though, or at least the anonymous authors of Ps 110 and Hebrews, read the story of Melchizedek closely. In doing so they find clues that other readers do not find on the surface. Interestingly, they notice not the explicit references to bread and wine or to a priest of the Most High, but they notice a particular ambiguity in the text. The authors notice what is not there, that Melchizedek has no genealogy. The writers of Ps 110 and Hebrews base their entire argument for Melchizedek

---

path of looking for deliberate foreshadowing.

Ezekiel's Temple, Typology, and Thesis

as a type on this lack of genealogy. In Ps 110, admittedly a small sample size, the text emphasizes Melchizedek as a "priest forever," the basis of which is the lack of genealogy in Gen 14 (Heb 7:3).[131] Like Melchizedek, Ps 110's priest-king is priest by oath and not physical descent (Ps 110:4).[132]

Heb 7:11–28 further develops the argument. First, the writer of Heb 7:11–14 states that two priestly orders exist, the Melchizedekian and Aaronic lines. Next, in Heb 7:16 he states that Jesus is priest not by bodily descent but by "the power of an indestructible life," a characteristic of Melchizedek's order (Heb 7:17). Thus, the *Steigerung* (escalation) in the antitype, according to Heb 7:25, is that Jesus always lives to make intercession, because he is a forever-priest. All of this theological development originates from an ambiguity in Gen 14. A surface reading would never notice whether or not a genealogy for Melchizedek is present. However, a close reading, especially in the context of the *toledot* of Genesis, indicates that the Genesis writer's presentation of Melchizedek states something theologically important by not giving him a genealogy.[133] At the same time, Heb 7:1–10 also mentions other typologically significant clues, which are Melchizedek's name and Abraham's tithe. These are important textual clues, but they are less ambiguous. Perhaps the unambiguous clues led the readers to look for more clues. Still, the major argument of Hebrews is not based on Melchizedek's name or Abraham's tithe, but on Melchizedek's beginning and end, due to the lack of a genealogy. Later writers were close readers of the text, detecting ambiguity.

Epochal Events

The next criterion for typology is that types relate to epochal events, persons, or institutions.[134] According to Clowney, the discipline of biblical

---

131. According to Longman III, *Psalms*, 383, features of the Psalm "... led to an eschatological interpretation." Many commentators focus here on the question of whether a priest can also be king. See Rowley, "Melchizedek and Zadok," 461–72. These investigations largely ignore the importance of the word "forever." However, Paul argues that the mention of a priest-king, which could not have been any of Israel's kings, necessitates a Messianic king who would reign and intercede forever. See Paul, "Order of Melchizedek," 195–211.

132. Paul, "Order of Melchizedek," 209.

133. On "gapping and blanking," using the *toledot* as an example, see Waltke with Yu, *Old Testament Theology*, 122.

134. Davidson, *Typology in Scripture*, 398, says, "The content of the correspondence [of type and antitype] extends even to details connected with the [type], but

theology looks at three horizons, the textual, epochal, and canonical horizons.[135] As previously noted, the textual horizon is when the reader first looks at the immediate text and studies the pericope closely. Next, for Clowney, one sees the epochal horizon in the structure of redemptive history. In his understanding, these epochs are YHWH's various covenants with his people.[136] However, seeing an event as epochal does not necessitate reading Scripture only in terms of a covenantal structure. Goldsworthy provides an alternate structure he calls "macro-typology."[137] This structure has three epochs, he says: "First, God's kingdom is revealed in Israel's history up to David and Solomon. Second, God's kingdom is revealed in prophetic eschatology. This recapitulates the first stage as that which shapes the future. Third, God's kingdom is revealed in the fulfillment of the Old Testament expectations in Christ."[138] This structure of macro-typology better encapsulates eschatological persons, events, and institutions that do not always directly relate to a particular covenant. Thus, when seeking for a type, one should look not just for foreshadowing facts, persons and events, but correspondences of entire epochs of salvation history.[139]

To determine epochal significance, one should examine whether or not the text shows the event or person to be theologically significant.[140] This includes the immediate context and that of the whole book. For example, the author of Genesis quite plainly presents Abraham as a theologically significant figure. One does not need the rest of redemptive

---

apparently always to such details as are already salvifically significant in the OT." As cited in Beale, *Handbook*, 20–21, Gerhard von Rad also describes narratives that are forward-moving, i.e., relating to *Heilsgeschichte*.

135. Clowney, *Preaching and Biblical Theology*, 88. Regarding the third horizon, the canonical, Clowney defines it as how a text is organically related to Jesus Christ. This section will not deal with this portion of his argument, since here we are concerned with typology developed merely in the OT.

136. For a similar approach, see Sequeira and Emadi, "Typology," 11–34; Schrock, "From Beelines to Plotlines," 35–56. Sequeira and Emadi, "Typology," 11, 24–25, root typology in a form of biblical-theological exegesis, wherein the Scriptures unfold along covenantal epochs.

137. Goldsworthy, *Gospel-Centered Hermeneutics*, 253. For further explanation see Goldsworthy, *Christ-Centered Biblical Theology*, 170–89.

138. Goldsworthy, *Gospel-Centered Hermeneutics*, 248.

139. Goldsworthy, *Gospel-Centered Hermeneutics*, 248.

140. The next criterion, "Old Testament Development," essentially applies the epochal horizon across the OT rather than to the immediate context, as practiced in this criterion.

history to understand his value. Typology develops, then, because later writers see the epochal significance already in the text, such as the "seed of Abraham" in Genesis. This is an intuitive step for typology, but scholars rarely mention this aspect.[141] For example, many intuitively take Aaron the high priest as a type of Jesus, but few discuss Phinehas as a type (Num 25). The difference is simply that Aaron is a far more important figure than Phinehas within Numbers and/or the Pentateuch, not least because he was the first high priest in Israel.[142] So the text itself, including the biblical book, presents people, events, and institutions as epochal.[143]

An example of the epochal horizon in typology is the narrative of Hagar and Sarah, developed in Gal 4:21–31. The passage is much debated, but here this study follows F. F. Bruce who states, "[Paul] is not thinking of allegory in the Philonic sense . . . [He] has in mind that form of allegory which is commonly called typology."[144] In other words, what Paul meant by ἀλληγορούμενος is not the method of allegorical interpretation that developed later in the church.[145] Additionally, scholars such as Caneday and Emerson see the Genesis text as narrating a historical event inherently laden with symbolic interpretation. The text itself provides a deeply symbolic contrast between a child of promise and a child of "works."[146] Paul did not interpret Genesis allegorically, but he read the text closely. Although much can be said about this example, for the present purpose the point is that Paul read Genesis as depicting the epochal significance of Isaac and Ishmael. These two children are more than two biological children in a long list of names in Genesis. Isaac is the promised child for whom Abraham waited by faith. Paul did not discern a type out of Abraham's other wife, Keturah, and her sons (Gen 25:1–6), because they are not epochally significant. Thus, within the context of the Genesis narrative, Isaac represents God's covenant by faith, whereas

---

141. Parker, "Typology and Allegory," 62.

142. For example, Ps 106 praises both Aaron and Phinehas, but the Psalm mentions Aaron first because it recounts Israel's history.

143. Goldsworthy, *Gospel-Centered Hermeneutics*, 253–56, provides a chart of events and persons both in original OT history and later prophetic development. Certainly, one could expand on this chart with even more specific references.

144. Bruce, *Galatians*, 217. See also the in-depth discussion in Provan, *Right Reading of Scripture*, 137–50.

145. Provan, *Right Reading of Scripture*, 131, cites Chrysostom's claim that here Paul calls an allegory here what is normally called a type.

146. Caneday, "Covenant Lineage Allegorically Prefigured," 50–77; Emerson, "Arbitrary Allegory?" 14–22.

Ishmael represents the opposite, one who seeks to secure God's blessing by one's own action. This criterion of epochal significance is the difference between the two pairs of brothers, Zimran and Jokshan versus Isaac and Ishmael. Based upon this epochal reading, Paul presents these two sons as types.

Epochal significance could be the main criterion that separates typology from allegory. Allegories are infamous for majoring on minors. For example, allegory makes the tent pegs of the tabernacle a symbol of Christ's resurrection because they are halfway out of the ground, or Rahab's rope a symbol of the blood of Christ because of its color.[147] The tabernacle is clearly important typologically, but the tent pegs are not. Rahab's importance in Jesus's genealogy is her gentilic status, not her rope. In Hebrews she is a paragon of faith, and in James she is a paragon of good works. Rahab is used as an illustration in Hebrews and James, not as a theologically important figure in redemptive history, and certainly her scarlet rope is never seen as particularly meaningful in the Scriptures. The general conquest of the promised land is epochally significant typologically (Heb 4), but not Rahab or her rope. Thus, epochal significance provides at least one control on appropriate typology.

Old Testament Development

Another criterion for textual typology is Old Testament development. In this case, the rest of the Old Testament canon provides clues that something is a type.[148] This feature is like the epochal horizon, except the event, person, or institution is developed throughout the Hebrew Scriptures and not just in one passage or biblical book. As Parker says, "Typology . . . *has development* and *takes shape* as later biblical authors build upon earlier written texts."[149] Herein lies another distinction from

---

147. For a real instance of the former example see DeHaan, *Tabernacle*, 65.

148. Again Beale, *Handbook*, 21–22, comes close to the view presented here, but he focuses instead on antitypes found in the OT, such as Noah being an antitype of Adam. The argument presented here is not just that there are OT antitypes, but that types are developed throughout the OT and into the NT as well.

149. Parker, "Typology and Allegory," 62 (Emphasis mine). This criterion can only apply to earlier OT texts. Later biblical writers (postexilic authors) cannot develop texts written near the end of OT Israel's history unless one includes the NT in this development. It would be more difficult to discern this criterion of typology, then, with a book such as Esther.

allegory, for allegory can connect various symbols although no connection of texts exists between type and antitype. However, if a text contains epochal events, logically writers will develop this significant event throughout the biblical canon.[150] Eichrodt already noted long ago that typology develops within the OT itself, using the exodus as his example.[151] OT typological development could be thematic, or a direct reference to a previous text. For example, Beale argues for a thematic development in reference to Eliakim, the one who holds the key of the house of David (Isa 22:22).[152] Beyond the immediate context of Isa 22, Beale claims, "Isaiah had generally understood the prior biblical revelation about Israel's coming eschatological ruler and David's heir . . . Thus, Isaiah supplied a little part of the revelation unfolded in the course of salvation history about kingship . . ."[153] In light of this example, one wonders why Beale insists on retrospection as a criterion, and places the burden of interpretation upon the NT writers, while yet saying that there is a ". . . forward-looking sense in the light of the whole OT canonical context."[154] With the example of Eliakim, Beale already shows how the OT canonical context clues the reader in to interpret the text as a type.

Several major examples of OT typological development occur in Scripture.[155] Two of these key examples are exodus and Eden imagery throughout the OT. Arguing for the validity of typology, Foulkes says, "The Old Testament itself points forward to divine acts more glorious than any in the past."[156] Perhaps no greater divine act than the exodus exists in the OT, yet even this act points forward to more glorious acts. Speaking of Exod 15, Lohfink writes, "In its literal meaning, the song of Moses already was composed in such a way that later saving acts of Yahweh could be introduced and read into its account of history, reduced as it was to a few basic images. Its very structure already assumed its typological application."[157] Regarding structure, Lohfink refers to the future-looking second half of the song. The enemies of Exod 15:13–15

---

150. Sequeira and Emadi, "Typology," 22.
151. Eichrodt, "Typological Exegesis," 234–35.
152. Beale, *Handbook*, 15.
153. Beale, *Handbook*, 15.
154. Beale, *Handbook*, 15.
155. See Baker, *Two Testaments, One Bible*, 171, for a list of many more examples.
156. Foulkes, *Acts of God*, 32.
157. Norbert Lohfink, "Song of Victory," 84.

are not the Egyptians, but the Canaanites and other foreign nations. The deliverance is not through the sea to escape the Egyptians, but to God's "holy abode" (Exod 15:13) and "mountain" (Exod 15:17). Some may say this speaks of Canaan, but one better understands this as ultimately about the tabernacle, temple, and a cosmic sanctuary.[158] Ninow, then, traces the development of the exodus type throughout the OT.[159] Isaiah in particular develops the exodus motif in Isa 11, 35, 40, and elsewhere as he prophesies hope for a regathering after the invasions of Assyria and/or Babylon.[160] Jeremiah, Hosea, Micah, Haggai, and Zechariah also speak of an eschatological heightening of the exodus event.

OT writers also develop Eden as a type throughout the biblical story. Fishbane, who argues for typology as a form of inner-biblical exegesis, sees Eden as "typology of space."[161] This typology, he explains, ". . . is achieved by the wholesale transfer of spatial imagery from one narrative topos to another."[162] Additionally, Morales ably shows how the Pentateuch develops Eden as the "cosmic mountain."[163] First, Morales shows how Exodus 15 contains Edenic imagery of God "planting" his people upon his holy mountain, his dwelling place (מִקְדָּשׁ; Exod 15:17). Later in Exodus, the writer describes the tabernacle in images and words resembling Eden. The language of God's holy mountain is also developed in Zion theology, such as Ps 48:1–3. Specifically, Ps 46 speaks of rivers and streams flowing from the mountaintop's holy tabernacle (מִשְׁכַּן; Ps 46:4). This Edenic tabernacle imagery is likewise reflected in the design of the Jerusalem temple. So, upon the temple's destruction, the prophets hope for a restored Eden. Ezekiel claims that the new land will be like Eden (Ezek 36:35), and his prophesied temple, atop a high mountain, contains a river of life flowing from its midst (Ezek 47). Using similar imagery, Joel prophesies a fountain coming from the temple, and mountains flowing with wine, milk, and water (Joel 3:18).

In sum, the OT itself develops Eden as spatial typology through the themes of the temple and Mount Zion. The NT then develops this typology further. John speaks of Jesus as the temple using Eden imagery when

---

158. Ninow, *Indicators of Typology*, 136; Also Morales, *Who Shall Ascend?*, 83–86; Morales, *Tabernacle Pre-Figured*.

159. Ninow, *Indicators of Typology*, 98–241.

160. Ninow, *Indicators of Typology*, 158–96.

161. For the section on typology see Fishbane, *Biblical Interpretation*, 350–79.

162. Fishbane, *Biblical Interpretation*, 368.

163. Morales, *Who Shall Ascend?*, 39–108.

Jesus says, "If anyone thirsts, let him come to me and drink... As the Scripture has said, 'Out of his heart will flow rivers of living water'" (John 7:37–38). The NT later explains that through Jesus, the source of the river of life, believers become living temples (1 Cor 3:16–17; 1 Cor 6:19–20; 1 Pet 2:5). Furthermore, Rev 21–22 provides the culmination of Eden typology. No temple exists in the new heavens and new earth, because the type gives way to the antitype. Eden is restored, even superseded, by the New Jerusalem on a great, high mountain, with the river of life flowing down from it. At last, the tabernacle (σκηνὴ), the dwelling place of God, is with man (Rev 21:3). So, in the case of Eden typology, the NT authors simply develop a theme the OT already developed.

One finds an example of lack of OT development in typology in the *Aqedah*, the story of Abraham binding Isaac. Scholars and preachers often claim this event as a type.[164] But is the *Aqedah* a type of Christ? The event meets the criteria of textual ambiguity and epochal events/persons. Interestingly, however, no OT writer develops this story later.[165] The OT canon makes no reference to this event, and even the NT mentions it very little.[166] The only other reference to Gen 22 is found in Heb 11:17–19. Even this passage, though, does not portray the *Aqedah* as typological of Christ. Instead, the writer emphasizes Abraham's faith, the fact that Isaac is the promised child, and that God was able to raise Isaac from the dead. The only possible typological connection in Heb 11:17–19 could be in the promise of resurrection, but the writer of Hebrews does not connect this story directly to the resurrection of Christ. In conclusion, there is no real basis for claiming this story as typological. Like the exodus or Eden, one expects to find further OT development if this event were so typologically significant.

Perhaps this last criterion defeats the entire argument of this study. If the argument is that we should not read NT interpretation back into the OT to find types, why should one use later OT texts to read earlier ones? Should we read backwards in an OT sense or not? In response, an

---

164. See, for example, Leithart, *Deep Exegesis*, 43–44.

165. The theme of sacrifice does appear throughout the OT, and Isa 53 presents the Servant as a sacrifice. The type many usually put forward, however, is that, just as Abraham gives up his son Isaac, God the Father gives up his Son to die. The notion of a father presenting his son as a sacrifice does not occur in the OT. Perhaps, then, one may say that the ram of Gen 22 is a type, but not Isaac.

166. There may be echoes in other OT events such as Jephthah sacrificing his daughter (Judg 11), but this echo does not develop the event as typological.

important distinction exists between Old and New Testament readings of previous texts. NT authors "discover" types from reading them already present in the OT, and one way to do so is to read the OT "backwards" to look for development. As to NT readings of the OT, Luke 24 does not indicate that once Christ rose, the apostles and early Christians suddenly were able to see Christ under every rock or "Jesus on every page."[167] Instead, Luke 24:27 indicates that readers, by the illumination of the Holy Spirit, now have the ability to see Christ wherever he is already prefigured in the OT, in "the things concerning himself." In fact, Jesus chastises the Emmaus travelers for not seeing what was already there in the OT (Luke 24:26–27).[168]

How, then, does one know where Jesus is prefigured? The argument here is that one way to do so is by looking at OT development. Later OT authors were able to discern textual clues from previous OT texts. One would expect the symbolism laden in earlier texts to be teased out over time, especially by the prophets.[169] Therefore, the NT writers, mostly steeped in their contemporary worldview of the Hebrew Scriptures, had their eyes opened to see the reality of the whole OT's typological presentation of the Messiah. This differs from a claim that the apostles had a unique, mystical insight into previously unseen types. So, for example, the Spirit does not give Matthew a unique apostolic insight into Hos 11:1 to be able to see that the exodus is a type of Christ, and that young Jesus's flight to Egypt is theologically significant. Instead, the Spirit enlightened Hosea to see the exodus as a type of something or someone greater to come, so Hosea writes his text. Matthew, then, applies the events of the life of Jesus as the antitype of the type already presented throughout the OT. As Beale says,

> The plausibility of suggestion that typological interpretation is normative and that we may seek for more Old Testament types than the New Testament actually states for us is pointed to by the observation that this method is not unique to the New Testament writers but pervades the Old Testament. The fact that later Old Testament writers understand earlier Old Testament texts typologically also dilutes the claim that the New Testament

---

167. Murray, *Jesus on Every Page*.
168. Provan, *Right Reading of Scripture*, 123.
169. Poythress, *Understanding Dispensationalists*, 112–13.

writers' typological method was unique because of their special charismatic stance.[170]

Thus, the Old Testament presents internal evidence of its own typological development.

Summary: Old Testament Criteria for Types

In sum, readers of the Bible face a dilemma: the Scylla of not seeing the Bible as a unity, and the Charybdis of reading the NT into the OT. Typology is currently a popular method of navigating the dilemma, but the method presents various issues. Undeniably, a distinction exists between the Testaments. God reveals the history of redemption is over time, culminating in Jesus the Messiah. Therefore, no one should claim that the OT fully shows every detail of God's purposes for the world in Christ. As Vern Poythress states,

> [T]he significance of a type is not *fully* discernible until the time of fulfillment. The type means a good deal at the time, but it is open-ended. One can anticipate in a vague, general way how fulfillment might come, but the details remain in obscurity. When the fulfillment does come, it throws additional light on the significance of the original symbolism.[171]

Poythress's words are true, yet the emphasis in this study is that the type "means a good deal at the time." Though one cannot fully comprehend the antitype without the NT, one can understand a great deal already from the OT. The section above attempts to show that one can look closely at OT texts themselves to see the latent typological features inherent in God's revelation. Rather than reading backwards, one can take the OT as the starting point and read forward.

So, to determine types in the OT, this study uses the following criteria.[172] First, the text must refer to a historical person, event, or institution.

170. Beale, "Positive Answer to the Question," 402.

171. Poythress, *Understanding Dispensationalists*, 115–16.

172. As mentioned earlier, this study does not use the prefiguration criterion of an ecclesiological aspect. Does this beg the question when applying typology to Ezek 40–48? In other words, does this study arbitrarily reject a criterion because it does not fit the conclusion that Ezek 40–48 is typological? First, as shown above, the present work rejects the ecclesiological aspect because it cannot be demonstrated in the texts Davidson studies. Second, even though this work does not use the criterion, Ezek 40–48 does actually include the ecclesiological aspect, for YHWH comes to dwell amongst

Second, the text should contain prophetic indicator(s). Third, later texts will show a heightened, eschatological fulfillment (*Steigerung*) of the type. Fourth, the type has a christological-soteriological context or fulfillment. Fifth, the text presents ambiguity as a clue to a type. Sixth, the text describes epochal events, persons, or institutions. Seventh, the OT develops the previous type.

Thesis: Ezekiel 40–48 as Typology

As this study has shown, many works in the past few hundred years have dealt with Ezek 40–48. The thesis of this study is that no work quite comes to a satisfying interpretation, or at least does not develop an adequate interpretation extensively enough. Throughout the next chapters, this study will interact with the positions described, as each portion of the argument is presented in turn. Nevertheless, here the study can summarize the basic problems with the aforementioned categories of interpretation.[173]

As to the arguments for a physical temple structure, these do not adequately deal with the considerations of genre. Ezek 40–48 incorporates many symbolic features. The temple is described in terms of a heavenly vision and has many features that can be called "proto-apocalyptic." The other "symbolic" perspective can also go too far, though, by saying the vision is purely symbolic and does not describe anything "real." Simply saying that the vision is a divine-enthronement pattern, a verbal icon, territorial rhetoric of kingship, or a symbolic description of heaven does not suffice to obviate the physical construction view. If these clues were sufficient, why the presence of such extensive details in the text? Instead, the extensive details show that the vision describes something that is in some sense "real."

Beale helpfully emphasizes the reality of the vision. While there is much to commend Beale's view, not least his extensive research, he errs in describing this as a vision of the actual heavenly temple, which he calls "real in non-structural form." The issue with his view is that, according to him, this heavenly temple of Ezek 40–48 is the city-temple that will

---

his people. YHWH's goal is to re-gather all his covenant people. Thus, Ezekiel's temple would still be a type if one includes the ecclesiological aspect.

173. This study agrees with Beale, *Temple and the Church's Mission*, 352, when he says, "In conclusion, it is best not to formulate the debate about Ezekiel's temple in a 'literal versus non-literal' framework." Nevertheless, historically the debate has proceeded using these categories.

descend in the last days, as described in Rev 21–22. In other words, Beale equates Ezek 40–48 with Rev 21–22. He states, "The picture of Ezekiel's temple that is integrated into Revelation 21:1—22:5 probably indicates its *consummated* fulfillment. The new heavens and earth are the holy of holies, as well as the new Jerusalem and new Eden, all of which are anticipated to varying degrees in the last segment of the book of Ezekiel."[174] Then he says, "We have contended . . . that John's temple is like Ezekiel's because *it is*, in fact, what Ezekiel prophesied . . . Ezekiel 40–48 itself was a prophecy of an eschatological temple . . . , and John's temple depicts the eschatological temple."[175] The thesis of this study differs from Beale by denying this conflation. The text presents far too many incongruities between Ezekiel and Revelation to say that they essentially describe the same place. In fact, the "heavenly temple" that descends in the new heavens and new earth is explicitly not a temple (Rev 21:22). Ezekiel sees a temple that is very different from any other described in the canon. The measurements and regulations are very specific in their details, features Beale does not adequately explain. The details in Ezekiel indicate something theological in themselves. Therefore, one must find a better way to explain Ezekiel's vision.

    The thesis of this work is that the best way to interpret the passage is under the rubric of typology. The benefit of typology is that the method helps the interpreter move past the rigidity of "literal" and "symbolic." Typology is not simply another way of describing symbolism. Symbols may or may not be rooted in reality. When the psalmist writes, "Even the sparrow finds a home . . . at your altars . . ." (Ps 84:3), he is not stating that there actually is a sparrow at the altar in Jerusalem. On the other hand, a type has its basis in an actual event, person, or institution.[176] Thus, to claim that Ezek 40–48 is a type is also to claim that the temple is presented as a real institution. In this sense, the vision describes a real temple, pointing forward to something real that is to come. In addition, typology clarifies the textual purpose of the prophet or author's writing. To say that the temple is "real" does not require that the author intended the temple to be built. In typology, the institution written about is inherently pointing forward to a heightened fulfillment (*Steigerung*). The method of typology shows how an institution can have a further referent beyond

---

174. Beale, *Temple and the Church's Mission*, 350.
175. Beale, *Temple and the Church's Mission*, 351.
176. This definition has been established since the work of Goppelt, *Typos*.

itself. In this case, the vision points forward to a greater fulfillment in the NT. Unlike Beale's claim, this study argues that the vision is not the same as that of Rev 21–22, but it does point forward to its heightened fulfillment. The study will show how the text of Ezek 40–48 shows typological features, and then it will demonstrate how later NT works develop these features in the Gospel of John and Rev 21–22.[177] These two books contain the most significant references to Ezek 40–48 in the NT.[178]

By showing that Ezekiel's temple is a type, this work shows that the temple is a way that God progressively revealed to his people how he would dwell among them. Ezek 40–48 provides the transition for seeing God's dwelling as outside a physical building. To quote Taylor again, "[Ezekiel] freed Israel from the last vestige of a belief in the localized presence of God in a building in Jerusalem."[179] The Gospel of John especially emphasizes the theology of the temple in its presentation of Christology.[180] In fact, this gospel contains the only direct reference in the NT to Jesus as the temple (John 2:21). Therefore, that Ezekiel's temple in particular influences the Fourth Gospel's presentation of Jesus as the temple is unsurprising. The book of Revelation also contains many examples of the influence of Ezekiel.[181] One writer states, "Pero Ezequiel ha dejado una profunda huella en casi todas sus páginas."[182] Ezek 40–48 also provides inspiration for Rev 21–22 in particular.[183] So far, though, no work in OT theology has emphasized the importance of Ezek 40–48 in the theology

---

177. Fishbane and Levenson show typological features in Ezek 40–48, but do not develop these in detail. See Fishbane, *Biblical Interpretation*, 368–71; Levenson, *Program of Restoration*.

178. Peterson, *John's Use of Ezekiel*; Beale, *Old Testament in Revelation*, Beale, *Revelation*; Fowler, "Ezekiel in the Fourth Gospel"; Hanson, *Prophetic Gospel*; Manning, Jr., *Echoes of a Prophet*; Vawter, "Ezekiel and John," 450–58.

179. Taylor, "Temple in Ezekiel," 70.

180. Barker, *King of the Jews*; Chanikuzhy, *Jesus, the Eschatological Temple*; Coloe, *God Dwells with Us*; Hoskins, *Jesus as Fulfillment*; Kerr, *Temple of Jesus' Body*; Kinzer, "Temple Christology in John;" Salier, "Temple in John;" Um, *Temple Christology in John's Gospel*.

181. Vanhoye, "L'utilisation d'Ezéchiel Dans l'Apocalypse," 436–76; Vogelgesang, "Ezekiel in Revelation;" Ruiz, *Ezekiel in the Apocalypse*; Fekkes, *Isaiah and Prophetic Traditions in Revelation*; Moyise, *Old Testament in Revelation*; Beale, *Old Testament in Revelation*; Beale, *Revelation*.

182. Sicre, *Introducción*, 293, "But Ezekiel has left a profound footprint on almost every one of its [Revelation's] pages."

183. Sicre, *Introducción*, 293.

of the temple as providing a transition from a physical temple and pointing forward typologically to a greater fulfillment.

Having explored the different views of the temple in Ezekiel, and the nature of typology, the next step is to examine the book of Ezekiel itself. What does the text actually say?

2

Evidence for a Type in Ezekiel's Temple Vision, Part I

The Vision in Context

Introduction

AN AXIOM IN BIBLICAL interpretation is that a text should be interpreted in its context. Therefore, as part of the exegesis Ezek 40–48, the reader must explore how the temple vision fits with the rest of Ezekiel's book. Ezekiel's message as a whole provides the proper lenses for understanding the prophesied temple as a type. A few presuppositions must be stated, however, before probing the book. This work will examine the entire book of Ezekiel, including its last nine chapters, as a whole literary unit. While taking into consideration some text-critical questions, this study uses a synchronic, final-form reading of the Masoretic Text (MT).[1] After all, the book of Ezekiel, and particularly Ezek 40–48, demonstrate a final unity.[2]

---

1. As it relates especially to Ezek 40–48, see the text-critical studies on P967 in Lilly, *Two Books of Ezekiel*; O'Hare, *Have You Seen?*; Crane, *Israel's Restoration*; Lust, "Use of Textual Witnesses," 7–20; Lust, "Ezekiel 36–40," 517–33; Díaz-Caro, "El Papiro 967," 245–53; Ribera, "El Targum y Las Versiones Antiguas," 317–28.

2. Many scholars question the unity of Ezek 40–48, the most well-known figure being Wellhausen, *Prolegomena to the History of Ancient Israel*, 123. Others followed him, such as Bertholet, *Das Buch Hesekiel*, xx; Hölscher, *Hezekiel*, 5; Gese, *Der Verfassungsentwurf*; Zimmerli, *Ezekiel 1*; Pohlmann, *Hesekiel*; Rudnig, *Heilig und Profan*. Many ably defend the integrity of Ezek 40–48, such as Joyce, *Ezekiel*, 7–16; Collins, *Mantle of Elijah*, 92–93; Block, *Ezekiel 1–24*, 17–23; Cook, "Innerbiblical Interpretation in Ezekiel 44," 193–208; Eichrodt, *Ezekiel*; Davis, *Swallowing the Scroll*.

As Duguid states, "The book of Ezekiel in its present form is a coherent and consistent whole."³ Even if different portions of the text developed at different stages, at the end of his ministry the prophet Ezekiel could easily have placed the texts together.⁴ In other words, the text appears as it does in the MT, and in its present order, because the final author intended to make meaning in this way, not because of competing ideologies or historical developments. Stevenson puts it well in saying, "The issue is not that someone pieced together scraps, but that someone wanted a quilt."⁵ The presupposition of the whole book's unity particularly matters when examining Ezek 40–48 in the book's context, for such an examination shows that the author places the temple vision at the end of the book to promote an eschatological message.

With these presuppositions in mind, we can now examine key texts which reveal connections to Ezek 40–48. Ezek 11:16; 20:33–34; and 34–37 show close textual and thematic links to Ezek 40–48. The passages underscore a typological reading of Ezek 40–48, for they show that YHWH intends a non-structural fulfillment of his covenant promise to dwell with his people.

The Context of the Book of Ezekiel

Scholars propose various ways to structure the book of Ezekiel.⁶ While in-depth discussion of structure is beyond the scope of this study, for proper interpretation one must understand the presence of a literary structure in Ezekiel. Some methods, especially redaction criticism, imply that the book of Ezekiel is a piecing together of disparate, if not contradictory, texts.⁷ Thus, as Mayfield notes, many structure the book based on perceived layers of redaction, detected through markers like oracle formulas ("The word of YHWH came to me, saying . . .").⁸ A better avenue is to look at the book of

---

3. Duguid, *Leaders of Israel*, 8.

4. Collins, *Mantle of Elijah*, 96; Block, *Ezekiel 1–24*, 22–23.

5. Stevenson, *Vision of Transformation*, 7.

6. In addition to the commentaries, works that specifically focus on the book's structure include van Dyke Parunak, "Structural Studies in Ezekiel"; Renz, *Rhetorical Function of Ezekiel*; Petter, "Mesopotamian City Lament?"; Mayfield, *Literary Structure and Setting*; Peterson, *Ezekiel in Context*; Hiebel, *Ezekiel's Vision Accounts*.

7. Notably, Garscha attributed only thirty verses to the prophet Ezekiel in Garscha, *Studien Zum Ezechielbuch*.

8. Mayfield, *Literary Structure and Setting*, 3.

Ezekiel synchronically, that is, as a literary work, and one way to structure a literary work is by theme.⁹ In the book of Ezekiel, several themes occur, often overlapping, such as the presence of the glory of YHWH, kingship, or the knowledge of YHWH (Zimmerli's *Erkenntnissformel*).¹⁰ Another appropriate way to structure the book thematically and literarily is by noting the visions of YHWH's glory.¹¹ Structuring Ezekiel's book according to theophanies is best because it highlights the interrelated themes of YHWH's glory, kingship, and recognition of his name, rather than ruling them out wholesale. Each account of YHWH's glory appearing to Ezekiel also stresses YHWH's kingship and name. Therefore, in reading the book as a literary unit, the theophanies of Ezek 1–3, 8–11, and 40–48 best reveal the structure of the book.

In the first structural marker, Ezek 1–3, YHWH's glory appears by the Chebar canal.¹² Although some believe the "storm from the north"

---

9. See Davis, *Swallowing the Scroll*, for a notable example of a synchronic literary reading. For structuring Ezekiel by theme see Kutsko, *Between Heaven and Earth*, 1. Mayfield, *Literary Structure and Setting*, 11, plainly states that books should not be divided by theme but by literary markers, which he argues should be, in the case of Ezekiel's book, the chronological formulas. About Kutsko's method, Mayfield says that ". . . [his] thematic reading of the book [may be] driving his structural analysis" (*Literary Structure and Setting*, 23). The argument here, though, is not that the following thematic structure is *the* literary structure for the book of Ezekiel, but simply one way to see thematic unity throughout the book.

10. On YHWH's presence, see Kutsko, *Between Heaven and Earth*; Hiebel, *Ezekiel's Vision Accounts*. On kingship, see Clark, "'I Will Be King Over You'"; Nevader, "Exile and Institution"; Nevader, *YHWH versus David*; Bechtel, "Politics of Yahweh;" Block, *Beyond the River Chebar*; Stevenson, *Vision of Transformation*. On knowledge of YHWH, see Zimmerli, *Erkenntnis Gottes*. This work is translated in Zimmerli, *I Am Yahweh*, 29–98. See also Joyce, *Divine Initiative and Human Response*. Zimmerli considers the *Erkenntnissformel* as a form marker to mark off a discourse.

11. The theophanies are linked in form. Beale, *Temple and the Church's Mission*, 337, notes three features in the introductions for each vision, 1) an initial comment on the date; 2) the hand of YHWH coming upon Ezekiel; 3) a statement that he saw visions. All the visions also occur at the Chebar river and concern a sight of the glory of YHWH. See also Hiebel, *Ezekiel's Vision Accounts*, 1–48; van Dyke Parunak, "Literary Architecture," 61–74.

12. The term "structural marker" indicates that not everything between these markers fits clearly into the theme. In other words, a number of different themes exist in the passages between, for example, marker two (Ezek 8–11) and marker three (Ezek 40–48). The argument here is not that Ezek 1–7, Ezek 8–39, and Ezek 40–48 make up the three main sections of the book, but that the three "markers" discussed here are like checkpoints which resume a theme woven throughout the book. Block, *Ezekiel 1–24*, 24–26, notes Ezekiel's literary style of "resumptive exposition," wherein he brings out a theme, drops it, and develops it later. Peterson, *Ezekiel in Context*, also

(Ezek 1:4) denotes coming judgment, the theophany more likely portrays a comforting image for the faithful such as Ezekiel.[13] The mobile throne introduces the theme of God's presence apart from the temple in order to, as Kutsko puts it, "... reassure [the] audience that Yahweh is present despite his seeming absence."[14] The passage ends with Ezekiel seeing YHWH's glory in the valley (Ezek 3:23). Importantly, then, the book begins with this theme of YHWH's presence.

YHWH's glory next appears in the second structural marker, the vision of Ezek 8–11.[15] At the vision's conclusion the prophet sees YHWH's glory alight from the temple and rest east of the city (Ezek 11:23). The third and final structural marker in the book is Ezek 40–48, where YHWH's glory returns from the east (Ezek 43:2), the direction in which Ezekiel last saw it (Ezek 11:23). YHWH's glory fills the temple (Ezek 43:5) and rests there forever (Ezek 43:7; cf. 44:1–2; 48:35). This brief outline of a literary structure shows that, rather than the writer appending Ezek 40–48 to the rest of the book after the exile, the temple vision is an integral part of the prophet's message.[16] Ezekiel is burdened to proclaim the return of YHWH's glory, even in the midst of present exile.[17] In fact, Ezekiel's pattern of halving oracles and composing symmetrical texts could explain why YHWH's glory begins and ends the book.[18] The

---

argues similarly for "structural peaks."

13. Duguid, *Ezekiel*, 58–59, states that the constant motion described in Ezek 1 is "ominous," using ANE background to view the chariot as the coming of a divine warrior, and the north being the direction whence Judah's enemies come. He claims, "The divine warrior is here approaching to wage war against his own people, not to deliver them." See also Allen, *Ezekiel 1–19*, 25. In response to Duguid, the divine warrior image is an appropriate description of the holiness of God, but need not represent his judgment. In Ezek 8–11, YHWH's judgment leaves the temple, i.e., away from the people. Thus, YHWH's appearance among his people in exile shows he moves towards them in mercy. Block, *Ezekiel 1–24*, 92, contends that the direction of the storm is either inconsequential or may refer to the north as the mythological location of the mountain of God, akin to Mount Zaphon.

14. Kutsko, *Between Heaven and Earth*, 2.

15. For connections between Ezek 8–11 and Ezek 40–48, see Kunz, "O espaço divino."

16. So Tuell, "Ezekiel 40–42 as Verbal Icon," 656. For connections between Ezek 1 and Ezek 40–48, see Nielsen, "Ezekiel's Prologue," 99–114.

17. Brettler, *How to Read the Bible*, 195, says, "If a main theme of the retribution section is divine abandonment, it should not surprise us that the main theme of the consolation section is the return of the divine Presence."

18. Greenberg, *Ezekiel 1–20*, 25–26, notes "halving" as a literary feature. This

book of Ezekiel develops a common theme of YHWH's glory coming to dwell among his covenant people, culminating in the final temple vision. In light of the literary theme of God's presence uniting the book, then, this section will examine a few texts in Ezek 1–39 that place the temple of Ezek 40–48 in an eschatological context. Clues in these texts indicate that YHWH's presence can be with his covenant people apart from the physical structure of a temple, further indicating that the temple of Ezek 40–48 should be considered a type.

A Little Sanctuary: Ezekiel 11:16

Ezek 8–11 concerns YHWH's judgment on Judah and his consequent departure from the temple. Eventually, YHWH's glory departs in Ezek 11:23. Yet before Ezekiel watches this transpire, YHWH gives him an oracle to proclaim (Ezek 11:14–21).[19] The relevant exegetical issue in this passage concerns Ezek 11:16, but the whole oracle is noteworthy. In Ezek 11:17–21, YHWH promises a covenant renewal, which includes giving the people of Israel a new heart. Using his method of resumptive exposition, Ezekiel develops this theme later in the book. In Ezek 36, YHWH promises to give the people a new heart and then, in Ezek 37:14, YHWH repeats that he will put his Spirit within them. Finally, in Ezek 37:26 he says he will make a covenant of peace with Israel. Thus, one finds the themes of a new heart/spirit and a covenant of peace in both Ezek 11 and 36–37. In this light, the term מִקְדָּשׁ ("sanctuary") provides another noteworthy textual link between Ezek 11:16 and 37:26, 28. Thus, exegesis of Ezek 11:16 cannot ignore a connection with these later chapters.

How, then, should one interpret Ezek 11:16? The text could refer to לְמִקְדָּשׁ מְעַט in a quantitative sense ("as a small sanctuary") or temporal sense ("as a sanctuary for a little while"). The best interpretation is that Ezekiel says YHWH was a "small sanctuary" among his people in exile

---

claim is tentative since the two texts (Ezek 1, 40–48) admittedly vary greatly in length, whereas "halving" implies a near equal number of words. Nevertheless, YHWH's presence bookends Ezekiel's work.

19. A number of scholars do not believe this text originally belonged to the unit. For example, see Brownlee, "Aftermath of the Fall of Judah," 393–404; Eichrodt, *Ezekiel*, 142. See, though, Joyce, "Dislocation and Adaptation," 49, who agrees with these scholars, saying, "We have argued then that Ezek 11:14–21 did not originally belong in its present setting, but it is certainly not by chance that these words are placed here." For a defense of the authenticity of this passage in light of intertextuality with Deuteronomy, see Gile, "Deuteronomic Influence in Ezekiel." 263–67.

(see the argument below). The temporal interpretation, "sanctuary for a little while," implies that a non-Jerusalemite presence was an anomaly. In that case, YHWH's presence in exile includes a planned obsolescence, with the permanent plan to remain present in the Jerusalem temple forever. In contrast, the quantitative interpretation, "small sanctuary," implies that YHWH can appropriately be present with his people apart from the temple in Jerusalem. Thus, in Ezek 11:16, according to Eichrodt, "Ezekiel gives us one significant glimpse of his thoughts about what exile could contribute to the relationship of Israel with God . . ."[20] God has not severed the exiles from his gracious presence.[21] In this period of redemptive history (exile), however, YHWH's presence is small, and not the totality of blessing that exists in the temple. Nevertheless, a small sanctuary presence provides hope that YHWH does not restrict his blessing to a physical temple.[22] Additionally, YHWH's small sanctuary says nothing about length of time, meaning YHWH can be present away from Jerusalem long-term.[23] Taylor says, "The suggestion is not that Yahweh has decamped to dwell permanently where he appeared to Ezekiel in Babylon, but that he has released himself from the Jerusalem Temple and has, as it were, gone walkabout. His absence from the Temple means his presence here, there and everywhere, in Babylon or anywhere, yes, or even in Jerusalem and Judah."[24] One may add that YHWH does not state when he will cease to "go walkabout," implying the possibility of an enduring presence outside the temple.

---

20. Eichrodt, *Ezekiel*, 145.

21. Eichrodt, *Ezekiel*, 145.

22. See Dus and Simian-Yofre, "Ezequiel," 421. Although they hold to the temporal view, they conclude, "La diferencia es que el Señor encuentra una solución alternativa, y, aun estando en Babilonia lejos del templo, se convierte él mismo en el santuario requirido." Author's translation, "The difference is that the Lord finds an alternative solution, and, even being in Babylon far from the temple, he converts himself into the required sanctuary."

23. Contra Allen, *Ezekiel 1–19*, 164, who claims that Ezek 40–48 teaches that the presence of God ". . . required the religious props of temple festivals and sacrifices." Allen sees Ezek 11:16 as an anomaly rather than a development in the theology of God's presence, moving away from a physical building, which opens the door for Ezek 40–48 to be interpreted in a non-physical sense.

24. Taylor, "Temple in Ezekiel," 67.

One's conclusion on the quantitative interpretation ("small sanctuary") versus the temporal ("for a little while") hinges on the meaning of the term מְעַט in Ezek 11:16.²⁵

YHWH says, וָאֱהִי לָהֶם לְמִקְדָּשׁ מְעַט בָּאֲרָצוֹת אֲשֶׁר־בָּאוּ שָׁם. Does the term refer to temporality or quantity (size)? As for the temporal sense, the majority of prominent English translations translate the phrase in this way.²⁶ One argument that the term is temporal is that immediately following (Ezek 11:17) YHWH promises a return to the land of Israel/Jerusalem.²⁷ The context of return makes this, as Duguid argues, "... a (positive) statement of the temporary nature of the Lord's presence among the exiles rather than a (negative) statement of the incompleteness of the Lord's presence with them ..."²⁸ Duguid also cites Hag 2:6 as an example, and states that the *waw* consecutive + imperfect (וָאֱהִי) shows a logical contrast between the first and second halves of Ezek 11:16.²⁹ In response to these arguments, however, each of the claims could also apply to the quantitative view. In other words, the context of the statement within the promise of return applies just as well to the "small sanctuary" as the "temporary sanctuary." In addition, the *waw* + imperfect contrast also holds in the second view. The sense would be that though the people were far off from Jerusalem, they could still worship YHWH because in a small way they still had a sanctuary.³⁰ Thus, the grammatical structure implying a contrast need not imply only a temporal contrast.

Scholars more commonly consider מְעַט quantitatively (in terms of size), though the view is less common among the English translations of Ezek 11:16.³¹ When the term refers to time, it is often conjoined to עוֹד, which does not happen in Ezek 11:16.³² Other OT usage of the term

---

25. Brownlee, "Aftermath of the Fall of Judah," 398, simply deletes the word based on the meter of the verse.

26. NIV; NRSV; RSV; ESV; CSB; HCSB; NASB. Some of these provide a footnote for the alternate rendering. Such wide usage is interesting considering that the KJV, the major text stream for many versions, uses the quantitative sense, "a little sanctuary."

27. Blenkinsopp, *Ezekiel*, 63–64; Duguid, *Ezekiel*, 151 fn. 17; Keil and Delitzsch, *Ezekiel, Daniel*, 87–88.

28. Duguid, *Ezekiel*, 151 fn. 17.

29. Duguid, *Ezekiel*, 151 fn. 17.

30. Zimmerli, *Ezekiel 1*, 264.

31. The KJV is the only major translation. JPS translates the phrase as "diminished sanctity." For an exegetical argument for the quantitative view see Joyce, "Dislocation and Adaptation," 45–58.

32. *TWOT* 1228a.

shows reference, Cooke argues, to "... degree rather than time" (cf. 2 Kgs 10:18, Zech 1:15).³³ He also mentions 2 Macc 5:19 as an indication that YHWH did not need the temple, but the people did.³⁴ Greenberg also argues for the meaning of size, stating that מְעַט is in apposition to מִקְדָּשׁ, similar to the apposition in Dan 11:34, "a little help."³⁵ Additionally, in OT usage מְעַט can sometimes be a temporal adverb, but is often taken qualitatively.³⁶ The LXX seems to buttress this interpretation, using the term μικρόν, and the vast majority of that word's usage in the NT refers to size or degree.³⁷ Additionally, Block admits the ambiguity of מְעַט, but holds to the size meaning in light of the claims of the Jerusalemites in the previous verses.³⁸

In conclusion, the understanding of מְעַט referring to size is more appropriate. Thus, Brettler communicates the meaning and significance of the phrase when he translates, "I will be for them a mini-Temple in the countries whither they have gone."³⁹ If this interpretation is correct, the verse carries important implications.⁴⁰ Regarding YHWH's temple presence outside the temple itself, Block says, "This statement is without parallel in the OT."⁴¹ This interpretation buttresses the argument of this

33. Cooke, *Ezekiel*, 125.
34. Cooke, *Ezekiel*, 125.
35. Greenberg, *Ezekiel 1–20*, 190.
36. BDB 589a; *HALOT*, 611; *TWOT* 1228a; *HAL* 578a.
37. E.g., Matt 11:11; 13:32; 18:6, 10, 14; Mark 15:40; Luke 12:32; John 7:33; 1 Cor 5:6; James 3:5; Rev 3:8. Only in a few instances does it refer to time (Mark 14:70; John 13:33). See Louw-Nida, *Greek-English Lexicon*, 59.15.
38. Block, *Ezekiel 25–48*, 350. Zimmerli, *Ezekiel 1*, 230, takes the phrase in terms of degree, not size, but also not temporally, translating, "... a sanctuary to them only a little." He considers this as a priestly variation of the covenant formula. Instead of, "I will be your God," this phrase adapts to, "I will be a sanctuary to you" (see also Zimmerli, *Ezekiel 1*, 262). The above, however, shows the greater evidence for the quantitative view.
39. Brettler, *How to Read the Bible*, 188.
40. The "size" view led to the Targum paraphrase, "Therefore I have given them synagogues second only to my holy temple, because they are few in number" (*B. Meg.* 29a, quoted in Blenkinsopp, *Ezekiel*, 63). In response, several scholars note studies that show synagogues did not exist at the time of the Babylonian exile. See Eichrodt, *Ezekiel*, 145 fn. 2; Brettler, *How to Read the Bible*, 188. Brettler cites Levine, *Ancient Synagogue*, 1–41. Cogan, "Into Exile," 360, argues, "It is just possible that an institution that might be termed a 'protosynagogue' took its first step at this period." Contra Cogan, Oded, "'Lemikdash Meat' (Ezekiel 11:16)," 103–14.
41. Block, *Ezekiel 25–48*, 349. Beale, *Temple and Church's Mission*, 347, disagrees because he argues people experienced God's cultic presence in many other ways

chapter, for Ezekiel implies that YHWH abandoned Jerusalem, but not his people.[42] He will reside amidst what Tuell calls "[his] true house."[43] The prophet introduced YHWH's throne as mobile in Ezek 1, then develops this theology here in Ezek 11:16, and resumes it in later texts of Ezekiel.[44] Beale draws out the significance of this for the temple vision when he claims, "Chapter 40 begins where chapter 11 left off: describing God's heavenly presence that had departed from the physical temple and had taken up invisible residence with the remnant of Israel in exile ([Ezek] 11:16, 23–25)."[45] Or as Tuell states, "The vision in Ezekiel 40–42 represents the fulfillment of these words [of Ezek 11:16]."[46]

"I Will Be King over You": Ezekiel 20:33–44

In Ezek 20, YHWH once again, in the midst of judgment, promises a future for Israel. The overwhelming tone of Ezek 20 as a whole is one of judgment, yet the text contains glimmers of hope.[47] These glimmers connect with later messages of hope in the book. First, YHWH states, אֶמְלוֹךְ עֲלֵיכֶם "I will be king over you" (Ezek 20:33).[48] Sometimes taken as a message of judgment, the phrase actually represents salvation. In the context

---

outside a building, such as in the Garden of Eden. Nevertheless, Ezek 11:16 explicitly states the concept for the first time.

42. Rom-Shiloni, "Ezekiel as the Voice of the Exiles," 1–45, distinguishes between the exiles who are not abandoned and those who remain in Jerusalem, whom YHWH has abandoned. In this verse, Rom-Shiloni, "Voice of the Exiles," 18, says, "[Ezekiel] crafts a new conception of exile . . . This ideology constituted the new exclusive status of the Exiles as away from the land of Israel, but not distanced from God . . . Hence, Ezekiel's consolation prophecy exemplifies the prophet's vital contribution to the evolution of an exilic ideology during the first years of exile." One can better understand this, however, not as an evolution but as a truth from other OT teaching that Ezekiel emphasizes in the exilic situation.

43. Tuell, "Ezekiel 40–42 as Verbal Icon," 657; Tuell, "Divine Presence and Absence," 107–8.

44. See Joyce, "Dislocation and Adaptation," 57, for connections in this text with Ezek 1 and its application to the exilic situation.

45. Beale, *Temple and the Church's Mission*, 339.

46. Tuell, "Ezekiel 40–42 as Verbal Icon," 657.

47. Partly because of the tone of judgment, many date this section as post-587 BC. Ganzel, "Descriptions of the Restoration," 197–211, argues for a pre-587 date.

48. For the literature on the semantics of the verb and the hypothesis of an annual deity enthronement, see Bechtel, "Ezekiel and the Politics of Yahweh," 141.

of this passage, YHWH speaks of taking this action in his wrath (חֵמָה).⁴⁹ Because of the failure of Israel's elders, YHWH would make himself king.⁵⁰ Nevertheless, for those in exile under a foreign king, the message also provides hope.⁵¹ Connections with later passages underscore the message of restoration. The concept of Israel's future king reappears in Ezek 37:22, 24. Not only do we find the term מלך there, but Ezek 37 also concerns the regathering of the nation in the land (Ezek 20:40//Ezek 37:21), on the mountain(s) of Israel (Ezek 20:40//Ezek 37:22), along with the *Erkenntnisformel* (Ezek 20:44//Ezek 37:28). Thus, despite a tone of judgment and wrath, YHWH in Ezek 20:33 promises to be king in an eschatological future. At some point his disposition will turn and he will accept (רָצָה) his people (Ezek 20:40). Duguid therefore claims, "The basic thrust of this section is one of promise, not judgement."⁵² In the book of Ezekiel, then, YHWH fulfills this prophecy when his glory returns in Ezekiel's temple vision.⁵³ As Stevenson says about the temple vision, "Kings build temples. YHWH built this temple. YHWH is king."⁵⁴ Just as the divine king abandoned his temple in Ezek 11, so he promises to return, both to reside in his temple and to assert his kingship.⁵⁵

The next link with the temple vision occurs when YHWH states that he will bring his people to הַר־קָדְשִׁי ("my holy mountain;" Ezek 20:40).⁵⁶ In this verse, Eichrodt notes, "We see the dawning glories of a new temple . . ."⁵⁷ The threefold repetition of שָׁם in the verse indicates the importance of the location. Using the term "holy mountain" for a

---

49. On the rhetorical purpose of this speech as YHWH defending his honor in Ezek 20, see Clark, "'I Will Be King Over You,'" 161–214.

50. Duguid, *Leaders of Israel*, 117–18, 126.

51. Bechtel, "Politics of Yahweh," 131.

52. Duguid, *Leaders of Israel*, 126. So also Zimmerli, *Ezekiel 1*, 414; Allen, *Ezekiel 20-48*, 7. Lust, "Ezekiel Salutes Isaiah: Ezekiel 20:32–44," 369, argues that Ezek 20:32–44 is a salvation oracle affixed to the judgment oracle of Ezek 20:5–26.

53. Levenson, *Program of Restoration*, 99, says, "Increasingly, the Exilic community saw the historical monarchy fulfilled in the eschatological theocracy. Ezek. 40–48 is, for some of that community, the expected theocracy." Bechtel, "Politics of Yahweh," 207–74, also takes Ezek 40–48 as an assertion of kingship in line with Ezek 20.

54. Stevenson, *Vision of Transformation*, 116.

55. Block, *Beyond the River Chebar*, 73–99.

56. The phrase is only used in Ezekiel here in this text, as noted by Allen, *Ezekiel 20-48*, 14. "Holy mountain of God," though, occurs in Ezek 28:14 in reference to Eden.

57. Eichrodt, *Ezekiel*, 282.

location characterizes Zion theology.⁵⁸ The phrase that follows, though, בְּהַר מְרוֹם יִשְׂרָאֵל ("on the mountain height of Israel") is an idiosyncrasy of Ezekiel's, which, Zimmerli claims, "... points to the temple mount in the light of the mythical mount of God."⁵⁹ The holy mountain here refers to the cosmic mountain of God. Since the term is also used in Ezek 40:2, one should interpret the prophesied temple of Ezek 40–48 in light of this passage and its cosmic mountain ideology.⁶⁰

The combination of YHWH's kingship and the return of his people to his holy mountain suggests an eschatological fulfillment.⁶¹ Characteristic of this book, Ezekiel further develops these themes in the following chapters of his book, culminating in the final temple vision.⁶² Duguid writes of this passage, "This looks forward in seed form to the full description of the renewed Israel at worship on a high mountain in chapters 40–48."⁶³ When YHWH retakes his throne in Ezek 43:7 on the holy mountain (Ezek 40:2), he asserts himself as king over Israel and fulfills the promise of Ezek 20:33.

58. Psalm 2:6; Isa 11:9; 56:7; 57:13; 65:11, 25; 66:20; Joel 2:1; Zeph 3:11.

59. Zimmerli, *Ezekiel 1*, 417. Also Eichrodt, *Ezekiel*, 282. Against Zimmerli, Block, *Ezekiel 1–24*, 656, states, "[This designation] fixes its geographical location. Since Ezekiel's interest in this oracle is exclusively national, this cannot be the cosmic mountain from which peace flows to the entire earth. As in [Ezek] 17:22–23 and [Ezek] 40:2, the expression refers to Jerusalem." However, although the context is national in some sense ("in the land"), Block's claim is too strong in that the phrase does not preclude a cosmic interpretation. For example, Isa 2:1–4 describes a cosmic mountain, yet the word of YHWH comes forth from Jerusalem. For prophets like Isaiah and Ezekiel, the land is the site of the cosmic mountain. Though Israel may be the main audience in Ezek 20, one cannot therefore exclude an international application.

60. Allen, *Ezekiel 20–48*, 16, sees an echo with the Song of the Sea (Exod 15:17–18). Levenson, *Program of Restoration*, 7, identifies this as the fulfillment of the promise in Ezek 17:22–24 to place the Davidic king on a הַר־גָּבֹהַּ וְתָלוּל ("high and exalted mountain"), along with the promise of renewed worship in Ezek 20:40.

61. Dus and Simian-Yofre, "Ezequiel," 438, suggest that Ezek 20:33–44 speaks of the exile, saying, "Ez 20,33–44 no habla de la vuelta del exilio, sino del destierro por llegar." Author's translation, "Ez 20:33–44 does not speak of the return from exile, but about the exile coming up." They base their reasoning, though, on dating the oracle before 587 BC. However, the date does not preclude a more distant fulfillment, for while Ezek 20:33–39 regards exile, the eschatological language of Ezek 20:40–44 suggests more than simply God's restoration in the exile.

62. See Block, *Ezekiel 25–48*, 497, for several more textual connections between Ezek 20 and Ezek 40–48.

63. Duguid, *Ezekiel*, 264. As Zimmerli, *Ezekiel 1*, 414, concurs, "In [Ezek 20:40ff] we can see a stage on the way to the concrete expectation of a new temple, as in chs. 40–48." So also Stevenson, *Vision of Transformation*, 179–80.

"My Dwelling Place Shall Be with Them": Ezekiel 34–37

Ezek 34 begins what Sicre calls one of the most important sections in the history of prophecy.[64] The chapter is a critique of Israel's kings, wherein YHWH provides his own kingship as the solution (Ezek 34:11–16) and emphasizes the future hope of Israel.[65] As Sicre writes, "Quizá lo que más debamos agradecerle (a él o a sus discípulos) es la ampliación de la esperanza y el hermoso desarrollo que hace de este tema en el capítulo 34."[66] Sicre states that this chapter begins the presentation of unconditional salvation.[67] From here on, Sicre writes, "Las tristes experiencias del pasado no se recuerdan para hundirse en la amargura; son el telón de fondo en el que se destaca más esplendorosa la salvación de Dios."[68] Although Ezek 34 does not relate extensively to Ezek 40–48, the chapter begins this important section on salvation (Ezek 34–48) and links to the texts previously discussed in this chapter.[69] The passage contains YHWH's repetition of the prophecy of Ezek 20 to be king over Israel followed by YHWH introducing the Davidic king over Israel, the נָשִׂיא (Ezek 34:24). The figure will reign in the context of the new covenant of peace (Ezek 34:25).[70] The result will be a fruitful land, described in Edenic language (Ezek 34:26–29). The text concludes with YHWH saying, "And they shall know that I, YHWH their God, am with them . . ." (Ezek 34:30). The book of Ezekiel repeats in later chapters these themes of the covenant of peace, a fruitful land, a prince/chief, and YHWH's presence.

---

64. Sicre, *"Con Los Pobres de La Tierra"*, 395.

65. Sicre, *"Con Los Pobres de La Tierra"*, 397. For the transition to hope, see also, Ganzel, "Restoration of Israel," 206.

66. Sicre, *"Con Los Pobres de La Tierra"*, 407. Author's translation, "Perhaps what we should most be thankful for (to him or his disciples) is the expansion of hope, and the beautiful development he makes of this theme in chapter 34."

67. Sicre, *"Con Los Pobres de La Tierra"*, 404. Albeit, Sicre bases this argument on Fohrer's three stages of prophecy—judgment, conditional salvation, and unconditional salvation. Similarly, Klostermann, "Ezechiel," 391–439, considers Ezek 3–24 the diary of a mentally ill prophet, while one sees the prophet's healing in Ezek 33–48.

68. Sicre, *"Con Los Pobres de La Tierra"*, 405. Author's translation, "The sad experiences of the past are not remembered so as to sink one into bitterness; they are the backdrop against which the salvation of God more splendidly stands out."

69. For a rhetorical analysis of the relationship of Ezek 40–48 to Ezek 33–39, see Renz, *Rhetorical Function*, 121–30.

70. Hwang, "נָשִׂיא in Ezekiel 40–48," 183–94, argues convincingly that the royal figure of Ezek 34–37 is the same as the one Ezek 40–48 speaks of.

Furthermore, Ezek 36 continues these themes. As Sicre puts it, Ezek 34 is like a door that opens into a new world, a world Ezek 36 develops.[71] Once again the prophet describes the future land of Israel as Edenic, with fruitful trees, fruitful people, and multiplying animals (Ezek 36:8–11).[72] After describing this vivified world, YHWH adds that he will do this for the sake of his name (Ezek 36:16–21), so that the nations will recognize that he is YHWH (Ezek 36:22–23). The *Erkenntnisformel* here continues the theme of YHWH's name and links this chapter with Ezek 20.[73] The next section then introduces a "new" covenant with the covenant formula in Ezek 36:28.[74] Cleansing (Ezek 36:25) and the gift of new hearts and new spirits (Ezek 36:26–27) begin the implementation of the new covenant. The covenant formula also links this text with preceding chapters, Ezek 20 and Ezek 34. Then, after providing the covenant formula, YHWH continues to describe the covenant by noting its effects, reiterating the productivity of the land (Ezek 36:29–36). In fact, YHWH states that passersby will say, "This land that was desolate has become like the garden of Eden . . ." (Ezek 36:35). In summary, this chapter states that YHWH will institute a covenant with his people again, such that the nations will know that he is YHWH, and the land will be like Eden. These themes surface in Ezek 37, and later in Ezek 40–48.[75]

Ezek 37 speaks of an eschatological day when YHWH revives Israel. The vision begins with Ezekiel prophesying to dry bones, resulting in YHWH bringing them to life (Ezek 37:1–10). Then YHWH explains the vision, stating he will bring his people back to the land (Ezek 37:11–14), with an oracle following the vision text (Ezek 37:15–28). The oracle begins with a sign act regarding the unification of the tribes of Israel (Ezek

---

71. Sicre, *Introducción*, 289, "Y esto [Ezequiel 34] dará paso a un mundo nuevo."

72. This Eden link does not preclude intertextual links with Lev 26 in this section, such that Ezekiel describes the reversal of those curses. See Lyons, *From Law to Prophecy*.

73. Block, *Ezekiel 25–48*, 358, contends, "This restoration oracle serves as a reflex of ch. 20." For more discussion of the links between Ezek 20 and Ezek 36, see Strine, "Repentance in Ezekiel," 488–91.

74. "New" is in quotation marks because Ezekiel does not use this term as Jeremiah does (Jer 31:31). Still, Ezekiel's covenant is clearly distinct from the old covenant of Sinai, for the people will receive new hearts and spirits.

75. Beale, *Temple and Church's Mission*, 339 fn. 13, connects Ezek 36 with Ezek 37 via the covenant formula. Gile, "Deuteronomic Influence," 238–46, shows how Ezekiel here draws on the covenant formula in Deuteronomy for his language of gathering from exile.

37:15–20), concluded by an explanation (Ezek 37:21–28). This explanation contains several features that link Ezek 37 to the previous oracles of restoration. First, YHWH states that one king will reign over unified Israel (Ezek 37:22). This links to Ezek 20, where YHWH stated he would be king, and Ezek 34, where YHWH stated both that he would shepherd Israel himself, and that the Davidic נָשִׂיא would be the shepherd. This text reiterates that David will be king/נָשִׂיא (Ezek 37:24, 26). Ezek 37:24b also links to Ezek 36 in saying that the people will obey YHWH's rules and statutes. Then, YHWH once again promises a covenant of peace (cf. Ezek 34:25). However, here YHWH exposits the earlier promise by calling it a בְּרִית עוֹלָם ("eternal covenant"). This expository comment makes explicit the eschatological nature of the covenant, and therefore colors the reading of all of Ezek 34–37, and even following chapters. Ezek 37:26b then uses the root רבה again, meaning in the Hiphil, "cause to multiply," recalling Eden (Gen 1:22). After all this eschatological and Eden language, YHWH uses temple language.

In Ezek 37:26c, YHWH states that he will set his sanctuary (מִקְדָּשׁ) among his people forever. Ezekiel quickly follows this statement with the promise that YHWH's dwelling place (מִשְׁכָּן) will be over (עַל) them, along with the reiteration of the covenant formula (Ezek 37:27). The preposition עַל here is noteworthy in comparison to the promise of Lev 26:11–12 that YHWH's dwelling place will be "in the midst" (בְּתוֹךְ) of his people. Ezekiel indicates that there will not merely be a building amidst the people, but that YHWH's glory will reside over them.[76] If, as argued here, the temple vision fulfills the hopes of Ezek 37, this leads to a view of the temple being more than a merely physical building. The oracle then concludes with YHWH stating that the nations will know he is YHWH, the one who sanctifies (מְקַדֵּשׁ) Israel, when his sanctuary (מִקְדָּשׁ) is among them forever. These terms further link the oracle to Ezek 11:16. Before, YHWH was a small sanctuary, not restricted to Jerusalem, yet these verses indicate the promise of the "full" sanctuary. This examination of Ezek 37 also shows that all these promises in Ezek 34–37—of one Davidic נָשִׂיא, new hearts, regathering in the land, Edenic fruitfulness, national unification, a covenant of peace—culminate in YHWH's presence among his people. In other words, YHWH fulfills this "new" covenant, an eternal covenant of peace, when he makes his full sanctuary among his people once again.

---

76. Beale, *Temple and Church's Mission*, 339.

Finally, the cosmic mountain theme provides a link between Ezek 37 and the temple vision. In Exod 15:17, the cosmic mountain is YHWH's sanctuary where he promises to plant his people. In Ezek 20:40, YHWH promises again to bring his people to his holy mountain. Ezekiel's temple vision then begins on a high mountain (Ezek 40:2), where the prophet sees a temple YHWH has built. In Ezek 48:10, Ezekiel describes the temple as the מִקְדַּשׁ־יְהוָה ("sanctuary of YHWH"). While the term מִשְׁכָּן is not used in Ezek 40–48, the term is interchangeable with מִקְדָּשׁ in Ezek 37. Thus, occurrences of מִשְׁכָּן in texts throughout Ezekiel shed light on the significance of the temple in Ezek 40–48. Though Andiñach states that Ezek 37:26–27 is unclear on whether YHWH refers to the temple or the presence of God, the connection with Ezek 40–48 indicates a temple.[77] Put simply, the temple of Ezek 40–48 is the permanent sanctuary YHWH promises in Ezek 37.[78]

Apparently, early interpreters also saw a close relationship between Ezek 37 and the temple vision. In the arrangement of P967, editors placed the text of Ezek 37 after Ezek 38–39 and right before Ezek 40.[79] Crane argues that the community that arranged P967 in this way did so to link the sanctuary in Ezek 37 to the temple in Ezek 40 under the leadership of the Davidic king.[80] Block disagrees with many scholars who see P967 as a witness to a pre-MT *Vorlage*, but nevertheless notes the significance of the artifact, saying, "Indeed, one could argue ... that the growth of apocalypticism in the late intertestamental period stimulated the rearrangement of oracles in this text-form, so that the resurrection of the dead is seen as the final eschatological event prior to the reestablishment of a spiritual Israel..."[81] This study does not necessitate a particular view on the date or origin of P967. The point raised here is simply that early interpreters saw a textual and theological connection between Ezek 37 and Ezek 40–48. This section shows many of the links that lead to such a natural conclusion. Thus, in the context of Ezekiel's book, readers should see Ezek 40–48 as the eschatological fulfillment and culmination of YHWH's promised covenant.[82] When all the prophecies of the covenant

77. Andiñach, *El Dios que está*, 258.
78. Block, *Ezekiel 25–48*, 498.
79. See Lilly, *Two Books of Ezekiel*.
80. Crane, *Israel's Restoration*, 251.
81. Block, *Ezekiel 25–48*, 341. Pohlmann, *Ezechielstudien*, 88, adds that Ezek 37 presents an appropriate transition into Ezek 40–48.
82. Ezek 38–39 describes the land being purged of its uncleanness. The problem

come to fruition, a new temple will exist and YHWH's glory will return.[83] One should interpret Ezek 40–48 in this light.[84]

Summary

The context of the book of Ezekiel shows that readers should understand the temple vision as the fulfillment of YHWH's eschatological, covenantal promise. The book of Ezekiel begins with an appearance of YHWH's glory (Ezek 1–3), followed soon after with YHWH's departure from the temple (Ezek 8–11). Amidst these theophanies, though, Ezekiel prophesies hope. Ezek 11 shows that YHWH does not restrict his sanctuary presence to a temple in Jerusalem, while Ezek 20 states that YHWH will be king over his people when he gathers them to his holy mountain, i.e., the temple. Ezek 34–37 shows a concurrence of many eschatological themes, such as a Davidic נָשִׂיא, an eternal covenant, and YHWH's sanctuary presence. These contextual insights shape the reading of the final theophany in Ezek 40–48, but exegesis of the actual vision is fundamental.

---

with Israel's uncleanness defiling the land (Ezek 36:17) is solved with a new heart and spirit (Ezek 36:26–27). Ezek 38–39 deals with the uncleanness of Israel's enemies such that outsiders cannot defile the land anymore either. This prepares the way for YHWH's sanctuary to be established once again. See especially Niditch, "Ezekiel 40–48 in a Visionary Context," 221–23; Nobile, "Ez 38–39 Ed Ez 40–48," 141–71. So also Milgrom, *Ezekiel's Hope*, 43. Feinberg, *Ezekiel*, 240, says, "These chapters [Ezek 40–48] are the fitting sequel to the series in chapters 33–39."

83. Sicre, *Introducción*, 289. Block, *Ezekiel 25–48*, 507–10, notes the similarities between this account and ANE temple-building after a god's victory over his enemies.

84. Alexander, *Ezekiel*, 134, claims that because Ezek 40–48 is apocalyptic, he says, "It is not a continuation of the previous chapters and their argument." However, this section on the context of Ezekiel's book shows clear textual connections.

3

Evidence for a Type in Ezekiel's Temple Vision, Part II

Exegesis of Key Texts in Ezekiel 40–48

BUILDING OFF OF THE contextual study, this chapter will show that the texts below describe a real temple, not a heavenly one. At the same time, the texts show typological features, indicating that the temple is eschatological and pointing forward to a greater, non-structural fulfillment. A few texts provide a hermeneutical roadmap for reading the entire vision, these being Ezek 40:1–4; 43:1–12; 47:1–12; and Ezek 48:35. These texts are used because, as the study will show, three of these passages occur at key structural markers in the vision, thus providing an appropriate map for the vision as a whole.[1] The other, Ezek 47:1–12, introduces the land, but the passage is also one of the clearest passages in the vision with typological features.

Ezekiel 40:1–4

The Date Formula

This text, the opening of the vision, provides a hermeneutical roadmap for what is to come in the following chapters of Ezek 40–48. These few verses include many salient details. First, the text contains a date formula,

---

1. Ezek 40:1–4 begins the vision, Ezek 43:1–12 lies at the center, and Ezek 48:35 concludes the vision.

mentioning the twenty-fifth year of the exile (573 BC; see Ezek 1:2).² Ezekiel intentionally places the vision here for a thematic purpose, not because it is the last-dated oracle of Ezekiel's book.³ The oracle in Ezek 29:17–21 dates to the twenty-seventh year of the exile (571 BC). Moreover, the nearest literary antecedent in terms of dated oracles (Ezek 33:21–22) comes twelve years prior to the temple vision. Therefore, Ezekiel places this vision here to conclude the book with the return of YHWH's presence. The date for this oracle is pregnant with theological meaning.⁴

Multiple scholars note that the twenty-fifth year likely symbolizes the halfway point to the Jubilee year (the fiftieth year; see Lev 25:8–22).⁵ Van Goudoever states that in apocalyptic literature adherents marked "mid-time," so possibly this conception of mid-time was also present in the exilic period.⁶ Bergsma provides another argument for the mid-Jubilee view by noting the phrase בְּרֹאשׁ הַשָּׁנָה בֶּעָשׂוֹר לַחֹדֶשׁ ("at the beginning of the year, on the tenth of the month").⁷ Normally a date formula

---

2. Joyce, *Ezekiel*, 222, calculates the date as April 28, 573.

3. For discussion of scholars who organize the book by the chronological formulas, see Mayfield, *Literary Structure and Setting*, 3–8.

4. Konkel, "Das Datum," 55, says, "[The date] sheds new light on the theological program of Ezek 40–48." Konkel argues for intertextual links with 2 Kgs 22, Josiah's renewal of the temple. Besides the Jubilee year discussed below, there may be another significant aspect of the date formula, which is that it is the tenth day of the first month. The Passover was to be commemorated during the first month of the year (Nisan; Exod 12:2), celebrating release from bondage. See Block, *Beyond the River Chebar*, 160; Alexander, *Ezekiel*, 136; Feinberg, *Ezekiel*, 240. In Ezekiel's new legislation, the Passover is celebrated beginning on the fourteenth day (Ezek 45:21). Thus, this vision arrives right before Passover begins. Gaebelein, *Ezekiel*, 276, believes that the date refers to the start of the civil year, in the month of Tishri, when Israel would celebrate the feast of trumpets and Yom Kippur (Lev 23:23–32). Thus, he connects this date to the trumpets of jubilee.

5. Zimmerli, "Das 'Gnadenjahr Des Herrn,'" 324. Bergsma, "'Built Jubilee' in Ezekiel 40–48," 75–85, further develops the argument. Other adherents include Levenson, *Program of Restoration*, 18; Greenberg, "Design and Theme," 190; Block, *Ezekiel 25–48*, 495. The prophet would be familiar with the Jubilee (cf. Ezek 46:17), assuming, as this study does, that the text of this vision postdates H. Odell, *Ezekiel*, 487, argues there is little foundation for the mid-Jubilee view. She claims the judgment does not begin until the destruction of Jerusalem, the eleventh year of exile, as Jerusalem's destruction is the focus of Ezekiel's ministry. In response, Ezekiel's prophetic ministry was to be a watchman (Ezek 3:16–21), and he did not begin his ministry until after the exile, so of course his ministry would concern Jerusalem's coming destruction. Moreover, Ezekiel mentions the exile as part of God's judgment (e.g., Ezek 11:16).

6. Van Goudoever, "Jobel Year," 347; cf., Dan 12:7.

7. Bergsma, "Restored Temple," 76–77.

mentions the month first. Therefore, Ezek 40:1 normally "should" say, "On the first month, on the tenth of the month." However, according to Bergsma's close reading, the text actually implies that the tenth day of the month *is* the beginning of the new year. Wellhausen points out that the only other place the year begins on this day is in Lev 25:9–10, the description of Jubilee.[8] The argument for mid-Jubilee does not depend entirely on such an interpretation of when the year begins, but Bergsma's insight supports an intentional link with the Jubilee year. In addition, multiples of twenty-five occur throughout the vision. Some rooms and gates are twenty-five or fifty cubits wide (e.g., Ezek 40:13, 15), reinforcing the significance of the number twenty-five.[9] Thus, the date notation matters because, as Block puts it, "The midpoint of the jubilee cycle marked a turning of the corner, turning the sights away from the tragedy of exile in the direction of renewal."[10] In light of the date, the temple is what Zimmerli calls "an edifice of liberation."[11] Bergsma also says, "The temple in some sense *is* Israel's jubilee; that is, it is in proper worship of the Lord that Israel experiences her true freedom."[12] He later states, "In fact, it is possible to read the entire vision of restoration in chs. 40–48 as an eschatological proclamation of the jubilee on the Day of Atonement."[13] So, even a detail such as the date formula provides a lens for interpreting the vision theologically (typologically).[14]

---

8. Wellhausen, *Prolegomena*, 110.

9. For more examples see Bergsma, "Restored Temple," 77–78.

10. Block, *Beyond the River Chebar*, 160. Contra van Goudoever, "Jobel Year," 344–49, who claims that Ezekiel marks the exile mid-way through the Jubilee, so the twenty-fifth year marks the end of the jubilee cycle.

11. Zimmerli, "'Gnadenjahr des Herrn,'" 329.

12. Bergsma, "Restored Temple," 79.

13. Bergsma, "Restored Temple," 80. See chapter four of this study for discussion on Yom Kippur, which is notably absent in this vision. Several scholars hold that Ezek 40:1 speaks of the first month, the month of Nisan, while Yom Kippur in Mosaic legislation is celebrated in the month of Tishri. See Block, *Ezekiel 25–48*, 513; Eichrodt, *Ezekiel*, 540–41. Greenberg, "Design and Themes," 190, argues for deliberate ambiguity to bring in themes of both Passover and Yom Kippur.

14. Those who argue for a millennial temple do not write about the mid-Jubilee date. See, for example, Gaebelein, *Ezekiel*, 276–77; Feinberg, *Ezekiel*, 240–41. Alexander, *Ezekiel*, 137, notes that the notation of the fourteenth year after Jerusalem's destruction shows the coming of God's new program for Israel in the millennium.

Divine Visions

Just like in Ezek 11, Ezekiel here is taken from his house to see YHWH's house (Ezek 40:1).[15] YHWH brings him שָׁמָּה ("there"), a specific location only described in the next verse. Perhaps Ezekiel places this indefinite word שָׁמָּה here to recall Ezek 20, where the term occurs multiple times in the context of salvation (Ezek 20:40), and to point forward to Ezek 48:35. Regardless, the next verse further explains the event. Ezekiel states that he was brought to Israel in מַרְאוֹת אֱלֹהִים (Ezek 40:2a). This phrase is commonly translated as "visions of God," but a better translation is "divine visions." Other theophanies exist in the OT (e.g., Exod 3; Isa 6), but this text is more than a theophany. In fact, YHWH's glory does not appear until Ezek 43:4–5, yet the whole vision is described as "divine." Milgrom adds that Ezekiel uses אֱלֹהִים as an appellative ("divinity") rather than a proper noun.[16] Thus, one better understands the genitive not in terms of content ("I saw God"), but in terms of genre ("I saw a divine vision"). The phrase only occurs in Ezek 1:1; 8:1; and 40:2, showing a close linkage between the texts.[17] Thus, as Block says, "The substantive parallels among these texts require that the same hermeneutical principles employed in the interpretation of the previous prophecies apply here, and that one interpret this block in the light of the previous visions of God."[18] The earlier visions did not, Cook says, ". . . relat[e] linear history and empirical facts. Rather, readers have seen his visionary gaze peer beyond observable reality to perceive *transhistorical* structures and truths."[19] He even calls the first divine vision an experience of a "parallel universe."[20] While Cook

---

15. Andiñach, *El Dios que está*, 258.

16. Milgrom, *Ezekiel's Hope*, 64. See *GKC* 124e.

17. Beale, *Temple and Church's Mission*, 337; Tuell, "Ezekiel 40–42 as Verbal Icon," 654–57.

18. Block, *Ezekiel 25–48*, 496–97. The Qumran community apparently read the text in the same way, seeing this vision as the cosmic temple in *Songs of Sabbath Sacrifice*. See Davila, "Macrocosmic Temple," 5–6.

19. Cook, *Ezekiel 38–48*, 112. This contrasts with Feinberg, *Ezekiel*, 241, who states, "The characterization of the prophecy as a vision in no wise detracts from the literal reality of what is depicted here, any more than it does in Daniel or Zechariah." Yet he also admits just before that, ". . . throughout the portion it will be seen that the natural and the supernatural are intertwined." Feinberg appears to come to the text with an *a priori* assumption of a "literal reality," without taking into context the genre of apocalyptic and/or divine visions.

20. Cook, *Ezekiel 38–48*, 112. Similarly, Niditch, "Visionary Context," 208–24, argues for reading Ezek 40–48 in light of Buddhist mandalas. While that particular

overstates some here, these scholars correctly note that this vision goes beyond a historical look at events in Israel.

What hermeneutical principles apply to a "divine vision"? Here the issue of symbolism comes into play. In Ezek 1, the prophet sees a puzzling vision of YHWH. This portrait of YHWH is different from the throne visions in Isa 6 or Rev 4. However, those who examine Scripture canonically do not normally conclude that these visions contradict each other, that one text must accurately describe God's throne while the others are wrong. Instead, most interpreters understand that these texts fall into a genre of prophetic visions, and therefore each detail should not be interpreted woodenly (see Num 12:6–8 on the mystery of prophetic communication).[21] A description of the glory of YHWH does not intend to literally describe every detail of YHWH and his throne. Instead, the purpose of each author is to present a portrait of the deity on his throne. Similarly, the emphasis of Ezek 40–48 is not necessarily how many cubits each room is, although each detail is relevant for the greater picture. Instead, the genre of "divine vision" emphasizes that the overarching purpose of the vision is to reveal YHWH and the return of his presence, rather than the details of the structure. As Apóstolo writes, "The visionary elements . . . highlight the *fantastic* dimension of the book."[22] In a small way, then, this phrase about a "divine vision" clues the reader in to read the text not as a physical blueprint but as a theological message to Israel.[23]

While Beale accurately sees the vision as more than describing a structure, he misunderstands the "divine vision" by saying that Ezekiel

---

conclusion is doubtful, she rightly argues for reading the genre as a vision rather than a staid building plan. The vision genre includes symbols, but this does not make it any less "real."

21. Dr. Iain M. Duguid personally provided insight to the author regarding the connection with Num 12.

22. Apóstolo, "Imagining Ezekiel," 1–30. This is not to say the writing in the book is not true, but to question whether Ezekiel intends to convey, as Apóstolo says, a ". . . literal rendition of things that happened . . . ," or instead if he intends to, ". . . tell, persuade, convince, teach, challenge and, last but not least, rebut opinions, create meaning and convey an all-round religious message."

23. Tuell, "Ezekeil 40–42 as Verbal Icon," 655–57, makes this argument, concluding that the vision is a "heavenly ascent," or that the vision itself functions as a kind of icon of entrance into a spiritual realm. The structure is "real" but not earthly. Likewise, Joyce, "Heavenly Ascent," 17–41, argues for a heavenly ascent. This study does not exactly argue that Ezekiel sees a heavenly temple, but the emphasis is right that this is more than earthly Jerusalem.

sees heaven in Ezek 40–48.[24] The prophet does not see YHWH's glory return until Ezek 43:1–5. If Ezekiel is describing a heavenly temple in Ezek 40–42, how can YHWH's presence be said to be absent until halfway through? YHWH's glory would always reside in heaven. Instead, Ezekiel says YHWH left the physical temple of Jerusalem, and Ezek 40 introduces not a scene in heaven but a cosmic mountain-temple. Nevertheless, one should recognize the similarity in genre of this passage with Ezek 1 and Ezek 8–11 so as to not interpret the passage woodenly. As Cook says, "Readers should seriously hesitate before applying normal categories of time and space to the vision's objects."[25] Ezekiel does open an alternative world, portraying it as the real world.[26] This is a vision of reality, but not necessarily a "literal" temple.

A Very High Mountain

The location to which YHWH's hand brings Ezekiel is ambiguous (Ezek 40:2).[27] YHWH brings him to the land of Israel and sets him on a הַר גָּבֹהַּ מְאֹד ("very high mountain"; LXX ὄρους ὑψηλοῦ σφόδρα). After YHWH brings Ezekiel to this mountain, the text then says that on it (עָלָיו) rests a structure like a city to the south. Two questions arise here. First, is the structure upon the mountain, or south of the mountain? Second, is the

---

24. Here the issue of genre comes into play, rather than a comparison of the actual theophanies. Beale, *Temple and Church's Mission*, 337–39, interprets the contents of the three theophanies in Ezekiel to be essentially the same, that is, visions of the heavenly throne room. Unfortunately, Beale's reasoning is flawed. Beale claims that Ezek 10 is a sight of the heavenly dwelling, based on parallels with Ezek 1. Ezek 1, though, never claims to describe a "heavenly temple," for the very point of the vision is that YHWH's throne is mobile. Ezekiel only sees a glimpse of YHWH's throne. So, Ezek 10 simply describes YHWH's throne leaving the physical temple. The return in Ezek 43 is to a physical temple. Ezek 40–48 is not describing a heavenly temple (which, after all, describes every part of the temple *except* the inner throne room that Beale claims Ezekiel sees in chapters 1 and 10). Yes, the three visions are similar in genre, but that does not lead to the conclusion that they are about exactly the same thing. One may give the same response to Joyce's similar claim in Joyce, "Heavenly Ascent," 25. However, Joyce rightly acknowledges the differences in Joyce, "Heavenly Ascent," 26–27, stating that these still do not remove the close similarities between the passages.

25. Cook, *Ezekiel 38–48*, 112.

26. So Apóstolo, "Imagining Ezekiel," 16.

27. Contra Beale, *Temple and Church's Mission*, 336, with his puzzling statement, "All commentators agree that the location is Jerusalem." Alexander, *Ezekiel*, 137, admits, "The high mountain is not identified."

structure Ezekiel sees here the temple described in Ezek 40–42, or the city described in Ezek 48:30–35?

In regards to the first question, most interpreters take the structure to be south of the mountain, but a better understanding is that the structure is on the southern part of the mountain. One reason for the former view is the supposition that such a large structure could not fit on top of the mountain, especially if one assumes this is Jerusalem. Nevertheless, the text uses the word for "upon." In fact, the objections given to the latter interpretation show Ezekiel's point. This is no typical mountain, nor is this even Jerusalem.[28] Jerusalem is only about 2,500 feet in altitude. With Mount Hermon nearly three times higher, Jerusalem is hardly "very high."[29] In addition, nowhere does Ezekiel mention Jerusalem in the vision. In fact, the text explicitly gives the city's name as "YHWH Is There" (Ezek 48:35).[30] Instead of Jerusalem's temple mount, the prophet writes of a cosmic mountain.[31] Why, then, mention of the "south"? The LXX attempts to smooth out the MT with ἀπέναντι ("opposite me"), based on a change from MT מִנֶּגֶב to מנגד.[32] This change, though, is not necessary.[33] Ezekiel does not mean that the structure is south of the mountain, but

---

28. Milgrom, *Ezekiel's Hope*, 64. Contra Zimmerli, *Ezekiel 2*, 347, who accedes, "[This is a] mythical divine mountain . . . ," but he takes this to be an elevation of the Jerusalem temple mount.

29. Cook, *Ezekiel 38–48*, 125; Block, *Ezekiel 25–48*, 501. Toy, "General Interpretation," xlvi, argues for a literal temple, but that this is not going to be a supernaturally elevated mountain. Instead, according to Toy, the mountain seems very high to Ezekiel because he is in the flatter Babylon. Such an explanation is unconvincing, for Ezekiel would have known Jerusalem well, so he would have known what a high mountain looked like. More importantly, the prophet knew the import of the Zion tradition. Beale, *Temple and Church's Mission*, 336, states that some believe this will be a literal reality in the millennium, when Jerusalem's topography will radically be altered. For example, Alexander, *Ezekiel*, 137, says he tends to favor Mount Zion as the mountain, noting geographical changes that transpire prior to the millennium (Zech 13; Rev 6–19). So also Gaebelein, *Ezekiel*, 298.

30. See the discussion on Ezek 48:35 below for the relationship of this name to Jerusalem.

31. Cook, *Ezekiel 38–48*, 125.

32. See Block, *Ezekiel 25–48*, 512; Zimmerli, *Ezekiel 2*, 331, who both argue for the LXX reading. Zimmerli states that the MT reflects a later redaction making the text refer to the new city south of the temple (Ezek 48:15–19).

33. Gese, *Verfassungsentwurf*, 10, argues for the MT as reflecting the original, saying that the emendation presupposes a distance between observer and observed, which is not the case in the vision of Ezek 40–42. See also Heibel, *Vision Accounts*, 173.

on the southern part of the mountain, at least from his vantage point.[34] In other words, Ezekiel simply means that the structure is south of him upon the mountain.

As to the second question, the text states that on this mountain the prophet sees כְּמִבְנֵה־עִיר ("something like the structure of a city;" Ezek 40:2).[35] Some think this refers to a city, since the city in Ezek 48:30–35 lies directly south of the temple.[36] Importantly, though, the prophet never claims to see the new city, only a structure that looks like a city.[37] Furthermore, the discussion above shows that the structure is on the southern slope, whereas the new city is further south. Since the vision goes on to describe the בַּיִת ("temple;" Ezek 40:5), a better understanding is that the prophet sees a temple structure so large that it is like a city.[38] In addition, Ezekiel does not see a wall between the outer and inner court. Instead, these sections are separated by elevation (Ezek 40:31). Thus, the structure is built more like a city, with possibly only one set of outer walls to mark off the structure from its surrounding territory.[39]

The temple's massive fortified outer wall does liken it to a fortified city.[40] Another interesting detail is that the text states in Ezek 40:3 that YHWH brought him "there," an unnecessary repetition of the end of Ezek 40:1, unless the text hints at a link between the temple and the city

---

34. Milgrom, *Ezekiel's Hope*, 45, describes it as the southern slope of the mountain, in comparison to the temple at Delphi on the southern slope of Mount Parnassus. So also Block, *Ezekiel 25–48*, 514.

35. Stevenson, *Vision of Transformation*, 44, translates it as "a form like a city."

36. Cook, *Ezekiel 38–48*, 125–26; Zimmerli, *Ezekiel 2*, 331; Joyce, *Ezekiel*, 222. Alexander, *Ezekiel*, 137, takes this to be Jerusalem, equivalent to the new city.

37. Zimmerli, *Ezekiel 2*, 347. Davila, "Macrocosmic Temple," 6, says that the Qumran community took the "something like a city" to mean that Ezekiel saw a heavenly city.

38. As Beale, *Temple and Church's Mission*, 340, says, "He saw a temple structured like a city, or perhaps a city structured like a temple."

39. Stevenson, *Vision of Transformation*, 44; Greenberg, "Design and Themes," 255–56; Zimmerli, *Ezekiel 2*, 355; Allen, *Ezekiel 20–48*, 232. Admittedly, as Patton, "Ezekiel's Blueprint," 156, says, one could assume the presence of a wall despite the absence of its description. Moreover, as this study will show below, a strong possibility exists that Ezek 42:15–20 describes another outer wall at the bottom of the mountain. Still, a wall like that would resemble a city wall.

40. Milgrom, *Ezekiel's Hope*, 64; Block, *Ezekiel 25–48*, 514; Allen, *Ezekiel 20–48*, 229; Tuell, *Law of the Temple*, 23. Eichrodt, *Ezekiel*, 541, calls it a "castle-like temple." Bechtel, "Politics of Yahweh," 220–24, also holds that the prophet equates the temple with the city, i.e., a political structure, showing that Ezekiel's God is also king.

of Ezek 48:35, where YHWH is there.[41] Moreover, the Qumran community shows influence from this text when they describe their temple as a "city of the sanctuary."[42] The *Temple Scroll* describes a temple with equivalent size to the city of Jerusalem in their day.[43] The text also fits with Jer 3:16–17, which states that Jerusalem will be called "The Throne of YHWH."[44] Here in Ezek 40, then, YHWH's throne, i.e., his temple, fills an entire city.[45] These details are relevant because, as Beale puts it, "The mountain is not only high but of extraordinary enough size to contain the entire city . . ."[46] A mountain large enough to contain an entire city is no standard mountain. Therefore, though describing the temple, the term "city" in Ezek 40:2, Tuell says, ". . . creates tension and suspense."[47] In typological terms, it demonstrates ambiguity.

If the above argument is correct, Ezekiel describes the equivalent of a cosmic mountain. On this very high mountain lies an enormous structure, the house of God.[48] Thus this verse is of major significance for interpreting the vision.[49] As Levenson says, "The Temple thus cannot be understood in purely historical and geographical terms, but must be seen, in part, in the light of mythic concepts of a cosmic mountain. It is only by allusion to this mythic realm that we can make sense out of the great emphasis upon the Temple liturgy in Ezekiel's restoration."[50] In cosmic mountain ideology, the temple is central to the cosmic order of the world.[51] The temple is called the "navel of the world" (cf. Ezek 38:12),

---

41. Milgrom, *Ezekiel's Hope*, 65.

42. *Temple Scroll* 40:12. See Levine, "Temple Scroll," 16; Patton, "Ezekiel's Blueprint," 136–37.

43. Patton, "Ezekiel's Blueprint," 136.

44. Beale, *Temple and Church's Mission*, 341.

45. This is not to claim that Ezekiel sees Jerusalem, but simply that both Jeremiah and Ezekiel envision YHWH's presence filling an entire city.

46. Beale, *Temple and Church's Mission*, 336.

47. Tuell, *Law of the Temple*, 73–77. Tuell says the argument that Ezekiel sees a city-like temple is unconvincing, for Ezekiel knows what a temple looks like.

48. Duguid, *Ezekiel*, 471–72, calls this "theological geography." In contrast to the valley of Ezek 37 representing the curse, here the high mountain represents restoration.

49. This cosmic mountain setting, Tuell, "Verbal Icon," 655, argues, ". . . evokes the final transformation of the world . . . ," and indicates that this is an eschatological temple.

50. Levenson, *Program of Restoration*, 8. Eichrodt, *Ezekiel*, 541, says the prophet ". . . transfer[s] these primitive mythical conceptions to Zion . . ."

51. Levenson, *Program of Restoration*, 10.

wherein the enthroned deity dwells and from which he rules the world. Thus, Levenson terms this tradition "supra-historical," relating less to actual history and more to a theological (he calls it "mythic") concept.[52] The mountain is eschatological, akin to the prophecy of Isa 2:2, "And it will be in the last days that the mountain of the house [or temple] of YHWH will be established as the highest of mountains, and will be lifted up above the hills, and all the nations will stream to it."[53]

At the same time, however, Ezekiel does not describe what Beale calls "... a temple set only in a symbolic geographical world of another dimension."[54] Beale equates the temple to the city, based on Rev 21:10, which describes the holy city, Jerusalem, on a great high mountain. Beale believes that Ezekiel does more than describe a temple using cosmic mountain imagery. Rather, Beale says, "The depiction of the mountain in Ezekiel 40 is different from figurative language applied to Israel's earthly temple."[55] Beale's point is that Ezekiel actually describes heaven. Against Beale, however, rather than Ezekiel describing another dimension, Ezekiel writes about an actual temple that he sees in a vision, large as a city, which he describes in cosmic symbolism.

An Angelic Tour Guide

In Ezek 40:3, the prophet sees a man like bronze (see Ezek 1:7; 8:2; Dan 10:6) holding a measuring rod and cord. Though called a man, in other apocalyptic literature similar beings are termed angels (Zech 1:9-14; 2:5-9; Rev 21:15). Thus, in this context one may appropriately consider the man in the vision as an angel or supernatural being.[56] The angel serves as a tour guide, taking Ezekiel around the already-built temple. He takes most prominence in Ezek 40-43, the description of the temple,

---

52. Levenson, *Program of Restoration*, 14. Cook, *Ezekiel 38-48*, 126, describes this temple as a "transfiguration," a glimpse, but not a realization, of the final reign of heaven on earth.

53. Zimmerli, *Ezekiel 2*, 347; Block, *Ezekiel 25-48*, 501; Beale, *Temple and Church's Mission*, 336.

54. Beale, *Temple and Church's Mission*, 337.

55. Beale, *Temple and Church's Mission*, 336.

56. Allen, *Ezekiel 20-48*, 229. Feinberg, *Ezekiel*, 241, argues that this man is the Angel of the Lord since, he says, "He is called Lord," citing Ezek 44:2, 5. However, Ezek 44:2, 5 refers to YHWH's glory entering in Ezek 43:1-5. In Ezek 44, although the angel still guides, YHWH speaks.

while in the section of legislation he fades into the background. He is missing in Ezek 44:5—46:18, but still present in some of the legislation material (Ezek 44:1, 4; 46:19, 21; 47:1–12). After taking Ezekiel through the river (Ezek 47:1–12), the angel suddenly drops out of the vision without any explanation or further mention. His absence is almost certainly due to the shift in genre, as the text moves to explaining the land (Ezek 47:13—48:35). How, then, is the angel significant to the interpretation of the vision, particularly the temple tour?

One aspect of his importance concerns the text's emphasis on the building plan. As Zimmerli points out, the presence of the guide consists of two actions, leading and measuring.[57] The main focus of the angel's work in the vision, however, is the measuring, which the text mentions nineteen times.[58] Cooke connects this to two Babylonian artifacts. First, Gudea statues have Gudea holding a stylus and rod with a temple plan on his lap. Second, a relief in Ur has the moon-god holding a measuring line and the "coiled line of the architect."[59] An additional parallel lies in the name of Gudea's assistant in the vision, Ninurta, meaning "Lord of Copper," similar to the bronze man in Ezekiel.[60] These ANE connections show a polemic of YHWH's kingship. The rod and cord, which in the ANE artifacts the king holds in his hand, symbolize true and righteous rule.[61] Thus, the tour guide's presence in Ezek 40–48 points to YHWH's righteous kingship.

In the midst of all these measurements, the angel provides almost no vertical measurements. Scholars propose different solutions to this enigma. Are vertical measurements absent because they are implied, and their mention is simply unnecessary? Are they absent because this is a two-dimensional "ground plan," indicating that the prophet is looking at blueprints when he goes into a trance?[62] Or do the horizontal measurements prove the exact opposite, that Ezekiel is not describing a blueprint but a "symbolic" temple? The absence of other aspects of a temple plan, such as describing materials and the purposes of each artifact (cf., 1 Kgs

---

57. Zimmerli, *Ezekiel 2*, 343.

58. Zimmerli, *Ezekiel 2*, 343.

59. Cooke, *Ezekiel*, 430.

60. Milgrom, *Ezekiel's Hope*, 65; Sharon, "Ezekiel 40–48 and Gudea," 106.

61. Cook, *Ezekiel 38–48*, 113.

62. Cooke, *Ezekiel*, 425. Similarly, Talmon and Fishbane, "Structuring of Biblical Books," 139, claim that the prophet actually discovered a blueprint in the (Jerusalem temple?) archives and bases his description here off of it.

6), leads one to conclude that the absence of vertical measurements is intentional. In this manner Ezekiel demonstrates that this is not a physical blueprint.[63] In addition, the "stylized" and symbolic nature of the measurements, being multiples of twenty-five, denote the particular style of vision.[64] The description is, in Eichrodt's words, ". . . [of] a purely visionary nature . . . The temple makes its appearance as a heavenly reality created by Yahweh himself and transplanted to stand on earth . . . There is nothing to suggest that it should have a human builder."[65] The presence of the angel underscores the eschatological, "non-physical" nature of the vision. While a common marker of apocalyptic is the presence of an angelic guide, the exilic prophet Ezekiel predates the time of full-blown apocalyptic literature as it appears in the Second Temple period.[66] Thus, perhaps the presence of an angelic guide shows that the book of Ezekiel lies on a point of transition to more apocalyptic literature, but Ezekiel's vision itself is not fully apocalyptic. The presence of an angelic guide, after all, is not the only criteria for apocalyptic. Thus, Ezekiel's vision is eschatological, but he does not see a temple in the heavenly realm.

"Declare All That You See"

The words in Ezek 40:4 provide more key information for forming a hermeneutical lens through which to read the whole vision. YHWH, via the angel, commands Ezekiel to look carefully, listen carefully, and "set [his] heart on," i.e., pay careful attention to, what the angel will show him.[67] Then, he commands Ezekiel to "declare" (הַגֵּד, Hiphil imperative

63. Zimmerli, *Ezekiel 2*, 343–44.

64. Zimmerli, *Ezekiel 2*, 344. While there are similarities between Ezekiel's temple and Neo-Babylonian temples, Ezekiel's vision is still "stylized." See Ganzel and Holtz, "Ezekiel's Temple in Babylonian Context," 211–26. The same can be said of the tabernacle, which has a physical fulfillment though it is "stylized" somewhat in its measurements. However, Ezekiel's temple is much more stylized than the tabernacle, having all measurements be multiples of the same number.

65. Eichrodt, *Ezekiel*, 542.

66. Collins, *Apocalyptic Imagination*, 5, in his classic definition of apocalyptic literature, says it is, "A genre . . . in which a revelation is mediated by an otherworldly being to a human recipient . . ." As it relates to Ezekiel, see Hanson, *Dawn of Apocalyptic*, 234. Note, however, that Hanson refuses to label Ezekiel as proto-apocalyptic or apocalyptic due to what he considers later editing of the Zadokite priesthood. See also the discussion in Pohlmann, *Ezechiel*, 85.

67. Note Block, *Ezekiel 25–48*, 512, who in his translation renders it, "Human,

of נגד) what he sees to Israel. This final phrase underscores that YHWH will show the prophet a building that already exists. The section on Ezek 43:1–12 will expound upon the relevance of the command to "declare." Suffice it to say here that YHWH does not command the prophet to draw up an architectural plan, but to preach (declare) a message concerning the vision.[68] The main point, though, is that YHWH enjoins the prophet to declare what he already sees built. Notably absent in the vision is any command to build, for instead YHWH is the one who prepares the temple, city and land.[69] In the words of Eichrodt, "There is nothing to suggest that it should have a human builder."[70] The vision contrasts markedly with the tabernacle in Exod 25:9, where YHWH shows Moses the pattern (תַּבְנִית) already built, but then tells them they will build (תַּעֲשׂוּ) accordingly.[71] Likewise, David provides Solomon a pattern (תַּבְנִית), but does so for the purpose of the son building the temple (1 Chr 28:10–12, 19).[72]

Levenson notices interesting parallels between this text and Ps 48 in regards to the importance of an already-built structure.[73] In Ps 48:4 [Eng 48:3], God is made known (נוֹדַע) as a fortress via the fortress of Zion. Therefore, people are commanded to set the city upon their hearts (שִׁיתוּ לִבְּכֶם) and pass through (פַּסְּגוּ) it, in order to recount (ספר) who God is to the next generation (Ps 48:13–15 [Eng 48:12–14]). In Ezek 40:4, the prophet is also told to set his heart (שִׂים לִבְּךָ) on all that he sees, so that he might declare (נגד) it to the people. The parallel with Ps 48 indicates a

---

look carefully and listen closely. Pay attention . . ."

68. Zimmerli, *Ezekiel 2*, 360–61.

69. Zimmerli, *Ezekiel 2*, 361.

70. Eichrodt, *Ezekiel*, 542. So also Block, *Ezekiel 25–48*, 505. Tuell, "Verbal Icon," 652, says, "The most decisive argument against reading Ezekiel 40–42 as a building program is that it nowhere claims to *be* a building program."

71. Cook, *Ezekiel 38–48*, 113; Milgrom, *Ezekiel's Hope*, 65, also notices this contrast, though he believes Ezekiel should pass these details on for the people to construct the building upon return from exile.

72. Stevenson, *Vision of Transformation*, 17. Strong, "Grounding Ezekiel's Heavenly Ascent," 206, uses this example to argue that Ezekiel's temple is, he writes, ". . . the first installment on a promise to be fulfilled at the end of exile." However, the distance in time is completely unequal. David hands the plan over to Solomon to build soon after. If Ezekiel intends for the temple to be built, that would take place many more years later (possibly twenty-five years later, per Ezek 40:1, but likely more). Moreover, why does Ezekiel say nothing about handing this plan over to others?

73. Levenson, *Program of Restoration*, 16; so also Zimmerli, *Ezekiel 2*, 361.

parallel in purpose. Just as the psalm explicitly states that the architecture is a theology lesson, so the architecture of Ezekiel's temple is, Levenson states, ". . . a public testimony to the nature of God."[74]

The lack of a command to build strongly indicates that YHWH does not intend for people to construct a physical building in Israel.[75] As Zimmerli says, "The common denominator by which the whole [vision] is to be understood cannot be missed. The prophet is charged by his vision with proclaiming to his downcast people that their God is already in the process of erecting his sanctuary in their midst in faithfulness to his earlier promise."[76] In addition, as Tuell claims, the absence of a command to build implies an eschatological temple that YHWH will build with his own hands in the last days.[77]

Typology in Ezekiel 40:1-4

Several features of typology, according to the criteria of this study, are evident in Ezek 40:1-4. First, the vision's introductory words here show that Ezek 40-48 describes a *historical institution*, the temple. The context of the vision is the historical reality of the exile (Ezek 40:1), and Ezekiel sees in a vision the actual land of Israel (Ezek 40:2). So, in contrast to Beale, Ezekiel does not see a heavenly city/temple.[78] No, the vision is

---

74. Levenson, *Program of Restoration*, 16.

75. Eichrodt, *Ezekiel*, 542, notes that some conclude that this is a building instruction because Ezekiel is told to pay attention to the measurements and pass them on. Eichrodt disagrees due to what he calls ". . . [the] purely visionary nature of the building represented here." For more on this see the discussion of Ezek 43:1-12.

76. Zimmerli, *Ezekiel 2*, 362.

77. Tuell, "Verbal Icon," 655-56. See also Eichrodt, *Ezekiel*, 452. Yadin, *Temple Scroll*, 185, also notes the mention of a temple built by YHWH in the *Temple Scroll* and in 4QFlorilegium. Block, *Ezekiel 25-48*, 504-5, uses the absence of a command to build as evidence that it is *not* eschatological. Beale, *Temple and Church's Mission*, 346, argues against Block, but he misses what Block is saying. Block makes his statement in the context of a discussion on "millenarian" views, and this is what he means by "eschatological," so Block dismisses the idea that people will build a physical temple. Block, Tuell, and Beale use the lack of a command to build to make essentially the same point, that Ezekiel does not describe a physical structure to be constructed in Israel, but, as Block, *Ezekiel 25-48*, 505, says, "spiritual realities." However, these scholars differ in their manner of explaining these spiritual realities. Beale and Tuell call these spiritual realities an eschatological temple.

78. Beale, *Temple and Church's Mission*, 336-37. This point is noted well by Odell, *Ezekiel*, 487-88, although she argues that, unlike Ezek 38-39, this text does

rooted historically, an important feature of typology that takes the vision beyond mere symbolism or a "spiritual sense" of the text.[79] Most importantly, however, Ezekiel's vision concerns the temple, a vital historical institution for Israel.[80] Therefore, one should expect typological development from the prophets, and in later texts like the NT, regarding an institution as important as the temple.

Next, the vision is clearly *prophetic*. As discussed above, Ezekiel sees "divine visions." Toy, who sees this as a literal temple, admits, "The fact that it is put in the form of a *vision* may be supposed to deprive it of literalness."[81] An angel also guides the prophet throughout much of the tour. Then, at the end of Ezek 40:1–4, YHWH tells him to declare the message as a prophet. Because the text is prophetic, even with some apocalyptic features, one should interpret the vision eschatologically. As seen above, the Qumran community interpreted this vision apocalyptically and further expanded its significance for their eschatological purposes. An upcoming chapter of this study will show how NT works also take the vision as prophetic-apocalyptic, thus developing its typology.

Another important typological feature of these verses is the *eschatological heightening* (*Steigerung*) latent here. The very high mountain, as shown above, represents a cosmic mountain. Thus, Ezekiel looks forward eschatologically to the day when YHWH's cosmic mountain will be established (similarly, Isa 2:1–5). Also, the nature and size of the temple, the "structure like a city" (Ezek 40:2), shows an eschatological heightening of the temple institution. Ezekiel's prophesied temple is not of the same scale as the Mosaic tabernacle or Solomonic temple, but is much larger. Finally, in regards to *Steigerung*, YHWH's command to Ezekiel

---

not describe a future event. She rightly shows, however, that, "Not only is the vision situated in time, it is also located in space." Thus she describes a ". . . tension between present vision and future reality . . . ," which typology clarifies.

79. Gaebelein, *Ezekiel*, 276–77, presents a false dichotomy when he says, "In the visions of God the prophet was brought into the land of Israel, which is conclusive evidence that the vision he is about to receive concerns the people of Israel and not, as the spiritualizing, allegorical school of interpreters claim, the church. Ezekiel knew nothing whatever of the church and therefore not a line of all his prophecies could intelligently be applied to the church of the Lord Jesus Christ." Again, typology allows for a text rooted in history, concerning Israel, but also pointing forward to other realities.

80. For an excellent study on the temples in Israel, see Haran, *Temples and Temple-Service*.

81. Toy, "General Interpretation," xlv, responds that all visions include an exhortation showing the "practical meaning" of the vision, and such are found in Ezek 43:10–11 and Ezek 44:5–9.

Evidence for a Type in Ezekiel's Temple Vision, Part II 69

to declare what he sees (Ezek 40:4) means the temple is already built. As noted above, YHWH builds the temple, not Israel. Therefore, the prophecy looks forward to a glorious day when YHWH's temple, something far greater than any human would build, will be established.

This part of the vision also shows *ambiguity* latent in the text. This section examined these ambiguities, including questions like whether Ezekiel sees a city or a temple, and whether the structure is on the mountain or south of it. The ambiguity demonstrates the possibility of typology. That Ezekiel calls it "a structure like a city" shows that this is no ordinary temple. That Ezekiel does not name the city Jerusalem, although he is taken to a temple in the land of Israel, shows that he does not wish to bring in the old connotations of that now-faithless city (Ezek 8–11). More importantly, the ambiguity of the temple-city's identity shows that the "city" is more likely a future, eschatological land, and the prophet does not want the reader to identify this with the particular land of Israel. Here again one sees the benefit of typology and its attendant ambiguity, which allows for historical rootedness alongside eschatological development.

Finally, Ezek 40:1–4 describes an *epochal* time in the history of God's people. Such is evident in the discussion above regarding the twenty-fifth year of exile, halfway to Jubilee. The context of the entire book indicates the failure of Israel to fulfill its part of the covenant, but YHWH promises an "eternal covenant of peace" (Ezek 37:26) of which the new temple is a major part. The date notation at the beginning of the vision gives more than a historical marker, for it also provides a clue that Jubilee is coming, and therefore that the temple is, as Zimmerli calls it, "an edifice of liberation."[82]

Ezekiel 43:1–12

Ezek 43:1–12 is a crucial passage for interpreting the vision because there YHWH explicitly describes the very purpose of revealing the temple to his prophet.[83] The passage is the culmination of the vision so far, and perhaps even the peak of the entire vision.[84] Levenson emphasizes the importance of this pericope when he claims, "In a sense, these lines are the

---

82. Zimmerli, "Das 'Gnadenjahr des Herrn,'" 329.

83. Alexander, *Ezekiel*, 146 agrees, saying, "The most significant event in these nine chapters is the return of the glory of God to the Temple." So also Feinberg, *Ezekiel*, 251.

84. Hals, *Ezekiel*, 288, calls Ezek 43:1–12 "... the central pericope for the organization of all chs. 40–48 ..." See also Cook, *Ezekiel 38–48*, 187; Bechtel, "Politics of Yahweh," 207.

crown and consummation of Ezekiel's life's work."[85] The preceding study of Ezek 40:4 relates to this key text. The two passages are linked by the command to "declare" (הַגֵּד) the temple to the house of Israel (Ezek 40:4; Ezek 43:10), providing a structural marker that shows Ezek 40:1—43:12 is the first main section of the vision.[86] Discussion of this passage will center on two main sections, the return of YHWH's glory (Ezek 43:1–7a) and the command to declare the "law of the temple" (43:10–12).[87]

The Glory of YHWH Fills the Temple

This passage (Ezek 43:1–7a) describes the third theophany in the book of Ezekiel. In Ezek 43:3, the writer directly mentions the previous two (Ezek 1–3, 8–11) and thus associates them.[88] Moreover, the description

---

85. Levenson, *Program of Restoration*, 10. Alexander, *Ezekiel*, 146, adds, "The whole argument and unity of the book is consummated in this act."

86. Hiebel, *Ezekiel's Vision Accounts*, 182; Konkel, *Architektonkik Des Heiligen*, 239; Greenberg, "Design and Themes," 189; Block, *Ezekiel 25–48*, 576; Talmon and Fishbane, "Structuring of Biblical Books," 138–53. Hals, *Ezekiel*, 286, sees the passage as a hinge between Ezek 40–42 and the rest of Ezek 43–46. This answers the objection of Joyce, "Heavenly Ascent," 17–41, who argues that Ezek 43 is not part of the core vision, and therefore the writer envisions a return to the earthly temple in Jerusalem.

87. This section will not study Ezek 43:7b–9, since the contents do not relate directly to the topic at hand. There are two relevant textual issues here in terms of the unity of Ezek 43:1–12. The first question is whether Ezek 43:10–11 belongs with Ezek 43:1–9. Fohrer and Galling, *Ezechiel*, 237–45, claim that Ezek 43:1–9 is an independent text that should be added to later passages (Ezek 44:1–2; Ezek 47:1–12). Allen, *Ezekiel 20–48*, 249–50, and Zimmerli, *Ezekiel 2*, 411, also separate the texts, claiming that Ezek 43:1–9 begins a new unit. However, Gese, *Verfassungsentwurf*, 39–43, argues for strong links between the two texts, as does Block, *Ezekiel 25–48*, 576–78. Block shows that 43:10–11 forms an *inclusio* with Ezek 40:3–4. Also, while Gese claims that the verses link to the next unit beginning in Ezek 43:13, Block argues that Ezek 43:1–10 links to Ezek 40–42. To do so, Block notes parallels with the tabernacle, Solomonic Temple, and ANE temple building, wherein the temple is first constructed (in this case, described), followed by an account of the deity's glory entering. See also Herrmann, *Ezechielstudien*, 52–53; Tuell, *Law of the Temple*, 35–42; Hals, *Ezekiel*, 304–6; Konkel, *Architektonik*, 80–82, who take the text as ending at Ezek 43:10. The second textual question regards the placement of Ezek 43:12. Does the verse on the *torah* introduce the new section of legislation following it, or is it a conclusion of the speech concerning the temple (Ezek 43:10–11)? The present study links Ezek 43:12 with its preceding passage, but this determination is largely based on how one understands the meaning of the "*torah* of the temple." The discussion in the section below will present the argument.

88. See van Dyke Parunak, "Literary Architecture," 70; Kunz, "Espaço divino," 215–25.

of YHWH's glory coming from the east (Ezek 43:1, 4) links to the second theophany. In Ezek 11:23, YHWH's glory departed the temple and went eastward to signify the judgment of YHWH. Therefore, the return of YHWH's glory in the present text signifies a restored relationship and a removal of judgment.[89] YHWH fulfills the earlier promises in Ezek 34–37, for the restoration comes after YHWH cleanses his people (Ezek 36:25).[90] Having cleansed the people, YHWH can set his sanctuary among them and make his dwelling with them (Ezek 37:26–28).[91] The context indicates that, according to Levenson, "The return of the [glory of YHWH] is the climax of the restoration vision of chs. 40–48."[92] The text marks a crucial place in the vision and in the whole book of Ezekiel.

An important question to examine in the text is the issue of where YHWH's glory resides. The text states that YHWH's glory fills the temple (Ezek 43:5), and that the prophet hears YHWH speak from the temple (מֵהַבָּיִת).[93] At that point, YHWH says, אֶת־מְקוֹם כִּסְאִי ("[This is] the place of my throne;" Ezek 43:7).[94] But what does "this" refer to? Many read these verses and assume that the text speaks of the most holy place or inner court, comparing with 1 Kgs 8:10–11, where the writer describes YHWH's glory filling the "house of YHWH," the temple (cf. Exod 40:34–35;

---

89. Block, *Ezekiel 25–48*, 578–79; Hiebel, *Ezekiel's Vision Accounts*, 227–31; Alexander, *Ezekiel*, 146–47. Van Dyke Parunak, "Literary Architecture," 72, also notes echoes of Sinai, e.g., Deut 33:2; Judg 5:4–5; Ps 68:8; Hab 3:3–4.

90. Ezek 37:1–14 also contains an element of cleansing. The human carcasses made the land unclean. Instead of disposing of the bodies in burial (as in Ezek 39:11–16), YHWH solves the problem of Israel's uncleanness by making the dead bodies alive.

91. Block, *Ezekiel 25–48*, 578, also notes the importance of the phrase, "the glory of the God of Israel," stating, "One of the central themes of the salvation oracles of chs. 34–37 is being fulfilled." Beale, *Temple and Church's Mission*, 340, says, "It is probable that Ezekiel 43 is developing the prophecy of the sanctuary in Ezekiel 37." Hiebel, *Ezekiel's Vision Accounts*, 184, says the only other place these terms are used together is in the narrative of the recovery of the ark, e.g., 1 Sam 4:21–22.

92. Levenson, *Program of Restoration*, 10.

93. Kunz, Espaço Divino," 222, notes that "Glory of YHWH" (Ezek 43:5) and "Glory of the God of Israel" (Ezek 43:2), also occur interchangeably in Ezek 8:3; 9:3; 10:19; 11:22.

94. Contra Wevers, *Ezekiel*, 312, when he notes, "MT does not have this is ... ," opting for LXX ἑώρακας ("you have seen"). A verbless clause in the MT is not noteworthy, yet even if the LXX is correct, what Ezekiel has seen refers to the glory in the temple in Ezek 43:5. So also Zimmerli, *Ezekiel 2*, 409. Hiebel, *Ezekiel's Vision Accounts*, 200, notes the anomaly here of a vision speech beginning with a verbless anacoluthon rather than a question or imperative.

Hag 1:7).⁹⁵ Thus, interpreters see this text as a temple dedication, just as happened with the previous dwelling places, leading to a "physical structure" view.⁹⁶ However, in the 1 Kgs 8 passage, the antecedent verses (1 Kgs 8:1–9) explicitly focus on the most holy place, specifically the ark of the covenant. Thus, the context of those verses shows that YHWH's glory emanates from the ark and fills the temple. In Ezek 43, though, such description of the ark or most holy place is conspicuously absent.⁹⁷ Although the Spirit brings the prophet to the inner court (Ezek 43:5), Ezek 43:5–7 only mentions YHWH's glory filling the temple (see Ezek 44:4).⁹⁸ So, as Cook notes, "In [the] place [of the temple furniture, such as the ark], there is a profoundly real presence of God filling the temple."⁹⁹

Furthermore, in Ezek 40–48, בית has a range of uses, but it always either refers to the entire temple area (Ezek 40:45–46) or simply to the temple building (Ezek 44:14).¹⁰⁰ The term never references merely the inner court, and so in Ezek 43 it must refer to the temple building.¹⁰¹ The difference between filling the temple and not merely the most holy place

---

95. Sweeney, *Reading Ezekiel*, 208, says, "YHWH enters the temple complex by the east gate in order to reside in the Devir or holy of holies of the temple where the Ark of the Covenant resided during the time of Solomon's temple." Also see Stevenson, *Vision of Transformation*, 51; Zimmerli, *Ezekiel 2*, 415.

96. So Alexander, *Ezekiel*, 146.

97. Block, *Ezekiel 25–48*, 580–81 says, "Ezekiel's portrayal of the temple itself rather than the ark of the covenant as the throne of Yahweh is striking." Joyce, *Ezekiel*, 227, argues that Ezekiel characteristically reworks and reapplies language for his own purpose, and does so here by reworking language about YHWH's presence in the ark to now speak of the sanctuary. See also Klein, *Ezekiel*, 176. Contra Zimmerli, *Ezekiel 2*, 415–16, who argues that YHWH's throne resides in the most holy place, yet the "revolutionary" aspect of Ezekiel's vision is that he does not mention the ark. In 1 Chr 28:2 David mentions the ark as the footstool of God. Thus, YHWH states not that the ark is returning but that the most holy place is now the "ark" or "footstool" of YHWH.

98. Milgrom, *Ezekiel's Hope*, 262. Zimmerli, *Ezekiel 2*, 414–15, also notes the similarities with Isa 6, though erroneously assumes that behind the hem that Isaiah sees lies the ark as the footstool of YHWH's feet.

99. Cook, *Ezekiel 38–48*, 187. Note that Cook, *Ezekiel 38–48*, 185–89, holds that YHWH's glory is a bodily, non-human presence that resides in the adytum. Yet he also admits that YHWH's glory may reside elsewhere, i.e., in heaven. Tuell uses the analogies of the *extra calvinisticum* and the Christian understanding of the hypostatic union of Jesus as the Son of God.

100. Stevenson, *Vision of Transformation*, 60; Milgrom, *Studies in Levitical Terminology, I*, 14; Milgrom, *Ezekiel's Hope*, 103, 138, 146–49.

101. Milgrom, *Ezekiel's Hope*, 146; Klein, *Ezekiel*, 176, argues that Ezek 43:7 states there will be no ark on which YHWH is enthroned.

is significant, for it indicates that this is no standard temple. YHWH's presence is not restricted to a mercy seat.¹⁰² As Milgrom writes, "Not just the adytum, but all of Ezekiel's sanctuary building was the symbolic residence of YHWH."¹⁰³ Herein lies more ambiguity inherent in typology. On the surface, the reader assumes YHWH's glory resides in the most holy place. After all, no one enters that room (Ezek 41:1–4), while priests and people enter the temple. After a close reading, however, evidently the text says otherwise—YHWH's glory fills the entire building. The location of YHWH's glory also shows an escalation (*Steigerung*), for Ezekiel prophesies a glory far greater and more extensive than any former temple (see Hag 2:9). Here, then, the text points forward to a future temple where YHWH's glory extends beyond its traditional confines, and instead YHWH's glory fills the entire temple.

The next significant portion of the text is YHWH's speech in Ezek 43:6–9. YHWH says, "This is the place of my throne, and the place for the soles of my feet" (Ezek 43:7). The location of YHWH's glory was discussed above, so here the meaning of the throne must be noted. The throne indicates royalty, and the soles of the feet show kingship and dominion.¹⁰⁴ At last, then, YHWH fulfills the promises given throughout the book, and the kingship of YHWH rights the wrongs of Israel's monarchy.¹⁰⁵ Interestingly, however, in contrast to Ezekiel, David links the footstool with the ark of the covenant in 1 Chr 28:2.¹⁰⁶ OT authors do not commonly refer to the temple itself as the footstool.¹⁰⁷ Still, some texts do so (Ps 99:5; 132:7; Lam 2:1; Isa 60:13).¹⁰⁸ Ps 99:5, in particular, associates the temple with the holy mountain as the place of YHWH's footstool. In line with these texts, which admittedly are a numerical minority, Ezekiel, by describing the temple as YHWH's footstool, emphasizes a different

---

102. Even though Sweeney, *Reading Ezekiel*, 208, believes YHWH fills the temple from the holy of holies, the image of filling the temple, he notes, "... would have been facilitated by the use of the ten incense burners placed in the Heikhal or palace of the temple. The smoke released by the incense burners would metaphorically represent the amorphous presence of YHWH to the people assembled before the temple." Thus, he argues that in reality the glory is filling the palace, not the holy of holies.

103. Milgrom, *Ezekiel's Hope*, 103.

104. Bechtel, "Politics of Yahweh," 207–20. Blenkinsopp, *Ezekiel*, 211–12, connects this passage to Ps 29:10, "YHWH sits as king forever."

105. Bechtel, "Politics of Yahweh," 219.

106. Block, *Ezekiel 25–48*, 581.

107. Wevers, *Ezekiel*, 312.

108. Zimmerli, *Ezekiel 2*, 415.

conception of YHWH's presence and kingship not limited to the ark of the covenant.[109]

The main claim in Ezek 43:7, though, is not about the location of YHWH's throne, but that YHWH will dwell among his people forever (so also Ezek 43:9b).[110] Kasher points out that this language implies a permanent residence, that is, that the temple is YHWH's house, and nothing the people do will make him leave.[111] Because of this, a millennial temple does not fit in this context, for such would imply that YHWH will reside in a physical temple in the millennium, but then the temple disappears and YHWH dwells in the new Jerusalem (Rev 21:22). Such a reading directly contradicts the promise to dwell in this temple forever.[112] Moreover, the text focuses not on YHWH dwelling in the temple but amidst his people.[113] The prophet, Eichrodt asserts, "Guard[s] against any crude localization of the world-God in a single building like the temple, such as had been a constant threat to temple-worship in pre-exilic days . . . ," with Ezekiel instead emphasizing ". . . the direct encounter with God . . ."[114] Stevenson points out the use of the term שָׁם (Ezek 43:7).[115] The term is not grammatically necessary, but it puts emphasis on "territoriality," that YHWH establishes a place where he will be with his people.

As noted earlier, then, the significance of this text lies in its fulfillment of eschatological promises, such as those in Ezek 37:26–28.[116]

---

109. Allen, *Ezekiel 20–48*, 256. Contra Feinberg, *Ezekiel*, 253, who argues for the ark as the footstool in the millennial temple.

110. Hals, *Ezekiel*, 288, says, "It is simply unmistakable that all that is being affirmed is the 'negative' point that Yahweh will never leave his people again." Ludwig, "Ezekiel 43:9: Prescription or Promise?," 67–78, regarding Ezek 43:9, shows that the statement is a promise rather than a command. See also Hiebel, *Ezekiel's Vision Accounts*, 201.

111. Kasher, "Anthropomorphism, Holiness and Cult," 195. The notion of YHWH's house further underscores that he fills the whole structure, not simply one room.

112. Feinberg, *Ezekiel*, 253, states this promise of eternal presence in a millennial temple but does not address this objection.

113. Zimmerli, *Ezekiel 2*, 416. Haran, *Temples and Temple-Service*, 256–57, claims that the throne or footstool are synecdoche for the house of God. He also states we must remember that the OT does not bind God to the throne/footstool. While true, Ezekiel's text emphasizes this point in a unique way.

114. Eichrodt, *Ezekiel*, 555.

115. Stevenson, *Vision of Transformation*, 50.

116. Beale, *Temple and Church's Mission*, 346. Block, *Ezekiel 25–48*, 506, argues against "forever" as eschatological in this context. Strangely, in previous comments Block, *Ezekiel 25–48*, 421–22, does see the words as eschatological in Ezek 37:26–28.

However, in light of the previous discussion, this promise takes on more profound meaning. YHWH does not simply reside in a small room in the midst of his people. The emphasis is not on a place, but on the relationship with his people.[117] In the words of Allen, "The framework ['I will dwell in the midst of the people'] interprets the vision in terms of Yahweh's immanence among his people, never to leave again."[118] Wherever God's people go, "YHWH is there" (Ezek 48:35), for YHWH's glory fills the entire temple-city. Once again, the text shows an underlying purpose deeper than what appears on the surface. The text does not simply describe a physical temple. Eichrodt says,

> In this way the outward forms of temple worship are to be penetrated, and their inward meaning laid bare. This is the purpose of this sober yet irresistibly logical structural outline of the buildings of the temple and the account of how God takes possession of them as he returns to his people. It provides us with an apt delineation of the objective at which the prophet aimed in his whole life work.[119]

Ezek 43:7 shows, then, that YHWH returns to his cosmic temple to dwell with his people in covenant forever.

The Law of the Temple

Ezek 43:10–12 also provides textual clues that the vision is not one of a physical blueprint for construction. At first glance, the command looks to be that Israel should "carry out" the vision, i.e., build the temple. Upon closer inspection, however, the interpreter sees that YHWH's command means something entirely different. This section will more closely inspect what Tuell rightly calls "an interpretive crux."[120] To do so, this section will proceed through the three verses looking at several key phrases.

Hiebel, *Ezekiel's Vision Accounts*, 201, writes, "In this perspective [Ezek] 40:1—43:10 is an illustration of the fulfillment of these promises; the perfect and everlasting temple is a symbol of the new and everlasting covenant YHWH is going to institute with Israel."

117. Zimmerli, *Ezekiel 2*, 416. See also Joyce, *Ezekiel*, 228. Therefore, this contrasts with Gaebelein, *Ezekiel*, 303, who argues forcefully that Ezek 43:7 must refer to a physical temple. He cites the promise in Hag 2:6–7.

118. Allen, *Ezekiel 20–48*, 256.

119. Eichrodt, *Ezekiel*, 555.

120. Tuell, *Law of the Temple*, 44. Joyce, *Ezekiel*, 229, says, "Verses 10–12 constitute an important section for the understanding of the overall purpose of chs. 40–48."

YHWH's first command to Ezekiel in this pericope repeats what the prophet heard before in Ezek 40:4. YHWH tells him, "Declare [הַגֵּד] to the house of Israel the temple." English translations usually render the verb in Ezek 40:4 as "declare," but translate the same verb in Ezek 43:10 as "describe."[121] LXX uses the more elastic term δείκνυμι, which means "make known," either in the sense of description (as the English translations have it) or to explain verbally (as argued below).[122] The LXX reflects the meaning of the Hebrew verb more accurately than the English translations. Here, then, the preferable gloss is "declare," i.e., preaching. If so, YHWH's following instructions should not necessarily be interpreted in the sense of a temple blueprint. If YHWH's or the prophet's intention was to have Israel construct the building, it is not likely that Ezekiel would provide a detailed list of measurements in sermonic form.[123] Such a format is not conducive to delivering a blueprint. "Describe," though, implies wanting others to write the measurements down.[124] Yet YHWH here commands the prophet to preach, not describe, the vision of Ezek 40–48, so that the people will live out the message. Why, then, does YHWH command him in Ezek 43:11 to "write it down"? Writing down the message after preaching makes the message even more persuasive.[125] The declaration, though, comes first.

---

121. See Ezek 43:10 in the CSB; ESV; NASB; NET; NIV; NKJV; NRSV. The KJV says, "shew."

122. Louw-Nida, *Greek-English Lexicon of the NT*, 1460.

123. This may be just what Feinberg, *Ezekiel*, 254, means when he says, "Minutely Ezekiel was to go over every feature of the temple . . . so that every detail of the will of the Lord would be carried out forthrightly and joyously."

124. Davis, *Swallowing the Scroll*, 37–39, argues that Ezekiel represents the transition in the role of prophet from primarily a preacher to primarily a writer. Certainly, the ultimate aim of the vision was for this text to be written down. This does not negate the possibility that Ezekiel preached this vision originally and wrote it down later.

125. Block, *Ezekiel 25–48*, 589; Davis, *Swallowing the Scroll*, 123; Stevenson, *Vision of Transformation*, 14. Simon, "Ezekiel's Geometric Vision," 431, argues that the writing is to reaffirm the vision. Simon contrasts with Allen, *Ezekiel 20–48*, 257, and Zimmerli, *Ezekiel 2*, 419, who claim that Ezekiel draws up a temple plan. Zimmerli's argument is based on the next word, לְעֵינֵיהֶם. He therefore translates this as, "draw [it] for them to see." The word is a noun, however, so a better translation is "write [it down] before their eyes." Stevenson, *Vision of Transformation*, 14, translates as, "for their eyes," but still concludes, "This phrase emphasizes the visual mode of the Narrator's rhetorical task . . . The task of the prophet is to produce a written document as the means of persuasion."

What, then, are the people supposed to do in light of Ezekiel preaching and writing down this message? YHWH explains in the rest of the passage. First, he says that they will be ashamed of their iniquities, for the size and measurements of the temple reflect the holiness of YHWH, while the rules of access underscore the sinfulness of the people.[126] Though ultimately certain people are allowed to enter the presence of YHWH which fills the temple, the vision typologically teaches their need for holiness. The next result for the people is that they will measure the proportion (וּמָדְדוּ אֶת־תָּכְנִית). The verb is a *waw* consecutive in the perfect tense, thus continuing the narration of what the people will do when the prophet describes the temple.[127] Here, according to Toy, ". . . we have merely the command to carry into effect all the particulars."[128] However, the discussion below will show that the purpose of measuring is not to build, but to induce shame. In fact, about this Stevenson says, "What is particularly significant is what is omitted. There is no instruction to *build* the house."[129] She demonstrates how, in contrast, the blueprints of the tabernacle (Exod 25:9) and the first temple (1 Chr 28:10–12) include a command to build. The discussion below will probe the phrase at the end of Ezek 43:11, "do them," which scholars often interpret as a command to build, to show that Stevenson is correct in noting an absence of a command to build. She accurately links the description of the plan not with the verb "to build" but with "to measure." The measuring, in the words of Block, ". . . calls for a mastery of the internal and external boundaries of sacred space."[130] At the interpretive crux of the vision, then, YHWH neglects to say that the people should build.

The people are to measure, then, but what are they measuring? This question also raises considerable debate. YHWH states they will measure the תָּכְנִית. Only one letter separates this term from the word תַּבְנִית, used in the context of the Solomonic temple and tabernacle (Exod 25:9;

---

126. Stevenson, *Vision of Transformation*, 37–78. Allen, *Ezekiel 20–48*, 257, makes virtually the same point, though he concludes that the message is an architectural plan intended to spur the people to build. Odell, *Ezekiel*, 498–500, argues that shame is the prerequisite for the people responding appropriately to the temple vision, rather than the result of the temple vision.

127. See the discussion in Stevenson, *Vision of Transformation*, 15–17, who surveys scholars who translate the *waw* as a conditional clause.

128. Toy, "General Interpretation," xlv–xlvi.

129. Stevenson, *Vision of Transformation*, 17. So also Odell, *Ezekiel*, 485.

130. Block, *Ezekiel 25–48*, 589.

1 Chr 28:11).¹³¹ English translations often use the same English word for both, something like "plan" or "pattern."¹³² While תַּבְנִית indicates a pattern, in the sense of a blueprint, תָּכְנִית should not be translated in the same way. In the cases of the תַּבְנִית texts, the author makes his purpose evident, which is to give instructions for those who will build.¹³³ Readers often assume such a purpose in Ezek 43:10, but do so unnecessarily.¹³⁴ Instead, the term תָּכְנִית indicates something more like "measurement" or "proportion."¹³⁵ This reading is underscored by the use of the term צוּרָה in Ezek 43:11, which means "form" or "design."¹³⁶ Cook shows that the Qumran community uses the same term in reference to angels, and the term stresses an ideal form.¹³⁷ With "proportion" as the proper understanding in Ezek 43:10, therefore, one understands that YHWH commands Israel to "measure the proportion."¹³⁸ This means, as Stevenson states, "The measurements of the structures are not given to provide a

---

131. As Cook, *Ezekiel 38–48*, 185, points out, this is especially interesting since Ezekiel often uses vocabulary from the Holiness School, but here does not.

132. These translations may also be assuming an emendation to the text of Ezek 43:10. While the MT uses תָּכְנִית, some scholars emend to תכנתו, from the root כון, glossed as "its layout." Zimmerli, *Ezekiel 2*, 410 appeals here to the LXX, Syriac, and Vulgate for this emendation, as does Allen, *Ezekiel 20–48*, 243. Block, *Ezekiel 25–48*, 586, disagrees, arguing that such a claim requires an unnecessary change to the root word. The Targum and Vulgate render identically the terms in Ezek 28:12 and Ezek 43:10. See also Stevenson, *Vision of Transformation*, 18.

133. Stevenson, *Vision of Transformation*, 17; Cook, *Ezekiel 38–48*, 185. Blenkinsopp, *Ezekiel*, 212, wrongly states that this vision is "... [e]xactly parallel to the vision at Sinai..."

134. Sweeney, *Reading Ezekiel*, 209, is one example of assuming without making an argument when he says, "YHWH... instructs him to teach the people the pattern (Heb., *toknit*) for the temple so they might measure it and implement its laws. YHWH is careful to state that Ezekiel will teach them the plan of the temple..." Gaebelein, *Ezekiel*, 306, also takes this view, concluding that a millennial temple will be built, but without providing a reason.

135. BDB, 10516. The only other place the OT uses this word is in Ezek 28:12, indicating proportion in the sense of "perfection."

136. HALOT, 1017. The term is a hapax, but see discussion in Milgrom, *Ezekiel's Hope*, 115.

137. Cook, *Ezekiel 38–48*, 185. Joyce, "Heavenly Ascent," 28–29, argues that Ezekiel sees the perfect heavenly temple, while Moses only saw the pattern after such (Exod 25:9).

138. Stevenson, *Vision of Transformation*, 18; Milgrom, *Ezekiel's Hope*, 112 fn. 333. Included in this term is the idea of a perfect proportion. Simon, "Ezekiel's Geometric Vision," 430–32, shows that part of the purpose of the measuring is to restore a sense of "taming" the sinfulness of the people.

building plan for structures, but to define the spaces which are created by the structures."[139] Thus, the term used in this verse provides another argument against seeing this temple as intended to be built.[140]

Interpretive issues still arise, however, in the following verses. In Ezek 43:11 YHWH gives a purpose clause, "that they may observe all its form and all its statutes, and do them" (וְיִשְׁמְרוּ אֶת־כָּל־צוּרָתוֹ וְאֶת־כָּל־חֻקֹּתָיו וְעָשׂוּ אוֹתָם). This clause provides the main crux of interpretation for the passage. The prophet is told to הוֹדַע ("make known") more information about the temple, including its צוּרָת ("form"; stated three times), תְּכוּנָתוֹ ("its arrangement"), מוֹצָאָיו וּמוֹבָאָיו ("its exits and entrances"), חֻקֹּתָיו ("its statutes"), and תּוֹרֹתָיו ("its laws"). Again, Stevenson gives a compelling argument, showing that these terms all relate to "territoriality," that is, boundaries of space and access.[141] The MT text states that the people should observe the "form" of the temple, not its laws.[142] As explained below, this provides important interpretive evidence against a physical temple blueprint.

Several more exegetical questions emerge in this verse due to ambiguous syntax. Does "keep/observe" refer to the form, or to both the form and the statutes? In turn, is Israel to "do" just the statutes, or "observe and do" both the form and the statutes? As to the first question, the suffix probably shows that not just the statutes, but also "all its form and all its statutes" are intended. Regarding the second question, many claim that "observe and do" are a hendiadys.[143] The hendiadys is likely, as the sentence ends with the direct object marker and third-person plural suffix.

---

139. Stevenson, *Vision of Transformation*, 18-19. See also Milgrom, *Ezekiel's Hope*, 114, who cites Eliezer of Beaugency.

140. So Cook, *Ezekiel 38-48*, 185, although this study disagrees with his conclusion that, in his words, "Ezekiel has viewed not a mere building plan but the perfect proportions of a real divine archetype."

141. Stevenson, *Vision of Transformation*, 13-19. Similarly, Milgrom, *Ezekiel's Hope*, 115.

142. While some emend the MT from צוּרָת to תּוֹרֹת, assuming a parallel with חֻקֹּת and reflecting the LXX δικαιώματά, such a change is unnecessary. Scholars who emend include Block, *Ezekiel 25-48*, 587-88; Cooke, *Ezekiel*, 474-75; Allen, *Ezekiel 20-48*, 243; Tuell, *Law of the Temple*, 43 n. 64; Zimmerli, *Ezekiel 2*, 411. Stevenson, *Vision of Transformation*, 14, does not emend, translating, ". . . so that they may observe all its forms end [sic] perform all its statutes."

143. Block, *Ezekiel 25-48*, 589. The conjunction of the two verbs, says Milgrom, *Ezekiel's Hope*, 115, ". . . yields the idiom 'observe carefully' (e.g., Deut 4:6)." The hendiadys also is found in Ezek 11:20; 18:21. Cooke, *Ezekiel*, 466 also mentions Deut 7:12; 26:16; 29:8.

So, then, what does it mean to "observe and do" the forms and statutes? An actual doing, or "carrying out" (ESV), of the laws implies the presence of a physical temple.[144] In that understanding, the people are to "carry out" either the construction project itself, or the laws that assume a physical temple.[145] In support of this construction view is the similar description of the tabernacle, where the people are commanded to "make" (עשׂה) it (Exod 25:9). The context is clear there that the verb refers to construction, since in the previous verse (Exod 25:8), YHWH says, "They will make me a sanctuary" (וְעָשׂוּ לִי מִקְדָּשׁ). Likewise, with the first temple (1 Chr 28:10), David commands Solomon to "do [it]" (עשׂה). The Chronicler also, though, provides the obvious context when he supplies another verb, "to build" (לִבְנוֹת). In Exodus and Chronicles, no ambiguity exists in reference to the verb עשׂה.

By contrast, in the Ezekiel text, the immediate referent for the verb is the form, its statutes, and even the temple's proportion (Ezek 43:10), not a sanctuary or a תַּבְנִית (a cognate of the verb "to build"). The text omits any reference to construction. Therefore, the meaning of "observe and do" is more along the lines of Cook's translation, when he says, "'They must come to terms with them,' that is with the temple's design and regulations."[146] This means "to live by its design and intent" (Message). Cook therefore claims, "The exhortation is not about building the utopian temple but about changing the real world upon engaging with its principles."[147] The temple need not be physically constructed, for the

---

144. Joyce, *Ezekiel*, 229, says the text ". . . seems to imply a definite expectation that the envisaged restoration of the temple will actually happen . . ." As Eichrodt, *Ezekiel*, 555, says, "The prophet's vision is reinterpreted and made into a set of directions as to how worship is to be conducted in the new temple. This has led to . . . the insertion of those laws and regulations without which the prophet's vision appeared to be incomplete in the eyes of disciples who were priests by profession." This difficulty is resolved when one sees the text as not in reference to obeying legislation in a new temple but "doing" the message of the vision.

145. According to Cook, *Ezekiel 38–48*, 186, Rashi and Radak interpret this as a command to order a construction project at the end of time, when the exiles will rise from the dead and return to Israel to rebuild the temple. Joyce, "Heavenly Ascent," 30–31, and Strong, "Grounding Ezekiel's Heavenly Ascent," 201–2, argue that here is the command to build the temple.

146. Cook, *Ezekiel 38–48*, 186, 192. He cites Ezek 7:27, 17:17, and 22:14 in translating the verb using the sense of "deal with."

147. Cook, *Ezekiel 38–48*, 186.

vision presents, in the words of Schweitzer, "... an alternative world that calls the present order into question at every turn."[148]

A final issue regarding this section concerns the meaning of Ezek 43:12. The text says,

זֹאת תּוֹרַת הַבָּיִת עַל־רֹאשׁ הָהָר כָּל־גְּבֻלוֹ סָבִיב ׀ סָבִיב קֹדֶשׁ קָדָשִׁים הִנֵּה־
זֹאת תּוֹרַת הַבָּיִת׃

("This is the law of the temple: the whole territory on the top of the mountain, all around, will be most holy. This is the law of the temple").[149] What is the law of the temple? Does the phrase refer to the upcoming legislation beginning in Ezek 43:13, the preceding vision (Ezek 40–42), or the immediate context ("the top of the mountain all around will be most holy")? This study argues for the third option.

Scholars such as Tuell, Block, Eichrodt, and Milgrom argue for the first option, that the phrase introduces the legislation from Ezek 43:13—46:24.[150] Tuell claims that from a form-critical approach the form of the text is legislative ("this is the law of..."), always designating a ritual ordinance, rather than referring to a general quality such as holiness.[151] In other words, a mountain being holy is not a *torah*, for a *torah* is an ordinance. Furthermore, Ezekiel mentions the term תּוֹרָה afterwards in Ezek 44:5, but not at all prior to Ezek 43:12.[152] Finally, some scholars argue that the phrase always introduces legislation (see Lev 6:2, 7, 18; Num 19:2; 31:21).[153] In response, other scholars show that the formula is also used to conclude legislation (Lev 11:46; 13:59; 14:32, 54).[154] Similarly,

148. Schweitzer, "Utopia and Utopian Theory," 18.

149. Allen, *Ezekiel 20–48*, 243, claims that the second occurrence of the term *torah* is "... superfluous ... not represented in LXX* Syr." Likewise, see Zimmerli, *Ezekiel 2*, 411. As seen below, though, the second clause is intentional.

150. Tuell, *Law of the Temple*, 45; Block, *Ezekiel 25–48*, 590–92; Eichrodt, *Ezekiel*, 556; Milgrom, *Ezekiel's Hope*, 115–16; Dus and Simian-Yofre, "Ezequiel," 466. Alexander, *Ezekiel*, 147, claims that this phrase introduces legislation to be lived out in the millennium. Blenkinsopp, *Ezekiel*, 195, argues that the text introduces legislation that was original to the narrative, but it was dropped from the original draft, since no legislation follows immediately after the announcement.

151. Tuell, *Law of the Temple*, 45.

152. Tuell, *Law of the Temple*, 45; Eichrodt, *Ezekiel*, 556, adds that it is "impossible" to describe Ezek 40–42 in terms of *torah*. Block, *Ezekiel 25–48*, 591, does note the use of the term in Ezek 43:11, but he understands it in terms of the following legislation.

153. Block, *Ezekiel 25–48*, 591; Cooke, *Ezekiel*, 466.

154. Eichrodt, *Ezekiel*, 556, points out this text but agrees with Tuell's position. Milgrom, *Ezekiel's Hope*, 115–16 also notes Lev 14:54–57, while Cook, *Ezekiel 38–48*,

Talmon and Fishbane, along with Milgrom, add that the Priestly text in Num 7:84–88 uses this formula to conclude a long list.[155] In response to the citation of Lev 14, Block claims that Lev 14:54–57 concludes prescriptive legislation, while Ezekiel's text concludes a lengthy description, and therefore it cannot be the conclusion of a *torah*.[156] Block makes a valid observation, but his argument assumes that Ezek 43:12 does not conclude the previous section. If it does, Ezek 43:12 is an instance of the phrase concluding legislation.

Continuing to argue for this first option, Allen says that terms like "law/instruction," "measurements," and "statutes" appear in Ezek 43:10–11 and then again in the "legislation" of Ezek 43:12, 13, and 18.[157] In response, these catchwords do not prove that the phrase refers to the following section, for catchwords may serve as a link, or hinge, from the past text into the following one.[158] The legislation beginning in Ezek 43:13 clearly does not appear from nowhere, but links to the vision of divine glory. This does not automatically mean, though, that Ezek 43:12 belongs with Ezek 43:13. Also, against this view are the similarities in terms between Ezek 40:1–5 and Ezek 43:10–12, demonstrating a literary *inclusio*.[159] If an *inclusio*, the "law of the temple" more likely refers to the preceding words rather than those following. In sum, the evidence shows that this

---

186, cites Num 6:21.

155. Talmon and Fishbane, "Structuring of Biblical Books," 140–42. Milgrom, *Ezekiel's Hope*, 116–17. Milgrom seems to side ultimately with Tuell, but he makes no strong claim, saying, "Why, then was it employed? It can be surmised that the first *torat habbayit* has in mind the prior list of instructions that have been imparted to the prophet by the guide, concerning the dimensions of sacred space in the sanctuary compound (Ezek 40–42). The second *torat habbayit*, however, may be anticipatory of the cultic instructions for the priests, *nasi*, and people (Ezek 44–46)." He adds that the "key" to unlock this meaning is the term בַּיִת. In the previous chapters, the term referred to a "secular building," but in the following chapters it refers to a sanctuary. Such a variation in meaning of the term is, however, simply unwarranted, for although YHWH's glory is physically present after Ezek 43:5, the building is exactly the same one, and the same term is used throughout.

156. Block, *Ezekiel 25–48*, 591.

157. Allen, *Ezekiel 20–48*, 250.

158. So also Cook, *Ezekiel 38–48*, 186, who attributes the term "hinge" to S. Dean McBride, Jr.

159. Milgrom, *Ezekiel's Hope*, 113. So also Cook, *Ezekiel 38–48*, 191. Zimmerli, *Ezekiel 2*, 420, agrees, though he takes Ezek 43:1–11(12) to be the work of later authors. Konkel, *Architektonic*, 80–82, 239, sees an *inclusio* with Ezek 43:10 as part of the primary vision material, but he does not include Ezek 43:11–12.

legislation formula can both begin and conclude legislation texts. Based simply on this evidence, it is difficult to prove that Ezek 43:12 begins the next section.

Talmon and Fishbane argue for the second option, that the *torah* of the temple concludes the first part of the vision, Ezek 40:1—42:20.[160] They note that this formula concludes cultic texts, especially in relation to the tabernacle (Lev 7:31; 13:59; 14:32, 54–57). They suggest that Ezekiel uses a "scribal-archival device" among priestly writings, a technique used to conclude cultic legislation.[161] They also add that writers can conclude legislation with an *inclusio* formula. For example, Num 7 concludes a cultic narrative about tabernacle offerings in Num 7:1–83 with a formula that contains its own *inclusion*: "This was the dedication offering for the altar . . ." (Num 7:84, 88). Thus, for them, the repetition of the phrase in Ezek 43:12 is not a result of scribal accretions, but instead it is an intentional *inclusio* to conclude a cultic section. Talmon and Fishbane appropriately show the possibility of an *inclusio*, but the *inclusio* of Ezek 43:12 does not come after Ezek 42:20. Their arguments that these words are a conclusion to a cultic text can equally apply to the other two views, for they could also conclude Ezek 43:1–9 or Ezek 43:10–11.

This study holds to the third option, that the "law of the temple" is the declaration concerning the sanctity of the area all around. In other words, the law of the temple is that ". . . the top of the mountain all around shall be most holy" (Ezek 43:12). In this view, advanced by Zimmerli, the prophet expresses the holiness of the area in his priestly role of giving *torah*.[162] Opponents argue that it is illogical to designate all the area "most holy," since that title is given already to the holy of holies (Ezek 41:4). Zimmerli responds that Ezek 41:4 adds the article, which designates a particular space, rather than simply defining its quality. Thus, the whole area could have that same quality, not just the room designated "*the* holy of holies." Zimmerli also takes the phrase to simply mean an indefinite sense of "sacred," rather than denoting any intensification of holiness.

---

160. Talmon and Fishbane, "Structuring of Biblical Books," 140–42. So also Cooke, *Ezekiel*, 466; Sweeney, *Reading Ezekiel*, 209, though he does not provide an argument.

161. Talmon and Fishbane, "Structuring of Biblical Books," 140.

162. The following argument is presented in Zimmerli, *Ezekiel 2*, 419–20. Klein, *Ezekiel*, 177; Joyce, *Ezekiel*, 229, also hold this view. Gaebelein, *Ezekiel*, 306, also claims this view, but he takes his conclusion in different directions. He states that "the Most Holy" fulfills Dan 9:24, and the law of the temple refers to the end of the "seventy weeks."

The use of the double term simply expands the reference to a larger area than commonly thought, rather than intensifying the quality of holiness.[163]

Next, Zimmerli sees a parallel in Ezek 42:20 and Ezek 43:12. Instead of simply describing measurements, the writer concludes the section on measurements with a purpose statement, which is "... to make a separation between the holy and the common" (Ezek 42:20). Thus, Zimmerli holds, "What in the final statement of the measurement report was a factual statement by the narrator here becomes an 'instruction' in the mouth of Yahweh himself."[164] Finally, as stated earlier, Zimmerli notices an *inclusio* with the initial vision in Ezek 40:2. He points out that the writer mentions the mountain only in Ezek 40:2 and Ezek 43:12, and so this indicates an intentional literary move.

Ezek 43:12, then, presents the latter part of an *inclusio* to sum up the meaning of the vision so far. The purpose of the verse is to show both the distinctive holiness of the temple area as well as the extension of holiness beyond the holy of holies. The distinctive holiness of the area can be discerned from the lack of an article in front of the second קֹדֶשׁ.[165] Many describe this as a comparative sense, comparing the area to its surroundings.[166] The temple area will be "[the] most holy," i.e., in comparison to the rest of the land, or the world. So, the reader should not take the temple area to equal the holy of holies, as Kasher argues.[167] However, even if technically the area is not the holy of holies, it is still the most holy place compared to everything else.[168] Cook makes reference to Ezek 45:3, where the entire sanctuary is designated קֹדֶשׁ קָדָשִׁים, "the most holy place." The writer uses

---

163. Joyce, *Ezekiel*, 229, describes the double term as "... the diffusion of the realm of the most holy."

164. Zimmerli, *Ezekiel 2*, 420.

165. Joyce, *Ezekiel*, 230, writes, "The absence of the article ... suggests that it could be the area as a whole that is described as 'a most holy place.'" Strong, "Grounding Ezekiel's Heavenly Ascent," 202, cites Ezek 41:4 with the article on the second word as evidence that Ezek 43:12 is adjectival, while Ezek 41:4 uses a noun. However, there is no debate that Ezek 41:4 refers to the room known as the most holy place. The argument here is that Ezek 43:12 extends YHWH's holiness, not that the whole temple is actually the most holy place.

166. Milgrom, *Ezekiel's Hope*, 113, 117; Block, *Ezekiel 25–48*, 592; Cook, *Ezekiel 38–48*, 186; Joyce, "Temple and Worship in Ezekiel 40–48," 156–57.

167. Kasher, "Anthropomorphism," 201.

168. Radak, cited in Cook, *Ezekiel 38–48*, 226, says, "Different points on the temple mount itself have varying degrees of holiness." In this case, however, the holiness gradations do not compare the different parts of the temple building, but the whole temple in comparison to all that surrounds it.

this superlative not in an absolute sense but, Cook says, "relative to its surroundings."[169] YHWH states that this new area is uniquely holy. Since YHWH's glory fills the entire temple (Ezek 43:5), such a conclusion is logical.[170] YHWH's holiness is not only distinct but also extensive. Allen says, "Not only the temple complex built on the mountain top (cf. [Ezek] 40:2) but also the surrounding reservation (see [Ezek] 45:1–3) partook of this holiness. So far did its aura spread."[171] Although some boundaries and gradation of holiness appear between the area and the rest of the land, this text emphasizes the extensiveness of the holiness.[172]

The final statement of this first half of the vision (Ezek 40:1—43:12), the words of Ezek 43:12b, significantly encapsulates the meaning of the entire vision thus far. The purpose of the temple, expressed as the vision's *torah*, is to show that the holiness of YHWH extends "all around." This is no standard temple, for YHWH's holiness is no longer restricted to one room. This shows what Hals calls "an eschatological advent" of the glory of YHWH.[173] The purpose of the vision and temple, then, is not physical construction. In Cook's words, "The goal is to change their own world, not make a beeline for Ezekiel's utopia [i.e., build a building]."[174] The purpose is to goad the people into action, not of construction but shame (Ezek 43:10). The perfection of the temple represents the moral perfection it should stimulate. As Simon says, "We thus see a confluence

---

169. Cook, *Ezekiel 38–48*, 226.

170. Kasher, "Anthropomorphism," 207, states, "In the Priestly source, only the enclosure reserved for the cult is considered holy; while the Holiness Source allows sanctity to transcend all boundaries and fill the entire land. Ezekiel 40–48 reflects, in a sense, an intermediate approach: not only the cultic area, but also its immediate environs, are holy—but not the entire Land of Israel."

171. Allen, *Ezekiel 20–48*, 257. Contra Cook, *Ezekiel 38–48*, 186, who propounds, "This is in no way a claim of undifferentiated, homogenous holiness across the temple mount." Also contra the translator of the *Vorlage* LXX, per O'Hare, *Have You Seen, Son of Man?*, 107–9.

172. Contra Hals, *Ezekiel*, 306, "Whereas Ezekiel concentrates on a holiness kept faithfully separated, others could look to an all-transforming holiness which would not require protective restrictions, but would extend forth so powerfully that in an ultimate pan-sacrality even the bells on the horses would be inscribed 'Holy to the Lord' (Zech 14:20)." Ezekiel actually hints here at "pan-sacrality." According to Joyce, *Ezekiel*, 230, this is especially surprising because of Ezekiel's priestly background.

173. Hals, *Ezekiel*, 306.

174. Cook, *Ezekiel 38–48*, 191. See also Liss, "'Describe the Temple,'" 141–43. Liss argues that the text itself becomes the "realization" for the temple.

of proper proportion in the moral and architectural realms."¹⁷⁵ The text is more than a moral lesson, however. Hals writes, "It is the assurance of a future new relationship . . . The 'law of the temple' in v. 12 is not a prescription to be carried out; it is the promise of a revelation to be longed for."¹⁷⁶ Therefore, in the words of Renz, "The book boldly declares itself to be Yahweh's means for transforming Israel."¹⁷⁷ YHWH transforms Israel when Ezekiel declares his message of his glory returning.

Typology in Ezekiel 43:1–12

The arguments above for proper interpretation of Ezek 43:1–12 lead to a typological understanding of the text. First, the text contains a clear *prophetic* indicator. YHWH tells Ezekiel, "Declare to the house of Israel the temple" (Ezek 43:10). The study above argues that this deals with verbal proclamation rather than a written blueprint. Second, the text consists of several *ambiguities* that later interpreters can mine. The study explored the ambiguities of whether Ezekiel is to "describe" or "declare" (Ezek 43:10), if the people are to "carry out/build" the instructions or "come to terms with them" (Ezek 43:11), and whether the law of the temple looks forward to coming legislation or describes the top of the mountain as most holy (Ezek 43:12). Likely the most significant of these is the final one, for a close reading of the text shows a radical perspective—YHWH's glory extends beyond the holy of holies. This insight coalesces with the discussion below concerning YHWH's glory in the new city (Ezek 48:35).

The text also shows aspects pointing to a *christological-soteriological* fulfillment. The study noted above that YHWH's glory returning from the east and filling the temple is a sign of his covenant salvation. Perhaps the zenith of the vision, YHWH's returning presence fulfills his promises in Ezek 36–37 that he would cleanse his people and make his dwelling among them again. Thus, when YHWH's glory returns, his people are no longer under judgment but under YHWH's covenant blessing. In addition, the text points forward to a christological fulfillment by showing that YHWH's presence of blessing can exist beyond the holy of holies. The argument above shows that YHWH's presence actually filled the whole

---

175. Simon, "Ezekiel's Geometric Vision," 431.
176. Hals, *Ezekiel*, 307.
177. Renz, *Rhetorical Function*, 130.

temple.¹⁷⁸ The NT will later say that Jesus is the temple (John 2:18–22) and that YHWH's glory resides in flesh (John 1:14). Such a notion only makes sense in light of a developing understanding that YHWH's glory does not dwell only in one room of a physical building.¹⁷⁹

The clearest typological feature in Ezek 43:1–12 is the *eschatological heightening* set forth when YHWH's glory returns to this new temple. First, as just mentioned, YHWH fills not just the holy of holies, but also the entire temple (Ezek 43:5). This heightening Hals calls "... [an] eschatological advent ..." of YHWH's glory.¹⁸⁰ Not only does YHWH's glory return, but this is also the greatest temple yet because his glory fills it all. The argument for a physical structure neglects this eschatological heightening. Those who hold to a millennial temple note that YHWH's glory does not return in the postexilic temple, so they say another physical temple must be built for YHWH's glory to return, as Ezekiel describes here.¹⁸¹ However, these proponents neglect the issue of the glory filling the whole house. Additionally, the text shows eschatological features because Ezek 43:10–12 demonstrates the building is already built. As argued above, the people are not commanded to construct a temple. Instead, this is a temple that YHWH establishes on top of the mountain. This new age, full of YHWH's covenant blessing and presence, will come not through the works of people, but because YHWH will bring his salvation.

---

178. This notion will further be developed in the discussion of Ezek 48:35.

179. This christological heightening is the aspect that Feinberg, *Ezekiel*, 252, misses when he states, "Thus Ezekiel was expressly given the privilege by the Spirit Himself of viewing the glorious return of the Lord to his abode and His people. God's glory may always be depended upon to fill His house; it has been so in the past and will be in the millennial era." Feinberg simply assumes that Ezekiel must be looking forward into a future event where YHWH's glory does actually fill the temple as it did in previous temples. Unfortunately, he does not discuss the issues in Ezek 43:1–12 that this study addresses.

180. Hals, *Ezekiel*, 306. Odell, *Ezekiel*, 497, calls it "... a perfect merging of the two realms [heaven and earth]."

181. Gaebelein, *Ezekiel*, 300–301.

Ezekiel 47:1–12

The Life-Giving River

This passage about the life-giving river, Ezek 47:1–12, presents one of the most compelling arguments for seeing the temple vision typologically.[182] As Taylor says, "So all this [Ezek 47:1–12] is of a piece with the interpretation of these nine chapters as idealized and essentially symbolic in character and intention. Those literalists who cherish the hope that they will one day be able to turn them into some kind of fulfillment in a Third Temple are doing a disservice both to the text and to the intention of the prophet."[183] This passage describes the effect of YHWH's habitation of the new temple (Ezek 43:1–12).[184] Here Ezekiel returns to the description of a part of the temple, while at the same time providing a transition to describe the new land (Ezek 47:13—48:29).[185] Some take the text to mean that the prophet hoped for an actual river flowing from the physical temple in Jerusalem.[186] However, one better understands the text as a theological presentation of YHWH's glory returning.[187] The river's description accentuates that YHWH dwells atop an eschatological cosmic mountain.

---

182. As stated initially, this study will read the text holistically. In the words of Block, *Ezekiel 25–48*, 689, "Because of its uncharacteristic lexical forms, doublets, repetitions, grammatical anomalies, substantive infelicities, and awkward interruptions, critical scholarship has not taken kindly to the text of 47:1–12." Since these issues do not substantially affect the interpretation of the text, however, this section will not deal with them. Wevers, *Ezekiel*, 333, claims that later "apocalypticist" scribes heavily edited the prophet's original vision. Nothing in this vision of the river, though, differs greatly from previous aspects of the temple vision, as seen, for example, in the angelic tour guide in Ezek 40. The apocalyptic nature of this text squares with what the prophet himself wrote previously (see also Eichrodt, *Ezekiel*, 582).

183. Taylor, "Temple in Ezekiel," 69. In this light, the statement is strange when Feinberg, *Ezekiel*, 271, claims, "Even many who take all from chapters 40–48 to be symbolical and figurative admit that this description is to be taken literally."

184. Zimmerli, *Ezekiel 2*, 509, holds, "Within chapters 40–48, 47:1–12 are most closely connected with the proclamation of Yahweh's eternal presence in the temple in 43:7–9."

185. Hals, *Ezekiel*, 287; Hiebel, *Ezekiel's Vision Accounts*, 191, 203–4, though she does not assign this text to the original layer of prophecy.

186. Alexander, *Ezekiel*, 156, states, "The river is a literal river." So also Gaebelein, *Ezekiel*, 332; Toy, "General Interpretation," xlvi–xlvii. See the discussion below.

187. Eichrodt, *Ezekiel*, 582. Hals, *Ezekiel*, 338, calls it "a prophecy of salvation."

The Physical River View

To explore this aspect of the vision, this section will first examine the arguments of those who take Ezek 47 to describe a physical river that will actually flow from the temple someday.[188] Some believe that a stream will flow from the millennial temple and then divide into two parts (see Zech 14:8; Joel 4:18), and so, as Ironside says, ". . . linking the Mediterranean Sea with the Dead Sea and giving the city of Jerusalem itself a water-harbor."[189] This idea of the splitting river comes from a harmonization of Zech 14:8 with the plural noun for "river" (נְחָלִים) in Ezek 47:9. One flaw in this thinking is that Ezekiel does not, in fact, mention the river splitting into two. Ezekiel's river flows directly to the Dead Sea (Ezek 47:8, 10).[190] The dual noun for river in Ezek 47:9 most likely refers to an ancient understanding of a double current rather than two rivers.[191] Moreover, it is geographically impossible for this river to flow from the temple mount to the Dead Sea. Besides the terrain the river would have to travel, the text explicitly states that the river begins as a trickle and grows with no tributaries adding to it, a physically impossible feat.[192] Another complication is that the fresh water overtakes the salty and purifies it (Ezek 47:8).[193] Therefore, as Duguid says, "[This cannot] be the result of an impressive civil engineering project."[194]

---

188. Likely based on this prophecy in Ezek 47, the *Letter of Aristeas* describes a spring from the Jerusalem temple in those days, but this claim is completely imaginary. For discussion of the *Letter* see Zimmerli, *Ezekiel 2*, 510.

189. Ironside, *Notes on Ezekiel*, 324. See also Gaebelein, *Ezekiel*, 334. Even Block, *Ezekiel 25–48*, 694, and Zimmerli, *Ezekiel 2*, 513, leave open the possibility of the river dividing into two but do not argue strongly for it.

190. Regarding the prophecies of Joel, Zechariah, and Ezekiel, Feinberg, *Ezekiel*, 271, says, "There is harmony of presentation." However, one would have to drastically alter the meaning of Ezekiel's text in order to read it as describing a river that splits, with half of it going to the Mediterranean.

191. Bodi, "Double Current," 22–37. The significance of this dual noun will be developed in a later chapter, as later NT interpreters pick up on its use here.

192. Duguid, *Ezekiel*, 532. Duguid points out that this is the only river of life in Scripture described as beginning in this manner. Regarding the terrain, Block, *Ezekiel 25–48*, 694, says, "In order for water to flow from Jerusalem to the Jordan Valley it must flow down into the Kidron, up over the Mount of Olives, and then cross a series of valleys and mountain ranges before it reaches its destination."

193. Beale, *Temple and Church's Mission*, 343.

194. Duguid, *Leaders of Israel*, 140.

Proponents respond that, although physically impossible, YHWH can perform a miracle, and so the river could actually exist, both in terms of geography and purity.[195] "Physical temple" proponents also argue that the presence of salt buttresses their view. Ironside argues that the presence of salt in the marshes (Ezek 47:11) must speak of the millennium, because in the eternal state there is no (salt) sea (Rev 21:1).[196] Also, salt represents the preservation of righteousness, which will not be needed in the eternal kingdom.[197] Similarly, Gaebelein claims that the presence of salt implies that Ezekiel does not speak of the "perfect, eternal age," so it must refer to the millennium.[198] In response, the presence of the salt need not indicate imperfection. As Block states, "The preservation of some pockets of saltiness is intentional, recognizing the economic benefit of the minerals found in and around the Dead Sea."[199] Cook also notes a theological meaning, a reminder of the covenant of salt (Num 18:19), and thus God's unending relationship with his people.[200] So, in terms of a physical fulfillment, Blenkinsopp strongly claims, "No amount of exegetical finesse or insistence on 'what the Bible plainly says' can transform the poetry of this passage into a topographically and ecologically realistic account of an event in time."[201]

---

195. Gaebelein, *Ezekiel*, 332–33, simply says, "We do not need to trouble ourselves about the manner in which the temple stream is to flow forth, nor do we need to solve the physical difficulties . . . Is there anything too hard for the Lord?" Also Feinberg, *Ezekiel*, 271–73; Toy, "General Interpretation," xlvii. Ellison, *Ezekiel*, 139–40, mentions this view but does not hold to it. Rabbinic exegesis also interprets the vision in this way. See *T. Suk.* 3:3ff; *Pirqe de Rabbi Eliezer*, 51.

196. Ironside, *Ezekiel*, 329.

197. Ironside, *Ezekiel*, 329. Ironside does not ultimately hold that there will be a physical river. His conclusion on the salt does not seem to fit his overall presentation, for he sees the trees and river as fulfilled in the land pictured in Rev 21–22.

198. Gaebelein, *Ezekiel*, 335. Feinberg, *Ezekiel*, 273, claims that the salt is for sacrifices in the millennial temple.

199. Block, *Ezekiel 25–48*, 695. So also Zimmerli, *Ezekiel 2*, 514, though one should not concur with him that, "The thoroughness of this transformation frightened a later writer who was aware of the possibility of the extraction of salt from the Dead Sea." Sweeney, *Reading Ezekiel*, 223, also adds that the salt is necessary in the diet and for food preservation. Cook, *Ezekiel 38–48*, 267, sees the necessity of salt for performing cultic functions.

200. Cook, *Ezekiel 38–48*, 267; Duguid, *Ezekiel*, 533. Dus and Simian-Yofre, "Ezequiel," 468, argue that the "mentality of minutiae" of the priesthood lies behind this text.

201. Blenkinsopp, *Ezekiel*, 231.

The Non-Literal River View

Many scholars hold that the book of Ezekiel presents in Ezek 47:1–12 a "fantastic," that is, a symbolic picture of restoration from exile.[202] Readers naturally recognize the supernatural elements present. Even elements of the apocalyptic genre return after a brief absence in the vision, namely, the angelic tour guide, measurements, and divine explanations.[203] Rather than reading the text "literally" as if this is an actual river that will descend from the temple, many take this as a picture of life and blessing in the presence of God. For example, Allen, who for the most part takes the "blueprint" approach to the entire vision, says, "Behind the vision stands the cultic concept of blessing, as the power of God which, crowning the worship of his pilgrim people, returns home with them and enriches their lives."[204] Later, he states, "The symbolism of theology [is] translated into the stuff of an imaginative vision . . ."[205] Even Ironside, who holds that Ezekiel describes a millennial temple, does not take the river to be literal, saying, "Now as we consider Ezekiel's vision it would seem to be but slavish adherence to literality which would deny the symbolic character of much that is here unfolded."[206] He compares Ezek 47 to the symbolism in the book of Revelation. The book of Revelation does not teach that an actual seven-headed beast will come upon earth, for the beast is a symbol of human government.[207] Similarly, a literal river here ". . . does not seem . . . either to be reasonable or in accordance with what we learn elsewhere in Scripture."[208] Block claims that the scene describes a miraculous act akin to the parting of the Red Sea, though here, in contrast to that event,

---

202. Block, *Ezekiel 25–48*, 690, 700–701. Block, *Ezekiel 25–48*, 701, calls the scene a ". . . literary cartoon with an intentional ideological aim." Allen, *Ezekiel 20–48*, 278, calls this "spiritual fantasy." Beale, *Temple and Church's Mission*, 345 says, "[It] is to be taken figuratively . . ." See also Dus and Simian-Yofre, "Ezequiel," 468.

203. Allen, *Ezekiel 20–48*, 277, says, "The tone of the narrative is much more apocalyptic than any of the other visionary accounts in chaps. 40–48 (cf. Zech 14:8)." Hals, *Ezekiel*, 338, says that, despite a lack of a cosmic ending, the label apocalyptic is "understandable."

204. Allen, *Ezekiel 20–48*, 280.

205. Allen, *Ezekiel 20–48*, 287.

206. Ironside, *Ezekiel*, 324.

207. Ironside, *Ezekiel*, 324. Similarly, Keil, *Ezekiel*, 359–60, compares this river vision to the prophecy of Joel that mountains will drip sweet wine, saying that a "literal" fulfillment is impossible.

208. Ironside, *Ezekiel*, 325.

water miraculously flows through dry land.²⁰⁹ Though the author provides symbols, Zimmerli humorously states, "[He] did not, in all this, intend to compose a fairy tale or blow a soap bubble."²¹⁰ Instead, the author desires to give a real promise to the people of Israel. Block contends that the river is a picture of "Ezekiel's national agenda" rather than a cosmic, eschatological portrayal.²¹¹ While true that the prophet focuses on the restoration of Israel (both people and land), and the river provides a rich symbol of blessing, the picture is also cosmic.²¹²

Though the vision directly relates to the land of Israel, one cannot rightly understand this passage without also a consideration of cosmic mountain ideology.²¹³ Clifford writes about the cosmic mountain myth in ANE literature. He notes, akin to Ezek 47, the presence of a sacred stream emanating from the deity's dwelling place in Ugaritic tradition.²¹⁴ El dwells at the source of two rivers, the waters of cosmic chaos.²¹⁵ Others note that the Gudea cylinder also bears an inscription describing waters which stream forth from a basin near the couch of the gods. The waters stream down to create large rivers bringing fertility to the land.²¹⁶ A seal of Gudea shows Ea enthroned with flowing jugs of water as the footstool.²¹⁷ Additionally, in the Mari palace, river goddesses stand at the base of the

---

209. Block, *Ezekiel 25–48*, 694. Zimmerli, *Ezekiel 2*, 513, also calls it a miracle, likening it to the healing waters in John 5:7.

210. Zimmerli, *Ezekiel 2*, 516.

211. Block, *Ezekiel 25–48*, 696–97; Cooke, *Ezekiel*, 516. In this regard, see especially Darr, "Wall Around Paradise," 271–79. Duguid, *Ezekiel*, 533, presents the matter slightly differently, saying that the river transforms all of God's covenant people, yet that includes native Israelite and resident alien (Ezek 47:22). Still, Duguid ultimately places the renewal within the land of Israel, contra Eichrodt, *Ezekiel*, 585–86.

212. Tuell, *Law of the Temple*, 69–71, adds based on similarities with ANE literature that the river describes much material prosperity.

213. Zimmerli, *Ezekiel 2*, 510, says, "This motif of the river of paradise, which flows down from the dwelling place of the gods, has been clearly at work in the formation of Ezek 47:1–12 alongside the bare natural phenomena of Palestine (wilderness of Judah, Dead Sea)." Also Eichrodt, *Ezekiel*, 583–84; Klein, *Ezekiel*, 181.

214. Clifford, *Cosmic Mountain*, 157–59.

215. Clifford, *Cosmic Mountain*, 48–57. Joyce, *Ezekiel*, 237, connects here the Ugaritic myth with the dual noun of the river (Ezek 47:9), suggesting ANE influence on Ezekiel.

216. Cook, *Ezekiel 38–48*, 262. For more similarities with water images, see Sharon, "Sumerian Temple Hymn," 99–109; Bodi, "Double Current," 22–37.

217. Cook, *Ezekiel 38–48*, 262.

inner sanctuary of Ishtar holding flowing jugs of water.[218] These ANE artifacts show what Bodi calls ". . . the motif of a vase with flowing streams . . ." connected with the temple.[219] Cook adds, "These are the cosmic waters of paradise."[220] Additionally, ANE streams often contain a sacred tree or plant as a symbol of life, such as in the seal of Gudea, and Ezekiel's vision also associates the stream with many life-giving trees.[221]

Moreover, Baal dwells atop his own cosmic mountain, Mount Zaphon.[222] The divine dwelling is called the navel of the earth, so that it is seen as ". . . the center or fulcrum of the cosmos."[223] In the vision of Ezek 47, the stone platform "corks" the primal waters, which Cook calls, ". . . [the] cosmic center, at the origin of all creation."[224] Since ANE mythology sees the sea as cosmic chaos, the life-giving river shows YHWH's conquest restoring cosmic order.[225] Zion tradition also contains this ideology of a stream that brings healing (Isa 33:20–24).[226] Ezek 47, therefore, develops most expansively on what Levenson calls "[t]he powers of the waters of Zion . . ."[227] The presence of a spring from under the temple teaches that YHWH's dwelling is "the holy center of creation."[228] In contrast to those who argue for only a national scale, the cosmic mountain background leads one to see the river as eventually transforming all of creation.[229] According to Levenson, "Zion has become the source of redemption; the Temple is the mechanism for the disbursal of abundant grace for the whole population. When the presence of God has returned

218. Cook, *Ezekiel 38–48*, 262.
219. Bodi, "Double Current," 30.
220. Cook, *Ezekiel 38–48*, 263.
221. Cook, *Ezekiel 38–48*, 264.
222. Levenson, *Program of Restoration*, 14; Block, *Ezekiel 25–48*, 501.
223. Levenson, *Program of Restoration*, 17.
224. Cook, *Ezekiel 38–48*, 268.
225. Duguid, *Ezekiel*, 530.
226. Zimmerli, *Ezekiel 2*, 510–11, also cites the "waters of Shiloah" of Isa 8:6–8 as part of the tradition in the background of Ezekiel's text.
227. Levenson, *Program of Restoration*, 13.
228. Sweeney, *Reading Ezekiel*, 221. Therefore this vision is not based on an idealized development of a physical spring either originally in, our outside, the temple, as Cooke, *Ezekiel*, 517–18, writes.
229. Sweeney, *Reading Ezekiel*, 222. According to Sweeney, the context also shows this, for the prophet follows up this vision with Ezek 47:13—48:35, a description of the new creation centered on the temple. This argues against Darr, "Wall Around Paradise," 277, who says the claim of universality is arbitrary.

to the navel of the world, the Land is transfigured through the life-giving stream thus renewed."[230] The connection with cosmic mountain ideology shows the eschatological nature of the temple, one of the criteria of typology. Like the vision of dry bones in Ezek 37:1–14, this passage describes a new creation in the eschaton.[231]

Typology in Ezekiel 47:1–12

As demonstrated above, the interpreter should not understand the passage as describing an actual miraculous river that will flow from a millennial temple. Nor, though, should readers understand this to be mere symbolism of a national restoration. The framework of literal versus symbolic does not do justice to the text, especially in the case of Ezek 47:1–12.[232] For example, the early church inappropriately saw in this text allegorical symbolism of various Christian truths.[233] Typology provides a way forward in understanding. In light of typology, one can see YHWH presenting a vision of a real temple with a real river.[234] The goal, however, is not for this temple and river to exist physically. The goal of the vision is the theological meaning behind it. With typology as a rubric, the temple, and in this case the river, can be real, yet not physical.[235]

---

230. Levenson, *Program of Restoration*, 13.

231. Hiebel, *Ezekiel's Vision Accounts*, 213; Dus and Simian-Yofre, "Ezequiel," 468.

232. Cook, *Ezekiel 38–48*, 267, also shows the limits of symbolism, but he wrongly concludes, "By now there is no doubt that throughout the temple tour of Ezekiel 40–48 the prophet has been engaged in what Carl Jung and others have called circumambulating a labyrinth or mandala. Moving with Ezekiel . . . readers have been practicing a devotion, engaging in a literary-spiritual exercise."

233. Zimmerli, *Ezekiel 2*, 515 cites the following, "The increase of the river represents the increase in the number of believers, the fourfold measuring [represents] the four gospels, the depth of the last measurement [represents] the depth of the fourth gospel (Theodoret), the river [represents] baptism (Polychronius) or then at the same time the Jewish people gaining new strength after the return from exile represents the church increasing in its number of believers . . . For Jerome the river is an image of the teaching of the church and of the grace of baptism . . ." Block, *Ezekiel 25–48*, 699, also lists multiple connections Theodoret draws.

234. Hence Feinberg, *Ezekiel*, 273, is correct about Ezek 43:10 to say, "Actual geographical sites are given, so there is no excuse for wild allegorizing." Although typology, for one, is not "wild allegorizing," it also allows for the "realness" of the vision in describing actual places in Israel. These details, however, may also point forward to greater fulfillment.

235. Niditch, "Visionary Context," 216–17, calls this cosmogonic, creating and

The cosmic mountain ideology and Zion traditions help to show this. The question of whether Zion as a cosmic mountain was "real" or not is the wrong question. The people saw Zion as the cosmic mountain, where YHWH dwelt. Levenson puts it well, although in the following quotation one could substitute "typological" for "supra-historical." He claims, "It should be clear that the Zion-traditions are supra-historical, in other words, informed by a mode of orientation better termed myth than history... Being more than natural and more than historical, it is immune to the onslaughts of all foes, legendary or historical."[236] So, in this vision, YHWH gives the people hope by showing them that he would dwell on his cosmic mountain once again. Thus, the vision in a sense has one foot in this world of history, describing the territory of Judea, yet in another sense has a foot in a transformed, eschatological world.[237] The passage also connects to previous eschatological promises, such as the fruitfulness of the land (Ezek 34:26–30; 36:30).[238] Ezekiel does not limit the transformation to Palestine, but instead, as Eichrodt says, "... [this] is of its very nature a universal event..."[239] Ezekiel emphasizes the role of Israel because that is his main concern.[240] Typology can take a symbol rooted in history, in this case a river that the writer clearly describes as part of the land of Israel, yet show its eschatological dimensions.[241]

Several other criteria of typology apply to the vision of Ezek 47:1–12. One is OT development. In this case, development occurs before and after this vision. Ezekiel develops previous traditions, and then several later

---

ordering a new world. The river connects the temple to the rest of the world.

236. Levenson, *Program of Restoration*, 14. Sweeney, *Reading Ezekiel*, 223, also notes the "mythological dimensions" of the trees that heal.

237. Eichrodt, *Ezekiel*, 584–85. Himmelfarb, "Temple and Eden in Ezekiel," 66, says, "In the vision of the restored Temple motifs drawn from Eden suggest a restoration better than anything history could possibly offer."

238. Zimmerli, *Ezekiel 2*, 514; Cooke, *Ezekiel*, 517. Joyce, *Ezekiel*, 236, adds the vision of dry bones in Ezek 37:1–14 as part of the motif of bringing the dead to life.

239. Eichrodt, *Ezekiel*, 585–87. He cites other prophecies like Hos 2:18; Isa 9:3; 32:15ff. Stevenson, *Vision of Transformation*, 142, adds, "[The river] serves a similar function in the text to the role of the Altar in Chapter 43. The Altar cleanses the House of the effects of chaos, while the stream heals the Land. The symbolism here is cosmic, involving a healing of the Land from the effects of chaos."

240. Eichrodt, *Ezekiel*, 586.

241. Hence the conclusion of Darr, "Wall Around Paradise," 277–79, is unnecessary. The text does not present an either/or, but a both/and regarding Israel and the world. See Tuell, "Rivers of Paradise," 188–89.

prophets develop Ezekiel's imagery. As to Ezekiel's use of prior traditions, Hals says, "Here traditions are being used and blended with the subtle creativity of an expert."[242] Ezekiel develops the original tradition of Gen 2:4–14 (cf. also Gen 1:20–23//Ezek 47:9–10).[243] Eden is a fruitful garden, with only one life-giving tree, and with one river flowing from the top of the mountain, dividing into four. Ezekiel transforms the tradition such that many life-giving trees fill the land.[244] The river provides life-giving properties to all natural life around it (Ezek 47:9), and Ezekiel describes one river, rather than a river that splits into four. The development of the Eden motif particularly points to typology.[245] As Fishbane notes, in history of religion studies, foundational events described as *axis mundi*, like Gen 2, provide a typological prototype for later events.[246] The transfer of Eden imagery to the river flowing from the temple identifies the latter as typology.[247] Citing Ezek 47:1–12, Fishbane claims, "The typological reuse of Edenic mythography in post-exilic prophecy is nowhere more forcefully evident than in connection with the new Temple."[248] Another oft-overlooked tradition that Ezekiel develops comes from the story of Sodom in Genesis 19. Sodom was a fruitful land, like Eden (Gen 13:10). When YHWH sent fire, brimstone, and sulfur down upon Sodom, the sea became uninhabitable.[249] In Ezek 16:53–55 YHWH promises to re-

---

242. Hals, *Ezekiel*, 339.

243. For discussion see Tuell, "Rivers of Paradise," 171–89; Himmelfarb, "Temple and the Garden of Eden," 63–78. Strangely, Cooke, *Ezekiel*, 517, says, "It is hardly possible to trace back the idea of a supernatural stream to the ancient myth of Paradise and its four rivers . . ." Tuell, "Rivers of Paradise," 172, shows how specific Eden terminology is used, so Ezekiel and Genesis are not merely drawing from the same Zion tradition that does not share those terms. Hiebel, *Ezekiel's Vision Accounts*, 208–9, also adds the flood narrative as a source for Ezekiel.

244. Himmelfarb, "Temple and the Garden of Eden," 65, argues that in Ezek 47 there is only "a great tree," referencing the tree of life in Eden.

245. Beale, *Temple and Church's Mission*, 341–42, argues for Ezek 47:1–12 as a development of and fulfillment of Eden, though he does not use the rubric of typology.

246. Michael Fishbane, *Biblical Interpretation*, 368.

247. Fishbane, *Biblical Interpretation*, 369–70.

248. Fishbane, *Biblical Interpretation*, 370. Fishbane here includes Ezek 40–48. The dating of the text is not essential to his point, since Ezek 40–48 does come after the destruction of the Jerusalem temple. Cook, *Ezekiel 38–48*, 269, says, "Ezekiel's temple is configured as Eden on earth, the fountain's locale."

249. Milgrom, *Ezekiel's Hope*, 229, says, "This area [the Judean wilderness] was like the Garden of Eden. Before the destruction of Sodom it was . . . [as] well-watered . . . as the garden of YHWH." See also Eichrodt, *Ezekiel*, 583.

store the land to its pre-Sodom state, a promise fulfilled when the river flowing to the Dead Sea restores the land of Sodom.

Ezek 47 also draws on the Zion tradition in Scripture, which itself expands on Edenic imagery of the river of life. Psalm 46:4 describes a river from the holy mountain, and Ps 87:7 describes a spring in Zion. Additionally, Ps 36:7–9, though not a Zion song, speaks of the "house" of God where YHWH is the "fountain of life," and in which the faithful "drink from the river of delights." Eighth-century prophets also prophesy about the barren wilderness transformed into fruitful land (Isa 29:17; 32:15–20; Amos 9:13).[250] Ezekiel's prophecy contains many commonalities with these earlier texts.[251] Ezekiel even previously identifies Eden as being on top of God's holy mountain, associating it with Zion (Ezek 28:13–14).[252] Surely the prophet, familiar with these images, intentionally develops them in Ezek 47:1–12.

Not only does Ezekiel develop previous OT images, but later prophets also develop Ezekiel's prophecy, namely in Joel 4:17–21 and Zech 14:8.[253] These two prophets "reinforce" Ezekiel's vision.[254] Joel states that YHWH will dwell on his holy mountain, and from his temple a fountain will flow that will water even the arid Valley of Shittim, while Zechariah prophesies that "living waters" will flow out of Jerusalem.[255] As mentioned earlier, unlike Ezekiel, he states that the waters will divide in two, so as to reach the Mediterranean and Dead Seas, presumably bringing life to everything in between.[256] Thus, before the closing of the OT, Eze-

---

250. Eichrodt, *Ezekiel*, 583. O'Hare, *Have You Seen, Son of Man?*, 185–87, also discusses how the LXX and *Letter of Aristeas* both present an idealized river that extends even further than the land of Israel.

251. Allen, *Ezekiel 20–48*, 279, cites the "trees in the desert" of Isa 41:19.

252. Tuell, "Rivers of Paradise," 175.

253. Eichrodt, *Ezekiel*, 584. Most commentaries mention these texts. Zechariah is well-known to be a postexilic text. While the date of Joel is ultimately unknown, many regard the work to be later than Ezekiel, not least because of Joel's use of earlier prophetic texts like this one. For an argument that Joel was written between 538–520 BC, see Ganzel, "Shattered Dream," 1–22.

254. Fishbane, *Biblical Interpretation*, 371.

255. Ewald, "Hezeqiel," 218, assumes that Ezek 47:1–12 comes later than Zech 14, but again, this study holds that the river vision belongs originally to the prophet Ezekiel. Alexander, *Ezekiel*, 157, believes that the rivers of Ezek 47 and Zech 14:8 will separately exist in the millennial age. The former flows from the temple outside Jerusalem, while the latter flows out of the city of Jerusalem itself.

256. Possibly Zech 14:8 picks up on the dual noun in Ezek 47:9. Instead of seeing the temple as the source of twin rivers flowing together, as in Mesopotamian literature,

kiel's prophecy, Zimmerli claims, "... has clearly already become a fixed element of eschatological expectation."[257] Keil goes so far as to call this a "... picture of the Messianic salvation ..."[258] Regardless, Ezekiel's vision significantly influenced later prophets.

As to another criterion of typology, some ambiguity also exists in Ezek 47:1–12 regarding its relationship to other aspects of the temple vision. The ambiguity concerns the lack of a few vessels in the temple and their relation to the river of life. These are ambiguous because, initially, one may not notice the absence of these items. In addition, interpreters are unclear as to whether the omission reflects theological meaning or is simply a case of the reader placing an unnecessary burden of proof on the writer.[259] One ambiguity is the lack of a lampstand, representing the tree of life.[260] While the garden of Eden contains the tree of life, the river vision mentions many trees (Ezek 47:12). Beale says, "Quite possibly the lampstand is no longer in the holy place because its redemptive-historical symbolism has begun to be fulfilled."[261] Beale argues that these "trees of life" outside the physical temple demonstrate that the "latter-day goal" of YHWH is an expanding, cosmic temple.[262] That claim is tentative, but regardless, the ambiguous lack of a lampstand likely points forward to a greater fulfillment.

A second ambiguity concerns the absence of a bronze water laver. Perhaps the laver is absent because the river of life flowing from the temple fulfills the symbol of the laver.[263] Instead of this water remaining in the

---

Zechariah takes things more "literalistically" in the sense of two distinct rivers flowing separate ways. See Cook, *Ezekiel 38–48*, 265. Keil, *Ezekiel*, 356, noting Hengstenberg's argument, takes the dual river to mean a river with very strong current, which fits with Cook's notion of twin rivers. Ewald, "Hezeqiel," 219, simply amends the text to make the noun singular.

257. Zimmerli, *Ezekiel 2*, 515.

258. Keil, *Ezekiel*, 351.

259. Greenberg, "Design and Themes," 193, writes, "Omissions cannot serve as a warrant for negative conclusions—unmentioned, therefore absent."

260. Beale, *Temple and Church's Mission*, 360.

261. Beale, *Temple and Church's Mission*, 360.

262. Beale, *Temple and Church's Mission*, 360.

263. Beale, *Temple and Church's Mission*, 360. Duguid, *Ezekiel*, 530, argues that the river replaces the laver, based on the source of the water from the south of the altar, where the laver would be located. Patton, "Ezekiel's Blueprint," 164–65, argues that the river replaces the river only as a secondary purpose, since the primary purpose is to feed and give life rather than to ritually purify.

temple, in Ezekiel's vision it flows out to renew the world. Beale then adds, "If this is a correct reading of Ezekiel . . . then we may deduce without too much speculation that the other unmentioned items in Ezekiel's temple are missing in order to indicate a radical change in the future cosmos."[264] Or, to apply Beale's words to typology, perhaps unmentioned items show ambiguity inherent in typology, pointing forward to a greater fulfillment.

Overall, the vision of Ezek 47:1–12 points towards a typological temple, not a physical building for construction.[265] As Hiebel says, "[T]he vision does not show a programme to be implemented by the people but a reality YHWH will bring about when and how he wishes."[266] Ezek 47:1–12, therefore, shows a number of typological features.

Ezekiel 48:35

The text of Ezek 48:35b says, וְשֵׁם־הָעִיר מִיּוֹם יְהוָה שָׁמָּה ("And the name of the city from that day will be: YHWH Is There").[267] Ezek 48:35 is the final main text that provides an interpretive key for the vision and indicates features of typology. The placement of the text at the very end of the vision shows its importance, as if the words provide a concluding summary of both the temple vision and the entire book of Ezekiel.[268] Moreover, with this conclusion, Ezekiel brings to a culmination his description of

---

264. Beale, *Temple and Church's Mission*, 361.

265. Joyce, "Heavenly Ascent," 30, argues that the lack of furniture points to a heavenly temple.

266. Hiebel, *Ezekiel's Vision Accounts*, 210.

267. The LXX re-points the Tetragrammaton and the final Hebrew word to render the meaning, "[that] will be its name," while Syriac says, "The Lord is his name." Based on context, the MT is the most appropriate reading. See the note and discussion in Zimmerli, *Ezekiel 2*, 545–47; Cooke, *Ezekiel*, 541.

268. Carson, "Lord Is There," 58, says, "But above all, the goal of these nine chapters is found in the very last line." Likewise, Klein, *Ezekiel*, 187, says, "It accurately points to the guiding theological motif in the final chapters as well as in the book as a whole . . . ," though he does not believe Ezekiel authored this section. Tuell, *Law of the Temple*, 74, points to the mention of the city here and Ezek 40:2 as an *inclusio* for the temple vision, showing that Ezek 48:30–35 is not a later addition to the text. Contra, for example, Gese, *Verfassungsentwurf*, 107; Zimmerli, *Ezekiel 2*, 547. As to the link with the entire book of Ezekiel, Hiebel, *Ezekiel's Vision Accounts*, 178, points out that the two chapters with the highest percentage of the term "city" are Ezek 9 and Ezek 48. This likely indicates an intentional link with the previous vision of YHWH's glory. Mayfield, *Structure and Setting*, 116–17, also shows that from a literary perspective Ezek 40–48 provides the culmination of the entire book.

the new city (Ezek 48), for, as Klein says, "The name—that is, the identity, meaning, and significance—of the city could now be wrapped up in the words 'Yahweh is there.'"[269] Andiñach states that, like a suspenseful novel, Ezekiel keeps the secret of the vision for the last line.[270] After giving the vision of the river (Ezek 47:1-12) and explaining the borders of the land (Ezek 47:13—48:29), YHWH describes the city by explaining its gates and dimensions (Ezek 48:30-35a). At the vision's end, Ezek 48:35b provides the name of the city. This conclusion describes the apogee of YHWH's salvation, or as Eichrodt claims, "... the essential content of the age of salvation in the eyes of Ezekiel."[271] Salvation for God's people means having the presence of God dwell with them, and the city represents just that. As Block notes, "The existence of the city is the evidence of Yahweh's eternal presence."[272]

The Meaning of the City's Name

What does the city's name mean? Or, to ask the question differently, where is YHWH? Some argue the name refers to the presence of YHWH's glory in the temple complex. The name, in that case, means, "YHWH is [over] there," in the temple, not "here" in the city.[273] In other words, "YHWH is thither."[274] In this view, if a traveler arrives at the city and sees a sign at its entrance saying, "יְהוָה שָׁמָּה," the sign would point north, referring to the temple. The presence of a final ה, perhaps a locative, provides evidence

269. Klein, *Ezekiel*, 189. Contra Block, *Ezekiel 25-48*, 735, who says Ezek 48:30-35 is a supplement to the book.

270. Andiñach, *El Dios que está*, 260. He says, "El texto tiene un vórtice, que lo es de la sección, pero también de todo el libro de Ezequiel, y en él se revela el nuevo nombre de la ciudad. Sostiene el secreto hasta las últimas palabras y, como en las narraciones de suspenso, crea un clima de tensión que no se resuelve hasta la línea final."

271. Eichrodt, *Ezekiel*, 593.

272. Block, *Ezekiel 25-48*, 581. Allen, *Ezekiel 20-48*, 285, also calls this title an "eschatological" name of the city. This contrasts with Ironside, *Ezekiel*, 336, who states, "[YHWH] will ... return in glory to His sanctuary and will dwell in the midst of His people throughout the kingdom age." No part of this text indicates that the dwelling is only in a limited, kingdom age. Instead, the verse implies that YHWH's dwelling is eternal and immutable.

273. Cook, *Ezekiel 38-48*, 296. The view goes as far back as Eliezer of Beaugency, according to Milgrom, *Ezekiel's Hope*, 261.

274. Cook, *Ezekiel 38-48*, 296. Kim, "YHWH Shammah," 187-207, also argues for the "thither" view. This usage goes as far back as Keil, *Ezekiel*, 381, who mentions Hävernick's argument for this sense.

Evidence for a Type in Ezekiel's Temple Vision, Part II   101

for this view (see the usage in Isa 34:12).²⁷⁵ Additionally, the perspective of the audience is not exile in Babylon, but Israel back in their land. If the audience were to say, "YHWH is [over] there" from Babylon, the name could refer generically to the area of Israel. However, Cook notes that the name of the city would be spoken within the city itself, thus pointing not to the land but the temple.²⁷⁶

Cook and Kim furnish further arguments for the view. Cook says, "Ezek 43:1–13 clarifies the deixis, leaving no doubt that YHWH is in the temple building, not in the city."²⁷⁷ Kim adds that intertextual exegesis shows connections here with Sinaitic theology, where YHWH is present atop Sinai and the people settle south, as opposed to Zion theology, where YHWH resides in the center of the people.²⁷⁸ Thus, the city's name shows that YHWH is present up north on the mountain, but the people cannot approach him, just like at Sinai. As Cook says in language reminiscent of Sinai, "If God were to directly contact the pilgrim city, it would cease to exist, since direct contact with the Holy is lethal. Thus, God hovers over the city, 'touching yet not touching.'"²⁷⁹ The meaning of the city's name as "over there" has important potential theological implications. Cook states that the city then becomes a rendezvous point with pilgrims looking towards a place they anticipate visiting.²⁸⁰ Ezekiel, therefore, provides

---

275. Cook, *Ezekiel 38–48*, 296.

276. Cook, *Ezekiel 38–48*, 296. Contra Kim, "YHWH Shammah," 203, who argues it must mean "over there" because the audience is in Babylon.

277. Cook, *Ezekiel 38–48*, 296. Kim, "YHWH Shammah," 192–93, additionally argues that the city is a transition place between the holy and profane, but bases his argument off of differences between Ezek 48:20 and Ezek 45, where in the latter text the city is not part of the portion (Ezek 45:6–7). One need not assume a contradiction, though. The reference to the "holy district" in Ezek 45:6–7 does not automatically mean the city is not part of the *terumah* ("Portion").

278. Kim, "YHWH Shammah," 200. Kim claims that, in terms of the city's relationship to the temple, Sinai imagery dominates over Zion/Eden imagery, but he provides no evidence for this claim. In Kim, "YHWH Shammah," 200–203, he simply shows that Ezek 40–48 uses Exodus language, but that point is not conclusive. The presence of Sinai imagery does not negate the dominance of Zion imagery. The fact that the city is named rather than the temple, as Zimmerli, *Ezekiel 2*, 538, says, "... testifies to the strength of the tradition of the holy city ... ," that is, Zion/Jerusalem ideology. Likewise, Allen, *Ezekiel 20–48*, 285, says, "These final verses seek to rehabilitate the old Zion traditions."

279. Cook, *Ezekiel 38–48*, 297. Here, "hovering over" seems to refer to his presence at the top of the mountain north of the city, not a Presence actually hovering like a cloud atop the city. See Kim, "YHWH Shammah," 198, who makes this point explicit.

280. Cook, *Ezekiel 38–48*, 297. He cites the similar texts Gen 19:20, 22; 21:13; Jer

the name not for the residents of Israel but for those seeking Israel's God in pilgrimage.[281] Such a notion does not fit with the tone of comfort for Israel, however. At this point in her history, Israel needs to know that YHWH is with them, not that he is available to pilgrim foreigners.

On the other hand, the more traditional view argues that the name of the city refers to the entire area, including the temple complex, city, and land. "YHWH Is There" is akin to *Immanuel*, meaning "God with us."[282] One scholar even translates the phrase as "Yahweh is here."[283] In other words, in this case, if travelers arrive at the city and see a sign at the entrance saying, "יְהוָה שָׁמָּה," they would think the sign refers to the city itself and the land as the place where YHWH's glory dwells.[284] Similar usage in Ezek 23:3 and Ezek 32:29–30 supports this sense, such that Keil argues that Ezekiel's sense is never "thither," with or without the final ה.[285] This interpretation means that YHWH's presence pervades the city and not merely the temple. Despite his belief that YHWH resides north of the city in the temple, Block says, "But with this new name the implicit symbolism of the design [of the temple] is made explicit: the city reflects the presence of Yahweh!"[286]

Although the city is "common" (Ezek 48:15), Block writes, "The aura of the divine presence will emanate forth beyond the sacred residence, pervading the entire reserve . . . Under the new order, where the people are, there is Yahweh. He does not only invite them to himself in the temple; he has come to them!"[287] Likewise, Zimmerli says, "What was reported in [Ezek] 43:1ff, the return of Yahweh to his temple, is here transferred to the city, which then once more, as in former times, is viewed

---

18:2. Cook nearly verbatim bases the claim off of Kim, "YHWH Shammah," 193.

281. Kim, "YHWH Shammah," 205.

282. Eichrodt, *Ezekiel*, 593.

283. Nielsen, "Ezekiel's Visionary Call," 111. She bases her claim on parallel usages like Isa 48:16; Prov 8:27. These texts do not convince, however, for they both make more sense with the rendering, "there."

284. Milgrom, *Ezekiel's Hope*, 261. According to Milgrom, *Ezekiel's Hope*, 259, the city is a microcosm of the land, possibly demonstrated in Ezek 48:30–35's NESW descriptions to reflect boundaries of land (47:15–20), rather than the previous NSEW description in 48:16.

285. Keil, *Ezekiel*, 381; Cooke, *Ezekiel*, 538.

286. Block, *Ezekiel 25–48*, 739. So also Eichrodt, *Ezekiel*, 593.

287. Block, *Ezekiel 25–48*, 740. Similarly, Keil, *Ezekiel*, 382.

in close relationship with the temple."²⁸⁸ In fact, Ezek 47:1–12 provides the key transition. The river symbolizes how, in a sense, YHWH's temple presence positively infects all the land.²⁸⁹ Cook, in arguing for the former view, actually provides more evidence for this latter view, claiming that other prophetic texts stand in tension with Ezek 48:35 because they describe God's presence in the city.²⁹⁰ Texts like Jer 3:17; Jer 33:14–18; Isa 60:14; and Isa 62:2–4 rename the city of Jerusalem to indicate YHWH's presence there in some sense.²⁹¹ Rather than seeing these texts as in tension with Ezekiel's text, they buttress the idea that YHWH's presence would be in the new city, similar to his presence in Zion.²⁹²

The location of this text at the end of the book serves as another argument for YHWH's presence in the city. Hals correctly notes that, formally, the vision report does not conclude with a final formula (cf. Ezek 3:15; 37:14). Due to this absence of a formula, though, he incorrectly states, "There is no real ending to chs. 40–48."²⁹³ The city's name, according to Hals, ". . . serves adequately to complete the small appended section of which it is a part [Ezek 48:30–35], but it does not fulfill that role for all of chs. 40–48, because the focus throughout is much more extensive than just the city."²⁹⁴ A better interpretation of this feature, though, is that Ezekiel very purposefully ends the book and the temple vision in this way. Ezekiel likely places these words here to show the opposite of Hals's argument, that is, to show that YHWH's presence is not merely in

---

288. Zimmerli, *Ezekiel 2*, 547; Allen, *Ezekiel 20–48*, 285; Klein, *Ezekiel*, 188, adds that a secondary author may be asserting his belief here that the temple should be in this city. Patton, "Ezekiel's Blueprint," 179, argues, "Throughout Mesopotamian history the name of the temple was an essential component in understanding the particular ideology embodied [sic] each particular temple." Thus, she states that the name more likely refers to the temple. However, though the temple is not directly named, the argument here is that the city and temple are closely equated. So, the name of the city fits with Patton's statement that the name is essential to understanding the ideology behind the temple vision.

289. Allen, *Ezekiel 20–48*, 276, says, "The common theme [of Ezek 47–48] is the essential bond between temple and land."

290. Cook, *Ezekiel 38–48*, 296. He also adds that these other prophets show a restoration of the monarchy, which he sees as a contrast to Ezek 40–48.

291. Hals, *Ezekiel*, 347, calls Ezekiel's description of the new city "semirealistic" and "less flamboyant" compared to these other prophets' texts.

292. Klein, *Ezekiel*, 188, adds that re-naming Jerusalem is a mark of postexilic authorship, but such a claim is unnecessarily speculative.

293. Hals, *Ezekiel*, 287.

294. Hals, *Ezekiel*, 287.

the city, but everywhere among his people. In Joyce's words, "[God] 'sit[s] loose' to the site itself, exhibiting a remarkable degree of detachment."[295] The words formally append the description of the city, but structurally conclude the entire vision.

The clear contrast between Ezekiel's city and the old city of Jerusalem provides further evidence that YHWH's presence resides in this city rather than just the temple. The Zion tradition holds that YHWH is in his city *because* he is in his temple (Isa 2:1–4). Though in this vision the temple is not located geographically in this new city, the Zionistic idea remains that YHWH is present here because he is in the temple (Ezek 43:1–12). Based on Jerusalem's faithless past, though, Ezekiel must ideologically distance this city from the old one, and does so in several ways. First, the location of the new city indicates a severing of ties with Jerusalem.[296] Milgrom claims that the city lies in the same area as the old Jerusalem, instead of symmetrically in between the six strips of land north and south (Ezek 47:13–23).[297] Such a move would imply that the new city replaces Jerusalem. However, some dispute this popular claim. Duguid asserts that the new city is north of the old Jerusalem and closer to Shiloh, noting the equal width of the tribal allotments (Ezek 47:14), with seven north of the *terumah* and five south.[298] In Duguid's view, Ezekiel may intentionally place YHWH's sacred presence further from the previously defiled Jerusalem.[299] Either way, however, the text makes a polemic against the old city.

Second, the city is purposely not named or identified in any way as Jerusalem, since, as Block says, "This name [YHWH Is There] announces the undoing of a past evil situation."[300] Previously in the book of Ezekiel,

---

295. Joyce, *Ezekiel*, 240.

296. Contra Gaebelein, *Ezekiel*, 346; Feinberg, *Ezekiel*, 279; Alexander, *Ezekiel*, 157, who plainly states, "Most would identify this city as the city of Jerusalem (cf. Zec 14:8)."

297. Milgrom, *Ezekiel's Hope*, 261; Also Block, *Ezekiel 25–48*, 711.

298. Duguid, *Ezekiel*, 544–45. See also Mackay, "Ezekiel's Division of Palestine," 29.

299. Duguid, *Ezekiel*, 545, also admits, "The shift in theological geography may also have been driven by a simple desire to locate the temple closer to the center of the land."

300. Block, *Ezekiel 25–48*, 739. Eichrodt, *Ezekiel*, 593, says the name ". . . answer[s] to the new state of salvation." This contrasts with Zimmerli, *Ezekiel 2*, 538, when he claims, "There can be no doubt that it is Jerusalem that is meant." He reasons, "Jerusalem is precisely too laden with tradition for Israel for that to happen [Jerusalem to be passed over]."

Jerusalem equated to idolatry and bloodshed, and, Block adds, "With its Canaanite origins, the name Jerusalem symbolized the city's degenerate and faithless past."[301] The replacement of Jerusalem with this city also shows the failure of the monarchy, corrected here by the kingship of YHWH.[302] Block argues, "[The new name] repudiates the notion of a political capital, linked with any particular tribe, as Jerusalem, the Judahite capital, had been."[303] However, as Zimmerli correctly points out, Jerusalem is not entirely out of the background of this text, for the capital city is known in the Zion tradition as the dwelling place of YHWH.[304] Therefore, Ezekiel takes the Zion tradition of YHWH's dwelling, previously in Jerusalem, and he cleverly translates those ideas to the new city without any mention of Jerusalem.[305] The new city with a new name, then, announces the reversal of the events of Ezek 8–11.[306] In this way the writer links the presence of YHWH in the city with his presence in the temple of Ezek 43.[307] Ezekiel contrasts here YHWH's presence in the new city versus the old city, not the new temple with the old temple (cf. Ezek 43:1–6).

---

301. Block, *Ezekiel 25–48*, 739. Odell, *Ezekiel*, 525, believes that Jerusalem is renamed Hamonah in Ezek 39:16, thus becoming a cemetery.

302. Stevenson, *Vision of Transformation*, 108. Per Stevenson, *Vision of Transformation*, 61, "there" is an important word in the vision, for it denotes boundaries for a territory, which consequently indicates power. According to Milgrom, *Ezekiel's Hope*, 262, this also is no longer the city of David, but belongs to all the tribes.

303. Block, *Ezekiel 25–48*, 738.

304. Zimmerli, *Ezekiel 2*, 547. Wevers, *Ezekiel*, 343, calls the new city, "Ideal Jerusalem." Hence, Tuell, "Divine Presence and Absence," 103–4, incorrectly asserts that Ezekiel severs ties with Jerusalem by describing the city as distinct from the mountain. Instead, the presence of YHWH overlaps in both the city and the temple, such that Zion traditions are still in play.

305. Renz, *Rhetorical Function*, 127, says, "The vision carefully reconstructs aspects of the Zion tradition, but resists any attempt to have a Davidic component in it."

306. Zimmerli, *Ezekiel 2*, 547.

307. Zimmerli, *Ezekiel 2*, 547. Zimmerli argues that a later redactor inserts this name to push against the "priestly reform project" that sees YHWH's glory only in the temple. Such a move is unnecessary, however. Zimmerli rightly points out that the text sees YHWH's glory equally in the city just as much as in the temple. These are not contradictions between authors, but ambiguities latent in the vision as a whole. So also, Dus and Simian-Yofre, "Ezequiel," 469.

Typology in Ezek 48:35b

If the name of the city indicates YHWH's presence in the city and land, the verse provides important information for interpreting the vision. Indeed, such a name for the city indicates more typological features. If the name of the city simply points to the presence of YHWH in the temple, the final words of Ezekiel's book do not add very much to what this study has already explored, beyond simply underlining the importance of YHWH's presence in the temple. However, since the study above argued for YHWH's presence in the city, not the temple, this section will show the typological importance of the city's name.

A "physical structure" interpretation presents problems, for then one must conclude that YHWH's presence may only be in the temple, as is typical of OT conceptions. If so, Ezek 48:35 would not make sense, since the text shows that the entire city, even land, will be like the holy of holies. The *inclusio* with Ezek 40:2 clarifies this notion.[308] This idea also fits with Ezek 43:1–12, which speaks of YHWH's presence beyond the holy of holies. In this respect, then, the text shows an *eschatological heightening*. The vision shows what Beale calls ". . . [a] widening [and] universally expanding . . ." vision of God's presence.[309] In previous temples, YHWH's presence was largely thought of as in the holy of holies. Ezek 43:1–12, though, describes YHWH's presence extending to the entire temple area, and here Ezekiel shows a heightening through the expansion of YHWH's presence.[310] Cooke says, "This goes further than [Ezek] 43:1–9 . . . but Ezekiel's own teaching promised that Jahveh would dwell above and in the midst of his people for ever, [Ezek] 37:26–28."[311] This language escalates typologically even more in the NT.

Additionally, because the text shows eschatological heightening, it naturally also includes the typological feature of *prophetic indicator*. Ezekiel prophesies that in the future the name of the city will be "YHWH Is There." Such a heightening is also *soteriological*, and fits with the exilic situation. Hopeless and under judgment, the people could have even greater hope that YHWH would be "among" them (see Ezek 37:27). In

---

308. Beale, *Temple and Church's Mission*, 340.

309. Beale, *Temple and Church's Mission*, 345.

310. Joyce, *Ezekiel*, 241, says, "This is a final striking case of Ezekiel both emphasizing the location of the holy, but also diffusing or spreading it."

311. Cooke, *Ezekiel*, 538. Duguid, *Ezekiel*, 547, also claims the vision is the fulfillment of Ezek 37:26–27.

Block's words, "Where God is, there is Zion. Where God is, there is also order and the fulfillment of all his promises."[312] Schwartz is therefore incorrect to say, "[YHWH] change[s] the name of the city to 'YHWH is there' (48:35), so that he can supervise his people's worship from close at hand and they will live in reverence (43:4–7)."[313] Such a statement sees the vision as a judgment. However, YHWH will give the people new hearts so that, without sacrificing his holiness, he may dwell with them instead of perennially censure them.[314]

This text also shows the typological feature of an *epochal* institution. Not only is the vision about the institution of the temple, but this text also specifically identifies the new "capital" city. As seen above, this city, for all intents, replaces the old Jerusalem. Sweeney identifies this city as "the new temple city."[315] Sweeney also underscores the epochal importance of this new city when he says, "YHWH stands once again in the holy center of the created world."[316] In addition, this epochal characteristic indicates the *historical* quality of this vision. Against Beale, the vision is not that of a heavenly temple.[317] Although "non-literal" features are present, such as YHWH's presence beyond the temple, Ezekiel still, after all, speaks of a city within the land of Israel. Duguid explains the historical rootedness and epochal significance well, saying, "This is not pure utopianism, since this Promised Land is not located somewhere over the rainbow . . . but rather in the land of Israel . . . This does not mean that we should therefore anticipate a 'literal' future fulfillment . . . This section is 'theology in the form of geography.'"[318] Typology, then, explains the historical rootedness of the city in Israel while allowing for non-literal features.

Another important typological feature in Ezek 48:45b is its *ambiguity*. Milgrom calls this text "a theological conundrum."[319] Specifically, the conundrum lies in the issue discussed above, whether YHWH resides only in his temple or in the city as well.[320] According to Milgrom, Ezekiel

312. Block, *Ezekiel 25–48*, 745–46.
313. Schwartz, "Ezekiel's Dim View," 62.
314. Milgrom, *Ezekiel's Hope*, 263.
315. Sweeney, *Reading Ezekiel*, 224.
316. Sweeney, *Reading Ezekiel*, 227.
317. Beale, *Temple and Church's Mission*, 336–37.
318. Duguid, *Ezekiel*, 548.
319. Milgrom, *Ezekiel's Hope*, 262.
320. Allen, *Ezekiel 20–48*, 286, expresses the ambiguity as well, writing, "The two parts of this final literary unit give expression to a biblical tension, the paradox of an

so far in the text made "... an incessant demand ..." to separate holy from common, but here the "secular" city contains the presence of holy YHWH. Moreover, Milgrom argues that previously YHWH "... locked himself inside his temple ..." (Ezek 43:7–9), yet here he is present in the city. Milgrom answers, "God is unbounded (hardly anthropomorphic) in space."[321] YHWH can operate in simultaneous spaces (cf. Ezek 37:27; Lev 26:12). Here the name of Ezekiel's city, then, clarifies the ambiguity of the vision and points forward to a heightened fulfillment. Milgrom concludes that Ezekiel's idea of God changes from anthropomorphic to ubiquitous, but a better way to state this is that Ezekiel's text is ambiguous.[322] After all, how does a mere mortal describe YHWH (see Ezek 1)? While interpreters seek to put texts into either/or categories, a better understanding is that the text has various shades. At times, YHWH may seem more anthropomorphic, while at other times ubiquitous. Duguid rightly says, "The language of God's dual presence is necessary in order to communicate both God's transcendence and his immanence."[323] Besides the question of YHWH's presence, the geography of the city is also ambiguous and points beyond a physical fulfillment. Cooke argues that the new city measures twice the size of present Jerusalem, and therefore he concludes, "The facts of topography are ignored in this ideal reconstruction."[324] In Ezekiel's final words, ambiguity stands out.

Conclusion

In the words of Levenson, "Ezekiel's tour of Zion is a foretaste of ultimate redemption granted [to] one who must otherwise dwell in history."[325]

---

immanent God who blesses his covenant people in lavish abundance, and of a transcendent God who, however immanent, must remain apart in his holiness of being." The two parts Allen refers to are Ezek 47:1–12 and Ezek 47:13—48:35.

321. Milgrom, *Ezekiel's Hope*, 262.

322. Similarly, Hals, *Ezekiel*, 346, says, "Manifestly the problem of the integration of these two different perspectives [YHWH's glory in the temple versus in the city] did not deter their being affirmed virtually side by side. Once again, it becomes clear that the intent of the vision is that of eschatological affirmation rather than practical clarification." Hals's underlying assumption is that multiple authors have competing views. He rightly affirms how the final text, however, presents this ambiguity purposefully to create an "eschatological affirmation."

323. Duguid, *Ezekiel*, 547. So also Joyce, "Heavenly Ascent," 37.

324. Cooke, *Ezekiel*, 535.

325. Levenson, *Program of Restoration*, 18.

This statement well sums up the typological nature of Ezek 40–48. The temple, river, and city are rooted in history, yet they also foretaste an ultimate redemption, an eschatological heightening. This chapter seeks to demonstrate this through examination of the temple vision in the context of the book and the key texts in the vision, Ezek 40:1–4; 43:1–12; 47:1–12; and 48:35b. Each of these texts provides a hermeneutical roadmap for interpreting the vision as a whole. Along the way, the study shows that these texts should be interpreted typologically. On one hand, a literal interpretation, one that sees the temple as intended for physical construction, does not adequately deal with the details of the text that show the symbolic nature of the temple and land. On the other hand, the texts also show that this is not merely symbolism, but rooted in Ezekiel's historical situation. Typology presents an adequate solution for this tension. Using the method of typology established before, this chapter shows how these features appear in the key texts of the vision. These are not the only texts, however, that make up this vision. What about the building measurements, leadership roles, sacrificial system, and land allotments? The following chapter will examine how a typological reading treats these elements of the vision.

4

Evidence for a Type in Ezekiel's Temple Vision, Part III

The Building, Legislation, and Land

Introduction

THE PREVIOUS CHAPTER ARGUED that specific texts in Ezek 40–48 show features of typology. In that way, the last chapter is a positive argument for why the vision should be interpreted typologically. This chapter looks at aspects of the text that many scholars claim argue for a physical fulfillment. In the words of Levenson, "The highly specific nature of the description of the Temple, its liturgy and community, bespeaks a practical program, not a vision of pure grace."[1] The previous chapter explained that key texts of the vision serve as a hermeneutical roadmap, influencing the reading of the rest of the vision. At the same time, an argument for typology cannot depend on only a few texts, but must take into account the entire vision. How, then, should an interpreter handle these aspects

---

1. Levenson, *Program of Restoration*, 45. In many instances Levenson's work undergirds a typological interpretation, yet he does not rule out a historical fulfillment. He writes, "The heavenly archetype and its human execution are not at odds in the mind of the prophet" (*Program of Restoration*, 75). He even notes tension in his interpretation of the vision when he concludes his work by saying, "Precisely because the program was more than practical, it could not survive intact in the world of practicalities. Yet, we suggest, this weakness within history of their program would not have troubled the authors of the program, for their glory was their very ability to look beyond history, to conceive a world the historian did not know" (*Program of Restoration*, 163).

of the vision that, on the surface, indicate that the prophet expects a very physical application of the vision? This chapter will explore the temple building and its measurements, the priesthood and leadership in this new envisioned society, and then the role of the legislation, such as the temple furniture, the sacrifices, and land allotments. A careful reading of the text shows that these aspects of the vision are idealized, and therefore typological, so the author does not intend for the audience to implement them literally.

The Temple Building

After the introduction of the vision in Ezek 40:1–4, the angelic guide immediately takes Ezekiel on a tour of the envisioned temple, what Milgrom regards as "... a riddle in spatial design."[2] In Ezek 40:5—42:20, Ezekiel describes the tour and the detailed measurements of what he sees.[3] While Ezekiel explains aspects of the temple in a few other places, such as the altar in Ezek 43:13–27 and the kitchen courts in Ezek 46:19–24, the main temple description takes place in Ezek 40–42. Thus, this section will examine the temple and its measurements in Ezek 40:5—42:20, providing numerous reasons for why the text does not present a temple intended to be physically constructed.[4]

The Detailed Measurements

If Ezekiel does not intend for his audience to implement this vision literally, why does he provide so many specific details regarding the building? Advocates for a physical temple view often present this point as a decisive consideration. For example, Toy writes, "On its face, the prophecy is literal:

---

2. Milgrom, *Ezekiel's Hope*, 41.

3. Van Dyke Parunak, "Ezekiel's Mar'ot Elohim," 71, shows a chiastic structure in the temple description as the guide leads Ezekiel from the outside to the inside of the temple, then back to the outside. Thus, rather than being a series of editorial accretions, the vision has an organized structure.

4. Block, *Ezekiel 25–48*, 506, takes Ezek 40:1—43:11 as the first section of Ezek 40–48. Chapter three of this study examined the structure of Ezek 43:1–12, arguing for an *inclusio* of Ezek 40:1–4 and Ezek 43:1–12. Thus, this study understands Ezek 40:1—43:12 as the first major section, aligning with Greenberg, "Design and Themes," 189. However, Ezek 43:1–12 was discussed in the last chapter so that aspect of the temple vision will not be examined here.

it relates to a real temple and state expected or hoped for by the prophet. This is the natural conclusion from the minute and exact statements of the dimensions of the temple and its territory . . . The measurements in chs. 40–42 are so minute that it would be hard to imagine their use unless a literal building was intended."[5] Since these measurements were not implemented in the postexilic temple (Ezra 6:3), some interpreters say the only other option is for Israel to construct this temple during an eschatological millennium.[6] Others like Milgrom do not hold to a millennial view but still claim that this temple description is realistic enough to reveal an intention for construction. Milgrom says strongly, "There is nothing miraculous about the structure . . . However, the area outside the temple is replete with miraculous data . . ."[7] Likewise, Cooke says, "In chs. 40–42 [Ezekiel] describes [the temple's] ground-plan, which is based partly on the lines of Solomon's temple, partly on the model of the walled and fortified sanctuaries in Babylonia."[8] For Milgrom, even the ten-foot-high and ten-foot-thick wall is feasible. He argues that a ten-foot-high wall is no real deterrent to an attacking enemy, so it is an appropriate size for a temple wall.[9] Milgrom presents an extensive comparison between Ezekiel's

---

5. Toy, "General Interpretation," xlv. See also the comment on Ezek 40:48–49 of Feinberg, *Ezekiel*, 244, who says, "Ezekiel continued to set forth detail after detail, making it increasingly difficult to interpret the whole in a figurative manner, in which case the abundance of minute details is worthless and meaningless." Gaebelein, *Ezekiel*, 279–80, presents a less convincing argument, merely saying, "That all this [the measurements] must have a deeper meaning we doubt not; and yet who can at this time give it to us in full? These instructions will be literally followed and carried out in the coming day of Israel's restoration."

6. Zimmerli, *Ezekiel 2*, 360, notes the contradiction between Ezekiel and Ezra's temples. Blenkinsopp, *Ezekiel*, 196, summarizes the millennial argument. See especially the commentaries referenced in this chapter by Gaebelein, Alexander, Feinberg, Ironside, and Ellison.

7. Milgrom, *Ezekiel's Hope*, 52.

8. Cooke, *Ezekiel*, 425.

9. Many note the similar size of this temple's gates and the preexilic gates found in the cities of Megiddo, Hazor, and Gezer. See Zimmerli, *Ezekiel 2*, 352, 359; Block, *Ezekiel 25–48*, 519; Allen, *Ezekiel 20–48*, 230; Duguid, *Ezekiel*, 473–74; Cook, *Ezekiel 38–48*, 128. What is unique about these walls, however, is not their size as city walls, but as temple walls. See Renz, *Rhetorical Function of Ezekiel*, 123. Patton, "Blueprint," 157–58, argues that the walls may have been intended for judges (the priests) to sit at the gates. Moreover, the walls are very large in proportion to the entire temple compound. For discussion on the proportion see Stevenson, *Vision of Transformation*, 45, 118; Joyce, "Heavenly Ascent?," 24; Zimmerli, *Ezekiel 2*, 359–60. Zimmerli, *Ezekiel 2*, 349, points out the oddity of a wall that is as thick as it is high. The unique size of the walls answers

temple and the temple at Delphi.[10] He admits, "Ezekiel's sanctuary design is not a ready-to-build blueprint. It lacks many structural details."[11] Still, since he believes Ezekiel's temple is based on Delphi's, he concludes that the temple could realistically be constructed.

Despite these claims, the minute details of the building should not lead to the conclusion that this is a blueprint for physical construction. Other explanations exist. First, cultural reasons explain the specificity. Through this genre of ANE temple instructions, Ezekiel expresses YHWH's kingship, regardless of whether the temple is actually constructed. Block shows that the detailed measurements fit with standard ANE conceptions of divine temple instructions, such as in the Hymn of Gudea.[12] Admittedly, these ANE temples were physically constructed. Nevertheless, ANE background shows that YHWH is manifesting his kingship by providing such a detailed plan. As the nation's god, he has every right to determine the exact nature of his dwelling.[13] In other words, Ezekiel knows no other way to make his point of divine kingship aside from a detailed temple plan, for this is how a god expressed kingship in ANE culture.[14]

Second, YHWH himself states the reason for the detailed measurements—to induce shame (Ezek 43:10).[15] Relatedly, he states that the

---

the objection of Strong, "Grounding Ezekiel's Heavenly Ascent," 197, who claims Ezekiel generally bases his description off of his memory of Solomon's temple walls.

10. Milgrom, *Ezekiel's Hope*, 44–53.

11. Milgrom, *Ezekiel's Hope*, 53.

12. Block, *Ezekiel 25–48*, 510. See also the work of Sharon, "Ezekiel 40–48 and Gudea," 99–109. Contra Patton, "Blueprint," 188, who says, "What is not represented in the Near Eastern texts is the plethora of detail found within ... Ezekiel ... We could not reconstruct the layout of any of these Mesopotamian structures if we did not have archaeological evidence to help us." Odell, "'The Wall Is No More,'" 339, notes major differences between Ezekiel and Gudea temples, notably that Ezekiel's temple is already built. These differences do not rule out the specificity of the temple instruction genre, though.

13. Block, *Ezekiel 25–48*, 510.

14. In addition to the claim of kingship, one may also consider Ezekiel's priestly background and how this vision reflects the Sinai event. At Sinai, YHWH concludes his redemption with setting up his sanctuary in the promised land (Exod 25–31). For the prophet-priest Ezekiel, YHWH's salvation also culminates in reinstating the cult. See Blenkinsopp, *Ezekiel*, 194. This is not to say, as Blenkinsopp does, that Ezekiel sees an actual heavenly temple. Still, the reason for Ezekiel laying out such a detailed temple has its background in the Sinai event as well.

15. Block, *Ezekiel 25–48*, 511. Patton, "Blueprint," 155, notes that features of the plan do not reflect a historical Israelite temple but rather serve as a critique of the past. Bechtel, "Politics of Yahweh," 241, claims that the meaning of the narrative temple

temple walls should separate the holy from common (Ezek 42:20).[16] The previous chapter showed that, instead of a command to build, YHWH commands the people to consider the proportions and be ashamed. YHWH's goal is not for the people to build the building, but to focus on the spaces.[17] In commenting on the hall of the inner temple, Block says, "The absence of any reference to its decoration, furnishings, or function reflects the primary rhetorical concern to define sacred space, not to provide a blueprint for a construction project."[18] These descriptions of spaces, in Block's words, ". . . reflect the sanctity of the territory within and the seriousness with which access to sacred space must be controlled."[19] This happens through measuring the spaces created by the structures, not measuring the structures themselves.[20] One sees this clearly in Ezek 41:9–11, where the prophet measures a free space, a space which becomes part of the measurements of the temple that add up to 100 x 100 cubits, a perfect square.[21] The text also describes concentric

---

tour does not come to light until the reader arrives at Ezek 43:10.

16. Patton, "Blueprint," 155, argues that the cells (the chambers) in these walls serve as transitional areas between sacred and common.

17. Stevenson, *Vision of Transformation*, 19, writes, "The issue in Ezekiel 40–42 is not the correct building of structures, but the creation of spaces, and even more importantly, keeping these spaces separate." Later she argues, "Many of the problems of interpretation concerning Ezekiel 40–48 are problems of genre, most notably that Chapters 40–42 are the 'blueprint' for the post-exilic temple in Jerusalem. The argument that this is territorial rhetoric rather than a blueprint depends on the definition of territoriality and a conceptual shift from structures to spaces" (*Vision of Transformation*, 163). Note however that in her conclusion Stevenson says, "I cannot prove it, of course, but I find it incomprehensible that the Rhetor of this text could imagine a society without an actual temple as the symbolic center of the society" (*Vision of Transformation*, 151). Also, Clark, "'I Will Be King Over You,'" 145, says, "There appears to be an intrinsic connection between physical detail and moral lesson in the vision."

18. Block, *Ezekiel 25–48*, 543.

19. Block, *Ezekiel 25–48*, 523.

20. Stevenson, *Vision of Transformation*, 19–30. The claim is somewhat exaggerated, for even Stevenson admits that sometimes in the vision the angel measures structures. Nevertheless, the general point is accurate, as the emphasis is on boundaries and spaces, and the spatial relationship of the structures to one another, rather than the actual structures.

21. Stevenson, *Vision of Transformation*, 25. Ezek 41:12–14 also mentions a yard between the בִּנְיָן and the temple. The בִּנְיָן plus the yard add up to 100 x 100 cubits, a perfect square in proportion with the temple building, which is also 100 x 100 cubits. Per Zimmerli, *Ezekiel 2*, 379, the yard is a restricted area. In addition, the LXX of Ezek 42:15–20 specifies that the guide measures the spaces, not the walls. See O'Hare, *Have You Seen, Son of Man?*," 105–6.

areas of sanctity, with holiness more prevalent on the inside and decreasing as one goes outward.²²

Moreover, the massive size of the temple and the thickness of the walls show the holiness of YHWH. The outer temple walls are greatly out of proportion to the rest of the temple.²³ The walls are thick (Ezek 40:5), not for self-defense but for separating YHWH's holiness from the "secular" areas.²⁴ That the measuring begins and ends with the outer wall (Ezek 40:5; 42:20) is telling, for it stakes the "territorial claim" of separation.²⁵ Likewise, the frequent mention of gates, rather than other cultic aspects of the temple, underscores the importance of access.²⁶ So Ezekiel shows not that YHWH needs to defend himself from political nations, but that he defends his holiness from the peoples' impurity.²⁷ Also along these lines, Bechtel notes that Ezekiel knows various terms to describe walls, but uses חוֹמָה, which refers to a city wall. Ezekiel does this to show YHWH's kingship, for a city is the domain of a (political) king.²⁸

Third, the detailed measurements show the holiness, and thus glory, of YHWH.²⁹ Ironside, in comments on Ezek 40:17–19, says, "We ... find ourselves more and more impressed with the glory and the grandeur of

---

22. Block, *Ezekiel 25–48*, 571; Blenkinsopp, *Ezekiel*, 202. Ganzel and Holtz, "Babylonian Context," 222, on the other hand, argue that analogous Babylonian temples also reflect gradations in sanctity. Still, Ezekiel's temple exaggerates this notion to the extreme. In addition, Ganzel and Holtz, "Babylonian Context," 226, admit, "We cannot say with any certainty that Ezekiel borrowed these features from his environment."

23. Tuell, *Law of the Temple*, 23. For more detail see Tuell, "Verbal Icon," 650–51.

24. Eichrodt, *Ezekiel*, 543. Allen, *Ezekiel 20–48*, 236, writes, "The massive gatehouses, as forbidding as those at the entrance to any city, warn all who come to worship of the awesome solemnity of the areas beyond. Access should not be lightly undertaken."

25. Stevenson, *Vision of Transformation*, 44. Zimmerli, *Ezekiel 2*, 348, points this out also, referencing Galling, but concludes that a secondary hand inserted the measurements of the wall in Ezek 40:5.

26. Stevenson, *Vision of Transformation*, 45. Ganzel and Holtz, "Babylonian Context," 216–17, count sixty-three verses in Ezekiel 40–42 devoted to walls, courtyards, and gates, with twenty-six devoted to the temple itself. Greenberg, "Design and Themes," 193, says over half of Ezek 40:1—43:12 is given to gatehouses and courts.

27. Zimmerli, *Ezekiel 2*, 361. Clark, "'I Will Be King Over You,'" 144–45, states that the greatest threat to Israel is not an enemy but YHWH himself. Patton, "Blueprint," 59–60, summarizes how this concept of separation is present in numerous ANE temples. Ezekiel, she says, "... exploited these concepts to the full ..." ("Blueprint," 60).

28. Bechtel, "Politics of Yahweh," 222.

29. Nielsen, "Ezekiel's Visionary Call," 99–114, argues that the details show the contrast with Ezek 1, and a reorientation of a world such that YHWH's glory can dwell permanently.

the vision. As Ezekiel gazed upon it, it must have been to him a marvelous picture indeed of that which Jehovah had in store for His people."[30] Relatedly, Eichrodt notes that little is said about the purposes of each room, nor of objects within the temple. Instead, as Eichrodt writes, "The description continually concentrates on the one point, that is to guarantee the dwelling of God among his people."[31] Even visually, Ezekiel's temple focuses on the glory of YHWH, since, unlike in previous OT dwelling places, the altar right in front of the most holy place lies exactly in the center of the complex.[32] Furthermore, the most holy place sits at the top of a three-level structure, making it the highest place in the building. Thus, were worshipers to walk in, their eyes would move to the altar, the highest and most central point. Eichrodt explains, "It catches the eye of the beholder through its dominating position and turns his thoughts to God enthroned above the universe as the Lord in all his glorious majesty."[33] The layout focuses the patron on the greatness of YHWH, showing that the main point of these detailed measurements of a building is to underline YHWH's holiness.

Fourth, the detailed measurements serve a literary purpose. Liss notes stereotyped language patterns as part of a claim for "literary reality."[34] The repetitive monotony of the detailed measuring puts the reader into the world of the temple, what Liss calls "diegesis."[35] There-

30. Ironside, *Ezekiel*, 285.

31. Eichrodt, *Ezekiel*, 549. In later pages, however, Eichrodt details where he believes later priestly editors changed this view by inserting their own descriptions of the purpose of rooms, sacrifices, etc. (e.g., Ezek 40:38–46; 41:15–26).

32. Milgrom, *Ezekiel's Hope*, 48–49; Patton, "Blueprint," 156. Maier, "Architectural History of the Temple," 34, argues that the altar at the center is the major difference between Ezekiel's temple and the *Temple Scroll* structure. Note, however, that Zimmerli, *Ezekiel 2*, 355, claims that the center of the temple is the most holy place, not the altar at the geometric center. He cites Ezek 41:21–22, which describes the altar as "in front of the Holy Place," rather than, "in the center of the court." Ezekiel's description is logical, however, since the prophet is actually seeing the holy place, not describing the overall space of the whole area. Besides this, the altar and most holy place should not be thought of as separate conceptually. The altar at the center also highlights the importance of the most holy place.

33. Eichrodt, *Ezekiel*, 549.

34. Liss, "'Describe the Temple,'" 126.

35. This notion is similar to Niditch, "Visionary Context," 208–24. Niditch argues for the temple as akin to a mandala, wherein the process of walking through the temple becomes a spiritual-mystical experience. Niditch explains Ezek 40–42 as the process of cosmogony, ordering a world. Simon, "Ezekiel's Geometric Vision," 434, sees the

fore, the descriptions need not imply physical construction, but instead function to create a literary effect. Liss also claims that fictional texts use patterns of spatial dimensions to symbolize non-spatial relations.[36] In other words, the extensiveness of the measurements shows they are symbols with theological meaning. In addition, since the man leads Ezekiel through a temple already built, the measuring produces a kind of map of the temple. Liss writes, "This existence on a map thus becomes not only transportable but also communicable to others. Thus, our text at hand functions as a 'map,' allowing the 'house' to exist outside of a geographically predetermined and permanent place. From that point in time on, the 'u-topian' temple finds its 'topos,' a location on a map, in the text."[37] Liss provides an analogy of the Forbidden City of Beijing. Citizens see a glimpse of the Forbidden City because otherwise the city is forgotten and has no relevance. Citizens may not access the city, however, lest the place lose its aura. Similarly, through the literary text, Ezekiel provides a temple full of mystique. The temple is inaccessible because of its holiness, but because of the text "map" readers can get a glimpse of the sacred realm. Liss concludes, "Only the 'literary temple' guarantees that the place and its holiness will never be violated again."[38] Thus, the focus here centers on the function of the text as a "topos" rather than an actual building.

The Size of the Temple

Aside from the detailed measurements, a major question concerning the physical construction argument relates to the size of the temple. At best, the temple as described in Ezek 40–48 cannot realistically be constructed in the physical realm of Ezekiel's time.[39] At worst (for those arguing for

---

geometric descriptions from a psychological standpoint as a means for the people to temporarily resolve anxieties in their relationship with God after the exile.

36. Liss, "'Describe the Temple,'" 126. Note that while Liss claims the text is fiction, she is responding to the historical-critical view that the text is a "constitution-draft" of the Persian period. Instead she argues for a description of "utopia," a "no-place." Rather than using the term "fiction," this study simply argues for a non-physical temple view, though several of Liss's points are relevant.

37. Liss, "'Describe the Temple,'" 136–37.

38. Liss, "'Describe the Temple,'" 143.

39. The wording here is intentional, for, as seen below, some think the geography of Israel will be massively transformed so as to make possible the construction of this temple on a high mountain.

construction), the temple's measurements make the structure physically impossible to build. Toy, who holds to a physical construction, sets forth the problem saying, "The dimensions of the temple-area may appear to be literally impossible, and thus designedly idealizing."[40] What is one to make, then, of the temple's size?

First, one must consider the size of the mountain on which the prophet sees the already-built temple (Ezek 40:2). The previous chapter argued that in Ezek 40:2 the prophet sees a temple as large as a city on the southern slope of the mountain, rather than a temple on the mountain with the new city (Ezek 48:30–35) south of the mountain. Thus, a mountain large enough to hold such a massive temple is difficult to picture. Beale says, "The mountain [in Ezek 40:2] . . . is not only high but of extraordinary enough size to contain the entire city of Jerusalem."[41] While the Solomonic temple (1 Kgs 8) lies atop a mountain, Beale adds that here the city is also set on the same high mountain. Therefore, he claims, "[The text portrays] a symbolic geographical world of another dimension."[42] In other words, this is not a mere temple, but a temple-city, or a city-like temple, and therefore practically impossible to construct on a mountaintop. Zimmerli adds that, due to the natural slope of the western side of the temple mount before Herod's temple, the 100-cubit building on the west side would not be possible in pre-Herodian days.[43] Although Ezekiel may not see "another dimension" as Beale claims, it cannot be that he sees his contemporary Jerusalem. Regardless of the exact size of the temple (see below), this temple is significantly bigger than Solomon's, and the text indicates that the mountain must also be bigger than the temple

---

40. Toy, "General Interpretation," xlvi.

41. Beale, *Temple and Church's Mission*, 336. Unfortunately, Beale does not state how he derives the measurements of the mountain. Note also the comment by Andiñach, *El Dios que está*, 259 [author's translation], "Anyone who would have read the text of Ezekiel in his day knew that Zion was not a high mountain, but low, surrounded by hills superior to it."

42. Beale, *Temple and Church's Mission*, 336–37. Beale is not clear here on whether he refers to the new city of Ezek 48:35, the new Jerusalem of Revelation, or the temple and its environs. He seems to equate the temple to the heavenly temple-city of new Jerusalem. Nevertheless, Beale's point holds, for in contrast to 1 Kgs 8, this passage describes a "structure like a city," an area bigger than Solomon's temple. Keil, *Ezekiel*, 273, commenting on Ezek 42:15–20, says, "[These verses] show most indisputably that the temple seen by Ezekiel was not to have its seat in the ancient Jerusalem."

43. Zimmerli, *Ezekiel 2*, 380.

mount in Jerusalem. How big, then, is the temple actually? Can it actually be built?

One's conclusion on the size of the temple depends on the standard of measurement used in interpreting the vision, especially Ezek 42:15–20, the summary of the guide's measurements.[44] The holy portion, Toy says, is a 25,000-unit square, and the entire temple complex a 500-unit square. If the "unit" mentioned equals a cubit of 21 inches, no difficulty in interpretation occurs, per Toy.[45] Block concurs, using a cubit of 20.5 inches, known as the long or royal cubit.[46] Thus he concludes that the whole temple area is about 850 x 850 feet, making the temple about the same size as the present-day temple mount.[47] On the other hand, if the unit used for calculation is a reed, i.e., six long cubits (about 10.5 feet; see Ezek 40:5), then that makes the holy portion 50 x 50 miles and the temple 1 x

---

44. According to Hals, *Ezekiel*, 286, many scholars conclude that Ezek 42:15–20 belongs to an initial expansion on the core of the vision (Ezek 40:1–37, 47–49; 41:1–4a).

45. Toy, "General Interpretation," xlvi.

46. Block, *Ezekiel 25–48*, 517, distinguishes in detail the difference between a normal cubit and the "long cubit." He concludes that Ezekiel used the long cubit (20.5 inches), based on 2 Chr 3:3 (Block incorrectly says 1 Chr 3:3), which says Solomon's temple was based on the normal ("old") cubit. Block does not mention the pre-Babylonian reed, as Beale does below. Keil, *Ezekiel*, 186–87, claims that the Mosaic or sacred cubit was longer, but that Solomon's builders used a shorter one. Therefore, for Keil, Ezekiel's long cubit reverts to the standard of the sacred cubit. See, however, Zimmerli, *Ezekiel 2*, 349, who claims that the Chronicler's "old cubit" is actually the same as Ezekiel's royal/long cubit. The Chronicler more likely means "old" in the Solomonic sense rather than "old" from the vantage point of the postexilic author looking back at the exilic period. Cook, *Ezekiel 38–48*, 113, agrees with this measurement of a long cubit. He mentions a wooden Egyptian cubit rod on display in the British Museum that measures to this length. In contrast, Sweeney, *Reading Ezekiel*, 199, uses a different standard for the regular and long/royal cubit. He states that a normal cubit is 20.68 inches, and a handbreadth is about four inches, so the long/royal cubit is 24–25 inches long. Thus, he measures one rod (6 cubits) as 144 inches or 12 feet. Cooke, *Ezekiel*, 430–31, also argues that the rod was six cubits long plus a handbreadth, not that each cubit was a cubit and handbreadth long. Cooke assumes, however, that the longer cubit only came into existence in the Persian period.

47. Block, *Ezekiel 25–48*, 570. So also Eichrodt, *Ezekiel*, 548; Zimmerli, *Ezekiel 2*, 360. Cook, *Ezekiel 38–48*, 178, in his own translation calculates the area to 875 x 875 feet. Cook, *Ezekiel 38–48*, 179, adds later, "Ezekiel's square temple complex would actually fit within the modern temple mount in Jerusalem. It is a large but realistically sized compound, perhaps more than twice the size of the preexilic temple courts . . . but nowhere near what Rashi calculates to be thirty-six times the original dimensions." See also Strong, "Grounding Ezekiel's Heavenly Ascent," 197–98.

1 mile. Toy responds, "But there is no difficulty even with these figures."[48] He states that the whole land of Israel, in Ezekiel's reckoning, is 230 miles long and 100 wide, plenty of space for a 50 x 50-mile portion of land. While one may object that the old temple mount is less than a 1 x 1 mile square, Toy responds that there is no need to restrict the temple to Mt. Moriah.[49] Instead, he claims that the whole land will be reconstructed, making the temple the center of Israel's life.[50] Toy is incorrect, however, in saying that such a large measurement presents no difficulty. Regarding the holy portion, great difficulty exists in positing that this area makes up over one-fifth of the entire land. Such a conclusion leaves very little land for the remaining twelve allotments. As to the argument for a change in topography, the claim is simply an assumption that cannot be proven. Ezekiel says nothing of such a change, a surprising fact considering the great vision of a life-giving river transforming the land, even to the Dead Sea (Ezek 47:1–12). Thus, such an assertion imports from a later text (Zech 14:9–11) a meaning non-existent in Ezekiel's vision. So, either one must use the smaller unit (royal cubit instead of reed), or Ezekiel purposefully describes an unrealistically sized building and does not intend a literal fulfillment.

Beale's conclusion aligns closely with Toy's second option, that the dimensions of the temple are about one mile long and one mile wide, making the building about the same size as the entire city of ancient Jerusalem in the second temple era.[51] He bases this calculation on what he calls the pre-Babylonian measuring reed, the one he says Ezekiel would have used, which was 6.2 cubits long.[52] By this standard, 500 reeds equates to 3,100

---

48. Toy, "General Interpretation," xlvi.

49. Toy, "General Interpretation," xlvi.

50. Toy, "General Interpretation," xlvi. Feinberg, *Ezekiel*, 249; Gaebelein, *Ezekiel*, 298, make the same argument, saying that Zech 14:9–11 prophesies a major change in topography. Ironside, *Ezekiel*, 299, also leaves open this possibility, stating that this temple is too large for Mt. Moriah.

51. Beale, *Temple and Church's Mission*, 341. Beale cites here Fairbairn, *Ezekiel*, 438, who provides an incorrect calculation that the temple is twice the size of ancient Jerusalem. Per Cook, *Ezekiel 38–48*, 179, Rashi also argues a similar view as Beale, but see the discussion below on Rashi's conclusion.

52. Beale, *Temple and Church's Mission*, 341 fn. 17. Unless otherwise specified, "cubit" in this context refers to the long/royal cubit, as this is the one most hold to be the standard for Ezekiel's vision. According to Beale, the Babylonian reed was 7 cubits. This would make the temple even bigger than as calculated here.

cubits.⁵³ If a cubit is 0.52 meters (20.5 inches, the reckoning Block also uses), this equals a little over one mile. Ultimately, the conclusion on specific measurements depends, first, on what size cubit the guide uses (the question discussed above), but, secondly, on whether Ezekiel describes the guide's measurements (Ezek 42:15–20) in reeds or cubits.

So, does the guide measure the area in reeds or long cubits? In Ezek 40:5, Ezekiel mentions that the angel's reed is six cubits long, and defines a cubit as the long cubit.⁵⁴ In addition, Ezek 42:15–20 appears to indicate the measuring of 500 reeds, rather than 500 cubits.⁵⁵ The passage only uses the word for cubit once in the *Kethib* MT (Ezek 42:16), while the rest of the passage uses "reeds," and the summarizing measurement for the whole area does not even specify the unit of measurement (Ezek 42:20).⁵⁶ So, Ezek 42:16 appears to contain a scribal error due to transposition of the first two letters of אמות ("cubit") and מאות ("hundred"). Alternatively, a scribe intentionally changed the word for harmonization purposes. Regardless, scribes in the *Qere* and the versions recognize the possible error in changing to "cubits." The LXX is initially ambiguous, saying in Ezek 42:16, 18, 19, πεντακοσίους ἐν τῷ καλάμῳ τοῦ μέτρου ("500 by the reed of measurement"). In Ezek 42:17, 20, however, the word πῆχυς ("cubit") is specifically used.⁵⁷ Why not, then, use "cubits" in each verse? Failure to do so in LXX leads to the likelihood of "reed" as an underlying reading. Moreover, the *Kethib* reading leads to "five cubits," a nonsensical

---

53. The calculation is similar to Rashi, *Ezekiel: Volume Two*, 378, who in his commentary on Ezek 42:20 argues for a total area of 3,000 x 3,000 cubits.

54. Contra Tuell, *Law of the Temple*, 27–29, who argues that a later Persian redactor inserted the phrase, "with a cubit and a handbreadth," into Ezek 40:5 to conform the text to a later-used measurement of the Persian period. He admits the tentative nature of his claim. Tuell bases his argument on 2 Chr 3:3, wrongly seeing "old" as a reference from the postexilic author's point of view rather than in reference to "old" in comparison to that before Solomon's time.

55. Because of the mention of reeds instead of cubits, many scholars see the text as a secondary redaction. Hiebel, *Ezekiel's Vision*, 181; Konkel, *Architektonkik Des Heiligen*, 70, see Ezek 42:15, 20b-e as the original layer of text.

56. Cooke, *Ezekiel*, 459, wrongly says "reed" refers to the instrument of measuring, and that confusion in LXX arose from misunderstanding this fact.

57. Contra Hiebel, *Ezekiel's Vision Accounts*, 173, who says, "The LXX does not represent קָנִים, leaving the reader to assume that cubits are meant."

conclusion.⁵⁸ Likely the use of "cubit" in MT Ezek 42:16 is a scribal error, so the text simply states "500 reeds," rather than "500 cubits by the reed."⁵⁹

Still, even following the LXX, others like Cook take the text in the sense of "500 [cubits] by the reed," arguing for an ellipsis of the term "cubit."⁶⁰ The hypothesis of an ellipsis is speculation, though, especially because of the intentional scribal notations. One would think a scribe would have inserted the term "cubit" in each verse of Ezek 42:16–20. Moreover, the ellipsis theory presents another difficulty. As Block shows, קָנִים should not be deleted.⁶¹ In that case, the reading "500 cubits reeds" does not make sense. As another hypothesis, Allen argues that the insertion of "cubit" in the *Kethib* explicitly identifies the cubit as a correction to the use of "reeds," but ends up displacing the word מֵאוֹת ("100").⁶² This theory, though, assumes many unverifiable steps, and it does not explain how mistakes could be found in a text intended as a correction. Cook adds that if the complex was so large (500 reeds), the guide would have used the cord in his hand, the instrument for longer measurements, rather than the reed.⁶³ However, the guide would not have needed the cord,

---

58. Block, *Ezekiel 25–48*, 568, agrees that the scribe made an error of metathesis and holds to the *Qere* reading, resulting in the gloss for "five hundred." So also Zimmerli, *Ezekiel 2*, 402.

59. On a separate but related issue, see scholars like Zimmerli, *Ezekiel 2*, 402; Allen, *Ezekiel 20–48*, 227; Gese, *Der Verfassungsentwurf*, 28–29, who delete the second קָנִים of Ezek 42:16 as a gloss. Scholars delete the word because, Block, *Ezekiel 25–48*, 568, states, "It creates inordinate interpretive problems . . ." The description of the temple in Ezek 40:15—41:13 does use the term for cubits, and seems to describe the temple as a 500 x 500 cubit square. On this issue, see the discussion forthcoming in this study. But do scholars also emend the text based on an assumption that the temple cannot be 500 reeds? Still, Block defends the MT's more difficult reading. Yes, the MT in this case should be kept, but contra Block, the prophet *is* describing the reed as a unit of measurement and not merely the instrument. Milgrom, *Ezekiel's Hope*, 101, on Block's claim of an instrument, says, "[It] lacks support." Milgrom replaces קָנִים with אַמּוֹת, resulting in "500 cubits rods." Milgrom is unclear as to how the text makes sense using both cubits and rods. Is "rods" meant to be taken appositionally to cubits?

60. Cook, *Ezekiel 38–48*, 179. He cites a long history of this interpretation, including Radak. So also Block, *Ezekiel 25–48*, 568. Allen, *Ezekiel 20–48*, 227, also holds this, citing ellipses in Ezek 43:16–17; 45:1; 46:22.

61. Block, *Ezekiel 25–48*, 568.

62. Allen, *Ezekiel 20–48*, 227; Zimmerli, *Ezekiel 2*, 402. Allen ends up deleting "reed" throughout Ezek 42:16–20, which Block, *Ezekiel 25–48*, 568, rightly disagrees with. Allen also rightly dismisses Barthélemy's hypothesis that only in this passage is a rod equivalent to a cubit.

63. Cook, *Ezekiel 38–48*, 179.

because many of the measurements were of smaller areas, though the final calculations total to a massive area overall. Ezek 42:15–20 is a summary, not a description of the guide measuring. The most likely scenario, after all, is that the *Ur*-text of Ezek 42:16–20 says "500 reeds."[64]

But does Ezek 42:16–20 actually describe the temple building? The conclusion that the temple measures to 500 reeds long and wide presents an apparent contradiction to Ezek 40:15—41:14.[65] In that passage, the prophet actually uses the word "cubit" as the standard of measurement. According to many scholars, then, the whole complex measures to 500 cubits long and wide.[66] Reading Ezek 42:16–20 as 500 cubits long and wide matches the measurements of Ezek 40–41 and, seemingly, the land plot in Ezek 45:2.[67] However, Ezek 45:2 actually does not use the term "cubit" until the end of the verse, to refer to the מִגְרָשׁ, the open land. The text simply states that the "holy place," the sanctuary, is 500 x 500 all around. The main difficulty, then, is the harmonization with Ezek 40–41. As Cook says, "A 500-reed-square walled zone finds no cross-reference elsewhere in Ezekiel 40–48."[68] Despite Cook's apropos point, the text of Ezek 42:16–20 makes the most sense as referring to 500 reeds on each side.[69] One possibility is that the sanctuary building is 500 cubits square while the entire area is 500 reeds square.[70] A better conclusion is that the

---

64. Hiebel, *Ezekiel's Vision Accounts*, 173, says, "The MT certainly offers the *lectio difficilior*. In addition, the entire passage appears to have been translated quite freely [in the LXX]." Keil, *Ezekiel*, 268–70, also argues for 500 reeds.

65. Beale, *Temple and Church's Mission*, 341, neglects this question though he holds to a 500-reed square measurement.

66. Block, *Ezekiel 25–48*, 570; Allen, *Ezekiel 20–48*, 227, 235; Zimmerli, *Ezekiel 2*, 404. The Mishnaic text *Babba Middot* 2:1 harmonizes the Herodian temple mount with Ezekiel's dimensions, listed as 500 x 500 cubits.

67. Gese, *Der Verfassungsentwurf*, 29; Allen, *Ezekiel 20–48*, 227; Cook, *Ezekiel 38–48*, 179.

68. Cook, *Ezekiel 38–48*, 179.

69. The *Temple Scroll*, in large part influenced by Ezekiel's vision, describes a temple far larger than 500 x 500 cubits, though the "court for men" at 500 x 500 cubits shows a concern for the square shape and the multiples of 25. Could Ezekiel's 500-reed complex have influenced the massive temple envisioned by this Qumran community? See Maier, "Architectural History of the Temple," 24–25, 33–35.

70. Greenberg, "Valid Criteria," 133, on determining secondary authorship, says contradiction is ". . . a weak ground unless the contradictory elements are close to each other and the contradiction cannot be accounted for on rhetorical grounds." In this case, the alleged contradictions are not close to each other, so there is more likely a better explanation.

measurements of Ezek 42:15–20 do not refer to the temple complex, but to another wall surrounding the whole area.[71] This may be what Rashi means when he says the 500-reed wall is "... the wall of the temple mount ... This was the wall that encompassed the entire mountain."[72] Perhaps a larger wall stands at the base of the mountain to guard the temple complex.[73] In this case, the guide measures a wall not measured before in Ezek 40–41, but possibly seen in Ezek 40:2. After all, Ezek 42:15 simply says the guide measures "all around," without specifying the area as that which he has already measured in Ezek 40:5–27. Keil also argues in this manner when he says,

> Vers. 15–20 does not refer to the space occupied by the temple and its courts, and therefore ... the wall which the measured space had around it (ver. 20) cannot be the wall of the outer court mentioned in ch. xl. 5 ... The meaning is rather, that around this wall, which enclosed the temple and its courts, a further space of five hundred rods in length and breadth was measured off ... *i.e.* a space which was intended to form a separating domain between the sanctuary and the common land. The purpose thus assigned for the space ... leaves no doubt remaining that it was not the length of the surrounding wall of the outer court that was measured, but a space outside this wall.[74]

Admittedly, it is unlikely that the guide would introduce a new measurement rather than concluding the previous tour, but the claim above is a possible solution.[75]

---

71. The LXX appears to more clearly point out that the guide measures the temple complex when it plusses the phrase διεμέτρησεν τὸ ὑπόδειγμα τοῦ οἴκου (Ezek 42:15). Cooke, *Ezekiel*, 462, argues that this is an enlargement recollecting Exod 25:9. See the comments below on the "trench" of Ezek 42:20, however. Hiebel, *Ezekiel's Vision Accounts*, 194, is an example of those who see the walls as the same due to redaction-critical concerns, i.e., seeing most of Ezek 41 as secondary.

72. Rashi, *Ezekiel: Volume Two*, 378.

73. O'Hare, "'Have You Seen, Son of Man?,'" 104–9, notes that "trench" may be an appropriate gloss for LXX Ezek 42:20, "προτειχίσματος," often thought of as separating holy from profane. In such a case, a large trench lies between the complex's walls and the rest of the people. Could early interpreters have understood this trench to be at the bottom of the mountain?

74. Keil, *Ezekiel*, 270–71.

75. Joyce, "Heavenly Ascent," 22, sees a literary *inclusio* marking this out as one vision. The *inclusio* supports the notion that the wall in Ezek 40:5 is the wall of Ezek 42:20.

If the temple measures 500 × 500 reeds, it seems impossible to build, barring a miraculous transformation of topography.[76] Thus, such a view indicates a temple not intended for construction. However, even if one takes the majority view that the temple measures to 500 cubits on each side, the temple is very large, and, in Tuell's words, "... highly impractical."[77] Cook, even holding to the latter size, says, "Ezekiel's terrace is immense compared with that of 'Ain Dara: about 766,000 square feet (thirteen football fields)."[78] Likewise, although many claim that the inner sanctuary is the same size in the Ezekiel and Solomonic temples, the former uses the longer cubit while the latter uses the normal cubit.[79] Thus, Ezekiel's temple is significantly larger than its predecessor. In fact, Solomon's temple was 20 × 60 normal cubits (1 Kgs 6:2), and his royal palace 50 × 100 normal cubits (1 Kgs 7:2), compared to Ezekiel's temple, which measures to 50 × 100 *long* cubits.[80]

Additionally, if the MT is the correct reading, the gateway porch is 60 cubits tall, about 105 feet (Ezek 40:14).[81] Interestingly, this is one

---

76. Alexander, *Ezekiel*, 145–46, argues for just this change in topography. Keil, *Ezekiel*, 273, writes, "It is true that the surface of Moriah supplied no room for this space of five hundred rods square; but the new temple was not to be built upon the real Moriah, but upon a very high mountain, which the Lord would exalt and make ready for the purpose when the temple was erected."

77. Tuell, "Verbal Icon," 650. Peterson, *Ezekiel in Context*, loc. 8119–20, interestingly observes that in ANE temple building accounts, the builders seek for the exact same foundations as the previous temple to build the new one upon it. This step is prominently missing in Ezekiel's vision, at least in part because of the vast difference in size of the two temples. Peterson concludes, "This concept is clearly lacking here in Ezekiel which reinforces my opinion that Ezekiel's temple perhaps was not intended to be made with human hands."

78. Cook, *Ezekiel 38–48*, 115.

79. Cook, *Ezekiel 38–48*, 148. See also the discussion above on 2 Chr 3:3.

80. Odell, *Ezekiel*, 490, incorrectly cites 1 Kgs 7:20 instead of 1 Kgs 7:2. Odell argues that Ezekiel's temple is intentionally the size of Solomon's palace, but she fails to distinguish the differing length of cubit used in Solomon's construction. The same problem occurs in Stevenson, *Vision of Transformation*, 114–15. In a footnote, Stevenson notes 2 Chr 3:3, which mentions that Solomon's builders used the "former cubit." Though she questions the historical reliability of Chronicles, she appears to agree that Solomon and Ezekiel used different cubits. She is unclear, however, as to whether Ezekiel and Solomon use merely the same dimensions (50 × 100) or the exact same measurements.

81. Cook, *Ezekiel 38–48*, 120. So also Keil, *Ezekiel*, 195–96, who points out the absence of the verb "measure," for such a height could not have been measured by the guide. The MT of Ezek 40:14 is extremely difficult to understand, so one should not press the argument here too far. The MT does not directly state that this is a vertical

of the few vertical measurements in the vision. The size of this gate, Greenberg says, "... verges on caricature ...," being half the length of the inner court.[82] Thus, Cook argues, the gate serves a symbolic function as a liminal hinge between earthly and heavenly realms.[83] The gate is extremely narrow, at 87.5 feet long and 43.75 feet wide (Ezek 40:13, 15), serving as an experience of passing through what Cook calls "different planes of reality."[84] So, this particular gate serves as an example of a symbolic world described in the text, not a blueprint for construction. Block, therefore, though holding to the smaller calculation of a 500-cubit square, concludes, "The shape and size of the entire complex reflect a lofty theological and spiritual ideal, according to which the residence of Yahweh must be perfectly proportioned."[85] While sections below will address the proportions of the temple, this section shows the importance of the temple's size. Whether a 500-cubit or 500-reed square, the temple is so large that it leads one to conclude the prophet did not intend for the temple he describes to be physically built.

More Details against a Physical Temple

Several other features of the building contend against a literal interpretation. Strikingly, few vertical dimensions of the building are listed (except in Ezek 40:5, 14; 41:8).[86] The term קוֹמָה ("height") is only used once in the vision (Ezek 40:5), yet used numerous times in the tabernacle and Solomonic temple descriptions. Relatedly, the prophet leaves out any construction materials, a stark contrast to the specificity of YHWH's former dwelling places.[87] Hals argues that labeling Ezek 40–42 under the genre of "blueprint" is inadequate, since, he says, "Crucial details and dimensions are omitted, so that no actual construction could ever have taken place

---

measurement and the angel is said to "make" the pilaster, not measure it.

82. Greenberg, "Design and Themes," 193.
83. Cook, *Ezekiel 38–48*, 128.
84. Cook, *Ezekiel 38–48*, 129.
85. Block, *Ezekiel 25–48*, 570.
86. Joyce, "'Heavenly Ascent,'" 24; Block, *Ezekiel 25–48*, 510–11; Beale, *Temple and Church's Mission*, 342. The text mentions vertical dimensions for the furniture in Ezek 41:22; 43:14–15. According to Stevenson, *Vision of Transformation*, 29–30, other horizontal measurements are absent in Ezek 42:1–12. One would not be able to construct the chambers simply based on these measurements.
87. Duguid, *Ezekiel*, 479; Zimmerli, *Ezekiel 2*, 343.

solely on the basis of what is said in chs. 40–42."[88] In response, despite the lack of vertical measurements, Alexander says that, "The detailed architectural plans in these chapters are sufficient for architects to draw plans and reconstruct models with a fair degree of accuracy."[89] Similarly, Allen actually sees the lack of vertical measurements as argument for planned construction, such that the present measurements show dependence upon an architectural ground plan.[90] In addition, Feinberg replies that we must interpret according to what we have, not what we readers wish we had.[91] The issue with these responses, however, is the presence of great detail in the text.[92] One wonders why Ezekiel provides so many details in many other respects, yet neglects to provide vertical measurements. The omission, then, appears intentional.

The author creates meaning by not including most vertical measurements. In the words of Stevenson, "The spaces are fully defined. This definition of space is the purpose of the measurements."[93] By defining horizontal spaces, YHWH accomplishes his purpose of separating holy and profane (Ezek 42:20). Vertical measurements are unnecessary for this purpose. Moreover, the lack of vertical dimensions focuses the reader on the motion of the guide and prophet from outside the complex to the inside.[94] That is, the reader only thinks of entering into the complex in a horizontal manner, and the thickness of the horizontal measurements show how difficult the access is.[95] Similarly, the mention of the measure-

88. Hals, *Ezekiel*, 299.

89. Alexander, *Ezekiel*, 138. Likewise Ironside, *Ezekiel*, 284; Feinberg, *Ezekiel*, 242.

90. Allen, *Ezekiel 20–48*, 228. Odell, *Ezekiel*, 489, similarly notes that lack of vertical measurements corresponds to the conventional accounts of other ANE building projects. Ganzel and Holtz, "Babylonian Context," 221, mention one two-dimensional Neo-Babylonian temple text.

91. Feinberg, *Ezekiel*, 245.

92. Tuell, "Verbal Icon," 652, hints at this notion.

93. Stevenson, *Vision of Transformation*, 19.

94. Liss, "'Describe the Temple,'" 135. Tuell, "Verbal Icon," 662, discusses how fixing the temple vision as a text forces the reader to experience the vision in the same way the prophet experienced it.

95. Liss, "'Describe the Temple,'" 135. Zimmerli, *Ezekiel 2*, 343, also notes that from the standpoint of the text's form, the guide does not speak until Ezek 41:4, when he shows the most holy place. Zimmerli concludes that the whole point of leading the prophet from outside to inside is to highlight this room. Hiebel, *Ezekiel's Vision Accounts*, 198, adds that precisely because one expects speech in a vision account, the vision underscores the holiness of this place. Similarly, Stevenson, *Vision of Transformation*, 54–56, shows the importance of territorial access based on the verbs of motion

ment of the outer wall's height (Ezek 40:5) also underscores the purpose of the temple to separate holy and profane.[96] A wall, in order to provide proper separation, by definition must be sufficiently tall.[97] The uniqueness of this vertical measurement in the vision underscores the separation.

Next, some other minor aspects of the temple show important symbolism and plead against a physical interpretation.[98] For example, the decorations are profound where noted. In fact, these features are more significant in light of the absence of any other decorations included.[99] As Cook writes, "The decoration of Ezekiel's temple departs markedly from Solomon's golden interior of 1 Kings 6. As elsewhere, the temple's beauty is expressed in geometry, not in bullion."[100] Tuell also notes the vast difference between this vision and the Gudea Cylinder regarding decorations.[101] The only prominent decorations described in Ezekiel are the palm trees and cherubim.[102] In Ezek 40, palm trees decorate the outer gatehouses. The trees designate the temple as what Cook calls ". . . a holy Edenic realm, the delightful, archetypal garden where God first dwelled with humanity."[103] In Ezek 41, Cook claims, "Ezekiel views a more central, sacred tree: the cosmic tree (*Weltbaum*)."[104] The entrance to the most holy place (Ezek 41:17–18) is decorated with cherubim standing guard

---

in the guide's tour.

96. Stevenson, *Vision of Transformation*, 37; Ganzel and Holtz, "Babylonian Context," 217. Hals, *Ezekiel*, 303, notes that the wall is too low to act as protection against an attack.

97. Duguid, *Ezekiel*, 472.

98. Cook, *Ezekiel 38–48*, 181, adds another argument based on a minor detail in the text, but the conclusion is unlikely. He argues that because in Ezek 42:15–20 the sides of the temple complex are called רוּחוֹת, the walls signify the four "basic winds" of the earth's cardinal directions. From this Cook concludes that the temple is the "compass rose" that orients all space on earth, and thus the cosmic center. Though interesting, Cook falls into the fallacy of illegitimate word totality transfer, since the term in this context is simply a word for side.

99. Eichrodt, *Ezekiel*, 549.

100. Cook, *Ezekiel 38–48*, 165.

101. Tuell, *Law of the Temple*, 30–31.

102. The temple also boasts two pillars (Ezek 40:49), present in the first temple, where they are named Jachin and Boaz (1 Kgs 7:21). Blenkinsopp, *Ezekiel*, 206, says these are a ". . . symbolic scheme underlying the architectural layout." Little can be surmised, however, about the meaning of the symbolism.

103. Cook, *Ezekiel 38–48*, 122.

104. Cook, *Ezekiel 38–48*, 167.

alongside palm trees. In ANE art, palm trees represent the tree of life.[105] The text, then, provides a picture of the garden of Eden, YHWH's original dwelling place.[106] Likewise, ANE cultures depict guardians (like cherubs) around the cosmic center of the world.[107] Cook argues that "archetypal trees" in many cultures serve as portals between different worlds.[108] Therefore, Cook claims, "Details such as these convey that Ezekiel's temple is something less than a final realization of heaven on earth."[109] The temple is not heaven itself, but does point forward to a greater dwelling place. Interestingly, Gaebelein sees these decorations as evidence for a physical temple. He takes the palms on the posts (Ezek 40:22, 26) as a symbol of victory, and therefore as fitting with a millennial age of blessing and glory.[110] The trees more likely represent Eden than victory, however. Even if they did signify only victory, this understanding would not necessitate a millennial timeframe.

Another unique feature of the temple is the בִּנְיָן, an enigmatic structure directly behind the temple on the west side that does not exist in the first temple.[111] Stevenson argues that the בִּנְיָן takes the place of Solomon's palace, for it is located in the same area.[112] Instead of the בִּנְיָן being used for a human king's residence, the building lies empty, forbidding access from the west, reserving the temple for YHWH's kingship alone (cf. Ezek

---

105. Allen, *Ezekiel 20–48*, 233. Zimmerli, *Ezekiel 2*, 388, adds that this is especially so when flanked by cherubim.

106. Cook, *Ezekiel 38–48*, 131.

107. Cook, *Ezekiel 38–48*, 165–66.

108. Cook, *Ezekiel 38–48*, 131.

109. Cook, *Ezekiel 38–48*, 126.

110. Gaebelein, *Ezekiel*, 281.

111. Blenkinsopp, *Ezekiel*, 207. Allen, *Ezekiel 20–48*, 233; Zimmerli, *Ezekiel 2*, 380, along with many, see this building as sealing off the back of the most holy place, making any access impossible. Cook, *Ezekiel 38–48*, states that the origin lies in storage for temple chariots, symbolizing YHWH fighting against his west-approaching enemy, chaos. Patton, "Blueprint," 163, suggests a similar point. This suggestion by Cook and Patton is unlikely, though.

112. Stevenson, *Vision of Transformation*, 117.

43:8).[113] The building serves, Zimmerli says, ". . . no useful function, but has been constructed on theological grounds . . ."[114] YHWH alone is king.

Finally, the numbers of the measurements in multiples of five, especially in increments of twenty-five cubits, point beyond a mere physical structure.[115] Notably, even a proponent for a physical structure, Ironside, says, "That all these measurements have a certain mystical significance I think is unquestionable, although it may not be easy to see always just what that significance is; but we cannot help but notice the frequent use of the number fifty, and of five and twenty."[116] Even if Ezekiel's temple is similar to ANE buildings and Solomon's temple, Ezekiel, Eichrodt says, ". . . reproduce[es] it in ideal proportions."[117] The shape and proportions in the increments of twenty-five reflect the temple's sanctity, for the perfect squares demonstrate YHWH's holiness. As Duguid says, "Once more the stakes have been raised from the arrangements of the Mosaic and Solomonic eras."[118] Only in Ezekiel's temple is the entire structure square, that is, completely holy. Liss therefore concludes, "One can see very clearly that Ezekiel's description hardly calls for an archaeological explanation. Instead, [it] . . . present[s] a priestly ideological program rather than a narrative outline of a blueprint."[119] The perfect square and proportions show the ideological program.

What, specifically, then, do the multiples of five and twenty-five mean? Blenkinsopp says that the measurements represent a "complex numerological system."[120] He admits, though, the difficulty in discerning the meaning of such a system. He concludes, "The main point is that in their regularity and homogeneity the measurements are part of a symbolic structure of meaning which transcends without entirely leaving

---

113. Zimmerli, *Ezekiel 2*, 380, writes that the building ". . . is clearly the product of an embarrassing situation [in the past]. Its intention is to forbid all access to the area behind the temple, that is behind the back of the Lord of the holy of holies who is facing forward i.e. eastwards."

114. Zimmerli, *Ezekiel 2*, 380.

115. Beale, *Temple and Church's Mission*, 342; Block, *Ezekiel 25–48*, 502; Cook, *Ezekiel 38–48*, 129.

116. Ironside, *Ezekiel*, 288.

117. Eichrodt, *Ezekiel*, 542.

118. Duguid, *Ezekiel*, 478.

119. Liss, "'Describe the Temple,'" 134.

120. Blenkinsopp, *Ezekiel*, 199.

behind the physical and historical reality of city and temple."[121] Cook speculates regarding several possible meanings to the number twenty-five.[122] The most likely of the options he mentions is that the importance of the number twenty-five relates to the date notation of Ezek 40:1.[123] The number shows the significance of Jubilee and Sabbath. Cook writes, "Sabbath and temple together are thus the Zadokites' twin foundations of Israel's sanctification. Therefore, in stressing the number twenty-five and its multiples, Ezekiel is likely embedding holiness and sanctification symbolism at the heart of his utopia. The design of the utopia appears to aim at making Israel holy."[124] Additionally, the idea of a "centered square" could be archetypally significant in providing order to chaos.[125]

Admittedly, the presence of the numerical symbolism does not rule out a physical construction. Many historical realities in the Scriptures also carry symbolic freight. The number is ubiquitous in the vision, however, suggesting a greater importance. Also, the vision contrasts greatly with previous OT dwelling places that do not include this numerical symbolism. Most likely, then, the idealism of the proportion implies that the vision goes beyond a physical building. Ultimately, as Haran states, "[The temple's] likeness, however, is reshaped in the spirit of the priestly school of which Ezekiel was a disciple. In accordance with the peculiar predilection of that school its plan is excessively schematized..."[126] Or,

---

121. Blenkinsopp, *Ezekiel*, 199.

122. Cook, *Ezekiel 38–48*, 13, claims that Num 8:24 allows Levites to begin serving in the temple at age twenty-five, so the Zadokite audience would imagine new priests preparing for duty. He hypothesizes also that the number "has elegant geometrical properties." Twenty-five is a square number (5×5). Also, the numbers three and four are included in twenty-five ($3^2 + 4^2$), digits that are also prominent in the measurements. Then, Cook adds that twenty-five is, in his words, "... a centered square number, that is, a number that when laid out as dots on a plane creates a square lattice pattern. The temple complex is laid out as such a lattice pattern of twenty-five dots." This demonstrates a hierarchical world of tiered zones of holiness. Cook concludes that, though one cannot know if Ezekiel knew such mathematics, Babylonian mathematicians would have worked with squares and tables of squares. On this, Odell, *Ezekiel*, 485, writes, "The preoccupation with numerical perfection is unprecedented in the Bible and may indicate familiarity with Babylonian metrology..."

123. Cook, *Ezekiel 38–48*, 130. Zimmerli, *Ezekiel 2*, 344, calls this "the decisive factor." See also Liss, "'Describe the Temple,'" 134.

124. Cook, *Ezekiel 38–48*, 130. Duguid, *Ezekiel*, 475, comments, "The inner courtyard is a perfect square,... for the square is the shape of the holy."

125. Cook, *Ezekiel 38–48*, 149–50.

126. Menahem Haran, *Temples and Temple-Service*, 45.

in another's words, "When we consider Ezekiel's measurements, they are round, they are grand, and as such, *they are ideal in character*."[127] The scheme of the numbers in this new temple, then, point to an eschatological heightening.

Summary

Typically, scholars see the specificity of the temple as evidence of a blueprint, yet a closer look at the details actually argues against that conclusion. Instead, the vision shows what Taylor calls "... the sheer impracticability ..." of building the temple.[128] While having some basis in earthly reality, Ezekiel sees a highly exaggerated version of a temple.[129] The main factors include the detailed measurements and the size of the temple. The detailed measurements actually serve a literary purpose of creating a textual "topos" rather than a physical blueprint. Additionally, they express YHWH's kingship and underscore his holiness. None of these interpretations necessitates the building of a real-world structure. The size of the temple, whether a 500-cubit or 500-reed square, shows that the temple cannot realistically be built. Other minor aspects of the description are also noteworthy, such as the absence of vertical measurements, the few key decorations in the temple, the mysterious בְּנְיָן, and the multiples of twenty-five. Each of these provides important theological insight as to the purpose of the vision.[130] So, in Clark's words, "The best way to understand the explicit temple measurements in the vision is not as a literal building plan. Rather ... these elements are intended to highlight Israel's need to pay more attention to the holy nature of their God ... In spite of sometimes providing detailed measurements, by and large the vision is idyllic."[131] Or, in other words, the vision presents a heightened version of a temple pointing forward typologically to an eschatological fulfillment.

---

127. Strong, "Grounding Ezekiel's Heavenly Ascent," 199.

128. Taylor, "Temple in Ezekiel," 68.

129. Strong, "Grounding Ezekiel's Heavenly Ascent," 200. Strong notes the tension of the vision, though ultimately he suggests that Ezekiel wrote the text on the walls of his house and archived it for future generations.

130. Hiebel, *Ezekiel's Vision Accounts*, 202, writes, "Alongside the lack of some essential dimensions, the idealized and even unrealistic proportions suggest that this is not about a building project but about a theological message."

131. Clark, "'I Will Be King Over You,'" 152.

Leadership in the New Society

Scholars have long mined the descriptions of leadership in Ezekiel's vision for an understanding of Israelite history. In the nineteenth century, Wellhausen argued that Ezekiel's vision, especially Ezek 44, demonstrates a transition from the Deuteronomistic (D) to the Priestly (P) cult.[132] Later, Gese's work shaped the study of Ezekiel's vision as he diachronically separated the text into three main sections, a core vision (Ezek 40:1–37, 47–49; 41:1–4), נָשִׂיא stratum (44:1–3; 45:21–25; 46:1–10, 12), and Zadokite stratum (44:6–16).[133] Since Gese's contribution, many have understood Ezek 40–48, in parts if not in whole, as a postexilic work meant to promote the Zadokite priesthood. Thus, Wellhausen, Gese, and others see the description of leadership in Ezek 40–48 as a window into the author's historical world. From this point of view, then, leadership in Ezek 40–48 demonstrates a society that either already exists in the author's world, or should exist. In that case, the writer of Ezekiel intends for the temple to actually be built.[134] After all, why would Ezekiel have Zadokite priests in his new legislation if he never meant for the temple described to actually exist?

Other scholars do not look for the history behind the text, but they argue for a literal fulfillment. Feinberg states the view well, saying, "Proper names [e.g., Zadok] serve to tie the revelation to historic reality and validity, calling for literal interpretation."[135] Is this, then, the only conclusion for such detailed description of Levites, priests/Zadokites, and a נָשִׂיא? While this section cannot delve into the entire history of scholarship on the OT priesthood, this study must defend a view of typology in light of these concerns. First, this section will examine the historical nature of the priesthood (Levites, priests, high priest, and Zadokites) that

---

132. Wellhausen, *Prolegomena to the History of Israel*, 123–24. Haran, *Temples and Temple-Service*, 72–73, concisely presents this view. Haran holds that Ezekiel reflects P theology.

133. See Gese's work *Der Verfassungsentwurf*. The three strata provide the basic structure but throughout the vision certain verses and portions thereof he deems to be part of various strata. In other words, the Zadokite stratum is not contained to Ezek 44:6–16 but includes various other verses throughout the vision.

134. For example, in 1996 Tuell wrote the article, "Ezekiel 40–42 as a Verbal Icon," arguing that the prophet Ezekiel sees a heavenly realm. Yet he earlier wrote *Law of the Temple* (1992), where he argues that postexilic redactors take the original vision and add legislation (Ezek 43–48), turning the whole vision into a Persian policy document.

135. Feinberg, *Ezekiel*, 243.

Ezekiel describes in the vision. After all, typology is rooted in history. The meaning of the priesthood in Ezekiel's vision, then, is based on a theological concern in the prophet's historical context. Second, this section will examine the role of the נָשִׂיא in Ezek 40–48. This figure, too, is typological, pointing forward to a greater fulfillment.

The Priesthood in Ezekiel 40–48

Several passages in Ezekiel's vision describe the priesthood of the new temple, with Ezek 40:45–46 and Ezek 44 as the most prominent.[136] Based on these texts, and supposed ideological emphases, scholars seek to decode various strata. Bechtel points out, however, "The multitude of redactional studies lacks definitive standards for how to distinguish the textual strata."[137] This study argues for continuity in texts on the OT priesthood, from Numbers and Deuteronomy to Ezekiel.[138] Ezekiel describes temple leaders as from the tribe of Levi, which by the monarchic period was narrowed down to the line of Zadok. The temple service was made up of priests who offered sacrifices, as well as priests who assisted in various aspects of temple service and worship. All of these were from the family of Zadok. At times, however, Ezekiel describes the assistants as "Levites," and the ones offering sacrifices as "the priests." In other places, though, Ezekiel refers to the assistants and the leaders both as priests (Ezek 40:45–46). Such terminology reflects Deut 18:1–8 (D), Num 3, and Num 18 (P).[139]

---

136. Other passages mention the priesthood, but these are either generic references or repeating information from the main texts listed. For example, the chambers of the priests are described in Ezek 42:13–14, and Ezek 48:8–14 distinguishes the land allotment of "priests, sons of Zadok," from that of "the Levites." Ezekiel 43:18–19 also mentions bringing a sin offering to, "the priests, the Levites, those of the family of Zadok, who draw near to me . . . to serve me."

137. Bechtel, "Politics of Yahweh," 210. See also Joyce, *Ezekiel*, 7–16.

138. Garrett, *Rethinking Genesis*, 207–32, argues that priests and Levites are one class with no distinction at any point in Israel's history. While correct as to class distinctions, the different groups held various roles (Num 1:47–54; 3:5–10; 18:1–7).

139. Betts, *Ezekiel the Priest*, 102, agrees that certain rituals are reserved for priests instead of Levites in P. In personal correspondence, Betts provided this caveat, "However, I did find a blurring of the priests and Levites at times. Sometimes there appears to be a distinction in roles and rank, yet at other times not so much in practice/roles. There appears to be fluidity based upon the needs of the occasion, even though they do appear to remember who was a Aaronic priest and who was a Levite at all times, keeping the hierarchy between the two in check. It makes sense, given the Levites were

Ezekiel 40:45–46

Ezek 40:45–46 describes

כֹּהֲנִים שֹׁמְרֵי מִשְׁמֶרֶת הַבָּיִת

("priests who keep charge of the temple") and

כֹּהֲנִים שֹׁמְרֵי מִשְׁמֶרֶת הַמִּזְבֵּחַ הֵמָּה בְנֵי־צָדוֹק הַקְּרֵבִים מִבְּנֵי־לֵוִי אֶל־יְהוָה לְשָׁרְתוֹ

("the priests who keep charge of the altar; these are the sons of Zadok, the ones who, of the sons of Levi, may approach YHWH to serve him").[140] Here the guide distinguishes Levites who may serve at the altar and those who may not.[141] Those who may approach the altar he describes as Zadokites. This permission for Zadokites to serve does not require, however, that only those who serve the altar are Zadokites.[142] The servants of the temple may also be Zadokites, for Ezek 40:46 merely says that, of the Zadokites, only altar priests may approach YHWH. That is, all who serve

---

there to help the priests. Sometimes the Levites seemed to step in and even do 'priestly' things if there was a need." This distinction is also helpfully examined by Duguid, "Putting Priests in Their Place," 44–47.

140. The meaning and translation of the priests' duty (שֹׁמְרֵי מִשְׁמֶרֶת) is debated. Block, *Ezekiel 25–48*, 537, argues that it means they perform guard duty (see 1 Chr 9:17–27). So also Greenberg, "Design and Themes," 193; Milgrom, *Studies in Levitical Terminology*, 8–16. This may be the meaning of that phrase, but other passages assign other duties to these officers. For example, Ezek 44:11 states that the Levites prepare the sacrifices and generally "serve" (שָׁרַת) the temple. After all, it is impossible that the Zadokite priests only keep guard of the altar, when clearly the vision describes a sacrificial system. See Zimmerli, *Ezekiel 2*, 358, for the generic meaning of "keeping [one's] duties." In conclusion, the priests and Levites had guard duty as part of their responsibility, emphasizing the area's sacredness, but had other duties as well. The rendering "keep charge" seems to encapsulate all the duties.

141. Contra Gese, *Verfassungsentwurf*, 57–65, who sees this text as independent but not yet reflecting a distinction between priests and Levites. Also contra Block, *Ezekiel 25–48*, 538, who claims scholars distinguish faultily between temple and altar, but that these terms are synonymous here and in Num 18:5. However, Num 18:3 does note a distinction between sanctuary and altar. Block, *Ezekiel 25–48*, 538, also says, "Distinctions drawn in [Num 18:5] are not between two groups of priests, but between Aaronid priests and other Levitical functionaries." This seems like just another way of saying there is some distinction in roles between priests and other Levites.

142. Gese, *Verfassungsentwurf*, 64–67, argues that Ezek 40:46b is a later insertion and part of the Zadokite stratum, promoting the Zadokites as the only true priests. So also Wevers, *Ezekiel*, 304.

at the altar are Zadokites, but not all Zadokites serve at the altar.¹⁴³ Ezekiel also notably describes both classes, temple servants and altar servants, as priests. This description is logical if the above is true, that both classes are not only Levites, but also Zadokites. Thus, the language resembles the priesthood described in Deut 18:1–8. Deuteronomy mentions כֹּהֲנִים הַלְוִיִּם כָּל־שֵׁבֶט לֵוִי ("priests, the Levites [or, the Levitical priests], all who are from the tribe of Levi"). Deut 18:1–5 mentions only priests, while Deut 18:6–8 discusses the Levites, though all are described as those who serve (שׁרת) before YHWH.¹⁴⁴ Deut 18 thus fits with Ezek 40 and its distinction of temple and altar servants. Does this text, though, square with the description of the priesthood in Ezek 44?

The Role of the Levites

In Ezek 44, YHWH speaks to the prophet and says that the Levites (הַלְוִיִּם) will serve in the sanctuary and temple (Ezek 44:10–11). Because of some past sin, they must "bear their punishment." Presumably this means this group of officers may not approach the altar to offer sacrifices, though they may slaughter the sacrifices (Ezek 44:11–14). YHWH contrasts this role with "a priest" (Ezek 44:13), and soon after (Ezek 44:15–31) develops the role of הַכֹּהֲנִים הַלְוִיִּם בְּנֵי צָדוֹק ("the priests, [that is] the Levites [or, the Levitical priests], the sons of Zadok"). While the title in Ezek 44:15, "Levitical priests," reflects Deut 18, as a whole Ezek 44 distinguishes between Levites who serve the temple (Ezek 44:10) and priests who serve the altar (Ezek 44:15).¹⁴⁵ Similarly, Num 3 describes Levites as those who guard

---

143. Duke, "Punishment or Restoration?" 74–75; Block, *Ezekiel 25–48*, 538, though he applies Ezek 40:46b to both sets of priests (Ezek 40:45–46a), which the syntax does not bear out.

144. Abba, "Priests and Levites in Deuteronomy," 257–67; McConville, "Priests and Levites in Ezekiel," 7–8. Emerton, "Priests and Levites in Deuteronomy," 129–38, argues for a distinction but also a rivalry between the classes. This goes against many scholars who see no distinction in Deut 18. They hold that D theology uses the term "Levitical priests," essentially simply Levites, to refer to all the priesthood, prior to P creating a distinction between priests and Levites. See Wellhausen, *Prolegomena*, 121–67; Haran, *Temples and Temple-Service*, 60–63. For more recent treatments see Fechter, "Priesthood in Exile," 27–41; Fechter, "Priesthood in Exile (2000)," 679–81; Klein, *Ezekiel*, 178. For a presentation of an anti-Levite polemic in the Persian period, see Tuell, "Priesthood of the 'Foreigner,'" 183–204.

145. For this reason, some scholars, e.g., Zimmerli, *Ezekiel 2*, 458, suggest that the term "Levitical priests" was inserted later into Ezek 44:15, but that the original perspective reflects the supposed P distinction of priests and Levites. Haran, *Temples and*

and serve the tabernacle (Num 3:6–9), distinct from priests (Num 3:6, 10). Likewise, Num 18 speaks of the duties of priests and Levites (Num 18:1–7). Interestingly, Num 18:1 says all the priests "bear iniquity," and later Num 18:23 says the Levites "bear their iniquity." Thus, in accord with the descriptions in Numbers, there is a general, though fluid, distinction between priests and Levites.[146]

The real insight into the purpose of Ezek 44 comes from understanding what it means for the Levites to נָשְׂאוּ עֲוֹנָם ("bear their punishment"). Many scholars view the text as a "demotion" of the Levites. According to them, in D the Levites served as priests at the altar. Due to sin, though, they were barred from offering sacrifices.[147] This common view is incorrect, however. Instead, in Ezek 44, YHWH restores the Levites to their original task. To probe this question, scholars attempt to discern what sin the Levites must have committed to cause the author of Ezek 44 to bar them from the altar.[148] McConville suggests that that there is no particular sin in mind. Instead, this is a "schema" of the Levites akin to other schemas of history like Ezek 20.[149] Probably the Levites failed in multiple ways over Israel's history, culminating in permitting the abominations described in Ezek 8–11. After all, Ezek 44 never describes any one particular incident. Although discovering a particular sin of the Levites appears impossible, the fact of their sin is clearly important.

Temple-Service, 83, however, suggests that "Levitical priests" in Deut is in contrast to unauthorized priests of another tribe, rather than a contrast with Aaronides.

146. McConville, "Priests and Levites in Ezekiel," 29. See also Haran, *Temples and Temple-Service*, 58–61; Fishbane, *Biblical Interpretation*, 183.

147. Wellhausen, *Prolegomena*, 123–24. Wellhausen argues that barring Levites due to sin is the author's stated reason, but the actual reason is that the Zadokites wanted to centralize worship in Jerusalem and thus ban the "Levitical priests" who served at the non-Jerusalemite high places. Similarly, see Wevers, *Ezekiel*, 318–20. For a view of this section as a Zadokite stratum after Ezekiel the prophet, see Hanson, *Dawn of Apocalyptic*, 264–69.

148. For summaries of the views on what sin the Levites committed, see Duguid, *Leaders of Israel*, 76–80; Levenson, *Program of Restoration*, 134–44. Awabdy, "YHWH Exegetes Torah," 685–703, argues that Ezek 44:7–9 serves as innerbiblical exegesis with Lev 22:25. The Levites allowed the uncircumcised to enter and perhaps serve in the sanctuary. The study of innerbiblical exegesis is valuable, but, as Awabdy admits in the end, does not fully answer the question of the status of the uncircumcised in the new society. Awabdy rightly opens the door for the possibility of a "circumcised foreigner."

149. McConville, "Priests and Levites in Ezekiel," 30. Cook, *Ezekiel 38–48*, 215, says, "Scholarly ink has been spilled in vain searching for historical events . . . behind Ezekiel 44. There simply are none."

Although the Levites are not "demoted," in some sense their sin affects their ability to serve at the altar. To prove this, several phrases in the text must be examined.

The first phrase is in Ezek 44:10, נָשְׂאוּ עֲוֺנָם ("bear their punishment," ESV; "bear the consequences of their sin," NIV, NASB).[150] Multiple questions influence interpretation. Does עָוֺן refer to a punishment or sin? Also, are the Levites bearing their own sin/punishment or that of others? Does נָשְׂאוּ כְלִמָּתָם ("bear their shame") in Ezek 44:13 parallel "bear punishment" in Ezek 44:10? "Bear punishment" is the most likely meaning, rather than "bear sin." Zimmerli claims Ezek 44:10 refers to the Levites bearing the punishment for their own sin, pointing to Ezek 14:10 and saying the phrase is a standard punishment formula.[151] Duguid also sees this as bearing punishment, connecting the phrase to the Suffering Servant of Isa 53.[152] This does not necessarily lead to the conclusion of a "demotion," however. Ezekiel envisions a day when the guilt is punished, but he does not explicitly connect the punishment to the inability to approach the altar (Ezek 44:11, 13).[153]

The next question concerns whether the Levites "bear punishment" for their own sins or the sins of Israel. In 1970, Milgrom argued that the phrase in question is a technical term regarding the duties of the tabernacle guards. The people, not the Levites, sinned (Ezek 44:6–8).[154] Due to the nature of their position, the Levites would "bear punishment" for the encroachment of the people. The Levites, then, were a "lightning rod," absorbing the punishment on themselves.[155] Though not the majority view, Milgrom's work led several exegetes to come to this conclusion.[156]

---

150. For discussion of the meaning of the phrase see Baruch Schwartz, "Term or Metaphor," 149–71; Milgrom, *Studies in Levitical Terminology*, 22–33; Zimmerli, *Ezekiel 1*, 164, 305, 351.

151. Zimmerli, *Ezekiel 2*, 452; Allen, *Ezekiel 20–48*, 251.

152. Duguid, *Leaders of Israel*, 77. He cites the research of Whybray, *Thanksgiving for a Liberated Prophet*, 31–57. Interestingly, several similar phrases are used in Isa 52:13—53:12, but this particular one is not.

153. Stevenson, *Vision of Transformation*, 63–78; Block, *Ezekiel 25–48*, 629.

154. Milgrom, *Studies in Levitical Terminology*, 84; Duke, "Punishment or Restoration?," 65.

155. Milgrom, *Studies in Levitical Terminology*, 22–33; McConville, "Priests and Levites in Ezekiel," 27; Wu, *Honor, Shame, and Guilt*, 143–45.

156. Duke, "Punishment or Restoration?," 63–64, comes to this conclusion, but he believes "they will bear their punishment" is a statement from God about the Levite's responsibility, not a threat of impending judgment. He argues that the "messenger

Milgrom later changed his view, however, as seen in his commentary on Ezek 38–48. He argues that the Levites bear punishment for their own sins, not for the sins of the people. Milgrom shows how in multiple ways the statement is an application, not a reversal, of Num 18, and he describes the view of Duguid and Whybray that in Isa 53 an individual bears punishment for his own sin.[157] Thus, the sin of the Levites is that their responsibility, according to Num 18, was to guard the sanctuary from encroachment, but they failed when they allowed foreigners to enter and worship idols (Ezek 44:6–8, 12). Thus, they will bear punishment for their sin. However, once again this need not imply demotion in the new temple era.[158] Instead, God restores the Levites to their previous position given in Num 18.[159] Milgrom's early argument, that guard duty is a punishment merely because it is dangerous, falls flat. The positions of high priest or watchman (Ezek 3), for example, are dangerous, but that fact need not imply inferiority. So, contrary to the classic view, no reason exists to see in the phrase "bearing their punishment" a negative view of the Levites.

The final exegetical issue in determining whether the Levites are being demoted is the phrase in Ezek 44:13 נָשְׂאוּ כְּלִמָּתָם ("bear their shame"). Unfortunately, some scholars simply equate this phrase with "bear their punishment," and thus assume it is a negative statement.[160] However, Block notes that Ezekiel previously uses "shame" in the context of salvation oracles (Ezek 16:53–63; 20:39–44; 36:31–32; 39:25–26; 43:10–11).[161]

---

formula" never introduces judgment. Duke also sees a parallel with the watchman of Ezek 3:16–21 ("Punishment or Restoration?," 66–67). Cook, "Innerbiblical Interpretation," 204, also argues this speaks of their responsibility, not punishment, but calls it a "rhetorical ploy" that is actually a restoration of the Levites, giving them the same function he believes they have in Num 18.

157. Milgrom, *Ezekiel's Hope*, 150–53.

158. Contra Milgrom, *Ezekiel's Hope*, 151.

159. Cook, "Innerbiblical Interpretation," 204; Cook, *Ezekiel 38–48*, 214; Odell, *Ezekiel*, 508.

160. For example, see Odell, *Ezekiel*, 508–9, where she resorts to the explanation that Israel replaced the Levites in their role as firstborn with their idols, such that they were "far from [YHWH]" (Ezek 44:10). The text gives little indication, though, of this theory regarding the firstborn. The phrase is not even discussed by some major works such as Zimmerli, *Ezekiel 2*, 452–56; Eichrodt, *Ezekiel*, 564–65; Allen, *Ezekiel 20–48*, 251, 261.

161. Block, *Ezekiel 25–48*, 632; Cook, *Ezekiel 38–48*, 106, 211. Contra Ganzel, "Descriptions of the Restoration," 204, where in her interpretation of Ezek 16:63 she says, "[Ezekiel] chides them for their intransigence."

So, Milgrom concludes, "Shame is a gift from God."[162] When one becomes aware of sin and consequently experiences restoration and forgiveness, at least one response is shame over past actions. Therefore, Duke writes, "The gracious restoration of the Levites to their position of cultic responsibility would remind them of their previous abominations and humble them."[163] Since Ezek 40–48 is a vision of restoration, "bearing shame" should be understood as part of the restoration process, not as a judgment. "Bearing shame" is not equivalent to "bearing punishment" in Ezek 44:10.

After a careful examination of key phrases in Ezek 44:9–14, the true role of the Levites in the new temple is clearer. Although many scholars since Wellhausen see the text as a demotion of Levites, the final analysis supports a different interpretation. First, the Pentateuch already supports a distinction between priests and Levites. Thus, Ezekiel's writing is not an "anti-Levite polemic" attempting to rewrite the history of the priesthood. Instead, because of the Levites's sin, Ezekiel creatively highlights the distinction already present in the Pentateuch. As Duguid claims, "Not only are the Levites not priests more clearly than ever before, but now they are not priests because of their own past sins."[164] One must remember, though, that this is not a demotion. The Levites's sin had apparently already been dealt with and as a consequence they "bear their shame." Now, in Ezek 44, the Levites are restored to their original position as described in Num 18. They are, as Block says, ". . . hereby fully rehabilitated and repatriated."[165] Moreover, they are actually given a further responsibility, that is, to slaughter sacrifices (Ezek 44:11). In the Pentateuch, this was the responsibility of the layperson (Lev 1:1–9). Thus, in one sense the Levites are actually "promoted."[166] In conclusion, then, the Levites are not presented in as negative a light as most assume. Ezekiel does not, per Wellhausen, ". . . hängt bloss der Logik der Tatsachen einen moralischen Mantel um."[167]

---

162. Milgrom, *Ezekiel's Hope*, 162.

163. Duke, "Punishment or Restoration?," 70. Similarly Block, *Ezekiel 25–48*, 629.

164. Duguid, *Leaders of Israel*, 79. Milgrom, *Ezekiel's Hope*, 151, presents a similar position.

165. Block, *Ezekiel 25–48*, 632. So also, Cook, *Ezekiel 38–48*, 210.

166. So also Block, *Ezekiel 25–48*, 630; Stevenson, *Vision of Transformation*, 66–78; Duguid, *Ezekiel*, 502. Contra Cook, *Ezekiel 38–48*, 214, who cites Num 16:9 as evidence that the Levites could approach the altar according to the Holiness School. That text, however, simply states that they serve the מִשְׁכָּן (in this case, the tabernacle), a generic enough term to harmonize with Ezek 44 (which uses מִקְדָּשׁ for the inner temple/sanctuary). Cook, *Ezekiel 38–48*, 216, incorrectly concludes that מִקְדָּשׁ refers to the altar.

167. Wellhausen, *Prolegomena zur Geschichte Israels*," 118. Author's translation,

Instead, as Joyce says, "[The Levites] hold responsibilities of some honour (vv. 11 and 14) and some statements about them are more positive than the Wellhausen theory can readily account for."[168] Ezekiel presents the role of the Levites as a very important one in the scheme of the temple and its cult. Duguid explains the relevance of all this when he says,

> Ezekiel's purpose in these regulations is not grounded in political propaganda against the Levites. Rather, his concern here is, as elsewhere in the temple vision, a priestly desire to heighten and strengthen the wall dividing the holy and profane. In pursuit of that goal, he utilizes and further develops old legislation to depict in visionary form a new future that restores things to the way they ought to have been in the past. The priests and the Levites are to be put back in their proper places.[169]

Rather than being only a window into Israelite history, herein lies the typological meaning of the Levites in Ezek 40–48. Ezekiel describes an office in Israel's history and cult, so the new temple is real in that sense. The meaning of the text, however, does not depend upon a physical temple being constructed. The purpose of the vision is to describe a new society where restoration has taken place. In Ezek 40–48 true worship is restored. No longer will YHWH's holiness be defiled and his sanctuary defamed. The reason particular offices are described is not to tie the vision to a future historical reality in Israel, but to use Israel's history to look forward to this eschatological fulfillment.

The Role of the Zadokites

What about the priests, that is, those often called the Zadokites? What is their purpose in this new temple? Ezek 44:15–31 introduces "the priests" in contrast to the Levites. In Ezek 44:10 the prophet draws a stark contrast from Ezek 44:9.[170] In Ezek 44:15, the writer also begins a section

---

"[Ezekiel] merely hangs a mantle of morality on the logic of facts."

168. Joyce, *Ezekiel*, 232, goes on to say that nevertheless the Levites are "in some sense demoted" and that the presentation of the Levites is "ambiguous." Still, he helpfully points out the positive presentation of the Levites. Also see Stevenson, *Vision of Transformation*, 81–83.

169. Duguid, "Putting Priests in their Place," 54.

170. Ezek 44:10 begins, "But the Levites . . ." On the disjunction see Waltke-O'Connor, *Biblical Hebrew Syntax*, 39.3.5d; Block, *Ezekiel 25–48*, 624.

with a contrast, but this one is not as strong.[171] Instead, the description of the Zadokites mirrors the previous description of the Levites in its form.[172] Just as Ezekiel highlights the previous sin of the Levites, so now he highlights the exoneration of the Zadokites. This should not be seen as rewarding the Zadokites for their faithfulness, but simply as a description of how the Zadokites behaved during the exilic period.[173] Nevertheless, many scholars find it impossible to believe that the Zadokite priests could have been so righteous during this time.[174] Ezekiel is surely aware of the failures of the priesthood he decried in Ezek 22:26 when YHWH says, "Her priests have defiled my law and done violence to my holiness..."[175] Though one should not gloss over the gravity of the sins in Ezek 22:26, they are not, however, the same as those of the Levites in Ezek 44:6–12.[176] All of the sins of the priests in Ezek 22:26 could take place without the type of idolatry described in Ezek 8–11. Moreover, YHWH accuses not only the priests, but also the people of similar actions.[177] Thus, the priests come away with, in Duguid's words, "... remarkably little blame."[178] In addition, the future description of the Zadokites takes into consideration these past sins and ensures they will be done away with (Ezek 44:23–24).

---

171. Odell, *Ezekiel*, 507. Ezek 44:15 begins, "But the Levitical priests, the sons of Zadok..."

172. Block, *Ezekiel 25–48*, 633–34.

173. Contra Duguid, *Leaders of Israel*, 80–81.

174. Zimmerli, *Ezekiel 2*, 456, believes the Zadokites must have sinned, saying, "It is... unthinkable that a whole class, united in one family, should be designated as having held true in a time of error and be adjudged worthy of subsequent reward. It is precisely this that happens when reference is now made to the 'Levitical priests, the descendants of Zadok.'" Also Gunneweg, *Leviten und Priester*, 203; Abba, "Priests and Levites in Ezekiel," 5.

175. Some, e.g., Odell, *Ezekiel*, 510, also argue that the priests failed to guard the sanctuary in Ezek 8–11 (see Ezek 44:6–8). The elders, however, were involved in the abominations of Ezek 8–11, not priests. For a convincing defense of this notion, see Duguid, *Leaders of Israel*, 67–72, 81.

176. See Ganzel, "Defilement of the Temple," 369–79, and her examination of "desecrate" in contrast to "defile" in the book of Ezekiel.

177. In Ezek 22:8 YHWH speaks similar judgments against the people saying, "You have despised my holiness and defiled my Sabbaths."

178. Duguid, *Leaders of Israel*, 75. Contra Milgrom, *Ezekiel's Hope*, 169, who argues that a non-Zadokite priesthood is abolished due to the sins of Ezek 22:26. His conclusions are based on the assumption of a history of the priesthood where there were different classes of priests such as the "countryside" ones.

Thus, this text is not a piece of Zadokite propaganda, for it honestly deals with the sins of the priests.

Still, if the Zadokites indeed sinned (Ezek 22:26), how can the text call them righteous? The best way to interpret their "righteousness" is in terms of degrees.[179] The priests are not entirely without blame, but they are more righteous than the Levites and the people of Israel. The priests demonstrated their righteousness in how they שָׁמְרוּ אֶת־מִשְׁמֶרֶת מִקְדָּשִׁי ("kept the guard of my sanctuary"), the role described in Ezek 40:46. Admittedly, the text nowhere speaks of the event(s) wherein the Zadokites did so, but they must have guarded the sanctuary in some sense. Moreover, YHWH is able to look upon the priests in this way due to the concept of "The Covenant of Grant."[180] The phrase שָׁמְרוּ אֶת־מִשְׁמֶרֶת ("kept the charge") in Ezek 44:15 indicates that such a grant may be in place here. Just as YHWH looked positively on Abraham and David despite their obvious sins, so he may look upon these priests because of his eternal covenant with the priesthood (Num 25:12–13).[181]

To conclude regarding the role of the priests, evidently Ezekiel creatively updates a previous *traditum* to create a new *traditio*.[182] The prophet does not edit the priestly regulations because of a new historical situation. Instead, he adapts or applies the Mosaic tradition to his present historical situation. The Zadokites are not "promoted" but restored to their rightful place. They are reinstituted to their important position of approaching YHWH's altar despite their grievous sins (Ezek 22:26). They, unlike anyone else, may approach YHWH to serve him. In this way, the Zadokites's role reinforces the theology of sacred space.[183] Those who are most righteous are able draw the closest to YHWH. Even despite their sins, these priests are righteous because of YHWH's covenant. Additionally, the text shows YHWH is intent on guarding the sanctity of his temple and his worship. Once again, rather than reflecting a historical situation in Israel's past, the text points forward to an eschatological future. Hals writes,

---

179. Duguid, *Leaders of Israel*, 82–83; Block, *Ezekiel 25–48*, 636–37.

180. Weinfeld, "Covenant of Grant," 184–205.

181. Levenson, *Program of Restoration*, 145–46; Duguid, *Leaders of Israel*, 82–83; Block, *Ezekiel 25–48*, 636.

182. Fishbane, *Biblical Interpretation*, 143.

183. Duguid, *Leaders of Israel*, 82; Block, *Ezekiel 25–48*, 637. Per Milgrom, *Ezekiel's Hope*, 164, the fact that the text here does not mention the priestly role of teaching also signifies the importance of guarding the sanctity.

> What Ezekiel offers is an eschatological promise of an extreme sort rather than a political attempt to restructure the priesthood ... Inasmuch as the rest of Ezekiel's descriptions of the new temple frequently border on the fantastic in order to make a point, is it not appropriate to expect that this section too belongs in that category, alongside a fantastically high and flat Zion (chs. 40–42), a miraculous advent (43:1–5), an amazing stream of water (47:1–12), and some most extraordinary land divisions?[184]

The priestly leadership, along with the temple's measurements, provides a vision of YHWH's holiness. Rather than buttressing the conclusion for a physical fulfillment, the passage supports an eschatological view of the text.

The High Priest

Ezek 40–48, mysteriously, does not explicitly provide legislation for a high priest (HP). Ezekiel sees the most holy place but may not enter it— only the guide may (Ezek 41:1–4). In the legislation of officers, namely Ezek 44, the text includes no description of a HP. Scholars have proposed a plethora of hypotheses in regard to this figure who is so important in the Pentateuch. Some take the position that the HP did not exist in Ezekiel's day, or at least was not very prominent, and that Ezekiel betrays evidence of an early stage of the history of the priesthood.[185] Others state that the HP desecrated the name and/or temple of YHWH, and therefore was punished by having his position completely stripped away.[186] Kasher argues that the position is abolished due to the nature of the new temple. YHWH's holiness is so prominent that no sinful human could approach his presence. Therefore, no need exists for a HP to minister in that area.[187]

---

184. Hals, *Ezekiel*, 319–20.

185. Wellhausen, *Prolegomena*, 121–67; Tuell, *Law of the Temple*, 147.

186. Milgrom, *Ezekiel's Hope*, 169–77. He argues that the reason for this is provided in Ezek 44:7–8, which apparently tells how the HP hired foreigners as watchmen. Though God blames the people, he says, surely the foreigners would not have been allowed entrance without the HP's consent. Moreover, the idolatry that was practiced, presumably what is described in Ezek 8–11, could only have taken place under the watch of the HP. Another key to the argument is that Ezekiel does not mention the HP anywhere in his book. Milgrom states that, in the book of Ezekiel, a leader who commits an egregious sin is not mentioned. Ezekiel eliminates not just the HP, but the king, prophets, elders, and officials.

187. Kasher, "Anthropomorphism, Holiness, and Cult," 197. Kasher says that

Duguid offers a different perspective with the suggestion that the writer vaguely mentions "the priest" in Ezek 44:30 and 45:19. At the time of Ezekiel, the HP would have existed, but not seen as having a very prominent role and thus would not be a dominant figure in Ezekiel's temple.[188] Relatedly, some assume that if Zadokites, of the lineage of Aaron, are present in the text, the text implies a HP.[189] Alternatively, for others the function of the HP is democratized among all the Zadokites.[190] Several scholars make this argument based on the restrictions that P places on the HP, which Ezekiel places on all the priests.[191] Finally, one scholar such as Block pleads agnosticism by saying, "Such questions cannot be answered."[192] This section will combine insights from different views to make an argument that the HP is implicit in the text but not present. In other words, YHWH's temple awaits a HP who had not yet arrived in Ezekiel's day.

First, the notion that no HP existed in Ezekiel's day should be rejected. As the above study shows, the Pentateuch provides a reliable history of the early priesthood, a system that included a HP. Moreover, Duguid convincingly argues that the HP existed in the Pentateuch and monarchic periods, even when the title הַכֹּהֵן הַגָּדֹל is not used.[193] The view that YHWH rejects the HP because of his sin also fails to convince. For one, Ezekiel points out the sins of the Levites, yet they are not rejected. One would assume that if YHWH restores the Levites, he would restore the HP as well. At the very least, if YHWH were to reject him, one expects an explanation.[194] Since the HP's position is even more important,

---

anthropomorphic language conveys that YHWH's glory dwells permanently in the temple in a very physical way (Ezek 43:1–8). The glory dwelling permanently thus creates all around it a sphere of supreme sanctity such that no human being may enter.

188. Duguid, *Leaders of Israel*, 59–64.
189. Levenson, *Program of Restoration*, 133, 140–44.
190. MacDonald, *Priestly Rule*, 92; Rooke, *Zadok's Heirs*, 104–19.
191. Milgrom, *Ezekiel's Hope*, 168; MacDonald, *Priestly Rule*, 56–113.
192. Block, *Ezekiel 25–48*, 637.
193. Duguid, *Leaders of Israel*, 59–64. From the wilderness period to the exile, the most common title for the HP is הַכֹּהֵן. As the cultic system becomes more complex in the monarchic period, more titles are used. Unless one is to take all of the texts mentioning a HP and place them after the exile, there is no escape from the conclusion that a HP existed before the exile.
194. Milgrom, *Ezekiel's Hope*, 176, claims that those who commit the grievous sin of polluting the sanctuary are wiped off the map, i.e., not even deemed worthy of mention. However, as previously shown, only the elders and people polluted the sanctuary.

his fall would be greater. If YHWH were to reject the HP, it would seem part of the prophet's project to denounce the position as he has done with other officials in the book. As to Kasher's argument about the nature of the new temple and its holiness, Kasher's emphasis does not explain the absence of a HP. His position could apply to the entire priestly system. If the whole territory is "most holy" (Ezek 43:12), according to the logic of Kasher's anthropomorphic conception no human being should approach the temple complex at all. Regarding the HP's role being democratized among the Zadokites, the evidence also presents problems. As Levenson notes, sometimes P's rules for the HP contradict Ezekiel's rules for the priests.[195] Indeed, no clear development of the evolution of priestly legislation occurs.[196] Sometimes Ezekiel seems to be updating legislation and sometimes he does not. Even if the legislation for the priests is "democratized," this does not automatically rule out the role of a HP. Possibly, Ezekiel knows of the legislation in P and feels no need to expand or contract the HP's powers. If it is not broken, he does not fix it.[197]

The arguments against a HP in the vision, then, do not convince. Milgrom incorrectly claims, "The evidence is incontrovertible that in Ezekiel's system there is *no place for a high priest*."[198] Instead, the text vaguely implies the presence of a HP.[199] Though Ezekiel does not list much temple furniture, he describes the table of the presence (Ezek 41:22). The Passover and some version of Yom Kippur are celebrated as well (Ezek 45:18–25).[200] Also, the text mentions Zadokites. These features naturally imply a HP.

Elders are not mentioned but people certainly are.

195. Levenson, *Program of Restoration*, 142. In Lev 21:11 the HP may not encounter a corpse, even that of his family. In Ezek 44:25, exception is made for priests to encounter the corpse of family members.

196. Hunt, *Missing Priests*, 124–44, notes how scholarship has read texts merely for their historical background and development. She argues that Ezek 44 may be less about what Ezekiel knows of P and instead be an innerbiblical interpretation of Ezek 23.

197. Rooke, *Zadok's Heirs*, 118; Greenberg, "Design and Themes," 203.

198. Milgrom, *Ezekiel's Hope*, 168.

199. Referring to other aspects of the vision, Greenberg, "Design and Themes," 193, says, "Omissions cannot serve as a warrant for negative conclusions—unmentioned, therefore absent." Also Rooke, *Zadok's Heirs*, 119.

200. Zimmerli, *Ezekiel 2*, 482; Allen, *Ezekiel 20–48*, 266. Contra Block, *Ezekiel 25–48*, 661–64. I say "some version" because Yom Kippur may or may not still exist on the calendar, but regardless this ritual serves a similar function.

Most importantly, the text does actually mention the priest.²⁰¹ When looking for the HP, one must first search for the correct term(s). Ezek 40–48 does not name הַכֹּהֵן הָרֹאשׁ or הַכֹּהֵן הַגָּדוֹל. The title most common in P, הַכֹּהֵן, does occur in Ezekiel, though.²⁰² Besides Ezek 1:3, a reference to the prophet's lineage, the title appears in Ezek 44:30 and 45:19. In Ezek 44:30, the text notably changes from plural to singular in the second reference.²⁰³ Some suggest the change exists simply to bring the text in line with Neh 10:38, which mentions a priest present alongside the Levites and other priests.²⁰⁴ Ezekiel, though, is more explicit that the worshiper should bring the tithe directly to the priest. More likely, Ezekiel speaks of a HP, as in Num 18:28, when Israel is instructed to give the tenth of the tenth to Aaron the priest (הַכֹּהֵן).²⁰⁵ In Ezek 45:19, הַכֹּהֵן offers a sin offering similar to Yom Kippur.²⁰⁶ The passage is odd in that, barring the reference to "the priest" in Ezek 45:19, the MT uses second-person singular in Ezek 45:18–20a (addressed possibly to Ezekiel), but then switches to second-person plural in Ezek 45:20b–21.²⁰⁷ This change implies that "the priest" and Ezekiel together make atonement for the temple.²⁰⁸ In Ezek 43:20, YHWH instructs Ezekiel to take the blood of the

---

201. Duguid, *Leaders of Israel*, 64.

202. Rooke, *Zadok's Heirs*, 116 fn. 30, argues that this term refers to a preexilic "chief priest" who, she says, ". . . is different from a post-exilic high priest." This study, though, does not argue for a postexilic kind of HP, but the kind that would have existed at the time of the exile. Even so, Zadok himself bears the title "the priest" (2 Sam 15:27; 1 Kgs 1:8, 1:26, 32, 34, 38, 39, 44, 45, 2:35; 1 Chr 16:39, 24:6), as does his son (1 Kgs 4:2).

203. Ezek 44:30 (emphasis added) says, "And the first of all firstfruits of all kinds, and every offering of every kind from all your offerings will be for the *priests*. And the first of your dough you shall give to *the priest*, that a blessing may rest on your house." Surprisingly, many scholars fail to note this change from plural to singular. Zimmerli, *Ezekiel 2*, 463, and Allen, *Ezekiel 20–48*, 264, do notice it, but only conclude that this part of the text must be a later addition.

204. Neh 10:38a says, "And the priest, the son of Aaron, will be with the Levites . . ." See Duguid, *Leaders of Israel*, 64; Gese, *Verfassungsentwurf*, 63.

205. This explanation also fits with the argument above that Ezekiel harmonizes with P and Num 18 in terms of the whole priesthood.

206. Ezek 45:19a states, "The priest will take from the blood of the sin offering and put it on the doorpost of the temple."

207. Zimmerli, *Ezekiel 2*, 480, concludes that v. 20b is a secondary expansion due to the seeming inconsistency in the versions. LXX backs up the switch to plural of the MT.

208. Block, *Ezekiel 25–48*, 662, argues that Ezekiel as the priest performs the ritual, with the final plural including the people as a whole. Other factors, though, go against seeing the people in view in v. 20. First, this text is similar to Ezek 43:18–27, where

bull and place it upon the altar. In contrast, in Ezek 45:19, though Ezekiel is present, he is not the one who places the blood on the altar. Instead, YHWH specifically instructs "the priest" to purify the altar. This text, then, presents a clear distinction between Ezekiel and the figure known as "the priest."[209] Therefore, the author intentionally brings in "the priest" for a second time in this vision so that he may perform this ritual.[210] Unlike Yom Kippur, where the HP enters the most holy place, here the HP only cleanses the altar, so this may explain why he takes a less prominent place in the text.

In addition, Ezek 45:18–21 is similar not just to Lev 16, but also the sin offering in Levs 4.[211] In that ritual we also find "the priest," a term used numerous times (Lev 4:6, 7, 10, 17, 20, 25, 26, 30, 31, 34, 35). He is not, though, a generic priest among many. The text also repeatedly terms him the "anointed priest" (הַכֹּהֵן הַמָּשִׁיחַ), a clear reference to the HP. The similarities between the passages buttresses the suggestion that the HP is also in view as "the priest" in Ezek 45:19.[212] Thus, upon closer examination, Ezekiel's vision does actually include the HP.

Ezekiel and the priests are instructed to purify the altar. In general, that passage uses the singular "you" until Ezek 43:26 where the text switches to third person plural and the priests make atonement for the altar. The plural there does not involve the people but Ezekiel and the priests together. This would be a clue that the same phenomenon happens in Ezek 45:18–20. Second, per Allen, *Ezekiel 20–48*, 266, the atonement of the altar is similar to the Yom Kippur ritual of Lev 16, where the HP makes atonement with no involvement from the people. Considering the separation of Israel in the new temple, such a change to allow them to make atonement is unimaginable. Biggs, "Role of Nasi," 51, argues that the context indicates the נָשִׂיא is responsible for the cleansing of the sanctuary. Though he does not perform the ritual, he ensures its execution. However, the text's switch from the second person pronouns to "the prince" in v. 22 obviates this view.

209. The suggestion that Ezekiel is the HP does not seem likely. Sweeney, *Form and Intertextuality*, 141, hints at this possibility. Ezekiel does reflect a "new Moses" in many ways throughout the book, but this parallel does not equate to him being a HP. After all, the original Moses had Aaron serve as HP.

210. Eichrodt, *Ezekiel*, 573, states that this passage is a "... priestly torah ... perhaps addressed earlier to the high priest ... ," but now the text is changed to address the prophet.

211. Duguid, *Leaders of Israel*, 64.

212. Berry, "Authorship of Ezekiel 40–48," 39, also sees the HP in view in Ezek 45:19, claiming that the term "the priest" is common for P. However, he states this as an axiom without providing much evidence. See also Cooke, *Ezekiel*, 502, who claims that this is the term in use at Ezekiel's time.

In light of the evidence, one must provide an explanation for the absence of a description of the HP. In this sense Milgrom is correct that the failure to mention the HP is intentional.[213] The proposal in this study is that YHWH sets up a temple system that includes a HP, but Ezekiel is not yet able to see or even understand who that HP is. In other words, the presentation of the HP is typological, ambiguously looking forward to an eschatological heightening.

The text states that during his tour Ezekiel does not enter into the most holy place, only the angelic guide does ("Then he went into the room and measured . . . ;" Ezek 41:3). This suggests that Ezekiel is not permitted to enter because he is a "son of man," the title YHWH often uses to address him. What would make this most holy place distinct from the previous ones in the tabernacle and Solomonic temple, where a mortal could enter? For one, this temple is God's eternal dwelling (in Ezek 43:7 YHWH says, "This is the place of my throne . . . where I will dwell . . . forever."). Also, here the presence of YHWH fills his abode in an unprecedented way.[214] Solomon himself acknowledged that the first temple could not contain God and be his dwelling (1 Kgs 8:27), yet Ezekiel sees how "the glory of YHWH" filled this temple (Ezek 43:5), which as a result completely transforms the city, the land, and all of creation (Ezek 47–48).[215] In addition, as shown above, the size, shape, and proportions of this new temple show the great holiness of YHWH. On account of this unprecedented level of holiness, no mere mortal may come into YHWH's presence. Block asks the question, "Did any human ever have access to this room?"[216] The answer is that no mere human being could, for all humanity is sinful. Yet if the presence of a HP is implicit, then Ezekiel's text leaves open the notion that a different kind of HP would one day come, perhaps one who was angelic or divine, or at least one who was more holy than the previous high priests. The prophet does not resolve the tension in this vision. Nevertheless, this presentation of the HP fits the message of Ezek 40–48. This temple space is sacred unlike any other. YHWH has revealed his holiness and glory in an unprecedented way, and therefore YHWH raises the standard of HP who may approach him.

---

213. Milgrom, *Ezekiel's Hope*, 174–75, says, "If it is not explicit then it does not exist." I do not agree with the statement, but he implies intentionality in the absence of the HP, contra Duguid, *Leaders of Israel*, 59–64.

214. Kasher, "Anthropomorphism," 192–98, especially see 197.

215. Sweeney, *Form and Intertextuality*, 141–42.

216. Block, *Ezekiel 25–48*, 637.

The נָשִׂיא in Ezekiel 40–48

Although much can be said about the one often translated as "the prince," this section focuses on the figure's role in the new temple.[217] The term "prince" often refers to a political figure (Ezek 34:23-24; 37:25), but he has a role in the cult here in Ezek 40-48.[218] Milgrom claims that the cult, in fact, is Ezekiel's main concern when it comes to the prince.[219] In other words, the absence of political functions or terminology does not imply that this is a different person.[220] Instead, this absence of political tasks reflects the previous failure of the Davidic monarchy (Ezek 43:7-9) and simply underscores YHWH's kingship. This may be why Ezekiel chooses the term more common in the premonarchic era instead of מֶלֶךְ ("king").[221] Therefore, while the author emphasizes the prince's cultic role, this need not rule out political leadership as well. The text, for theological reasons, simply does not discuss this political aspect.[222] Ezekiel mentions the

---

217. For an examination of this term throughout the OT, see Speiser, "Background and function," 111-17. The term can denote tribal leaders in the Pentateuch (Num 1:16) and Joshua (Josh 22:30), then later can refer to a king (1 Kgs 11:34; Ezek 12:10) or prince (Ezra 1:8). Hence the term can generically refer to a leader, a tribal chief, or the nation's king.

218. Block, *Beyond the River Chebar*, 82. Block equates the prince with the Davidic shepherd-king, answering objections in Block, *Beyond the River Chebar*, 89-94. Levenson, *Program of Restoration*, 57-69, also argues for the figure as a Davidic king. Feinberg, *Ezekiel*, 258, claims he cannot be the king and that his position emphasizes the theocratic reign of Jesus Christ in the millennium. Gaebelein, *Ezekiel*, 314, says that the prince is not called Davidic in the temple vision, so he cannot be the Messiah. This is based, however, on the assumption that the prince cannot be the figure of Ezekiel 34 and Ezekiel 37.

219. Milgrom, *Ezekiel's Hope*, 173. Hence he is not called מלך. Note Levenson, *Program of Restoration*, 64, however, who shows the parallelism of the two terms in Ezek 7:27; 32:29.

220. Hwang, "נָשִׂיא in Ezekiel 40-48," 183-94. Hwang makes several arguments for continuity between the prince in Ezek 34, 37 and 40-48. First, the final author makes no comment on the figures being different, so canonically one would naturally read the book as if they are the same. Second, the text supports a close connection between Ezek 33-37 and Ezek 40-48, strongly implying the figure is the same. Third, condemnation of monarchic abuses does not inherently imply abandonment of the Davidic ruler. Fourth, the land size of the prince implies significant standing (Ezek 48:2). Hals, *Ezekiel*, 252, 274, 288, also argues that the prince is the same Messiah of Ezek 34 and Ezek 37.

221. Speiser, "Background and Function," 113, demonstrates the prominence of the term נָשִׂיא in the premonarchic era. Tuell, *Law of the Temple*, 106, agrees.

222. Bechtel, "Politics of Yahweh," 230, says, "The [prince] must be a royal figure,

prince in Ezek 44:3; 45:7–8, 17; 48:21, giving the longest exposition in Ezek 45:21—46:12.²²³ In Ezek 44:1–3 the prince has special access to the outer gate and may exit the temple by the same gate he entered (Ezek 46:8). This privilege is not extended to the people (Ezek 46:9). He has the same restrictions of access to the inner sanctum as the laypeople, however (Ezek 46:1–7). The prince also has special territory for himself (Ezek 45:7–9; 48:21) and is not allowed to acquire any more land (Ezek 46:18). Finally, the prince is responsible to provide the sacrificial animals for all the people on the feast days (Ezek 45:21–25).

Though the vision portrays the prince in realistic terms (i.e., not as an idyllic king), he has an important role considering the context of the vision.²²⁴ Since this version of the temple is "radically theocentric," the prince is not called to build the temple, appoint priests, and plan the worship, as David and Solomon did in their day.²²⁵ Instead he is, in Block's words, "... the appointed lay patron and sponsor of the cult."²²⁶ He makes preparations for the worship of YHWH (Ezek 45:17), in contrast to Solomon, who offered sacrifices (1 Kgs 8:63).²²⁷ In other words, the emphasis

---

a king, in view of [Ezek] 43:7 'they and their kings ... shall not again profane'; Ezekiel envisions a future with a monarchy." Bechtel is incorrect, though, in his argument that the king is an "impotent" figure.

223. Gese, *Verfassungsentwurf*, 108–23, claimed that some of these texts were part of a "נָשִׂיא stratum." See the discussion in Duguid, *Leaders of Israel*, 27–31.

224. Duguid, *Ezekiel*, 501. Also Bechtel, "Politics of Yahweh," 231, says, "The [prince's] duties and privileges identify his unique connection with Yhwh ... His role within Yhwh's kingdom is pivotal." Levenson, *Program of Restoration*, 113, calls him, "A figure of great honor, however impotent," and an "A-political Messiah" (*Program of Restoration*, 75). Also see Biggs, "Role of Nasi," 50. Contra Tuell, *Law of the Temple*, 108, who concludes that the prince is only messianic in a narrow sense, being a Davidide, but is more of a historical and political figure than an eschatological hope. Tuell, *Law of the Temple*, 115–17, ultimately concludes that the figure represents the governor of Yehud under Persian dominance.

225. Patton, "Blueprint," 101; Stevenson, *Vision of Transformation*, 116. On the radical theocentricity of Ezekiel, see Joyce, *Divine Initiative and Human Response*, 89–105. On the restriction inherent in the term נָשִׂיא, see Hwang, "נָשִׂיא in Ezekiel 40–48," 185, who cites 1 Kgs 11:34 as an example. Likewise, Tuell, *Law of the Temple*, 103–4. Levenson, *Program of Restoration*, 64, writes, "Solomon's 'demotion' to *nasi*' may be the 'lashes of mankind,' but it is not the retraction of grace (2 Sam 7:14–15)."

226. Block, *Beyond the River Chebar*, 93. So also Duguid, *Leaders of Israel*, 50–55; Tuell, *Law of the Temple*, 108–10.

227. Contra Latto, *Josiah and David Redivivus*, 191–92, who argues that the prince also offers sacrifices in Ezek 45:17. See Hwang, "נָשִׂיא in Ezekiel 40–48," 188, for reasons why the text says "provide" rather than "sacrifice." As for Solomon in 1 Kgs 8:63,

on the "blandness" of the prince only serves to emphasize the centrality of YHWH and his presence in the temple and the land.[228] Levenson probably goes too far in the suggestion that the role of the prince becomes, he says, ". . . absorbed into the personality of YHWH . . . ," yet it is true that the role of the prince underscores YHWH's theocratic reign.[229] The role of the prince thus continues the theme of holiness and separation.[230] YHWH's presence resides in the temple, so only authorized personnel may draw near. The prince may draw nearer than the people, for he may stay at the gate of the inner court (Ezek 46:2) and the people only the outer court (Ezek 46:9-10). At the same time, in his grace YHWH appoints someone to sponsor worship of him.[231] Moreover, the above does not imply that the prince's role is unimportant. Instead, he has a position of great honor.[232] Thus the term prevents an understanding of, as Levenson calls it, ". . . sultan-like imperialism," but also does not preclude him from identification as the Davidic Messiah.[233]

The prince, then, is not a historical figure present in the days of the book's completion.[234] He is a typological figure in Ezekiel's temple vision. He is one who holds a position of great honor, a messianic figure, a son of David, who fulfills the eschatological hope in Ezek 34:23-24 and 37:25.[235] He is the patron of Israel's worship. He is one who will not op-

---

he surely did not slaughter 142,000 animals himself. However, the text appears to indicate that Solomon had some part to play in actually offering sacrifices, though he also must have played provider of the animals.

228. Duguid, *Leaders of Israel*, 54-55. Levenson, *Program of Restoration*, 80, claims, "YHWH is to the messiah as Nebuchadnezzar is to Zedekiah [cf. Ezekiel 17]." In other words, the messiah is essentially a vassal/puppet of YHWH the king.

229. Levenson, *Program of Restoration*, 99; Bechtel, "Politics of Yahweh," 235.

230. Smith, *To Take Place*, 59-60.

231. Block, *Ezekiel 25-48*, 677. Contra Milgrom, *Ezekiel's Hope*, 137, who downplays the prince's importance by saying, "[He] has no role in the cultic service." Technically he does not lead the cult, but as the provider, the cult would not exist without him.

232. Levenson, *Program of Restoration*, 113; Tuell, *Law of the Temple*, 107. Contra Hals, *Ezekiel*, 288, who says, "To put it crassly, the prince's value is solely to be unlike the past kings (see 43:7-9), one whose cultic role is modest, whose property rights are so modest as to be minimal (see 45:7-8a and 48:21-22), and whose further role in connection with property is presented in a totally negative way."

233. Levenson, *Program of Restoration*, 67; Duguid, *Leaders of Israel*, 14-16; Cook, *Ezekiel 38-48*, 204; Bechtel, "Politics of Yahweh," 233-35.

234. Tuell, *Law of the Temple*, 115-20, holds this position.

235. Contra Procksch, "Fürst Und Priester Bei Hesekiel," 99-133, who argues that

press YHWH's people and will use just measurements (Ezek 45:8–12), ruling under the kingship of YHWH himself.

Ezekiel's portrayal of the prince contains several typological features. The prince reflects a historical figure, that is, the Davidic king and the prophesied Messiah. Clearly, the figure is also prophetic, for Ezekiel speaks of a future society in his prophetic vision. As shown above, the leadership in the new society is prophetic, not a description of the author's time period. The figure is also eschatological. He is not a governor of the Persian period but the one who will exist when YHWH's glory returns (Ezek 43:1–12) and when the land is transformed (Ezek 47:1–12). The presence of the Messianic prince also shows the aspect of christological-soteriological typology. The prince also reflects an epochal institution, the monarchy, a pillar of Israel's society.[236] The figure also shows OT development since Ezekiel presents an unexpected development in the presentation of the Messiah by emphasizing YHWH's kingship instead of that of the human ruler.[237]

The prophecy also contains the typological feature of ambiguity. This ambiguity leads to numerous differing interpretations, for several questions arise when one thinks of the prince as the messianic figure. In addition to his reduced role as king, the text presents a few aspects that seem to preclude a christological interpretation.[238] For one, the text indicates that the prince has sons to whom he may give his inheritance (Ezek 46:16–18). In Christian Scripture, Jesus of Nazareth fulfills the messianic prophecies. He does not have sons and, after dying, rises from the dead to live forever (Ps 16:11; Ps 110:4; Heb 7:25), so he cannot die and leave his inheritance to anyone. Another concern is that the prince may not

---

the prophecies of Ezek 33–37 and Ezek 40–48 are so radically different that they must speak of distinct periods. Thus, the former speaks of the eschatological age, while the temple vision only prepares for such. Hence the prince takes on the role of the high priest. Besides the unity this study has demonstrated between the two sections of Ezekiel, another problem is with the picture of YHWH's kingship in the temple vision. How could such be said to only be an *interregnum* until the true Messiah appears?

236. Block, *Ezekiel 1–24*, 8. The pillars are covenant, temple, land, and king.

237. According to Cook, *Ezekiel 38–48*, 204–5, later OT texts may develop Ezekiel's presentation of the prince. Zech 4, in particular, notes a "diarchic polity," i.e., the two rulers, civic and cultic, leading worship (cf. Ezek 44:3).

238. Ellison, *Ezekiel*, 143, rightly states, "For the literalist the identity of the prince must be a major problem, for he cannot be the King who has returned, Jesus the Messiah."

approach past the gate to the inner court (Ezek 44:3).[239] Thus, he may not enter into the most holy place. Relatedly, the prince offers sacrifices, presumably for his own sins (Ezek 46:2, 12). The NT church held that Jesus is sinless and therefore need not offer sacrifice for his own sins (Heb 7:26–28). Because he is sinless, he is able to enter into the presence of YHWH (Heb 9:11–28).[240] Thus, these facts appear to contradict the NT presentation of Jesus as the messianic antitype.

These concerns need not rule out a typological interpretation. Typology does not mean that every detail finds its exact fulfillment in the antitype. For example, the early church saw Jesus as the fulfillment of the promised kingly descendant of David (2 Sam 7:14; Heb 1:5). Yet that very text, 2 Sam 7:14, speaks of that son as one who sins. Similarly, Heb 2:13 applies a prophecy of Isaiah and his biological children (Isa 8:18) to Jesus and his "spiritual" children. Therefore, concerns about details need not rule out typological interpretation. What matters is the meaning behind these regulations for the prince. The rule on inheritance intends to preclude the prince from abusing his power and taking land from the people (Ezek 46:16–18). The message is that the Messiah will deal equitably, unlike previous kings. Like the prophecy of Isa 8, one can interpret the prophecy of the prince's sons in a spiritual sense as those who belong to Jesus through union with him. As to the restriction of entrance to the most holy place, this again underscores YHWH's holiness. The text also underlines the significance of the HP. Ps 110 is the only passage that explicitly describes the Messiah as both priest and king, so one should not expect the kingly figure here to fulfill a priestly role. One must await the eschatological heightening of the antitype. Finally, as to the prince's sacrifices, this is simply the prophet's way of describing the prince's worship. He is one who himself is involved in worship of YHWH. The issue of the sacrificial system will be discussed in the section below. Suffice to say, the ambiguous nature of the prince in the vision points forward to typology, rather than arguing against it.

---

239. For example, Alexander, *Ezekiel*, 150, says, "He is not the Messiah. He is said to 'eat bread before [Yahweh]' (44:3). If he were Yahweh, this would be contradictory. In addition, he is to make sin offerings . . . for himself." Alexander concludes that the identity of the prince is unknown. Similarly, Gaebelein, *Ezekiel*, 314. As discussed below, the problem here is expecting a literal fulfillment (matching every detail) rather than a typological one.

240. Per Feinberg, *Ezekiel*, 257–58, the Messiah also functions as a priest, while here Ezekiel bars the prince from such activity.

Legislation: Furniture, Sacrifices, and Land

Ezekiel's new legislation begins in Ezek 43:13 and includes directions on the cult, priestly leadership, and land allotments. Excepting civil laws, Ezekiel's legislation regulates similar aspects of Israel's religious life as Moses's legislation does. As a result, some scholars focus on the historical development of the legislation, that is, the chronological relationship between Mosaic and Ezekielian legislation.[241] Regardless, Ezekiel's legislation never took root in Israelite society. Thus, the purpose of this part of the vision is not immediately apparent. Did Ezekiel, or later hands, actually intend for this legislation to replace the Pentateuchal version? How does this practical law-code fit with the lofty vision that surrounds it? Even Eichrodt says that the book goes from, as he calls it, "... the character of a great vision, a prophetic glimpse of God's act of fulfillment in the midst of his people ... [to] proclamations of divinely ordained statutes which depart from what is seen in visions and come down to earthly realities with all their sins and imperfections."[242] Due to the differences, Eichrodt unnecessarily concludes the presence of various hands of authorship. Other scholars, based on these apparently "earthly realities," conclude that the author intends for the legislation to be enacted.[243] Some believe this legislation should be enacted in the millennium.[244] Ellison rightly shows what is at stake when he says, "The sacrifices provide the real crux in [the vision's] interpretation. Make the sacrifices symbolic and the temple becomes symbolic too; take the temple literally and we have to agree that there will be animal sacrifices in the Millennium."[245] This section will answer the argument that the author of Ezekiel intends for his new legislation to actually be implemented at some point in the future, the millennium or otherwise. If he does not, then what is the legislation's purpose? While this study cannot examine each detail of the legislation,

---

241. Toy, "General Interpretation," xlvii, says that Ezekiel's legislation contradicts Deuteronomy and Leviticus, so Ezekiel presents a historical development.

242. Eichrodt, *Ezekiel*, 530. So also Feinberg, *Ezekiel*, 235–36.

243. Milgrom, *Ezekiel's Hope*, 55–60; Allen, *Ezekiel 20–48*, 269–70. Milgrom, *Ezekiel's Hope*, 60, says, "Ezekiel's utopia of the equal subdivision of the land is pure fantasy ... But the laws concerning the sanctuary, its personnel, and the *nasi* are viable and enforceable."

244. Rooker, "Evidence From Ezekiel," 119–34; Scofield, *New Scofield Reference Bible*, 883–84; Feinberg, *Ezekiel*, 234–35.

245. Ellison, *Ezekiel*, 140.

this section will discuss the main categories, that is, the sacrificial system, including the temple furniture, and the land allotments.

Temple Furniture

While for the most part the prophet describes the temple furniture during the temple tour, this section discusses the items in relation to the sacrificial system. The main issue respecting the temple furniture is that Ezek 40–48 does not mention some prominent aspects of the tabernacle and Solomonic temple. The absence of certain furniture may indicate changes in sacrificial legislation and thus impacts the vision's interpretation. Greenberg cautions against assuming meaning behind their absence, saying, "Omissions must remain obscure."[246] Admittedly, arguments from silence are difficult to make, and the prophet never explicitly states that the furniture is intentionally omitted.[247] Because of the importance of these items, however, their omission is more likely intentional.[248]

Notable omissions in this temple include a table of showbread (for the bread of the presence of YHWH), the bronze basin, the golden lampstand (menorah), and the ark of the covenant.[249] Haran suggests a historical reason for the absence of this furniture. He simply explains that Ezekiel's vision is based on the temple in its state after the deportation of Jehoaichin.[250] At that point, sauys Haran, the Babylonians had already taken the vessels, and, for Ezekiel, furniture out of sight is furniture out of mind. Haran's conclusion is unlikely, however. As Cook says, Ezekiel's

---

246. Greenberg, "Design and Themes," 193. He initially wonders if the omissions are meant to eradicate any "mythological" conception of God, but then he states that the presence of the table argues against this notion. Therefore, he remains agnostic on the issue.

247. Likewise Beale, *Temple and Church's Mission*, 355, admits, "Arguments from silence are difficult to prove or disprove. Therefore, whatever position is finally taken on this issue will be difficult to substantiate."

248. Beale, *Temple and Church's Mission*, 356, claims that the omission of nine major features of the traditional temple cumulatively imply an explanation beyond omission or merely a different focus on the writer's part.

249. In Ezek 41:21–22, Ezekiel sees an altar table. Some think this is the table of the showbread, since he calls it the "table before YHWH." The present table, though, is plainer, indicating it is not the table of showbread. The table of showbread was made of acacia wood overlaid with gold, while this one is simply made of wood. See Beale, *Temple and Church's Mission*, 354–55.

250. Haran, *Temples and Temple-Service*, 45.

vision is not held by such restraints.²⁵¹ The vision is not a historical description but a future projection. Moreover, Ezekiel surely knew of the items in the ancient tabernacle and first temple, so he could have incorporated them if he so desired. A different kind of explanation relates to the nature of the vision as that of a heavenly temple. Joyce argues that the bread of presence and menorah are not present because they are not necessary. Ezekiel, he says, sees the realities to which those items point (YHWH's glory and angels, respectively).²⁵² Joyce adds, "Such is Ezekiel's focus on YHWH himself that much else is simply eclipsed."²⁵³ Here Joyce exaggerates, though, since Ezekiel focuses on "much else," even precise measurements of doorjambs. As to seeing the heavenly temple, this view does not take into account other aspects of the vision that "localize" the temple, such as the land allotments.²⁵⁴

A better explication for the missing furniture is that the author shows an ideological intention in his omissions. The purpose is not to describe what items are and are not in a future physical temple, but to make theological claims. Commenting on Ezek 41:1–2, a description of the hall into the inner temple, Block says, "The absence of any reference to its decoration, furnishings, or function reflects the primary rhetorical concern to define sacred space, not to provide a blueprint for a construction project."²⁵⁵ What claim, then, does the author make? Kasher argues that the lack of objects in the temple shows YHWH's "bodily" occupation of the temple.²⁵⁶ Now that YHWH is physically present, objects symbolizing his residence are no longer necessary. However, Patton accurately points out that the absence of these items has the opposite effect of showing YHWH's physical presence.²⁵⁷ If YHWH were indeed present "anthropomorphically," items such as a table, lamp, and seat would be necessary for his physical presence. The items actually argue for anthropomorphism, so there must be another explanation for their absence.

The absence of certain furniture items, in fact, shows the typology of the vision, for this feature points forward to a greater fulfillment. The

---

251. Cook, *Ezekiel 38–48*, 165.

252. Joyce, "'Heavenly Ascent,'" 30.

253. Joyce, *Ezekiel*, 225.

254. Joyce, "'Heavenly Ascent,'" 17–41, sees Ezek 40–42 as the core vision of the temple, with other aspects accruing to the text later on.

255. Block, *Ezekiel 25–48*, 543.

256. Kasher, "Anthropomorphism," 197.

257. Patton, "Blueprint," 154.

absence of the ark of the covenant, as well as the table of bread for YHWH's presence, indicates that there is no longer a need for the localized presence of YHWH.[258] As the previous chapter detailed, YHWH's glory fills the entire temple (Ezek 43:5) and the land (Ezek 48:35). The absence of the ark aligns with the prophecy of Isa 66:1, "Thus says YHWH, 'The heavens are my throne, and the earth a footstool for my feet. What is this house that you would build for me and what is this place of my rest?'" YHWH no longer limits himself to a temple or the most holy place (the ark). Likewise, according to Jer 3:16–17, no need exists for the ark since YHWH's presence presides over all Jerusalem. While on one hand Ezekiel emphasizes YHWH's separation from sinners via his presence in the temple, the prophet also points forward to a heightened fulfillment. As the next chapter will show, this points to an understanding of YHWH's presence through Jesus (John 2:19–21), and the new heavens and new earth, where there is no ark or temple (Rev 21:22).

Other missing items demonstrate cosmic symbolism in the vision. The bronze sea basin represents the cosmic waters over which YHWH reigns. Likewise, the lamp (menorah) represents the tree of life. These items were discussed in the previous chapter, in light of how Ezek 47:1–12 portrays cosmic symbolism as the explanation for these items' absence. One final item with important ideological symbolism is the altar in Ezek 43:13–27. The altar description reflects language of the cosmic mountain, with the altar understood as the "bosom of the earth" and its highest point the "mountain of God."[259] The former term appears in Ezek 43:14, traditionally understood as the "base on the ground" of the altar. Block takes this to be a trench to catch the blood of slain animals.[260] The word חֵיק seems to best indicate the term "bosom," however. The phrase,

---

258. While the tabernacle/temple were never meant to contain YHWH physically, for he dwells in heaven (1 Kgs 8:27), nevertheless Israel saw YHWH as present among his people in the land in a unique way via the tabernacle/temple. YHWH was never hypostatically present over the ark, yet it represented his dwelling among them. Ezekiel's vision implies that this special dwelling extends beyond one room.

259. Fishbane, *Biblical Interpretation*, 370. Fishbane cites Albright, *From the Stone Age to Christianity*, in support. Block, *Ezekiel 25–48*, 600, claims that Albright erroneously derives the notion of "mountain of God" from an etymological link with an Akkadian cognate which Albright claimed to mean "mountain of the gods." Block contends that the Akkadian word does not actually have that sense. Unfortunately, though, Block does not address the possibility of the Hebrew word in Ezek 43:15 actually being הַר אֵל.

260. Block, *Ezekiel 25–48*, 597–98.

Block says, also links to the Akkadian designation of the platform of Marduk's temple, which was considered the bosom of the earth/underworld.[261] Next, the term for "mountain of God" is found in Ezek 43:15, הַהַרְאֵל. This is often translated as "altar hearth" since the context is a description of the altar (LXX says αριηλ, "altar"). The term also looks similar to אֲרִאֵיל, meaning altar or hearth.[262] Therefore the term is traditionally thought of as a *hapax*, a unique version of the word for altar, without a *yod* and with an added *he*. However, in ancient scribal practice of writing with no spaces (or vowels), the word exactly resembles הַר אֵל, the mountain of God. Moreover, the remainder of Ezek 43:15–16 uses the traditional terms for altar hearth. Only the first term (Ezek 43:15a) is different. Therefore, interpreters need not assume a *hapax*. Even if the first term refers to an altar hearth, however, perhaps the author intentionally changed this word to insert an echo for the reader that this temple is indeed the mountain of God.[263] Thus, these hints link to an ideological understanding of the temple as the cosmic mountain.

For Beale, the alteration of the temple furniture reflects a future alteration of the cosmos under Christ.[264] He rightly reacts against "literal" interpreters who see Jesus's physical reign as replacing the items of the furniture. However, his conclusion on the cosmos' alteration is unnecessary. Ezekiel does not actually see the new heavens in his vision. Instead, YHWH reveals a forward-pointing version of the temple.[265] The hints explained above in regards to the cosmic mountain demonstrate the underlying symbolism of the temple vision. The temple's furniture, and lack thereof, demonstrate the ideological intention of the text, rather than a description of a physical structure. The symbolism of this historical institution reflects a prophetic indicator in the text and points forward to an eschatological heightening. The meaning of certain items, such as the

261. Block, *Ezekiel 25–48*, 597; Fishbane, *Biblical Interpretation*, 370.
262. Block, *Ezekiel 25–48*, 600.
263. Milgrom, *Ezekiel's Hope*, 120.
264. Beale, *Temple and Church's Mission*, 358.
265. Beale, *Temple and Church's Mission*, 359, later approximates this view when, of his argument, he says, "Perhaps this last difficulty is *partly* [emphasis mine] solved by understanding that prophets typically 'depict the future in terms which make sense to its present' and 'clothe the purposes of God' in the thought-forms of the contemporary culture and learned tradition . . .'" Beale here essentially describes the nature of typology, but note he says this only partly solves the difficulty of his argument, since he does not ultimately hold a typological view. He must admit, though, to the presence of progressive revelation.

missing lampstand, demonstrates a soteriological context. Finally, the text shows ambiguity in that the author does not explicitly say that items are absent, or why. A close reading, however, leads one to see the omission as purposeful. Thus, this aspect of the vision reveals several indicators of typology.

The Sacrificial System

A significant portion of the legislation in Ezek 40–48 expounds the new sacrificial system. Due to the extensive detail present, some interpreters argue that the author must intend for the system to be implemented literally. For some who see a unity in the canon of Scripture, the implication must be that these sacrifices will be offered in an eschatological future. After all, Israel did not enact Ezekiel's new sacrificial legislation upon their return from exile.[266] Therefore, some conclude that Jews must implement this system in the time Rev 20:1–6 describes, the millennium. Alexander mentions the differences between this legislation and the Mosaic as proof that a new type of worship will exist in the millennium.[267] Since chapter 3 of this study already addressed the overall purpose of the sacrifices, to induce shame (Ezek 43:10–12), this section will examine the premillennialist arguments and demonstrate why their assumptions of a millennial enactment are unnecessary. Instead, the sacrificial system described is typological, pointing forward to an eschatological fulfillment in Jesus Christ.

Premillennialists generally provide three possible categories for understanding the sacrifices in the millennium. Some consider the sacrifices as a memorial akin to the Lord's Supper, others as a temporal forgiveness of sins, and yet others as "hypocatastasis."[268] The memorial view holds that the sacrifices are not effective in themselves to provide atonement. Instead, they look back to the sacrifice of Christ, and from thence derive their effectiveness.[269] Next, the "temporal forgiveness" position states that, just like previous sacrifices in the OT, the ritual accomplishes forgiveness of sins, but only temporarily or in a ceremonially cleansing

---

266. Rooker, "Evidence From Ezekiel," 129.

267. Alexander, *Ezekiel*, 133.

268. For a presentation of these views and a defense of sacrifices offered in Ezekiel's temple during the millennium see Rooker, "Evidence From Ezekiel," 131–34.

269. Rooker, "Evidence From Ezekiel," 131. See also Scofield, *New Scofield Reference Bible*, 908; Feinberg, *Ezekiel*, 234.

sense (Lev 1:4; 4:26–31; 5:16). All of these sacrifices throughout the OT ultimately find their efficacy only in the work of Jesus on the cross.[270] Alexander makes an analogy with the NT Christian's confession of sin. The confession does not actually accomplish forgiveness, but serves as a reminder. Similarly, the OT sacrifices were "picture lessons" to remind one of forgiveness.[271]

The third view is hypocatastasis. Hypocatastasis describes a figure of speech where the author refers to an object with one term, but without mentioning that object. Rooker provides the example of how prophets described future battles using language of spears, bows, and arrows, while in reality any contemporary fulfillment of such battles would not involve said weapons.[272] In the case of the legislation, Ezekiel uses the language of atoning sacrifices, but he does not actually mean that they are atoning. He simply has no concept or language for expressing Christ's atoning sacrifice in a way other than the sacrificial rituals of his day. In Ironside's words, "Prior to the work of the cross there could be no other way of presenting that work prophetically than by directing attention to such offerings as the people understood."[273] The notion of hypocatastasis developed to account for the objection that the sacrifice of Jesus abolishes the OT sacrificial system (Heb 7:27; 9:12, 26). As Scofield says, "The reference to sacrifices is not to be taken literally, in view of the putting away of such offerings [in Hebrews], but is rather to be regarded as a presentation of the worship of redeemed Israel, in her own land and in the millennial temple, using the terms with which the Jews were familiar in Ezekiel's day."[274] Rooker concludes, then, that Ezekiel describes future worship, but not the actual slaughtering of animals.[275]

One response to the memorial view is that, while the argument deals with the sacrifice of Christ, it does not adequately address the institution

---

270. Rooker, "Evidence From Ezekiel," 132. See also Alexander, "Ezekiel," 874.

271. Alexander, "Ezekiel," 874.

272. Rooker, "Evidence From Ezekiel," 133.

273. Ironside, *Ezekiel*, 305. Cited in Rooker, "Evidence From Ezekiel," 133. Ironside goes on to say, however, that Christ's sacrifice abolishes the sacrifices. He states in Ironside, *Ezekiel*, 288–89, that the sacrifices will be re-instituted at the time of great tribulation, but not in the millennial temple.

274. Scofield, *New Scofield Reference Bible*, 888.

275. Rooker, "Evidence From Ezekiel," 134. Ironside, *Ezekiel*, 288–89, argues that Christ fulfills the Ezekielian sacrifices.

of the Lord's Supper (Luke 22:14–23; 1 Cor 11:17–34).[276] According to the NT, Christ already instituted a ritual to remember his sacrifice, the Lord's Supper. What need would there be in the millennium to offer more sacrifices to remember the sacrifice of Christ?[277] Would not the converted Jews observe the ritual already instituted, the Lord's Supper (itself an observation of the Passover feast)?[278] Alexander holds that the Lord's Supper actually argues for the sacrificial system, for it provides an analogy of non-efficacious remembrance.[279] However, he simply states that they should be able to coexist without recognizing the hermeneutical trajectory of typological fulfillment. In other words, the Lord's Supper fulfills the role of the memorial of Christ's death that the sacrifices (e.g., Passover) anticipated. Another response is that the Lord's Supper and animal sacrifices are very different memorials.[280] The Lord's Supper is inherently backwards looking (Luke 22:19; 1 Cor 11:24–25), while the animal sacrifices look forward to a permanent cleansing for the one making the offering (Heb 9:9–13). Animal sacrifices also involve death, which the atonement of Christ intends to put away (Heb 9:22). How can sacrificial death be reinstituted after Christ's work? Additionally, Ezekiel does not call the sacrifices memorials, but states that the sacrifices make atonement.[281]

As to the second view of temporal forgiveness, one can scarcely reconcile such a position with Jesus's work on the cross accomplishing complete atonement. What would need would there be to return to a temporal sacrificial system when the permanent one has arrived? The author of Heb 10:18 describes the abolishment of sacrifices once complete

---

276. The following argument assumes a canonical reading of Scripture.

277. Ellison, *Ezekiel*, 142, writes, "In addition they [who disagree with Scofield] cannot see why, when water, bread and wine have met the symbolic needs of nearly a thousand generations of Christians, the Millennium will need more."

278. Feinberg, *Ezekiel*, 108, argues that the Lord's Supper will cease at the millennium and Ezekiel's sacrifices will replace it. Again, this does not square with the teaching of Hebrews or the commandment of Jesus. See Beale, *Temple and Church's Mission*, 345. Alexander, "Ezekiel," 876, states that the Lord's Supper will be for the church and the sacrifices for the Jews.

279. Alexander, "Ezekiel," 876.

280. Feinberg, *Ezekiel*, 234, makes an analogy to the Lord's Supper and the sacrificial system as equivalent memorials, thus for him validating the presence of sacrifices in the millennium.

281. Rooker, "Evidence From Ezekiel," 131; Beale, *Temple and the Church's Mission*, 344.

forgiveness is accomplished.[282] Alexander retorts that Heb 10:18 does not describe the abolishment of sacrifices that serve as "picture lessons." He claims, "Since the sacrifices were only pictures, they could never conflict with the sacrifice of the Messiah."[283] His argument fails to convince, however. The context of Hebrews is the Mosaic sacrificial system and the offerings abolished are Mosaic sacrifices. Whether or not the sacrifices are mere pictures or effective for atonement, the antitype has come, so the type fades into the distance (Heb 8:13).

Regarding the third view, hypocatastasis has some merit in the sense that Ezekiel is pointing forward typologically. However, merely using the term hypocastasis does not account for the extensive temple system Ezekiel describes. In other words, if the temple will physically be set up in the millennium, hypocatastasis means it remains empty of activity. Why, then, such detail of a temple to be set up? The activity Ezekiel describes in that temple is the sacrificial system. In the view of hypocastasis, one must explain the purpose of physical kitchens, a physical altar, an actual liturgical calendar, and more, in the context of an actually rebuilt temple. For example, will the people still gather for worship on these particular calendrical feast days, but simply not offer sacrifices? Thus, the view of hypocastasis falls short in a literalistic reading. Ellison writes, "Make the sacrifices symbolic and the temple becomes symbolic too."[284] One must provide a more developed explanation for what will actually occur during the millennium if this temple is a physical one.

A unique proponent of the premillennial view is Hullinger, in that he denies the memorial and hypocatastasis view of the sacrifices.[285] Hullinger states that the sacrifices, like those in the Mosaic legislation, will actually be effectual. However, he argues that "effectual" does not mean that they actually provide atonement. For him, they were never meant to. Hullinger's entire argument depends on his view of atonement. He states that atonement in the Levitical context indicates wiping, erasing, or cleansing rather than covering or propitiation.[286] Therefore, Hullinger

---

282. Ellison, *Ezekiel*, 141, says, "I require stronger evidence than this vision to accept against all the weight of New Testament evidence that the Levitical sacrifices will be reintroduced."

283. Alexander, "Ezekiel," 876.

284. Ellison, *Ezekiel*, 140.

285. Hullinger, "Millennial Sacrifices, Part 1," 40–57; Hullinger, "Millennial Sacrifices, Part 2," 166–79.

286. Hullinger, "Millennial Sacrifices, Part 1," 48.

says, cleansing will be necessary in the millennium because people will come to salvation but not have glorified bodies.[287] Without cleansing they may not be in the presence of YHWH's glory. He further states that the five references to atonement deal with cleansing inanimate objects or the people being made fit to approach God in worship (Ezek 43:20, 26; 45:15, 17, 20).[288] Hullinger then examines each sacrifice in Ezek 40–48 in light of its Levitical context. The burnt offering (Ezek 45:15, 17) shows complete devotion to God, which is not at odds with Christ's sacrifice.[289] The grain offering demonstrates dedication to God and a tribute to the deity.[290] The peace offering does not make peace with God, but expresses that one is already at peace with him.[291] The purification/purgation offering, he says, provides purification when one sins unintentionally, or contracts uncleanness for various reasons.[292] Moreover, the offering does not purify people but objects. Thus, in Ezek 40–48 the offering will purify the sanctuary from uncleanness, not forgive sin. The guilt/reparation offering, Hullinger says, means one is "liable to pay" a damage done.[293] One makes the offering when misappropriating items in the sanctuary, commits suspected transgression, or defrauds a neighbor. Apparently, the suspicion of transgression, rather than certainty, indicates to Hullinger that the sacrifice does not effectually cleanse sin. Thus, in Ezek 40–48, he says, the reparation offering does not imply atonement for sin. Therefore, Hullinger argues that each of the offerings in Ezek 40–48 serves a purpose other than atoning for sin in the sense of propitiation of wrath or removal of guilt.

Hullinger's argument falls short primarily in that he inaccurately redefines the meaning of atonement. For Hullinger to claim that the sacrifices in Ezek 40–48 do not contradict the sacrifice of Christ also applies necessarily to the Levitical sacrifices, thus meaning that Jesus's work does not fulfill those sacrifices either. The sacrificial system in Leviticus would still be in effect if they were merely modes of worship and not effectual for sin in any sense. On the contrary, Jesus's sacrifice abolishes

---

287. Hullinger, "Millennial Sacrifices, Part 1," 49–50.

288. Hullinger, "Millennial Sacrifices, Part 1," 51–52.

289. Hullinger, "Millennial Sacrifices, Part 1," 55.

290. Hullinger, "Millennial Sacrifices, Part 1," 56–57.

291. Hullinger, "Millennial Sacrifices, Part 2," 166. For mention of the peace offering see Ezek 43:27; 45:17; 46:2, 12.

292. Hullinger, "Millennial Sacrifices, Part 2," 169–73.

293. Hullinger, "Millennial Sacrifices, Part 2," 175.

the Levitical sacrificial system because they are both of the same nature, i.e., intended to remove guilt (Heb 7:27; 9:11–28; 10:11–14). Jesus's sacrifice is a propitiation making atonement and removing guilt (Rom 3:25; Heb 2:17; 1 John 2:2). Simply put, then, the sacrifices in Leviticus were intended to remove guilt and cleanse from sin, not merely to wipe away uncleanness. Ezekiel's vision does not explicitly alter this meaning in any instance.[294] Therefore, the natural reading of Ezekiel's vision is that in the new temple worshippers offer sacrifices for forgiveness of sin.[295] This view cannot square with a physical temple under Christ's reign in the millennial age. Furthermore, even if atonement was simply cleansing and not propitiation, Heb 9:12–14 presents the sacrifice of Christ as the once-for-all purification offering.[296]

Arguments for the observance of the sacrificial system in the future fall short. How, then, do the sacrifices fit into the vision? First, one must explain them in light of Mosaic legislation.[297] Then, one must show how they fit with the NT and the work of Christ. Regarding the differences with the Pentateuch, Toy presents the problem with a literal fulfillment, saying, "In any case, the supposition that Ezekiel's picture is symbolical does not remove the difficulty, since the prophet sets up as his standard of perfection something different from that of the Pentateuchal books."[298] In other words, why would Ezekiel alter the divinely ordained pattern of worship? The differences, in fact, demonstrate the typological nature of the legislation. Attempts, therefore, at harmonizing the legislation are misguided. Ezekiel does not intend to provide a new legislation for implementation, but to make distinct theological points by his changes.[299]

---

294. Differences in details occur between P and Ezekiel's sacrificial system, as shown in Milgrom, *Ezekiel's Hope*, 201–6. These differences relate to method, not meaning.

295. Cook, *Ezekiel 38–48*, 233, argues for the translation "propitiation" rather than "cover" or even "expiation" as better fitting the Zadokite understanding of YHWH's holiness (Ezek 45:15). Zimmerli, *Ezekiel 2*, 479, adds, "The expiatory significance of the sacrifice is emphatically expressed."

296. Duguid, *Ezekiel*, 521, fn. 21. Clearly, at least, the "atonement" for the altar in Ezek 43:19–20 is a purification offering for cleansing. See Block, *Ezekiel 25–48*, 609. This does not mean all further sin offerings described are only for cleansing.

297. Block, *Ezekiel 25–48*, 498, writes, "Perhaps the most significant issue in the interpretation of Ezek. 40–48 is the relationship of this vision to the Mosaic Torah."

298. Toy, "General Interpretation," xlvii. Recall that, overall, Toy argues that Ezekiel intends a literal fulfillment, but Toy cannot harmonize the Mosaic and Ezekielian legislations.

299. These changes are charted in Milgrom, *Ezekiel's Hope*, 219–20; Block, *Ezekiel*

Rather than trying to fit a text into an interpretation of Scripture, interpreters should ask, as Duguid puts it, "What distinctive truth does this particular passage teach?"[300] For example, Milgrom notes the changes in the offering of Ezek 45:18–25 as reflecting, he says, ". . . Ezekiel's obsession with purifying the sanctuary in preparation for the *pesah* . . ."[301] Ezekiel several times reinforces the need for purity by his changes.[302] He adds a bull offering for sin/purification on the fourteenth day of *Nisan*, at the beginning of Passover (Ezek 45:21–22; cf. Lev 23:5–7; Exod 12:1–14).[303] Ezekiel also adds a public Passover with a purification bull to purge the sanctuary (Ezek 45:18–20; cf. Num 9:1–14, where Passover is observed by families).[304] He prescribes sacrificing seven bulls rather than two (Ezek 45:23–25; cf. Num 28:17–23).[305] The Sabbath and new moon sacrifices are also generally greater in Ezekiel (Ezek 46:4–7).[306] In Block's words,

---

25–48, 673–77. Alexander, "Ezekiel," 872, argues that changes in Ezekiel exist to harmonize all the biblical covenants. He points to the absence of Yom Kippur and a high priest (the latter being disproven in this chapter). Alexander's point does not justify other changes, however. Changing the number of bulls sacrificed does not seem to help a new covenant believer at all. In addition, Alexander, "Ezekiel," 873–74, makes a very unsure argument for these aforementioned major changes, using words like "presumably," "argument from silence," and "it is difficult to be certain."

300. Duguid, *Ezekiel*, 522.

301. Milgrom, *Ezekiel's Hope*, 202.

302. As Duguid states, in addition to increased purity rites, Ezekiel's legislation has more animals sacrificed in the rites. Duguid, *Ezekiel*, 522, writes, "God is doing something greater than the former things, a greatness that shows itself in . . . the number of the sacrifices." Cook, *Ezekiel 38–48*, 249, adds, "Rather than 'contradicting' Mosaic Torah, Ezekiel 46 aims at *intensification*."

303. Milgrom, *Ezekiel's Hope*, 202.

304. Block, *Ezekiel 25–48*, 662–64, argues that the ritual of Ezek 45:18–20 is a onetime purification of the sanctuary rather than an annual preparation for Passover. On the other hand, note Cook, *Ezekiel 38–48*, 236–37. Per Cook, the context of this text is the annual rituals, rather than a one-time altar cleansing like Ezek 43. The decision on this question does not affect one's view on the nature of the sacrifices themselves, though a one-time sacrifice does more clearly point typologically to a future fulfillment. As to the public nature of Passover, Cook, *Ezekiel 38–48*, 238, points out that under Hezekiah and Josiah the feast was already centralized and communal. Still, Ezekiel diverges from Mosaic legislation.

305. Milgrom, *Ezekiel's Hope*, 208. Note, interestingly, that the new moon offering of P includes two bulls (Num 28:11) while in Ezekiel it includes only one (Ezek 46:6–7), so this example describes a decrease in sacrifices. Block, *Ezekiel 25–48*, 666, helpfully traces the evolution of the Passover, while noting that the people in Ezra 6:19–22 return to the original Mosaic form.

306. See charts in Block, *Ezekiel 25–48*, 673–74. In the new moon sacrifice Ezekiel

"The cult of the new order is preoccupied with holiness..."[307] Thus, Milgrom concludes, "One has to concede that Ezekiel is more than a priestly tradent. He is an *innovator*, a lawgiver, another Moses."[308] He presents, in Duguid's terms, "... vision in the form of legislation."[309] Ezekiel innovates to reflect the theology of his particular situation.

Next, how does the sacrificial system fit typologically with the NT work of Christ? Ezekiel's description of sacrifices fits the criteria of typology.[310] Again, the view of hypocastasis comes close to this notion. One correct aspect of hypocatastasis is that Ezekiel speaks only in language and concepts that he knows.[311] Ezekiel cannot describe a completely different type of worship any more than he can write his book in Chinese. The divine Author communicates through human authors with concepts they know. The difference between hypocatastasis and typology, though, is that typology does not require a physical temple to be constructed. So, Ezekiel's sacrificial legislation points typologically to the work of Christ in a way similar to how Levitical legislation does. Ezekiel describes the same offerings as Moses, only with some variations.[312] The original

---

legislates more grain offerings but fewer animals for slaughter. However, the daily offerings may be lesser in Ezekiel (see Ezek 46:13–14, cf. Num 28:1–8). Only one lamb is sacrificed, and only one ritual a day occurs, unless Ezekiel assumes the evening sacrifice. See on the evening sacrifice, Block, *Ezekiel 25–48*, 676. Cook, *Ezekiel 38–48*, 249, explains the lessening of new moon animal sacrifices as a way to elevate the Sabbath. Cook, *Ezekiel 38–48*, 248–49, also explains the fewer daily offerings (i.e., the lack of an evening sacrifice) as a reflection of the concern to shut the inner gate. Such an explanation also fits with Ezekiel's heightened concern for purity.

307. Block, *Ezekiel 25–48*, 667.

308. Milgrom, *Ezekiel's Hope*, 218.

309. Duguid, *Ezekiel*, 22. Block, *Ezekiel 25–48*, 677, calls this "... an ideational cultic calendar for the new age."

310. The criteria are a historical institution (sacrificial system), prophetic indicators (vision of the future), a heightened fulfillment (more rigorous purification), a soteriological context ("I will accept you;" Ezek 43:27), ambiguity, epochal institutions (a major development in the sacrificial system), and OT development (developing previous legislation).

311. Beale, *Temple and Church's Mission*, 343, writes, "Hence, it is not incorrect to say that Ezekiel speaks in the language and images familiar to his audience in portraying sacrifices in a temple to prophesy about the escalated redemptive-historical realities of Christ's sacrifice..." Ironically, Alexander, "Ezekiel," 871, makes statements that sound very similar. He describes the vision as being to Israelites past, present, and future, having Israelite concepts, with the purpose of providing hope.

312. Ezekiel includes the burnt offering (Ezek 40:38–39; 43:18, 24, 27; 44:11; 45:15–25; 46:2, 4, 12, 13), grain offering (Ezek 42:13; 44:29; 45:15–25; 46:5, 7, 11,

purposes for each offering are unchanged, as Ezekiel does not explicitly redefine any of them.[313] The relevant offerings do effect atonement in Ezekiel's system (Ezek 45:17).[314] These atoning sacrifices point forward to the one provided by Christ.[315] Hence, in the new heavens and new earth, heavily based on Ezekiel's vision, neither temple nor sacrificial system exists, for "... its temple is the Lord God the Almighty and the Lamb" (Rev 21:22b). Ezekiel's sacrificial legislation points forward to the fulfillment in the sacrificed Lamb.[316] Moreover, the changes in Ezekiel's vision reflect a heightened burden for holiness and purity. This burden points typologically to the future purity of God's people. Through the sacrificial work of Jesus Christ, the bride is clothed with fine linen, bright and pure, fit for the presence of YHWH (Rev 19:6–9).

According to the canon of Scripture, then, Ezekiel's sacrificial legislation will not be enacted in the future any more than the Levitical sacrificial legislation will be restored, for both are types. As described in this section, Ezekiel's sacrificial system reflects a historical institution, but is prophetic, eschatological, and christological-soteriological. Ezekiel's legislation also contains ambiguity, hence Rabbi Hananiah ben Hezekiah's burning of three hundred barrels of oil to reconcile the legislation with the Pentateuch.[317] The sacrifices also reflect an epochal change of the in-

---

13–15, 20), peace offering (Ezek 43:27; 45:15, 17; 46:2, 12), sin offering (Ezek 40:39; 42:13; 43:19, 21–22, 25; 44:27, 29; 45:17, 19, 22–23, 25; 46:20), and guilt offering (Ezek 40:39; 42:13; 44:29; 46:20).

313. For an explanation of the offerings in Leviticus, see Morales, *Who Shall Ascend?*, 122–43.

314. Block, *Ezekiel 25–48*, 532, says, "The primary function of the holocaust [עֹלָה] was propitiatory, to turn away divine wrath, and expiatory, to atone for sin." According to Morales, *Who Shall Ascend?*, 125, "While the precise understanding of the Hebrew verb ... typically translated 'atone', has been complicated by its possible roots and cognates, its scriptural usage implies a twofold meaning: ransom from death and purification from pollution—both functions being involved by varying degrees in atonement, according to context."

315. Block, *Ezekiel 25–48*, 612–13, discusses this as an implication for a Christian reading of the sacrificial system in Ezekiel.

316. See the following chapter for discussion of Rev 21–22. Block, *Ezekiel 25–48*, 659, writes, "It is evident from these lists [Ezek 43:13–17], that in Ezekiel's new order sin will continue to be a problem for the nation." This is correct if one expects a literal fulfillment. But seeing the sacrifices typologically eradicates the need to include sin's presence in the future. Sin is dealt with, and *that* is the point of presenting the sacrifices. The system is Ezekiel's way of describing that, in this new society, sin is dealt with through sacrifice. The canon later explains this sacrifice as being that of Jesus the Christ.

317. For the story, see again *B. Shabbat* 13b, cited in Duguid, *Ezekiel*, 17–18.

stitution, moving away from the Mosaic legislation and towards a greater fulfillment. In fact, the only element of typology missing here is further OT development, for the OT does not mention Ezekiel's legislation in later texts, though Ezekiel develops earlier Mosaic legislation.[318] Typology, then, explains why Ezekiel does not simply prophesy a sinless world without a need for sacrifice (akin to Isa 65:17–25).[319] While perhaps he could have done so, this was not his method, nor need it have been. Instead, he presents an eschatological world in his own terms, yet not literally describing a system to be implemented. Through the sacrifices he typologically depicts a holy God and a purified people.

The Land

A final matter in Ezekiel's vision may point to a typological fulfillment, that is, the prophet's description of the boundaries of the new Israel (Ezek 47:13—48:29). Here again a number of scholars believe the very detailed physical descriptions of land measurements and boundaries show evidence for a literal fulfillment.[320] In a comment on Ezek 48:15–20, Feinberg writes,

> Notice once again the great minuteness of detail. This is more than strange, it is inexplicable, if all the statements are to be taken symbolically. As far as we are aware, no such abundance of details occurs anywhere else in Scripture outside the instructions for the construction of the tabernacle and its priestly service, which no orthodox expositor feels called upon to interpret other than with strict literalness. Then it is only consistent to do the same here. No commanding considerations indicate otherwise.[321]

---

318. Haggai, however, prophesies a greater glory in the temple, while Malachi condemns the corruption of the contemporary sacrificial system. Neither of these prophets explicitly develops Ezekiel.

319. Cook, *Ezekiel 38–48*, 234, objects, "A literary utopia is *not* the eschaton, where evil and death are defeated by God, but an alternate world that exits [sic] alongside present reality and challenges it."

320. A few interpreters like Scofield, *New Scofield Reference Bible*, 883–95, and Ellison, *Ezekiel*, 137–44, hardly discuss the land. Possibly they take for granted that if the text speaks of a millennial period, the land description in Israel will be fulfilled literally.

321. Feinberg, *Ezekiel*, 277.

Elsewhere he says, "Suffice it to say, the geographical locations are so exact that they cannot mean other than literal places."[322] Alexander also reads the vision in the context of YHWH's promise in Ezek 37:22, 25 to regather all of Israel into the land.[323] In his mind, Ezek 40–48 surely describes such a fulfillment. As with the previous sections, though, the details of the text actually indicate a different understanding. The prophet presents the boundaries as idealized, i.e., replete with theological meaning, what Duguid calls "theolog[y] in geographical form."[324] Block puts it similarly, saying, "[O]ne should construe this document not as a literary photograph of the land of Israel but as a cartographic painting by an artist with a particular theological agenda."[325] This section will present three aspects of the text that show theological intentions—the extent of the boundaries, the mention of all tribes, and the topological features of the boundaries.

As to the extent of the boundaries, Ezekiel basically reflects influence from Num 34:1–12, a description of the "promised land" (Gen 13:14–17; Ezek 47:14).[326] Notably, Israel never fully inherited this land (Josh 13–21).[327] Interestingly, though, Ezekiel's land does not include certain portions the people inherited under Joshua and David, namely, the Transjordan. Block contends that this is because YHWH never promised the Transjordan to Israel.[328] Also, the author of Num 32:6, 13–15, Cook notes, "... [is] *particularly negative* about Gad and Reuben's proposal to occupy the Transjordan."[329] Therefore, Ezekiel's prophecy describes the long-awaited

322. Feinberg, *Ezekiel*, 274.

323. Alexander, "Ezekiel," 871.

324. Duguid, *Ezekiel*, 541.

325. Block, *Ezekiel 25–48*, 723. Blenkinsopp, *Ezekiel*, 233, writes, "We are therefore invited to read [the boundary description] more as a utopian statement ... than as a program for national emancipation."

326. Duguid, *Ezekiel*, 541; Block, *Ezekiel 25–48*, 710–12. The northeast portion of the land is larger in Ezekiel's plan than in Num 34 and includes the areas of Damascus and Hauran (see Ezek 47:18; Block, *Ezekiel 25–48*, 716–17). The prophet provides no explicit reason for this expansion.

327. See Cook, *Ezekiel 38–48*, 277, where he cites his helpful diagram located at https://goo.gl/FDxxky. Ezekiel's prophesied land is far bigger than Joshua's conquered territory.

328. Block, *Ezekiel 25–48*, 716.

329. Cook, *Ezekiel 38–48*, 279. Cook explains this as a theological submission to the Priestly tradition. Another small detail in describing boundaries is that Ezekiel begins his description in the north and moves counterclockwise, whereas Numbers begins in the south moving counterclockwise. Cook, *Ezekiel 38–48*, 288–89, argues helpfully that the ordering of the tribes in Ezekiel reflects the ordering around the

fulfillment of YHWH's promise to give Israel the land. Not only does YHWH provide the land of Canaan he swore to Abraham, and the land he promised to Moses, but even more land in the northeast sector around Hauran. Like the river of Ezek 47:1–12, the prophet gives a theological picture of YHWH's overabundant blessing on Israel in the future.

The second important point of the text lies in the distribution of the land to the tribes (Ezek 47:21–23). Levenson calls this manner of distribution "... a deliberate attempt to recreate the archaic period in Israel's history."[330] All twelve tribes of Israel receive an inheritance, for they are reunited in fulfillment of the promise of Ezek 37:16–23.[331] Since the tribe of Levi does not have its own allotment, Ephraim and Manasseh each receive one so as to keep the portions at twelve. Also, Judah's territory moves slightly upward, ironically making it practically a northern tribe.[332] In addition, the sojourner receives part of the inheritance, whereas Levitical law allowed sojourners to live among Israel (Lev 19:33–34) and convert (Exod 12:43–48), but always to be in dependence on others economically (Deut 24:17–22).[333] A sojourner receiving inheritance, Levenson writes, "... [is] more radical than anything else in all the legal corpora of the Hebrew Bible."[334] One can see, then, the theological intentions of apportioning the land. This feature does not automatically rule out a literal interpretation, but a literal fulfillment raises questions like why Judah's territory would move north.

Finally, in how YHWH draws the land boundaries, Ezekiel provides a significant clue for reading the text. Allotments run east to west on straight lines, with the portions stacked one on top of the other, ignoring geography (Ezek 48:1–7).[335] Scripture typically arranges Israel's geogra-

---

wilderness tabernacle in Num 2–3.

330. Levenson, *Program of Restoration*, 112.

331. Duguid, *Ezekiel*, 542; Block, *Ezekiel 25–48*, 708–9, 722.

332. Cook, *Ezekiel 38–48*, 288; Levenson, *Program of Restoration*, 188; Duguid, *Ezekiel*, 544. Brodsky, "Utopian Map in Ezekiel," 20–26, argues for a democratization in the tribal allotments.

333. Block, *Ezekiel 25–48*, 717–18, adds that inheritance falls to long-term residents, not just any sojourner.

334. Levenson, *Program of Restoration*, 123. Thus, as Block, *Ezekiel 25–48*, 718, argues, this passage fits well with Isa 56:3–8, a text that scholars often pit against Ezek 44 in its vision of the foreigner coming to worship YHWH. Thus, one should better understand Ezek 44 as forbidding the idolatrous foreigners from entering the temple as they did in preexilic and exilic times.

335. Beale, *Temple and Church's Mission*, 342. Beale cites Ellison, *Ezekiel*, 139, for

phy north-south, Block notes, with its coast on the west, central spine, and Jordan River on the east.[336] Ezekiel's east-west division provides some equality among tribes, but, in Duguid's words, "It is far more fundamentally a way of orientating the entire land along the sacred east-west axis of the temple."[337] Block writes, "The effect is highly artificial," and Cook calls the division ". . . fine-tuned and geometrically precise, but also geographically implausible."[338] The borders, he adds, ". . . run roughshod over all preceding history and tradition of inhabitation . . . ," and they ignore geological factors and terrain that provide natural boundaries, unlike the outer boundaries Ezekiel describes.[339] Brodsky writes, "The description of tribal allocations . . . is entirely symbolic. The tribal territories seem to hover over the land, since no landmark anchors them in place."[340] The territories make an ideological (theological) claim rather than intending to describe a literal land.

Such a division ignoring geographical features is practically impossible to implement. Proponents of a physical fulfillment respond that the land will be transformed supernaturally.[341] Feinberg says, "This approach [that the land distributions are geographically impossible] is unsatisfactory from a number of angles, but chiefly because it bases all on a naturalistic foundation without due recognition to the supernatural features inherent in the chapters."[342] Feinberg's claim, though, is unfair. This study does not argue that supernatural changes are impossible, but that the text never describes any supernatural changes taking place, especially not in

---

pointing out this feature first. Contra Greenberg, "Idealism and Practicality," 59–66, who argues that, though the map is ideal, it is still realistic.

336. Block, *Ezekiel 25–48*, 722.

337. Duguid, *Ezekiel*, 544. Block, *Ezekiel 25–48*, 722–23, also argues that the east-west distribution promotes equality among tribes. He adds, though, that some inequity is present because the northern tribes inherit far more land, seeing as the border goes to Hauran. Thus Block, *Ezekiel 25–48*, 723, argues against an "ideal map," rather calling it "an artificial ideal." Still, Block agrees that Ezekiel's map is theological geography.

338. Cook, *Ezekiel 38–48*, 287.

339. Cook, *Ezekiel 38–48*, 287. Block, *Ezekiel 25–48*, 722, also notes the rejection of historical precedents, calling some correspondences coincidental.

340. Brodsky, "Utopian Map in Ezekiel," 22.

341. For example, Alexander, "Ezekiel," 868, argues, "Geographical changes will be necessary prior to the fulfillment of chs. 45, 47–48; therefore, one should not look to past or present fulfillments of these chapters but to the future."

342. Feinberg, *Ezekiel*, 236.

a millennium.³⁴³ Ezekiel's descriptions are very matter-of-fact. The miraculous river (Ezek 47:1–12) certainly could physically exist if YHWH desired to supernaturally create one. However, the argument here is that the text shows a more profound fulfillment than a merely physical one. An assumption of changed topography is thus unwarranted. Ezekiel's message, then, is that of an "idealized" map. The land's straight boundaries reinforce one of the purposes of the temple precinct's boundaries, to provide order amidst chaos and trauma.³⁴⁴ Additionally, as the section on Ezek 48:35 noted, the geography draws attention to YHWH's sanctuary.³⁴⁵ Though the *terumah* is not literally in the center, the map revolves around the sacred area. Overall, though, this description of the new land shows that the map is highly ideological.

These three features—the extent of the boundaries, the mention of all tribes, and the topological features of the boundaries—reveal typology in the text. The historical land of Israel provides a referent to which the prophet gives a prophetic indicator. The greater extent of the land shows a heightened fulfillment. The return of all tribes shows the soteriological context and links the text with the earlier promise of Ezek 37. The text shows ambiguity when it comes to the straight east-west boundaries. Some think this division of land can literally be implemented, but the notion seems impossible, and therefore must point to a theological rather

---

343. Ezekiel never uses the term millennium, but clues hint that he describes an eschatological event (contra Block, *Ezekiel 25–48*, 504–5, who denies the presence of eschatological language). Thus, one could interpret the text as describing something akin to the new heavens and new earth, where there may be changed topography. However, such a conclusion must be derived from studying Rev 21–22, not reading that text back into Ezek 40–48. Premillennialist scholars, on the other hand, read Rev 20:1–9 back into Ezek 40–48. Feinberg, *Ezekiel*, 271, also begins his section on the land saying, "Throughout the prophets of the Old Testament (see notably Zech. 14) there is a constant line of truth indicating that in the age of earth's climax amazing and far-reaching physical and geographical changes will take place in the earth, especially in the land of promise itself." So, Feinberg also includes other OT prophecies in his reading of Ezekiel. This study argues that Ezekiel's vision *in se* points typologically forward, but does not itself describe any change in topography.

344. Simon, "Ezekiel's Geometric Vision," 414.

345. Duguid, *Ezekiel*, 544–45, argues that the temple is located more centrally among the tribes. He argues that the tribal strips are equal (Ezek 47:14) and since seven are north of the *terumah* and five are south, the new temple is close to Shiloh, thirty miles north of the old temple mount. Cook, *Ezekiel 38–48*, 290, argues that Duguid takes Ezek 47:14 too literally. Cook is more likely correct, for the tribes north of Reuben inherit far more land to the east. The equality probably relates only to the straight lines.

than literal fulfillment. As for OT development, though later OT texts like Ezra-Nehemiah do not reflect fulfillment of Ezekiel's prophecy, Ezekiel clearly develops previous understandings of the land by heightening the promise of Num 34 and the physical fulfillment in Joshua. Thus, rather than arguing for a physical fulfillment, the land description fulfills the criteria of typology.

Conclusion: Legislation, Sacrifices, Land

One of the most forceful arguments for a physical temple is the presence of Ezekielian legislation. On the surface, the presence of a sacrificial system and land allotments brings the vision "down to earth."[346] However, a closer look shows a far different picture. The answers above to these objections deal a severe blow to the "literal" temple view. The text itself actually contains its own clues that the legislation and land should not be implemented. Why, then, so much detail in the sacrificial legislation and the land boundaries? Each piece of the text shows either ideological differences with the Pentateuch to state a theological point or contains a clue that points toward a typological fulfillment. The texts at each point show most, if not all, of the criteria for typology. In discussing the rhetorical function of these aspects of Ezekiel's vision, Ezekiel's purpose is, Renz says, ". . . to provide a vision for the people as a whole, an exilic community which was tempted to assimilate to its environment."[347] In other words, Ezekiel's words are not merely to elevate a certain school (Zadokites) above the people, as many claim to be the purpose of such great detail, but to provide hope for the people. The hope lies in the vision's eschatological fulfillment. Renz further writes,

> Just as the book of Ezekiel may well have inspired those who decided to return, so the fact that a return took place and the temple was rebuilt lends further credibility to the book. Even if the return from exile was a less remarkable event than anticipated, it was necessary for the establishment of a paradigm by which future experiences could be interpreted. Only then could Ezekiel's vision receive an eschatological and cosmic interpretation and the question whether Israel had really returned or was still in exile . . . could arise. In fact, it might well be that the influence of Ezekiel in later times was greatest among those who

346. Recall Eichrodt, *Ezekiel*, 530.
347. Renz, *Rhetorical Function*, 245.

were not content with seeing the fulfillment of Ezekiel's vision in the Jerusalem establishment.[348]

Another way to explain Renz's words is via the lens of typology. Ezekiel establishes a paradigm for a future eschatological fulfillment. Indeed, later interpreters saw the text this way because of these typological features inherent in the text. To these later interpreters, particularly in the NT, this study will now turn.

---

348. Renz, *Rhetorical Function*, 240–41.

5

Ezekiel's Temple Vision in the New Testament

(Gospel of John, Revelation 21–22)

Introduction

TYPOLOGY INHERENTLY LOOKS FORWARD. The previous chapters argued that the text of Ezek 40–48 contains many features of typology. Key texts demonstrate the forward-looking, eschatological, and christological-soteriological character of the vision. Additionally, aspects of the vision that some claim point to a physical temple actually indicate typology. Tellingly, then, no future generations have physically constructed Ezekiel's temple. The author of Ezra-Nehemiah describes the postexilic regathering and rebuilding of the temple, but the temple and land looked nothing like what Ezekiel prophesied. Legislation was more Mosaic than Ezekielian. Nor does the subsequent Herodian temple reflect much influence from Ezekiel.[1]

Even so, Ezekiel's vision did not disappear from the consciousness of religious communities dependent on the OT.[2] Later interpreters meditated on the vision and developed different symbolic understandings. Ezekiel influenced the *merkabah* tradition that developed among a

---

1. The second temple period does reflect the influence of the Zadokites in the priestly lineage.

2. One can find a helpful summary of how communities in the intertestamental period used Ezek 40–48 in Robinson, *Temple of Presence*, 32–77; Stevenson, *Power and Place*, 187–213.

mystical Jewish community, not only with Ezek 1 but also Ezek 43:1–12.[3] More substantially, the Qumran community looked to Ezekiel's vision to understand their identity.[4] The *Florilegium* shows that the group saw themselves as the true spiritual temple, spiritualizing the OT teaching on tabernacle/temples.[5] The *Songs of Sabbath Sacrifice* (4Q400–407), also shows particular influence from Ezek 40–48 regarding the community's understanding of what the heavenly temple looks like.[6] Martínez writes, "Pour l'aueteur des *ShirShabb* et pour la communaute qumranienne le temple future d'Ezechiel est une realite presente dans le ciel."[7] Even though they opposed the Herodian temple, the members of the Qumran community did not see Ezek 40–48 as the true temple they should build on earth.[8] Furthermore, another intertestamental text, *1 Enoch*, uses language from Ezek 40–48 to describe a vision of heaven.[9] In light of the eschatological character of Ezekiel's text, though, one should not be surprised that later interpreters "spiritualized" Ezekiel's temple or viewed it as symbolic in different ways.[10]

The nascent Christian community, accepting the Hebrew Bible as Scripture, also demonstrates in the New Testament (NT) how Ezek 40–48 shaped their theology. A canonical reading of Christian Scripture shows that the NT depends significantly on Ezekiel, including Ezek

---

3. Boustian, "Hekhalot Literature," *DEJ*, 719–21; Newsom, "Merkabah Exegesis," 11–30.

4. Martínez, "Qumran," 441–52; Gurtner and Perrin, "Temple," *DJG*, 941; Beale, *Temple and Church's Mission*, 338; Manning, *Echoes of a Prophet Ezekiel*, 42–48.

5. The *Florilegium* speaks of the temple as a "sanctuary of men," indicating their conception of a non-physical temple (4Q174). See Vermes, *Dead Sea Scrolls*, 525.

6. Vermes, *Dead Sea Scrolls*, 329–39. For discussion see Davila, "Macrocosmic Temple," 1–19.

7. Martínez, "Qumran," 448. Author's translation, "For the author of the *Sabbath Songs* and for the Qumran community, the future temple of Ezekiel is a present reality in heaven."

8. Martinez, "Qumran," 441–52. The Dead Sea Scrolls also contain a temple plan in "The Temple Scroll" (11QT), with similarities and differences to Ezekiel's temple. See Vermes, *Dead Sea Scrolls*, 191–220. Whether all these documents represent a monolithic theology or that of different communities is difficult to parse.

9. *1 Enoch* 14–15 in particular shows Ezekiel's influence. For more, see Nickelsburg, "Temple According to 1 Enoch," 7–24.

10. Robinson, *Temple of Presence*, 77, after examining second-temple literature, concurs, saying, "The hypothesis that Christian authors, such as John [in Revelation], might have used Ezekiel's visions to communicate their own distinctive ideologies is, thus, thoroughly plausible."

40–48. As demonstrated earlier, typology is one way that early Christians saw Jesus as the fulfillment of the OT Scriptures (Rom 5:14; Rom 15:4; 1 Cor 10:6; Heb 7:15; 1 Pet 3:21). Indeed, the writers of the NT, or at least of the Gospel of John and Revelation, used Ezek 40–48 as typology, not as describing a physical structure to be built in the future. This chapter examines John's Gospel and Revelation because these works provide the most extensive inner-biblical exegesis with Ezek 40–48.[11] They are the clearest examples of typological fulfillment of the passage. For the Gospel of John, Ezekiel's temple is a type of Jesus Christ. For Revelation, the temple points forward as a type to the new heavens and new earth, that is, the new Jerusalem.

The Gospel of John: Ezekiel's Temple Is a Type of Jesus

Introduction

A significant amount of scholarly literature on John in recent times contends for the importance of the temple in the Fourth Gospel's theology.[12] Köstenberger even holds that the second temple's destruction propelled the writing of the gospel and consequently its presentation of Jesus as the true temple.[13] Alongside these studies of the Fourth Gospel, scholars have developed important biblical-theological studies of the temple that include John's Gospel.[14] Even so, scholars have not explored in as much detail the particular role of Ezekiel's temple vision (Ezek 40–48) as a background for John's presentation of Jesus as the temple.[15] A few studies have

---

11. Unfortunately, space does not permit an extensive look at the entire NT and its typological use of Ezek 40–48. That important endeavor should be undertaken in the future.

12. See the recent studies by Barker, *King of the Jews*; Chanikuzhy, *Jesus, the Eschatological Temple*; Hoskins, *Jesus as Fulfillment of the Temple*; Um, *Temple Christology in John's Gospel*; Coloe, *God Dwells with Us*; Kinzer, "Temple Christology in the Gospel of John," 447–64; Salier, "Temple in John," 121–34.

13. Köstenberger, "Composition of the Fourth Gospel," 69–108.

14. See the discussion of temple in John's Gospel in Gurtner and Perrin, "Temple," 944–45; Clowney, "Final Temple," 156–89; Beale, *Temple and Church's Mission*; Morales, *Who Shall Ascend?*, 257–307; Köstenberger, "John," 415–512.

15. For example, only one sentence is given to Ezek 40–48 on the article for the biblical theology of the temple in McKelvey, "Temple," 806–11. Keener, *Spirit in the Gospels and Acts*, 159, states, "The use of Ezekiel's new-temple image is probably more significant for the Fourth Gospel than has been hitherto realized . . . Jesus is the new temple . . . Some of John's conception of that new temple is apparently derived from

dealt with the book of Ezekiel as a background or source of temple theology for the Gospel of John, but these studies do not treat the topic in sufficient detail.[16] While the garden of Eden, the tabernacle, and Solomon's temple are important sources of information for a biblical-theological understanding of Jesus as the temple, Ezek 40–48 also provides worthy consideration. In light of the gap in the literature, this section will argue that Ezekiel's temple vision is an important background for understanding the Gospel of John's theology of Jesus as the temple. To prove this claim, the study will examine the major texts from the Gospel of John that deal with Jesus as the true temple. These include the prologue (John 1:14), the temple cleansing (John 2:13–22), the Samaritan woman conversation (John 4:19–24), the living water proclamation (John 7:37–39), and the farewell discourse (John 14:1–3).[17] In each section, the study focuses on lexical, thematic, and/or theological connections John makes with Ezek 40–48.[18] This section contends that Ezekiel's vision influenced John's explanation of a new eschatological temple, one made without hands, the temple of Jesus's body, where God's presence would dwell among his people.[19]

Ezekiel." One recent work is Peterson, *John's Use of Ezekiel*, though he does not focus exclusively on Ezek 40–48.

16. See Manning, *Echoes of a Prophet*, 150, commenting, "Although John certainly presents Jesus as the new temple at times, it is difficult to establish verbal parallel to any passage in Ezekiel." Vawter, "Ezekiel and John," 450–58, compares Ezekiel and John, but totally neglects the temple theme. The best treatment is found in Fowler, "The Influence of Ezekiel in the Fourth Gospel." However, Fowler only focuses a few pages of his work on Ezekiel's temple.

17. Some texts that may advance temple theology but cannot be dealt with here are John 1:51, John 10, and John 17. Connections with Ezek 40–48 are less obvious in these texts.

18. In this work "John" simply refers to the traditional author of the book. Space does not permit a defense of Johannine authorship, and its relevance to the matter at hand may only lie in the dating of the book, which would tie the thrust of the Gospel's message to the destruction of the temple. The connections with Ezekiel, however, do not depend on who authored the Fourth Gospel.

19. Fowler, "Influence of Ezekiel," 121, writes, "It would appear, then, that Jesus' claim to rebuild the Temple . . . is best understood in light of the eschatological expectation that was inspired, in a large measure, by the vision of Ezekiel."

The Word Dwelt among Us (John 1:14)

The prologue (John 1:1–18) serves as the introduction to the Gospel of John, highlighting many of the themes that will recur in the narrative.[20] Thus, the presence of a temple theme in the prologue strongly indicates that this is a major theme of the Gospel as a whole. The prologue introduces Jesus as the Word (λόγος), which is not directly a temple image. However, John 1:14 says that the Word became flesh and dwelt (ἐσκήνωσεν) among us, a strong allusion to the tabernacle. Yet Ezekiel's temple helps illumine the concept of the Word dwelling among mankind.

By the use of σκηνόω (John 1:14) the writer alludes to the tabernacle or tent of meeting motif in the Pentateuch.[21] The noun form of the word occurs in Exod 25:9 LXX to refer to the tabernacle and in Exod 33:7 to the tent of meeting. The author of the Fourth Gospel, then, shows that the Word and glory that previously dwelled with Israel comes to earth to dwell among his people.[22] Another possible allusion to the tabernacle in John 1:14 is the term δόξα ("glory"). The Hebrew word for tabernacle, מִשְׁכָּן, and the verb to dwell, שָׁכַן, are both cognates of the later rabbinic term שְׁכִינָה, which means "glory." The tabernacle (מִשְׁכָּן), where God dwelt (שָׁכַן), was the manifestation of YHWH's glory (שְׁכִינָה).[23] Therefore, in the Fourth Gospel, the claim that "we have beheld his glory" (John 1:14) is a claim of beholding the fulfillment of the cloud that dwelt with the people in the tabernacle and/or temple.[24]

What does this text, then, have to do with Ezekiel's temple? In the OT, God's dwelling place shifted from the tabernacle to the temple

---

20. Carson, *John*, 111.

21. Koester, *Dwelling of God*, 100–107; Ridderbos, *John*, 50–51; Beasley-Murray, *John*, 14; Schnackenburg, *John: Volume One*, 269–70; Carson, *John*, 127–28. Others see a reference to Wisdom making her dwelling as in Sirach 24:8. On this see Haenchen, *John 1*, 119; Lindars, *John*, 94. However, a reference to Wisdom does not rule out the tabernacle theme, since the text in Sirach appears to be an "intermediary" between the Pentateuch and Prologue. So Raymond E. Brown, *John I–XII*, 33.

22. Carson, *John*, 127. Kerr, *Temple of Jesus' Body*, 121–23, provides an extensive look into the Exodus background of this verse.

23. Evans, *Word and Glory*, 82. The rabbinic term comes after the first century and one cannot be sure that it was in use by the time of the Fourth Gospel. However, Brown, *John I–XII*, 33, writes, "The theology of the *shekinah* was known at that time ..."

24. Carson, *John*, 128; Köstenberger, "Destruction," 98; Evans, *Word and Glory*, 185–68.

during Solomon's reign (2 Sam 7; Ps 43:3 [Eng.]; 46:4–5 [Eng.]).[25] However, YHWH's glory departed the temple in the Babylonian exile, just as Ezekiel prophesied (Ezek 8–11). Ezekiel, though, later promised restoration, saying, "And I will set my sanctuary [מִקְדָּשׁ] among them forever. And my dwelling [מִשְׁכָּן] will be with them, and I will be to them their God, and they will be to me a people" (Ezek 37:26–27).[26] The LXX for "dwelling" in this passage is κατασκήνωσίς, which has the same root as the "dwelling" in John 1:14. This promise harkens back to Lev 26:1–13, where God promises the covenant blessing of dwelling among his people. God's covenant promise in Ezek 37, then, is the fulfillment of the promise of Lev 26 and the previous tabernacle.[27] Since Ezekiel's vision in Ezek 40–48 is a resumption of the promise in Ezek 37, this indicates that Ezekiel's temple fulfills God's "tabernacling" presence.[28] In the temple vision, Ezekiel portrays the spiritual reality of Ezek 37:26–27 in what Block calls "concrete terms."[29] God says that in this temple he will dwell (שָׁכַן) forever (Ezek 43:7).[30] Moreover, the end of the vision (Ezek 48:35) indicates the theme of the vision, proclaiming, "YHWH is there!"[31] According to Ezekiel, YHWH makes his tabernacle dwelling among his people through the new temple.

Considering the context of Ezekiel, one should read John 1:14 not just in view of Exodus references, but Ezekiel's temple as well. As Koester says, "The promise of God's tabernacling presence [including Ezek 37:27] was realized when the Word became flesh."[32] In addition, John says that the flesh of Jesus replaces the tabernacle as the place of God's dwelling. This, then, also fulfills the expectation of Ezek 43:7.[33] Ezekiel

25. Schnackenburg, *John: Volume One*, 269, notes how the themes of tabernacle, temple, and glory converge in John 1:14.

26. Unless otherwise indicated, all translations are the author's.

27. Evans, *Word and Glory*, 82; Koester, *Dwelling of God*, 18–19, 104. Also see Morales, *Who Shall Ascend?*, 79, who notes the LXX of Lev 26:11, "I will place my covenant among you." God's presence equals his covenant, which is echoed in Ezek 37.

28. Block, *Ezekiel 25–48*, 497, calls Ezek 40–48 "resumptive exposition" of the previous promises.

29. Block, *Ezekiel 25–48*, 506.

30. Interestingly, the LXX has changed אֶשְׁכָּן־שָׁם ("I will dwell there") to κατασκηνώσει τὸ ὄνομά μου ("my name will dwell"), perhaps a notable change in light of John's concern for Jesus as the revealer of YHWH's name. See Brown, *John I–XII*, 33.

31. Fowler, "Influence of Ezekiel," 127.

32. Koester, *Dwelling of God*, 104.

33. Um, *Temple Christology in John's Gospel*, 153; Block, *Ezekiel 25–48*, 590;

witnesses the glory of YHWH filling the temple (Ezek 43:1–5; 44:4).³⁴ Just as Ezekiel presents what Block calls "... optical reinforcement of verbal pronouncements ... ," in the same way John emphasizes that "... we have *beheld* his glory" (John 1:14).³⁵ So, as Duguid points out, "The solid walls of the Old Testament temple have once again [as with the tabernacle] become flimsy material."³⁶ The new temple of Ezekiel concerns God manifesting his glory and making his dwelling among his people in the new covenant era. John declares that these two themes find their culmination in Jesus Christ.³⁷ Thus, John 1:14, and its background in Ezekiel, plays a role in introducing Jesus as the new temple.³⁸

The Temple of His Body (John 2:13–22)

The episode of Jesus cleansing the temple provides the key to unlocking John's temple Christology, for only here (John 2:21) does the author explicitly connect Jesus to the temple.³⁹ Moreover, the presence of this narrative near the beginning of the gospel likely provides a hermeneutical key for interpreting Jesus as the new temple throughout the rest of the book.⁴⁰ The passage indicates that Jesus is or will be the replacement of the physical temple, a reality linked intricately to the death and resurrection of Jesus (John 2:19–22). Therefore, as the Fourth Gospel progresses, one can expect further links to temple theology within the context of Jesus's death and resurrection, not merely his coming (John 1:14).⁴¹ Therefore,

---

Brown, *John I–XII*, 33. O'Day, "John," 522, notes the association with Ezek 37:27 but does not discuss Ezekiel's temple.

34. Um, *Temple Christology in John's Gospel*, 154.

35. Block, *Ezekiel 25–48*, 582. Brown, *John I–XII*, 34, also connects Ezekiel seeing God's glory to the Word's glory becoming visible. Some commentators miss this point when they focus the discussion on whether or not the writer(s) of the Prologue was an eyewitness to Jesus. See Haenchen, *John 1*, 119–20; Schnackenburg, *John: Volume One*, 270.

36. Duguid, *Ezekiel*, 481.

37. Block, *Ezekiel 25–48*, 590; Peterson, *John's Use of Ezekiel*, 45–46.

38. Hamid-Khani, *Revelation and Concealment of Christ*, 280.

39. Hence Hoskins, *Jesus as the Fulfillment*, 108, places discussion of this text first in his monograph.

40. Coloe, *God Dwells with Us*, 84.

41. Hoskins, *Jesus as the Fulfillment*, 116. As will be seen, the notions of Jesus providing "living water" (John 7:38) as well as "preparing a place" (John 14:3) both connect to Christ's death and resurrection.

this section will first explain the claim of Jesus to be the "new temple" in the context of John's narrative. Then, the section will show how Ezekiel provides a background for this text in John. To examine the Ezekielian background, this section will explore Ezekiel's promise of a cleansed (non-corrupted) temple.

The historical context of Jesus's temple cleansing in the Gospel of John is the corruption of the Herodian temple. Debate arises as to what constitutes the corruption in Jesus's day. Some suggest that it involves exclusion of the Gentiles from the outer court, others extortion within temple precincts, or even that Jesus is abolishing the sacrificial system.[42] Though the Synoptic portrayal may provide additional information, this section focuses on John's account and his portrayal of Christology. In John, the lips of Jesus name the abhorrent action, which is making the ". . . Father's house a house of trade" (John 2:16). Jesus does not condemn corrupt business or the sacrificial system. He reproves the very existence of trade within the temple precincts.[43] The reference to Zech 14:21, "In that day there will no longer be a trader in the house of the Lord," supports this view.[44] The merchants could have traded elsewhere, yet they set up shop in a place designed for worship. Knowing of the temple's corruption, Jesus indicates that it will be destroyed (John 2:19). Though some believe the predicted destruction refers only to Jesus's body, the context of judgment provides reason to believe Jesus hints at the destruction of the physical temple building as well.[45] The people respond not just in misunderstanding, but also incredulity that their temple could be destroyed (John 2:20).

---

42. For the first view, see Carson, *John*, 179. Carson argues that merchants should not be in the temple area at all, much less in the court of the Gentiles. For the second view, see Borchert, *John 1–11*, 163. He states that whether cheating is happening is "not clear," yet he emphasizes details such as the expense of the animals. For another argument that Jesus condemns corrupt trading, see Evans, "Jesus' Action in the Temple," 270. For the third view, see Lindars, *John*, 137; Haenchen, *John 1*, 187; Schnackenburg, *John: Volume One*, 356.

43. As Gurtner and Perrin, "Temple," 944, state, "Jesus' concern . . . is the restoration of pure worship . . ." See as well Morris, *John*, 172; O'Day, "John," 543–45; Beasley-Murray, *John*, 39–40; Brown, *John I–XII*, 121–22; Michaels, *John*, 160–61.

44. Dodd, *Fourth Gospel*, 300. Contra Schnackenburg *John: Volume One*, 347, who sees no allusion in Jesus's saying.

45. Köstenberger, "Destruction," 100; Chanikuzhy, *Jesus, the Eschatological Temple*, 309–12; Beale, *Temple and Church's Mission*, 193. Contra Carson, *John*, 181, who argues that Jesus referred only to his own death.

John's portrayal of Jesus's critique of the temple finds similarities in Ezekiel.[46] The first temple's destruction sets a precedent for God's condemnatory destruction of the next temple. The prophet Ezekiel warns a corrupt people with a corrupt temple that their sanctuary would be destroyed under God's judgment, yet also foretells that God would "raise up" a new temple. Ezekiel concerns himself with purifying the temple of practices besides YHWH worship. From Ezekiel's perspective, the main issue is the idolatry of the religious leaders (Ezek 8–9).[47] In response, Ezekiel portends a "cleansed" temple, that is, a temple of "sacred space." The prophet states it best in Ezek 43:12, "This is the instruction regarding the temple: On the top of the mountain, all the territory all around will be most holy. Behold, this is the instruction regarding the temple." YHWH also tells Ezekiel to make known the description of the temple so that the people may be ashamed of their iniquities (Ezek 43:10). In other words, the purpose of the temple is to provoke repentance, leading to the establishment of a holy territory.

In addition to this description of sacred space, Ezekiel's temple vision rebukes the religious leaders for their corruption of the old temple.[48] For example, at several points in the tour, the angelic guide tells Ezekiel that there is to be a division between Zadokite and non-Zadokite priests, for only the Zadokites were relatively righteous during the time of corruption (Ezek 40:46; 43:19; 44:6–41). Jesus, via his temple cleansing in John, likewise rebukes the religious leaders of his day.[49] Also, interestingly, John's account is the only one that mentions the animals (John 2:14). This could merely be the detail of an eyewitness, but could also be a possible connection with Ezekiel's mention of the corrupt priests who make images out of beasts (Ezek 8:10).[50] The beasts in Ezek 8:10 are

---

46. At least one scholar suggests that Isaiah and Ezekiel are in the background of the temple cleansing. See Draper, "Temple, Tabernacle and Mystical Experience in John," 263–88. Evans, "Jesus' Action in the Temple," 251, also briefly notes a connection.

47. For exposition on the sins of the "elders" of Israel, see Duguid, *Leaders of Israel*, 111–16. In contrast, the prophet Jeremiah (Jer 7:1–15) lays the blame on the people who turn the temple into a "den of robbers" (Hoskins, *Jesus as the Fulfillment*, 69).

48. For a detailed study see Duguid, *Ezekiel and the Leaders of Israel*.

49. Evans, "Jesus' Action in the Temple," 248–64; Peterson, *John's Use of Ezekiel*, 107.

50. Peterson, *John's Use of Ezekiel*, 122–23. The connection is tentative, since, after all, no one is worshipping the animals in the temple of Jesus' day.

likely not unclean animals, but the sacrificial animals of the same kind that Jesus drives out in the second temple.

In conclusion, this section demonstrates that John portrays Jesus's concern for the sacredness of the temple precincts, which had become defiled largely due to the failure of the leadership. In response, Jesus promises a new temple that would be cleansed from its corruption, and he portends the cleansing by driving out the traders. This eschatological temple that Jesus promises refers to his own body, which will undergo death and resurrection in order to allow mankind to dwell in God's presence.[51] In a similar way, Ezekiel condemns Israel for its corruption of the first temple, led by the idolatry of the elders within the precincts. Ezekiel provides a solution in the form of a cleansed temple. His description of the new temple emphasizes sacred space, a territory that is holy and has been cleansed from its defilement. Since Ezekiel gives such prominence to a cleansed temple, his vision provides an important background for John's presentation of Jesus in this passage.[52] Moreover, since this text stands as one of the most important passages for John's temple Christology, the passage provides good basis for understanding Ezek 40–48 as a background for John's temple theology as a whole. Not only does John present YHWH's glory as dwelling among mankind (John 1:14), but as Duguid says, "The walls [of the temple] needed to be flimsy ... so that they could be torn down in a final cataclysmic temple-cleansing, achieved through the breaking of his body on the cross ... There on the cross the radical focus on sacrifice of Ezekiel's temple found its full expression, as the new temple itself was made a complete sacrifice for sin, by which God's people were cleansed once and for all."[53] Ezekiel's temple points forward to a fulfillment in the destroyed temple of Jesus's body.

---

51. Chanikuzhy, *Jesus, the Eschatological Temple*, 316. According to Brown, *John I–XII*, 122, the Qumran community also made reference to Ezek 40–48, even after the Second Temple's destruction, in the hopes of an eschatological temple that would be purified from corruption. For more on the hopes of the Qumran community for an eschatological temple, see Chanikuzhy, *Jesus, the Eschatological Temple*, 31–43; Martínez, "L'Interpretation La Torah D'Ezechiel," 441–52.

52. Hoskins, *Jesus as the Fulfillment*, 72.

53. Duguid, *Ezekiel*, 481.

Worship in Spirit and Truth (John 4:19–24)

John further develops his "temple Christology" as he records the account of Jesus conversing with a Samaritan woman. Jesus explicitly identified himself as the temple in the cleansing episode, and in this narrative he goes on to explain the implications of that claim. This section will examine especially John 4:19–24 to explicate John's theology of worship through a non-physical temple.[54] Part of the background for this concept is Ezekiel's temple vision.

Jesus's claim about true worship lies in the immediate context of the woman's claim that Jesus is a prophet (John 4:19). Since the conversation takes place near Mt. Gerizim, the woman takes this opportunity to ask the prophet about the proper location for worship. In her understanding the question equates to the proper location for the temple.[55] Jesus first responds by saying that worship will not take place at Gerizim or Jerusalem (John 4:21), then corrects the woman by telling her that true worship must include true knowledge of God (John 4:22). After this, Jesus makes the claim that the hour has come when true (ἀληθινοί) worship is ἐν πνεύματι καὶ ἀληθείᾳ (John 4:23). The context indicates that part of what characterizes true worship is that it need not take place at Gerizim or Jerusalem, but instead is "in S/spirit and truth."[56] Scholars debate the meaning of this phrase, but the key is Jesus's statement that the basis for worship is that πνεῦμα ὁ θεός ("God is spirit"; John 4:24). Thus, God's nature as spirit implies that worship of him need not be bound to a physical location. As Coloe puts it, "Material temples can no longer be sufficient."[57] Moreover, not only does "God is spirit" refer to the presence of God

---

54. Other avenues from this pericope could be explored. The "living water" motif will largely be dealt with in the next section. According to Coloe, *God Dwells with Us*, 109–12, another possible connection lies in the harvest discussion of John 4:34–38. Ezek 47:22 LXX promises that foreigners (paralleling Samaritans) will have an inheritance and "eat" (φάγονται; cf. MT, יִפְּלוּ, "have an allotment") with the children of Israel.

55. Hoskins, *Jesus as the Fulfillment*, 137. Morris, *John*, 236, believes "... [it] seems more probable that she is simply trying to change the subject ..." to distract from talking about her sin. The mention of Jesus as "prophet," though, seems to indicate a genuine concern on the woman's part.

56. Hoskins, *Jesus as the Fulfillment*, 140. Detailed discussion of the exact question Jesus addresses can be found in Um, *Temple Christology in John's Gospel*, 167–78. Brown, *John I–XII*, 180, is right that Jesus is not contrasting external (ritual) worship with internal worship.

57. Coloe, *God Dwells with Us*, 103. For the same conclusion see also Köstenberger, "Destruction," 102; Schnackenburg, *John: Volume One*, 435.

untethered to a location, but also to the eschatological life that God provides, that is, a new spiritual life (cf. eschatological life to the dead by the Spirit in Ezek 37). Therefore, Jesus is calling for, as Um says, "... a new worship empowered by the reality of eschatological life found in the True Temple of God."[58] This worship, as John claimed previously in his book, comes through the true temple of Jesus.

Ezekiel's temple provides a backdrop for Jesus's statements to the Samaritan woman.[59] YHWH promises through Ezekiel that he will be a sanctuary among the people *in a foreign land* (Ezek 11:16). The prophecy of Ezek 11:16–21 actually points *towards* a non-structural fulfillment, for it demonstrates that YHWH can still be God of his people even outside Israel and without a physical temple. The prophet himself is aware of this, since while in Babylon he sees firsthand the glory of YHWH seated on his throne (Ezek 1). That initial vision intends to convey God's presence with his exiled people.[60] Ezek 11:16 further reinforces this radical theology. As Block says, "This statement is without parallel in the OT."[61] The contrast in Ezek 11 is not between a sanctuary in exile versus a sanctuary in the land, but between a sanctuary "for a little while" and a sanctuary "forever."[62] The eternality of the sanctuary is the focus of Ezek 40–48, but not necessarily its location in the physical land. Thus, YHWH provides a new understanding of temple worship as not bound to a building in Jerusalem.

In conclusion, passages such as Ezek 11:16 and ultimately the vision in Ezek 40–48 reveal a radically new theology of the temple. YHWH is able to dwell with his people even without a physical building. Though this theology is not explicitly developed throughout Ezekiel's book, it finds its culmination in the temple vision. Taylor expresses it well in saying, "Ezekiel's great legacy was that he freed Israel from the last vestige of a belief in the localized presence of God in a building in Jerusalem, however this may have been understood, to the possibility that Yahweh

---

58. Um, *Temple Christology in John's Gospel*, 173. Similarly, Brown, *John I–XII*, 180, says, "Jesus is speaking of the eschatological replacement of temporal institutions like the Temple..."

59. Oddly, even in his discussion of John 4, Hoskins, *Jesus as the Fulfillment*, 138, cites Ezek 46 as an example of eschatological prophecy that a physical temple would one day be re-built.

60. Block, *Ezekiel 1–24*, 108.

61. Block, *Ezekiel 1–24*, 349.

62. Peterson, *John's Use of Ezekiel*, 45.

was a God of movement ... and that he was forever moving on with his people."⁶³ The Gospel of John takes up this theology and develops it further.⁶⁴ Ezekiel's prophecy sets a precedent for Jesus's claim to the Samaritan woman that true worship does not take place on a physical mountain, but "in spirit and truth."⁶⁵ Furthermore, in Jesus's conversation with the woman, he offers her living water, connecting worship and temple theology with life-giving water. Ezek 47 provides a background for this claim as well.⁶⁶ Such connections reinforce the thesis that Ezekiel's temple is a background to John's temple Christology. However, since "living water" appears again in John 7:37–39, the study will detail these links in the next section.

Rivers of Living Water (John 7:37–39)

The present text continues to build on the previous narratives in John. Not only has Jesus identified himself as the true temple (John 2:13–22), and further explained that true worship is "in spirit and truth" (John 4:23), but he has also identified himself to the Samaritan woman as the source of "living water" (John 4:7–14). The concept of living water also has its roots in temple theology, and John 7:37–39 especially shows how Ezekiel's temple provides a background for John's temple theology.⁶⁷

---

63. Taylor, "Temple in Ezekiel," 70.

64. Block, *Ezekiel 1–24*, 349, says, "The closest analogues [to this temple theology] are found in the NT ... ," and he cites John 2:19–22 and John 4:21–23. Peterson, *John's Use of Ezekiel*, 52, connects Ezek 1 with John 4.

65. Um, *Temple Christology in John's Gospel*, 186, writes, "The Jewish expectation of a structural, end-time Temple building is depicted by John as finding its fulfillment in the new creational age when the true messianic Temple will represent the eschatological presence of God." Clarity is in order. This study argues that some Jews expected not a structural temple but, appropriate to Ezekiel's prophecy, a heightened fulfillment. In other words, NT authors did not come up with this idea, but saw it in the OT.

66. Um, *Temple Christology in John's Gospel*, 148–50; Manning, *Echoes of a Prophet*, 188. See Manning, *Echoes of a Prophet*, 159–66, for a more extensive discussion specifically of John 4:10–14 and Ezek 47. This information can also be applied to John 7:37–39. Less convincing is Coloe, *God Dwells with Us*, 95–96, in her argument that Jesus sitting upon the well reflects Ezekiel's temple sitting on top of the cosmic waters, from which the river flowed.

67. Taylor, "Temple in Ezekiel," 70, argues, "[O]ur Lord's memorable words on the great day of the feast in John 7 are perhaps the most significant ..." of Ezekiel's influences on the NT. This in contrast to Walther Zimmerli, *Ezekiel 2*, 515, where he refers to John 7:38 as "... a more heavily veiled echo of Ezekiel 47."

John presents Jesus as the temple in this text by showing him as the source of living water. Jesus says in John 7:37, "If anyone thirsts, let him come to me and drink." In the next verse, though, the text contains ambiguity as to whom the living water will come from. John 7:38b states, ποταμοὶ ἐκ τῆς κοιλίας αὐτοῦ ῥεύσουσιν ὕδατος ζῶντος. The difficult exegetical issue is whether the water comes from Christ's belly or the believer's belly. The most immediate preceding nominative is the believer (ὁ πιστεύων), yet grammatically the referent could actually be Jesus.[68] Manning claims that if the source is Christ, this helps the interpreter understand the OT Scripture being quoted, as the Scripture would more likely refer to a messianic figure that promises water.[69] Whatever the referent, though, Jesus is ultimately the source of living water.[70] Even if the believer is the one from whom the water flows out, that water is the Spirit (John 7:39), and Jesus is the sender/source of the Spirit (John 7:39; 16:7). If the water comes from Jesus's belly, still the believer goes to Jesus to drink the water. Also, even if this passage claims that living water will come from Jesus's belly, Jesus earlier said that water would spring up from the believer (John 4:13-14). In conclusion, then, whether Jesus is the direct source of living water (coming out of Jesus's belly) or indirect source (by giving the Spirit to indwell the believer), Jesus makes an explicit claim to be the source of living water. Having established this, the next step is to examine how the living water motif has its roots in the imagery of Ezekiel's temple.

Ezek 47 provides part of the background for John 7:37-39. What "Scripture" John 7:38 references is a puzzle to scholars. Some believe the text refers to the water YHWH provided during the wilderness wanderings. Neh 9:15, 19-20 explicitly connects the giving of water in the wilderness with YHWH giving his Spirit.[71] Others see a tight connection between John 7:37-39 and the Feast of Tabernacles, and thus consider

---

68. Thus the rendering, "Jesus stood up and cried out, 'If anyone thirsts, let him come to me and drink, whoever believes in me. As the Scripture has said, 'Out of his heart will flow rivers of living water.'" See Manning, *Echoes of a Prophet*, 174. In reference to "him" being the believer see Carson, *John*, 323–25; Ridderbos, *John*, 273; Lindars, *John*, 300–301. For Jesus as the referent see Brown, *John I-XII*, 320; Beasley-Murray, *John*, 115; Schnackenburg, *John: Volume Two*, 154; Haenchen, *John 2*, 17.

69. Manning, *Echoes of a Prophet*, 175–76.

70. Carson, *John*, 323; Hoskins, *Jesus as Fulfillment*, 162–63.

71. Carson, *John*, 326–27. For much further detail, see Shidemantle, "Use of the Old Testament in John 7:37–39."

Zech 13–14 and Joel 3:18 as a background.[72] Narrowing the reference to one single text is difficult. This section merely seeks to demonstrate that one of the primary references is Ezek 47.

First, there is slight lexical evidence for a relationship. Like John 7:38, the LXX of Ezek 47:9 uses the term ὁ ποταμός (though in Ezek 47 the water is not called "living").[73] Interestingly, the LXX uses the singular form, but the MT uses the plural נְחָלִים.[74] This Hebrew form led to a tradition that two rivers came from the temple. Thus, John's use of the plural (ποταμοί) could be based on this Ezekiel MT tradition.[75] Another slight piece of lexical evidence is Jesus's use of the term κοιλίας. While some propose an allusion to Jesus's side as the reason for this term, another alternative is more likely.[76] Significantly, the temple altar is called the "bosom of the earth" (חֵיק הָאָרֶץ; LXX κοιλώματος) in Ezek 43:14 and several other texts (Ezek 38:12; Jub 8:19). The temple is the center of Israel and Israel is the center of creation.[77] As Kerr says, "This would be a very fragile connection if it were not for the fact that both Zech. 14.8 [which also uses the plural] and Ezek. 47.1–12 are strong contenders as sources of the quotation of [John] 7.38."[78] Also, while Zechariah states that the waters come from Jerusalem, only Ezekiel claims that they come directly from the temple. Thus, the details of Ezekiel's temple fit better

---

72. Manning, *Echoes of a Prophet*, 177–78; Michaels, *John*, 465–66; Schnackenburg, *John: Volume Two*, 155–16. Brown, *John I-XII*, 321–23, argues for a composite picture of Zechariah, Ezekiel, and Ps 78:15–16.

73. However, apparently a writer of the Qumran community interpreted the future temple's river(s) as "living waters," inspired by Ezek 47. Likewise Rev 22:1 mentions "the river of the water of life." See Um, *Temple Christology in John's Gospel*, 161.

74. Oddly, of the seven occurrences of this term in Ezek 47:1–12, only one (Ezek 47:9) appears in the plural.

75. See Manning, *Echoes of a Prophet*, 178–79, for evidence from Zechariah, Qumran, and the Targumim of post-Ezekiel interpretation.

76. For the allusion to John 19:34, see, for example, Schnackenburg, *John: Volume Two*, 156; McKelvey, *New Temple*, 83. Even less convincing is Bauckham's theory that the side of Ezekiel's temple equates to the side/shoulder of Jesus. On this, see the discussion in Um, *Temple Christology in John's Gospel*, 157–59.

77. Sweeney, *Form and Intertextuality*, 142; Levenson, *Program of Restoration*, 9. In the period of the Qumran community especially, as Gurtner and Perrin, "Temple," 941, write, "The temple took on cosmological symbolism, with its earthly practices thought to reflect that of its heavenly counterpart."

78. Kerr, *Temple of Jesus' Body*, 239.

with John's presentation of Jesus.[79] John says Jesus is the temple (John 2:19–21), and in Ezek 47 the waters flow from the belly of the temple.

Biblical-theological evidence also argues for a relationship between Ezek 47 and John 7:37–39, based on the setting of the Feast of Tabernacles. At the feast, the leader took a pitcher of water and processed through the Water Gate, which Jews identified as the future south gate of Ezekiel's temple.[80] Then, the water from the pitcher was poured into a basin. Celebrants saw this ritual as a symbol of the river flowing out of Ezekiel's temple (*Tosefot Sukkoth* 3:5–9).[81] Undoubtedly, a large part of the feast imagery does come from the "water from the rock in the wilderness" motif. The feast itself is a memorial of the wilderness wanderings. The "water from the rock" motif can be seen as typology, though, which later writers further developed to include the imagery of water flowing from the temple. Zech 14:8, 16 clearly connects water flowing from the temple with keeping the Feast of Tabernacles, and the Zechariah text was read at the celebration of the feast. However, several traditions also connect Ezek 47 with the feasts and with Zechariah.[82] In other words, one finds a "stream" of tradition that begins with the wilderness motif, develops into Ezekiel's thought of river(s) flowing from the temple, further develops in Zechariah's connecting the outpouring of water with *Sukkoth*, and then finally leads to John's theology of Jesus. The theological concept of "living water" connects the theological "streams" of John 7, Zech 14, and Ezek 47. As noted above, both John and Ezekiel speak of ποταμοὶ that give life (Ezek 47:9; LXX ζήσεται). When Jesus speaks of "living water" both in John 4 and in John 7, he does not mean merely "running water" but life-giving water.[83]

---

79. Keener, *Spirit in the Gospels and Acts*, 159, states, "Although I believe that John makes most use of the new-temple material in Ezekiel, I concur with those scholars who argue that John regularly blends various texts midrashically and that he is following that practice here." See also Coloe, *God Dwells with Us*, 132; Kerr, *Temple of Jesus' Body*, 241. Um, *Temple Christology in John's Gospel*, 157, mentions Ezek 47:1 as the primary referent.

80. Brooke, *Dead Sea Scrolls and the New Testament*, 289.

81. See Manning, *Echoes of a Prophet*, 179. The ritual also is related to Zech 13–14, but that text is itself dependent on Ezek 47. For a detailed description of the water ritual, see Carson, *John*, 321–22.

82. Hoskins, *Jesus as the Fulfillment*, 165. For Zechariah's dependence on Ezek 47 see Block, *Ezekiel 25–48*, 696–701.

83. Köstenberger, "John," 438, calls it a double entendre. Borchert, *John 1–11*, 291, explains, "The flowing water as a symbol of God's provision is likewise epitomized

Understanding Ezek 47 as a background to this text provides a grid for seeing John's treatment of Jesus as the temple.[84] The vision of the river takes place amidst Ezekiel's prophecy of restoration. The river is the source of life for a restored land and people, but YHWH only shows Ezekiel the river after the restoration of the temple and worship.[85] In particular, the glory of YHWH returns in Ezek 43:1–5, which leads to restoration.[86] Additionally, Ezekiel had previously promised that YHWH would sprinkle water on the people's hearts to cleanse them, associated with the giving of the Spirit (Ezek 36:25–27). Therefore, when YHWH gives his Spirit, the people are cleansed, and only then restored as a people and restored to their land.[87] Thus, Ezekiel associates the presence of the temple river with the cleansing, healing, life-giving presence of the YHWH.[88]

John 7:37–39 parallels the pattern of Ezekiel. John remarks that the Spirit would not come until Jesus is glorified. In the Gospel of John, Jesus's glorification primarily consists of his atoning work at the cross (John 12:23–28; 13:31; 17:1), and John 7 refers to this as well.[89] So, Jesus must accomplish the sacrificial purging (the temple of his body must be destroyed), but then restore the temple (rise from the dead; John 2:19–22), thus reinstituting proper worship (John 4:23–24). Then he sends the life-giving water of the Spirit (John 7:39), the presence of YHWH with his

---

in Ezekiel's temple vision . . ."

84. The following is partially based on Manning, *Echoes of a Prophet*, 179–83.

85. Block, *Ezekiel 25–48*, 686–87.

86. Ng, *Water Symbolism in John*, 178.

87. The clear similarities between Ezek 47 and Gen 1–2 indicate that the temple river is not just a picture of physical restoration but of spiritual restoration to purity, healing, and life. See Sweeney, *Form and Intertextuality*, 142, who notes connections with the creation account and sees the exile as a purging in order that creation might be restored in Ezek 40–48.

88. The writers of Zech 13–14, Joel 3:18, and Isa 44:3 also show this link. For rabbinic sources see Carson, *John*, 328–29. See also Ng, *Water Symbolism in John*, 178; Allison, "Living Water," 143–57.

89. Köstenberger, "John," 455. For a study on Jesus's glorification in connection with temple theology, see Hoskins, *Jesus as the Fulfillment*, 147–59.

people.⁹⁰ Thus, Ezek 47 provides a background for understanding how Jesus as the temple will send the life-giving Spirit.⁹¹

In conclusion, John 7:37–39 reveals lexical, thematic, and structural parallels with Ezek 40–48, especially Ezek 47:1–12. In fact, when it comes to the Gospel of John, this text reveals the clearest connection with, and fulfillment of, Ezekiel's vision because of its reapplication of the river of living water. Moreover, John 7:37–39 describes the most overt development of Ezekiel's vision in the NT apart from Rev 21–22.⁹² In addition, the river vision is not the only aspect of the vision that John develops, for John relates Jesus's words to the establishment of the temple (Jesus's body) and return of YHWH's glory.

The Father's House (John 14:1–3)

At the beginning of the Farewell Discourse, Jesus, after washing his disciples' feet and predicting that a disciple would betray him (John 13), seeks to comfort his disciples (John 14:1). As part of his message of comfort, Jesus uses temple theology.⁹³ As with the other sections, this section will demonstrate not only that John 14:2 contains temple theology, but specifically how Ezekiel's temple vision further clarifies John's theological message.

---

90. Other scholars also connect the "resurrected temple" with the giving of the Spirit in John 20:22 as a fulfillment of John 7:37–39 and Ezek 47. See Peterson, *John's Use of Ezekiel*, 196; Beale, *Temple and Church's Mission*, 198–200. Kerr, *Temple of Jesus' Body*, 244–45, links John 7:37–39 with the water flowing from Jesus's side (the crucifixion) and the giving of the Spirit.

91. Manning, *Echoes of a Prophet*, 185; Hoskins, *Jesus as the Fulfillment*, 166–67. In contrast to Alexander, "Ezekiel," 918, who states but does not explain, "That Ezekiel 47:1–12 is being 'fulfilled' by John 7:37–39 is problematic in the least. 'Fulfillment and interpretation' must be distinguished from 'comparison and analogies' and other uses of the OT by the NT." Presumably, Alexander means that John 7:37–39 cannot fulfill Ezekiel's prophecy interpreted according to his "literal" grammatical-historical hermeneutic.

92. As Duguid, *Ezekiel*, 533, writes, "In the New Testament, apart from Revelation 22 . . . , the Gospel of John develops this vision of Ezekiel [the life-giving river] most fully."

93. Bryan, "John 14," 187–98. Bryan presents extensive research of Jewish literature that cannot be fully explored here. See also Walker, *Jesus and the Holy City*, 170–74. Contra Köstenberger, "Destruction," 106, who claims, "[T]he fourth evangelist is silent on the temple in the second half of his Gospel." Per Kinzer, "Temple Christology in John," 450, many scholars see the key temple texts as limited to the Book of Signs.

The presence of temple language begins in John 14:2, "In my father's house are many rooms; if it were not so, would I have told you that I go to prepare a place for you?" Jesus uses a phrase here nearly identical to one in John 2:16, when he references the Jerusalem temple.[94] John 2:16 says, "τὸν οἶκον τοῦ πατρός μου," while John 14:2 states, "ἐν τῇ οἰκίᾳ τοῦ πατρός μου." In addition, only John's temple cleansing account uses the term "my Father's house," while the other gospels reference the "house of prayer" (from Isa 56:7). If in John 2 Jesus's body replaces the temple (the Father's house), dwelling in the Father's house (John 14:2) likely speaks of union with Christ, the "temple" who himself is united to the Father (John 10:30)?[95] John 14:3 underscores the notion, with Jesus saying, "I am coming to take you to myself."[96]

Alternately, others do not see a link to the temple here.[97] For example, Köstenberger believes the reference more clearly speaks of Jesus as the direct mediator to the Father through prayer. In effect, John already considers the temple obsolete, though this text is not a direct reference to such teaching.[98] Instead, Köstenberger takes the "dwellings" (μοναί) as a description of heaven, a dwelling similar to a typical extended household of the day. He adds that "father's house" in literature outside the NT simply designates a patriarch's family.[99] Another argument against a temple understanding is the use of μοναί instead of a more direct reference to a temple dwelling such as σκηνόω (cf. John 1:14) or ναός. In the LXX the root of μοναί never refers to a temple context. Others see a temple

---

94. Kinzer, "Temple Christology in John," 451; Coloe, *God Dwells with Us*, 160; Kerr, *Temple of Jesus' Body*, 277. See also Luke 2:49.

95. Brown, *John XIII–XXI*, 627, allows for the possibility of interpreting John 14:2 "parabolically" as a reference to union with the Father through the body of Jesus. For an argument that this text refers to union with Christ, see Gundry, "In My Father's House," 68–72.

96. Kerr, *Temple of Jesus' Body*, 293.

97. McCaffrey, *House with Many Rooms*, 49–50. McCaffrey's argument is that only the term οἶκος designates the temple, not οἰκία. Many commentators take Jesus's words to be a reference to heaven. So Morris, *John*, 567; Beasley-Murray, *John*, 249; Lindars, *John*, 470–71; Borchert, *John 12–21*, 103–4; Michaels, *John*, 767–68; Carson, *John*, 488–89. In contrast, O'Day, "John," 740, states, "It is critical to the interpretation of Jesus' words here that the reference to 'my Father's house' not be taken as a synonym for heaven." However, O'Day, "John," 740–41, believes the text refers to the disciples' relationship with the Father, not the temple.

98. Köstenberger, "Destruction," 106.

99. Köstenberger, *John*, 425–27. For evidence of the "patriarch's family," he cites McCaffrey, *House with Many Rooms*, 50–51.

connection, but they argue that the new messianic community is the temple in this text.[100]

Despite these important concerns, ample reason remains to see a temple reference in John 14:2. Barker provides two of the reasons.[101] One is an episode in *1 En* 90:29 where Enoch has a vision of the temple, "... a new house greater and loftier than the first ... ," referring to its size and ability to house all the Lord's sheep. *1 En* 90:37 continues, "And I saw that that house was large and broad and very full." A tradition exists, then, that God's future "house" would be larger than the previous temple and would house all of God's people. However, this alone is not a strong argument that the house is equivalent to God's temple.

A second argument considers the OT context of the wilderness wanderings. In the Pentateuch, YHWH tells his people not to fear, for he promises to "go before" them so that they can know where to encamp (e.g., Deut 1:33). In like manner, Jesus tells his disciples not to be afraid, for he will go before them to prepare a place (John 14:1–3).[102] Furthermore, one should link the promised land to the temple of YHWH, since Exod 15:13, 17 speaks of God bringing his people to the place where YHWH permanently dwells.[103] Ultimately, the song of Exod 15 points to the heavenly reality of YHWH's "cosmic mountain," reflected in the various tradition streams of the OT (Sinai, Zion).[104] One also finds this language in the intertestamental period, with God promising to "plant" his people in the land and dwell with them (*Jub.* 1:16–18; 1QS 8:4–8).[105] Therefore Jesus's words in John 14 appropriately connect with other texts that convey God's going before his people to prepare his temple.

Coloe also argues that the "Father's house" refers to the temple.[106] She argues that John 14 frequently uses the verb form of the "many rooms," μένω. While other interpreters take the "rooms" to refer to

100. Walker, *Jesus and the Holy City*, 169; Gundry, "In My Father's House," 68–72.

101. Barker, *King of the Jews*, 402. Kerr, *Temple of Jesus' Body*, 278–92, makes another argument, more tenuous and beyond the scope of this section, based on the context of John 13, where he sees the footwashing episode as a cleansing rite in preparation for Jesus's discussion of the temple in John 14.

102. Brown, *John XIII–XXI*, 625, also believes Jesus's words reflect the promised land mentioned in Deut 1:29, 33.

103. Barker, *King of the Jews*, 400.

104. Morales, *Who Shall Ascend?*, 83–85.

105. Brooke, *Dead Sea Scrolls*, 241.

106. Coloe, *God Dwells with Us*, 162–63.

believers abiding in the Father's dwelling, actually in this chapter God (Father, Jesus, and Paraclete) dwells with the believer (John 14:10, 17, 23, 25). God's indwelling draws on the OT imagery of God descending to dwell in the tabernacle/temple.[107] Thus, the language of dwelling and rooms reflects God dwelling with his followers as he did in the temple. Furthermore, Coloe argues (as Barker does, but with different evidence) that the language of "preparing a place" comes from OT temple language. In the MT the terminology almost always refers to the ark of the covenant (e.g., 1 Chr 15:1). In the LXX the terminology also refers to the temple (2 Chr 3:1).[108] Indeed, in ANE cultures elaborate rituals took place to prepare the temple for the deity's dwelling.[109] Coloe also notes connections with the Targums, one of which says, "The glory of my Shekinah [dwelling presence] will accompany amongst you and will prepare a resting-place for you (*Targum Neofiti* Exod 33:14)." There is, therefore, a possibility that this terminology of preparing a resting place already was current by NT times when speaking of the tabernacle/temple.[110] In conclusion, then, though perhaps the presence of temple theology is more tenuous here than in previous texts, a plausible case remains that John has temple language in mind. Since John continuously presents Jesus as the new temple, cumulative evidence makes the reference to a temple in John 14 more likely.[111]

If, in fact, John 14 contains temple language, and so far Ezek 40–48 is a background for John, Ezekiel's temple vision probably influences John here as well. First, the passages share similar theological contexts. Preparing his disciples for his departure, Jesus comforts them by providing a future hope that he will dwell with them once again. In the same way, in the midst of exile, YHWH comforts his people through Ezekiel by giving them a promise of his returning presence (Ezek 48:35), a restored "house" and restored land.[112] In both contexts, the true source of comfort is the presence of YHWH.[113] The disciples' comfort lies not in having a physical space to live in, but in the hope that Jesus will one day

---

107. Coloe, *God Dwells with Us*, 162–63. Not until John 15, when the metaphor shifts to a vine, do believers abide with God.

108. Coloe, *God Dwells with Us*, 164.

109. Walker and Dick, *Induction of the Cult Image*.

110. McNamara, "'To Prepare a Resting-Place for You,'" 106–7.

111. Kerr, *Temple of Jesus' Body*, 278.

112. Peterson, *John's Use of Ezekiel*, 46, 154, 189.

113. Peterson, *John's Use of Ezekiel*, 114.

return to be with them in that dwelling place (John 14:3). Likewise, the high point of Ezekiel's vision is Ezek 43:1–9, when Ezekiel sees YHWH's glory return to the temple, where God "... will dwell in the midst of the people of Israel forever" (Ezek 43:7). The vision ends with the proclamation of YHWH's presence for eternity (Ezek 48:35). This chapter has already noted a connection with Ezek 43, Ezek 48, and John 1:14. However, the fulfillment of Ezekiel's prophecy does not find its full resolution with the "tabernacling" presence of the Word coming to reside in first-century Palestine. The full completion consists of the disciples of Jesus dwelling with the Word and beholding his glory for eternity.

A second allusion to Ezek 40–48 may reside in Jesus's reference to "many rooms" and the inclusion of many rooms in Ezekiel's temple.[114] Admittedly, Ezek 40–48 LXX does not use the term μοναί as found in John 14:2. The word translated "chambers" is παστοφόρια (MT לִשָׁכוֹת; Ezek 40:17; 41:6). After all, the chambers are used as stopping points, not living spaces. The temple includes some of the chambers for priests to change into vestments, gather supplies, or perform a ritual. The purpose of other chambers is for worshipers to meet or to eat during a festival.[115] Such use clearly differs from the living spaces Jesus promises.

Nevertheless, Ezekiel's vision describes many chambers, more than in Solomon's temple. Ezekiel's temple contained thirty chambers as well as four rooms for kitchens in the outer court (Ezek 40:17; 46:21–24). The inner court includes two main chambers for the priests (Ezek 40:45–46) and eight "side chambers" (Ezek 41:9–11). The sheer size of Ezekiel's temple also relates to the "many rooms" Jesus speaks of. Recall that *1 Enoch* speaks of a temple large enough to accommodate all the flock of God.[116] Perhaps after gathering "one flock" (Ezek 37:15–24; John 10:16), a larger house is needed for the people to come and worship God. Moreover, although Ezekiel is notorious for not allowing foreigners into the sanctuary (Ezek 44:9), the eschatological temple is often associated with the gathering of the Gentiles.[117] As mentioned before, Ezekiel does speak

---

114. Kerr, *Temple of Jesus' Body*, 300; McCaffrey, *House with Many Rooms*, 68; Ironside, *Ezekiel*, 285, 297. Feinberg, *Ezekiel*, 248, dismisses the notion, simply saying, "The thought may be heartwarming to some, but there is no intended parallel or type of this character in the text. Even as an analogy it leaves much to be desired."

115. Block, *Ezekiel 25–48*, 524.

116. Barker, *King of the Jews*, 402; Gurtner and Perrin, "Temple," 941, also connect this passage in Enoch to the vision of Ezekiel.

117. Kerr, *Temple of Jesus' Body*, 302.

of reuniting with Samaritans (Ezek 37:19–27), so Ezekiel simply has a different perspective of how other nations will become part of God's flock. Thus, the many chambers of Ezekiel's temple may convey typologically that there will be plenty of space for many to worship YHWH.[118]

A third connection between John 14 and Ezek 40–48 lies in the mention of a prepared τόπος ("place") and the preparation of the land in Ezekiel.[119] The study earlier showed how Jesus's statement reflects YHWH's promise to go ahead of Israel to prepare the "place" of the promised land.[120] However, the terminology of τόπος requires examination. The term τόπος, though common, often refers especially to God's dwelling (notably Deut 12:11; 2 Sam 7:10; Ps 76:2 LXX) or the promised land (Josh 1:3).[121] Eventually, in extrabiblical literature, "place" became a frequent reference to the eschatological temple.[122] In Ezek 40–48 the term does not refer to Ezekiel's temple as a whole, but a "holy place" where the priests place the sacrificial offerings (Ezek 42:13), where the priests live, and to house the sanctuary (Ezek 45:4). So, a slight lexical relationship between texts exists, but the idea of preparation of the place provides a stronger connection. The episode of Gog and Magog's destruction (Ezek 38–39) reveals YHWH's purpose to purify the land completely before he can establish his new temple (Ezek 40–48).[123] Once the temple is established and YHWH's glory returns (Ezek 43:1–5), the land becomes fruitful (Ezek 47), and the people come and live there (Ezek 47–48). In Ezek 40–48 YHWH prepares a place with a temple so that his people can dwell with him, and so in John 14:1–31 Jesus says he departs to prepare a place for his disciples to reside with the temple, Jesus himself.

Typology of Ezekiel 40–48 in John's Gospel

This section evaluated the theme of temple Christology in John in light of Ezekiel's temple vision. If Ezek 40–48 contains typology, later writers like the author of the Fourth Gospel should expect a non-structural

---

118. Kerr, *Temple of Jesus' Body*, 302.

119. Kerr, *Temple of Jesus' Body*, 302–6, connects "place" with the temple but fails to discuss Ezek 40–48.

120. Köstenberger, *John*, 427.

121. Contra Bryan, "Eschatological Temple," 194–95.

122. Kerr, *Temple of Jesus' Body*, 304–5.

123. Milgrom, *Ezekiel's Hope*, 6.

fulfillment of the OT temple. Indeed, the Gospel of John weaves the theme of Jesus as the new temple throughout its narrative. Major texts in John show Jesus as the new temple, and each includes theological connections to Ezek 40–48, though some connections are stronger than others.[124] The collective evidence shows that the Gospel of John presents Jesus as the typological fulfillment of Ezekiel's temple.[125] This study does not argue that Ezekiel is the only or even the main influence on the theme of John's temple Christology. However, scholars often fail to give due attention to the role of Ezekiel's vision when considering the temple in biblical theology. This study demonstrates the major contribution Ezek 40–48 provides to a fuller understanding of this theme in John. As William Fowler writes,

> Does John intend to communicate Jesus as the fulfillment of Ezekiel's promise of a new Temple? . . . The answer to the above would seem to be in the affirmative . . . [There is] a case for viewing Ezekiel as a major contributor to the new Temple image in John. It would be difficult to imagine the shape that the new Temple theme would take in the Fourth Gospel if there were no Ezekiel.[126]

Typology inherently moves forward to an antitypical fulfillment, and the Gospel of John shows part of that fulfillment as understood in Christian Scripture.

---

124. Dumbrell, *End of the Beginning*, 69, notes John 2:12–25; 4:20–24; 7:37–38 as texts reflecting analogies to Ezekiel's new temple.

125. Duguid, *Ezekiel*, 481.

126. Fowler, "Influence of Ezekiel," 144.

Revelation 21–22: Ezekiel's Temple Is a Type of the New Heavens and New Earth

Introduction[127]

The book of Revelation provides the "canonical capstone" for the Christian canon of Scripture.[128] As such, the writer of Revelation fills the book with OT allusions.[129] Since the temple is a major theme of OT theology, one expects that theme to reach its culmination in Scripture's capstone.[130] Indeed, Revelation, and the entire Scripture, arrives at its crescendo in Rev 21–22 using the temple theme. Though the author explicitly states that there is no temple (Rev 21:22), he fills Rev 21–22 with temple imagery and allusions.[131]

Moreover, the writer provides no description of the temple in Rev 20:1–10, making a physical fulfillment in the millennium, in Tabb's words, "... implausible and unwarranted."[132] Such an ending to Revelation indicates that the temple (in all its OT iterations) is typological, pointing forward to a greater eschatological fulfillment.[133] Just as the OT sacrificial

---

127. The authorship of Revelation is not a major issue for the purposes of this study, which uses a synchronic, canonical reading. In this section "John" refers to the traditional author of Revelation as well as the self-identified or "implied" author within the book, "the Seer" (Rev 1:1–4, 9–11). The hypothesis that the same author wrote the Fourth Gospel and Revelation is intriguing for seeing a link in their temple theology, but space does not permit an exploration of such an issue. Regardless, without presupposing a link, this study will demonstrate a unity in theology between the Fourth Gospel and Revelation, rather than unity under one author.

128. Tabb, *All Things New*; Tõniste, *Ending of the Canon*.

129. Revelation does not directly quote OT passages. On assessing the validity of allusions see Mathewson, "Assessing Old Testament Allusions," 311–25; Paulien, "Criteria and the Assessment of Allusions," 113–29. As demonstrated below, structural correspondence with Ezek 40–48 increases the likelihood that lexical similarities also show some relationship to Ezekiel's vision. As Mathewson points out, we can determine if the texts cohere even while being unable to prove the author's intention.

130. Bauckham, *Climax of Prophecy*, xi, writes, "[Revelation] is a book designed to be read in constant intertextual relationship with the Old Testament. John was writing what he understood to be a work of prophetic Scripture, the climax of prophetic revelation..."

131. Robinson, *Temple of Presence*, xxiv, aptly comments, "The puzzling issue for interpreters is why John chose to utilize Ezekiel's *temple* vision if he desired to dispense with the temple."

132. Tabb, *All Things New*, 179.

133. Contra Block, *Ezekiel 25–48*, 503, who writes, "Although the skeletal parallels [of Ezekiel 40–48 and Rev 21–22] are impressive, the major divergences in detail point

system points forward to a sacrifice that abolishes the system (Heb 7:27; 10:18), the temple points forward to Jesus as the temple (John 2:19–21), thus abolishing the need for a physical temple in the eschaton. Rev 21–22 demonstrates this *telos*. Thus, building off of temple themes in the Gospel of John, Taylor writes, "So the way is prepared for the rich development of Ezekiel's symbolism in the book of Revelation."[134] As the author of Revelation presents the fulfillment of the OT temple, he capitalizes on imagery and language from Ezek 40–48.[135] Mathewson claims, "[John's use of Ezek 40–48] extends beyond verbal and conceptual similarities to include broader contextual correspondences and an interaction with whole sections of biblical texts."[136] Such use indicates that not just the temple, but also specifically Ezekiel's temple, is typological. This section of the study will proceed methodically through Rev 21:1—22:5, dividing the text according to its major parts.[137]

God's Dwelling Place (Revelation 21:1–8)

As Revelation concludes, John sees in his apocalyptic vision a new heaven and new earth, with "the holy city, new Jerusalem coming down out of heaven" (Rev 21:1–2). Even the macro-structure of Revelation's book probably reflects Ezekiel's macro-structure.[138] In Ezekiel, the apocalyptic battle of Ezek 38–39 leads to the establishment of a new temple. In Revelation, Babylon falls (Rev 19), an apocalyptic battle takes place (Rev

---

to two different fulfillments." For Block, John simply takes from and adapts Ezekiel's vision for his own eschatological vision. Unfortunately, Block, who interprets the temple as "ideational," never fully explains how Ezekiel's temple should be fulfilled, for he also denies a physical construction in the millennium.

134. Taylor, "Temple in Ezekiel," 70.

135. The author of Revelation also alludes to many other OT books, notably Isaiah. Thus Vogelgesang, "Ezekiel in Revelation," 71–72, and Töniste, *Ending of the Canon*, 108, overreach in concluding that John uses Ezekiel as a *Vorlage* and structural base, although Revelation uses Ezekiel throughout. See Vanhoye, "L'utilisation Du Livre d'Ezéchiel," 436–76.

136. Mathewson, *New Heaven and a New Earth*, 221.

137. Rev 21:1—22:5 describe the vision of the new city. Rev 22:6–21 concludes the entire book and mostly rehearses major themes of Revelation. Moreover, the latter pericope does not reflect much influence from Ezek 40–48. See the discussion of OT allusions in Rev 22:6–21 in Töniste, *Ending of the Canon*, 184–93.

138. Fekkes, *Isaiah and Prophetic Traditions*, 226.

20:7–10), and then the new city/temple comes down from heaven.[139] At the mention of the city's descent, the text also reflects influence from Ezek 40–48, for YHWH also takes Ezekiel in a divine vision to see a city (Ezek 40:1–4).[140]

The name of the new city also coheres with Ezekiel's vision. Block claims that the difference in names between Ezekiel's city, "YHWH Shammah," and John's, "new Jerusalem," indicate discrepancy, not fulfillment.[141] This work, however, demonstrated previously how Ezek 40:1–4 and 48:35 link with Jerusalem. While Jerusalem is explicitly not named due to corruption in Ezekiel's time, the theology of Jerusalem remains latent. Behind Ezekiel's new city lie concepts of Zion theology and cosmic mountain ideology. Also, Ezekiel's city lies on the southern slope of the cosmic mountain, the mountain of God, while John sees the new Jerusalem on the "great, high mountain" (Ezek 40:2; Rev 21:10), showing that John intends for this city to fulfill Ezekiel's.[142] Moreover, the meaning of the name "YHWH Shammah" finds consistency with the details of John's new Jerusalem.[143] As "YHWH Shammah" denotes, God dwells in new Jerusalem with his people (Rev 21:3), and his glorious presence gives light (Rev 21:23). Finally, Rev 3:12 seems to equate the name of new Jerusalem with the name of God.[144] Therefore, unlike Ezekiel, John may feel freedom to use "Jerusalem" once more because Babylon replaces the old Jerusalem as the anti-God city.[145] The next section will provide more details on the new Jerusalem, but here one sees consistency in the presentations and how the new Jerusalem fulfills Ezekiel's prophecy.

---

139. Presser, "La Escatología de Ezequiel En La Revelación de Juan," 129–46; Robinson, *Temple of Presence*, 112; Osborne, *Revelation*, 712; Vanhoye, "L'utilisation du livre d'Ezéchiel," 440–41; Vogelgesang, "Interpretation of Ezekiel," 68; Moyise, *Old Testament in Revelation*, 67–68; Mathewson, *New Heaven and a New Earth*, 29.

140. Contra Robinson, *Temple of* Presence, 123, with the puzzling claim, "Immediately obvious is that Rev 21:2 bears little resemblance to Ezekiel 40:2." Interestingly, Ironside, *Ezekiel*, 281, though a premillennialist, also agrees that the similarity in the openings notes a similar genre, so that one should take aspects of Ezekiel's vision symbolically just as with Revelation.

141. Block, *Ezekiel 25–48*, 503.

142. Discussion of the "great, high mountain" follows in the section on Rev 21:10.

143. Duguid, *Ezekiel*, 548.

144. Beale, *Temple and Church's Mission*, 348. The conqueror will have both the name of his God and the name of the new city on him, which seems to equate the two names. See also Rev 22:4 and the discussion in Robinson, *Temple of Presence*, 177–78.

145. Duguid, *Ezekiel*, 548.

John also, in what appears as a relative side note in the passage, states that in the new heavens and earth the sea is gone (Rev 21:1). Generally, this means that chaos and rebellion are eliminated, for the sea represents the forces of chaos (Ps 89:9–10; 93:1–5; 104:5–9; Dan 7:3).[153] Additionally, in Revelation the sea represents the sinful world (Rev 13:1; 17:11).[154] Ezekiel's temple vision may also influence this passage, however.[155] Although Ezekiel mentions the Dead Sea (Ezek 47:8, 10), the temple itself contains no water basin representing the sea.[156] As Cook notes, "[The basin] had represented the cosmic abyss. It bore the name of the Canaanite god of chaos and conveyed primordial vastness through its shear [sic] enormousness by ancient standards."[157] Additionally, Ezekiel's temple altar "corks" the cosmic chaos (Ezek 47:1), providing another reason why a basin is unfitting.[158] The previous chapter examined temple furniture and argued that, while arguments from silence cannot be definitive, the lack of description of major articles is likely intentional. Ezekiel's lack of a water basin points forward typologically to the time when YHWH's coming to dwell in glory eliminates the forces of chaos. As Cook concludes, "Rev 21:1 affirms Ezekiel's vision: 'The sea was no more.'"[159] Thus, the opening of the vision already demonstrates Ezekiel's influence.[160]

---

153. Barker, *Gate of Heaven*, 19; Robinson, *Temple of Presence*, 167; Mathewson, *New Heaven and New Earth*, 64–65. Mounce, *Revelation*, 381, calls this "plausible" but opts for a slightly different conclusion. Beale, *Revelation*, 1042, lists five options, all of which relate to sin/evil, and opts for a combination of all five meanings.

154. Caird, *Revelation*, 262.

155. Mathewson, *New Heaven and New Earth*, 65–69, argues for the Exodus motif as a background to this passage and quotes numerous OT texts, but none from Ezekiel.

156. Tuell, *Ezekiel*, 290, argues that the absence of the basin is not due to historical circumstance, since Ezekiel mentions bronze pillars (Ezek 40:49) despite their destruction in the first temple (2 Kgs 25:13–17).

157. Cook, *Ezekiel 38–48*, 271.

158. Cook, *Ezekiel 38–48*, 268.

159. Cook, *Ezekiel 38–48*, 271.

160. Robinson, *Temple of Presence*, 122–23, argues that Isaianic allusions dominate Rev 21:1–9, while Ezekiel comes to the forefront in 21:9–17. Similarly, Mathewson, *New Heaven and New Earth*, 69. However, this study shows that Ezekiel is prominent throughout, even though the book may not take the forefront in this passage, while Isaiah plays an important part in other texts as well.

As the passage continues, the writer makes an important statement in Rev 21:3, the covenant formula and promise of God's dwelling. Here, the covenant formula fulfills the promises of Ezekiel, first in Ezek 37:26–28, then Ezek 43:7, and finally Ezek 48:35.[146] In particular, the phrase echoes Ezek 43:7, where YHWH promises to dwell (κατασκηνώσει) with his people forever.[147] Here in Rev 21:3 the author echoes God's dwelling in the wilderness tabernacle with the term σκηνή, just as John 1:14 does.[148] Thus, this passage describes the ultimate fulfillment of the promises in Lev 26:11 and Ezek 37:27, and by extension the promise of Ezek 40–48.[149] The connection is explicit in the statement, "God himself will be with them" (Rev 21:3), a fulfillment of the promise in Ezek 48:35, "YHWH is there." In addition, Rev 21:3 uses the plural "peoples," a strong hint that God's covenant people includes the nations.[150] In Ezekiel, too, YHWH provides a means for the foreigner to become part of God's people (Ezek 47:21–23). The typical OT covenant formula is applied to the church in the new covenant (Rom 9:25; 1 Pet 2:10), and one aspect of that formula in the OT is God dwelling with his people. The "dwelling place" overtly reflects the temple in the OT, but the NT fulfillment does not speak of a physical building for dwelling. This trajectory shows that Rev 21 describes the ultimate fulfillment of OT dwelling places, one that does not include a physical temple.[151] So, as Ezekiel's temple points forward to, YHWH's covenant dwelling with his people find its consummation not in a physical temple, but in John's new Jerusalem.[152]

---

146. Tabb, *All Things New*, 196; Tõniste, *Ending of the Canon*, 107. Mathewson, *New Heaven and New Earth*, 50–51, argues that John particularly uses the Ezek 37 formula rather than the one in Lev 26.

147. Beale, *Revelation*, 1046; Robinson, *Temple of Presence*, 130.

148. Caird, *Revelation*, 263–64; Mounce, *Revelation*, 383. Tõniste, *Ending of the Canon*, 107, writes, "Revelation uses the term 'tabernacle' recalling the incarnation of Christ..."

149. Beale, *Revelation*, 1046, also notes that *Jubilees* 1:17 describes God's promise, "I will build my sanctuary in their midst, and I will dwell with them, and I will be their God and they will be my people."

150. Beale, *Revelation*, 1047; Robinson, *Temple of Presence*, 133; Mathewson, *New Heaven and New Earth*, 52; Vogelgesang, "Interpretation of Ezekiel," 84, though Vogelgesang inappropriately comes to a universalist conclusion. In this study the term "international" is preferred over universalistic.

151. Morales, *Who Shall Ascend?*, 300, states, "The covenant formula's use here demonstrates that this reality of life with God in the new earth is the substance of covenant theology, unifying the covenants as their one definite *telos*."

152. Mathewson, *New Heaven and New Earth*, 55–56.

The New City (Revelation 21:9–21)

From this point on, John's vision tour (Rev 21:9—22:5) directly reflects the order of Ezek 40–48.[161] Ezekiel's vision begins with the guide taking him through the temple, then describes the city, and finally explains the land, starting the last part with a tour of the life-giving river. Similarly, in John's vision an angelic tour guide shows him the "city-temple," and the vision ends with the river of life.[162] In Rev 21:9—22:5, the author recapitulates Rev 21:1–8, since in Rev 21:10 he sees the same new Jerusalem as he saw in Rev 21:2.[163] Thus, one should read about this new temple-like city in light of the previous section, the fulfillment of YHWH's covenant promise. Moreover, John does not appear to describe a literal city. Instead, in Mounce's words, "Although a few writers take the New Jerusalem in John's vision to be an actual city, it is far better to understand it as a symbol of the church in its perfected and eternal state."[164] Multiple times John describes the city as the bride (Rev 21:2, 9), which is the church (Rev 19:6–10). This line of interpretation makes more sense of the similarities between new Jerusalem and Ezekiel's temple even while the structures (city versus temple) are different. The comparison is more likely since Ezekiel's vision pointed forward to a non-physical fulfillment, and John's city is not a physical one.

As a new vision commences, the description of the city in Rev 21:9—22:5 shows clear similarities with, and thus influence from, Ezek 40–48, beyond simply the macro-structure of the books.[165] Similarities include the Spirit carrying the person away (Rev 21:10; Ezek 40:1–2; 43:5), the high mountain (Rev 21:10; Ezek 40:2), the appearance of God's glory (Rev 21:11; Ezek 43:2, 5), twelve gates inscribed with Israel's tribes

---

161. Beale, *Revelation*, 1061; Deutsch, "Transformation of Symbols," 114.

162. John's vision contains no temple, but the description of the city parallels Ezekiel's description of the temple. So also Robinson, *Temple of Presence*, 126, though she does not agree that in Ezekiel the city lies upon the same mountain.

163. Beale, *Revelation*, 1062; Mathewson, *New Heaven and New Earth*, 94; Vogelgesang, "Interpretation of Ezekiel," 119. Deutsch, "Transformation of Symbols," 109–10, calls Rev 21:9—22:5 the "Jerusalem appendix" to Rev 21:1–8.

164. Mounce, *Revelation*, 382. So also Beale, *Revelation*, 1062, 1066; Mathewson, *New Heaven and New Earth*, 55. The writer explicitly identifies the city as the bride (cf., Rev 19:6–10). Moreover, the parallelism between Rev 21:2 and Rev 21:10b–11a shows that God's glory is the bride's adornment.

165. Block, *Ezekiel 25–48*, 502–3; Vogelgesang, "Interpretation of Ezekiel," 38–39; Tabb, *All Things New*, 177; Beale, *Temple and Church's Mission*, 351; Stewart, "Future of Israel," 563–75. Each provides very similar charts.

(Rev 21:12; Ezek 48:31–34), an angel with measuring rod (Rev 21:15; Ezek 40:3), symmetrical measurements (Rev 21:16; Ezek 45:2), emphasis on residents' purity (Rev 21:27; Ezek 43:12), the river of life (Rev 22:1; Ezek 47:1), and the life-giving trees (Rev 22:2; Ezek 47:12). This study will address each of these in turn and explore how Ezekiel's temple points forward to each aspect of the new city.

First, the Spirit and angel carry John away to a mountain. Ezek 40:1 states that the hand of YHWH brings Ezekiel to a mountain, but in Ezekiel the hand of YHWH is synonymous with the Spirit (Ezek 2:2; 3:12, 14, 24; 8:3; 11:1, 24; 37:1; 43:5).[166] Thus, though the angel is not initially present in Ezekiel, the introductions to these visions in Ezekiel and Revelation are essentially the same. YHWH by his Spirit, with an angelic guide, shows both John and Ezekiel a vision of his glory.[167] By John linking his vision to Ezekiel's at the outset, Mathewson claims, "John suggests that the readers' perception of their future inheritance is to be shaped by ... Ezek. 40–48 ..."[168] These details show aspects of apocalyptic vision, and thus mitigate the likelihood of a physical fulfillment. Beale also notes a rhetorical parallel with Rev 17:1–3.[169] The parallel shows that the likelihood of this city physically existing on earth equates to the likelihood of an actual harlot riding on a giant seven-headed beast on earth someday.[170] Nonetheless, the means by which God gives the vision shows a clear connection between the Ezekiel and Revelation texts.[171]

---

166. So also Robinson, *Temple of Presence*, 128–31. Beale, *Revelation*, 1065, argues that Rev 21:10 combines Ezek 43:5 (the Spirit taking up Ezekiel) with Ezek 40:1–2 (YHWH's hand upon him). However, the cited texts show that the combination happens elsewhere in Ezekiel, so one cannot argue indubitably from this that John combines these two aspects of Ezek 40–48. He may simply be influenced by other parts of Ezekiel (e.g., Ezek 3:14). Bauckham, *Climax of Prophecy*, 158, notes the parallel of "in the Spirit" in Rev 17:3 and Rev 21:10, an intentional theological contrast of Babylon and Jerusalem. Interestingly, Ezekiel's vision also takes him from Babylon to Jerusalem.

167. In Rev 21:10, John sees heaven open and the city come down. In Ezek 40:1–4, Ezekiel sees a city, and later in Ezek 43:3, he sees YHWH's glory. Ezekiel describes YHWH's glory as being like the vision in Ezek 1, where he sees YHWH's throne in heaven.

168. Mathewson, *New Heaven and New Earth*, 122.

169. Beale, *Revelation*, 1064.

170. Even the premillennialist Ironside, *Ezekiel*, 324, says the same.

171. Mathewson, *New Heaven and New Earth*, 97, writes, "John's description corresponds most closely to the similar phenomenon in Ezekiel."

Aside from the prophets being carried away in a vision, significance lies in the Spirit setting Ezekiel on a ὄρους ὑψηλοῦ σφόδρα (LXX; "very high mountain") versus setting John on a ὄρος μέγα καὶ ὑψηλόν ("great and high mountain").[172] Interestingly, Levenson says "very high mountain" (Ezek 40:2) is ". . . substantially the same . . ." as the "high and lofty" mountain of Ezek 17:22.[173] In turn, from Ezek 17:23 one sees that Ezek 17:22 refers to the mountain of the heights of Israel (Mount Zion), and also to "my holy mountain" in Ezek 20:40. Thus, though using slightly different wording, all these references in Ezekiel use Zion language and speak of the cosmic mountain. If so, then it is notable that LXX Ezek 17:22 uses the term ὄρος ὑψηλόν to translate הַר־גָּבֹהַּ וְתָלוּל ("high and lofty mountain"). The LXX does not appear to translate תָּלוּל, or combines the two terms into one word. In essence, then, no substantial difference in meaning appears. All the terms refer ideologically to the cosmic mountain. One could even speculate that John takes the Hebrew wording of Ezek 17:22 but, unlike LXX, actually translates תָּלוּל with μέγα.

The connection with the cosmic mountain and Eden (as in Ezek 28:13–14) also buttresses the idea that Revelation, which also contains Edenic language, uses this theology.[174] Morales's words on Rev 21:1 are relevant here when he writes, "Here the cosmogonic pattern of redemptive history comes to an end, the final exodus: once God's people are brought to this mountain, singing the song of Moses and the Lamb ([Rev] 15:3), there is no more sea (cf. [Rev] 20:13)."[175] YHWH finally and irrevocably plants his people on his holy mountain (Exod 15:17). In addition, while a reader may initially assume the Spirit carries John to a mountain to look up to heaven and see a city, the text could mean that John sees a city coming out of heaven to rest on a mountain.[176] The latter understanding also

---

172. Robinson, *Temple of Presence*, 125, argues, "Although none of the terms are particularly distinctive, the similar phraseology, sustained lexical linkages, and comparable literary contexts add weight to the allusion [of Revelation to Ezekiel]."

173. Levenson, *Program of Restoration*, 25.

174. Levenson, *Program of Restoration*, 26–34, where he speaks of the association of Eden with the mountain in Ezekiel. Also Töniste, *Ending of the Canon*, 159. Dumbrell, *End of the Beginning*, 24, sees Ezekiel's temple-city as Zion, as reflected in Rev 21–22, but he also emphasizes Sinai traditions.

175. Morales, *Who Shall Ascend?*, 299.

176. Mathewson, *New Heaven and New Earth*, 99–100; Beale, *Revelation*, 1065. John could be standing on the same mountain or elsewhere. Mathewson adds that regardless of geographical location, John intends for the reader to think of Mount Zion (*New Heaven and New Earth*, 100). Contra Dumbrell, *End of the Beginning*, 31, who

accords with Ezekiel's vision.[177] This interpretation, then, understands Rev 21:9 to show the cosmic mountain ideology as expressed in Zion theology (Isa 2:2; Micah 4:1) and even later in *1 En* 18:8, 24–25, where God's throne is on a garden-mountain.[178] As Ellison puts it, "The New Jerusalem is the mountain of God that fills the earth."[179] In addition to other sources, John uses the concept developed in Ezek 40–48.

John's vision continues with a sight of the new city coming down out of heaven (Rev 21:10; cf. Rev 21:2). A standard aspect of apocalyptic literature is a vision of heaven opening. The prophet/seer gets an "inside look" at the secret mysteries of God. While Ezekiel does not directly state that heaven opens for him, he too is carried in a "divine vision" (Ezek 40:2).[180] Interestingly, the character in *1 En* 90:28–29 also envisions a temple coming down from heaven. In the coming verses (Rev 21:10—22:5), John describes the city. The link with *1 Enoch* indicates that John takes a standard motif of a heavenly-temple vision, along with Ezekiel's vision that includes both temple and city, and modifies it to a vision of a city with no temple. Finally, the city coming down out of heaven implies that no human builds it, just like Ezekiel sees an already-built temple, implying that no human will build it.[181]

---

argues a contrast with Ezekiel, saying heaven comes down to earth and transforms all earth into a paradise. In response, first, the similarities with Ezekiel indicate a greater likelihood of similarity here. Second, the city coming down onto the mountain does not exclude Dumbrell's point. The mountain could represent, or even be, the entire earth.

177. Caird, *Revelation*, 269–70. Contra Mounce, *Revelation*, 389, who writes, "In a vision the angel transports John to a great, high mountain to watch the descent." Vogelgesang, "Interpretation of Ezekiel," 111–12, argues that John's new city lies on a plain, and the river does not flow down from a mountain, a major change from Ezekiel. The reasons he provides are that the new city *is* the new world, not, like Zion, on a mountain for the world to travel to. Also, he argues John alludes to Rome and Babylon. In light of Zion theology and Ezekiel's influence, though, the idea that the city lies on the mountain is more likely, especially since John's text is vague.

178. Caird, *Revelation*, 270; Mounce, *Revelation*, 389; Eichrodt, *Ezekiel*, 541. Also connecting Ezek 40:1–4 with Isa 2:2 are Duguid, *Ezekiel*, 471; Allen, *Ezekiel 20–48*, 229.

179. Ellison, *Ezekiel*, 143.

180. See the comments on Rev 21:2 for the claim that Ezekiel sees heaven opened.

181. Similarly on this point regarding the city in Rev, see Caird, *Revelation*, 271. Mounce, *Revelation*, 390, says, "That the city comes down from God means that the eternal blessedness is not an achievement of people but a gift from God." One can say the same about Ezekiel's temple. See Stevenson, *Vision of Transformation*, 116, who writes, "Kings build temples. YHWH built this temple. YHWH is king."

Next, in Rev 21:11 the city has "the glory of God." Just as YHWH's glory dwelt in the temple, so now he dwells in the city, that is, the bride.[182] Beale argues that "the glory of God" here refers to Isa 58:8; 60:1–2, where YHWH's glory resides in Jerusalem. However, in light of the immediately upcoming description of the wall and gates of this city, a clear reflection of Ezek 48:30–35, YHWH's glory at least equally relates to Ezek 43:1–12.[183] Rev 22:3 also provides a parallel with this verse and an echo of Ezek 43. Just as YHWH's glory dwells in the center of the temple (Ezek 43:7), here God's throne is in the middle of the new city.[184] In addition, the glory of God has "... radiance [φωστήρ] like a precious stone" (Rev 21:11), while Ezek 43:2 says the earth shone with the radiance [LXX φέγγος] of YHWH's glory all around.[185] God's glory filling the city thus fulfills Ezek 43:1–12 and 48:35.[186] As Ezekiel prophesied, in Rev 21:11 YHWH fills his temple-city with his glory.

John's description of the city in Rev 21:12–14 directly reflects Ezekiel's temple, even while there is no temple.[187] Even the literary structure follows Ezekiel's, as both texts move immediately from introduction to describing the wall and gates of the temple/city (cf. Ezek 40:5–27).[188] Recall from the exegesis of Ezek 40 that Ezekiel sees a "city-like temple." In this light one understands why John's city and Ezekiel's temple are very similar.[189] John appears to merge Ezekiel's description of temple walls

---

182. Beale, *Revelation*, 1066.

183. Mathewson, *New Heaven and New Earth*, 100. After making the claim about Isaiah, Beale, *Revelation*, 1066, later claims an allusion to Ezek 43 regarding the "radiance" in Rev 21:11. See also Robinson, *Temple of Presence*, 133; Vogelgesang, "Interpretation of Ezekiel," 86–87; Töniste, *Ending of the Canon*, 160.

184. Mathewson, *New Heaven and New Earth*, 203; Robinson, *Temple of Presence*, 176. Vanhoye, "L'utilisation du livre d'Ezéchiel," 437, shows that Rev 1:15 and Rev 18:1 also quote Ezek 43:2.

185. John earlier describes God's glory as a radiant precious stone (Rev 4:3). LXX uses φωστήρ only four times, in reference to the creation of sun and moon (Gen 1:14, 16). In contrast, LXX uses φέγγος 19 times. Hence the different usage between Revelation and Ezekiel is not surprising.

186. Morales, *Who Shall Ascend?*, 300; Robinson, *Temple of Presence*, 134.

187. Robinson, *Temple of Presence*, 136–49. Töniste, "Measuring the Holy City," 269–93, argues for a similar rhetorical purpose between what Stevenson calls "territorial rhetoric" in Ezek 40–48 and Töniste's "architectural rhetoric" here in Rev 21:12–21.

188. Beale, *Revelation*, 1068.

189. Peterson, *John's Use of Ezekiel*, 189–90, argues the same. Blenkinsopp, *Ezekiel*, 239, argues that Ezek 48:35 brings together city and temple. Other Zion texts prove, he says, "... this was no innovation." He calls Rev 21:12–14 a "Christian targum" on

(Ezek 40:5–27) and city walls (Ezek 48:31–34), since John describes twelve gates.[190] This explains the apparent difference between Ezekiel's three gates around the temple (Ezek 40:5–27) versus the twelve gates of new Jerusalem.[191] Like Ezekiel's temple wall, John describes "a great, high wall" (Rev 21:12). Like Ezekiel's city gates, John describes four groups of three gates with names of Israel's tribes inscribed.

Some details of the new city's gates initially appear to contradict Ezek 40–48, but ultimately reflect influence from Ezekiel. In Rev 21:12, the gates each have an angel, a detail Ezekiel does not mention. However, Fekkes argues that the cherubim stationed at the "temple" of Eden (Gen 3:24) and engraved in the temple in Ezek 41:25 influence the writer of Revelation.[192] Also, both Ezek 42:15–19 and Rev 21:12–13 describe the gates in order of east, north, south, and west.[193] Caird writes, "Out of the many possible Old Testament precedents [John chose] the most erratic."[194] The erratic nature indicates that surely John chose this order intentionally. Robinson argues that John choosing Ezekiel's temple-gate order shows that he presents his city as the temple fulfillment.[195] Finally, Rev 21:14 says the wall has twelve foundations with the names of the apostles inscribed on them.[196] While this reflects a clear difference with Ezek 48:30–34, with the names of the tribes inscribed, the notion of inscribing names still reflects Ezekiel's influence.[197] Here, John simply describes an eschatological

---

Ezek 48:35.

190. Beale, *Revelation*, 1068. Robinson, *Temple of Presence*, 144, adds, "[This is] consistent with John's condensing tendency." Vanhoye, "L'utilisation du livre d'Ezéchiel," 464, shows this condensing tendency.

191. Duguid, *Ezekiel*, 482, points out this distinction.

192. Fekkes, *Isaiah and Prophetic Traditions*, 265. So also Mathewson, *New Heaven and New Earth*, 103–4. Contra Robinson, *Temple of Presence*, 144, who argues that the angels reflect Ezek 28 and Eden imagery. Mounce, *Revelation*, 379, argues for Isa 62:6 as background, and Beale, *Revelation*, 1069, sees all as viable backgrounds.

193. Beale, *Revelation*, 1068; Feinberg, *Ezekiel*, 249. Ezek 48:30–34 describes the gates in the order of east, north, south, and west, but John reflects Ezekiel's temple gates rather than city gates.

194. Caird, *Revelation*, 272.

195. Robinson, *Temple of Presence*, 144. Also Töniste, *Ending of the Canon*, 160; Mathewson, *New Heaven and New Earth*, 102–3.

196. The number twenty-four (the names of the tribes and apostles) represents the completeness of God's people. Beale, *Revelation*, 1069–70, sees Isa 54:11–12 as background.

197. Vogelgesang, "Interpretation of Ezekiel," 91, notes that here an element is added where otherwise John abridges Ezekiel, showing how John draws special attention

heightening. Since Jesus Christ is the cornerstone of God's people (1 Pet 2:6), the apostles represent the foundation of the church (Eph 2:20). Thus, the names of the apostles represent the union of OT Israel and Gentiles as God's people built upon the foundation of Christ's church.[198]

Next, in Rev 21:15–21, an angelic tour guide measures the city, its walls, and gates. Once again, the presence of the angel reflects Ezek 40–48's influence (Ezek 40:3–5).[199] In both, the guide holds a "measuring reed," the only difference being that in Revelation the rod is made of gold. In fact, in Rev 11:1–2 the Seer receives a measuring rod, and God tells him to measure the temple.[200] Likely, then, John provides another indication that the new city *is* the new temple, in the sense that it contains God and the Lamb's presence.[201] In that case, this text reflects Ezekiel even more closely. Then, as the angel measures, John states that the city is square, with length and width equal (Rev 21:16–17). This coincides with Ezekiel's temple, which the tour guide measures off as a perfect square (Ezek 45:2–3; 42:15–20). Ezekiel's new city is also square (Ezek 48:31–35).[202] Vogelgesang writes, "The purpose of this procedure is to 'show' the city to the prophet . . . and to convey the idea of its perfection, plan, and eternal preservation."[203] Such fits precisely with YHWH's instructions in Ezek 43:11, where he tells Ezekiel to declare the temple's proportions.

---

to this point of unity in Christ.

198. Mounce, *Revelation*, 390–91; Ellison, *Ezekiel*, 143; Robinson, *Temple of Presence*, 147–49.

199. Mounce, *Revelation*, 391; Beale, *Revelation*, 1072; Robinson, *Temple of Presence*, 149; Vanhoye, "L'utilisation du livre d'Ezéchiel," 441. Or, possibly the figure is simply a common characteristic of apocalyptic literature (cf., Zech 2:1). See Collins, *Apocalyptic Imagination*, 5; Hanson, *Dawn of Apocalyptic*, 234–46. Even so, the connection between texts pertains.

200. Tabb, *All Things New*, 175; Robinson, *Temple of Presence*, 152–53; Beale, *Revelation*, 561. Töniste, *Ending of the Canon*, 163, points out that in Rev 11:1–2 the guide has a standard rod, while here the rod is gold. She concludes that the former reflects more influence from Zech 2, while this text reflects Ezekiel's influence more.

201. Vogelgesang, "Interpretation of Ezekiel," 39, notes, "Only the specific temple-language of Ezek 40–48 is missing. Some of these 'missing' elements are found in Rev 11:1–2 and probably Rev 3:12."

202. Beale, *Revelation*, 1075, also notes that Ezekiel mentions the holy place, altar, and offering of land as squared (Ezek 41:21; 43:16–17; 48:20). Also Mathewson, *New Heaven and New Earth*, 106.

203. Vogelgesang, "Interpretation of Ezekiel," 92. Similarly, Töniste, "Architectural Rhetoric," 286, writes, "The purpose of measuring is to show that God's church, the new Jerusalem, conforms to God's intended perfect design. It is complete."

The new Jerusalem measures to 12,000 stadia.[204] The wall measures to 144 cubits, about 216 feet (Rev 21:17). In these numerical details, Revelation does not reflect the measurements in Ezek 40–48. Notably, Ezekiel uses multiples of twenty-five in his measurements, but John uses multiples of twelve.[205] However, both visions contain unexpectedly large and highly schematized numbers.[206] In fact, John's city is larger than the promised land that Ezekiel describes as the inheritance from YHWH (Ezek 48:1–29).[207] Perhaps John reflects on Ezekiel's use of large measurements and is inspired to heighten them even further.[208] Moreover, Rev 21:16 also mentions the city's height, indicating its equal measurement in length, height, and width, and thus making the city a perfect cube. Ezekiel's vision is noteworthy for its general lack of vertical measurements, but in Ezek 40:5 the angel measures the height of the temple wall. Perhaps Ezekiel's rare wall measurement explains the mention of the wall in Rev 21:17.[209]

---

204. Mounce, *Revelation*, 392, explains that this equals about 1,400 miles each direction. In a previous chapter this study argued that around Ezekiel's temple the guide measured an outer wall of 500 x 500 reeds. This makes the entire temple complex about one mile on each side. Such a structure is large for a temple, but not for a city. The new Jerusalem is far bigger than the 25,000 cubit square *terumah*, the city with its surrounding portion (Ezek 48:20).

205. Mathewson, *New Heaven and New Earth*, 105.

206. Vogelgesang, "Interpretation of Ezekiel," 95–96, argues that the wall is not very high in proportion to the 12,000 stadia-high city. While true, 144 cubits is still enormously high for a city gate. Moreover, the disproportionality simply shows that John's presentation is more theological than structural.

207. Vogelgesang, "Interpretation of Ezekiel," 95, argues that the city is approximately the size of the known Hellenistic world. See also Beale, *Revelation*, 1074; Robinson, *Temple of Presence*, 151, for evaluation of other theories.

208. The heightening may also serve to show an inclusion of other nations. Beale, *Revelation*, 1074, notes the mention of a human measurement (Rev 21:17) and says, "This comment might provide the key to understanding John's simplifying and abbreviation of details from the Ezekiel 40–48 vision together with his universalization of some of the elements from that vision." John emphasizes with this comment God's intention to dwell with mankind (i.e., Jews and Gentiles). Contra Caird, *Revelation*, 273, who argues that the human versus angelic measurement refers to the standard of measurement for a cubit.

209. After all, the height of this wall is greatly out of proportion with the height of the city. Contra Robinson, *Temple of Presence*, 142, who concludes that the wall is 144 cubits in breadth, not height. See Beale, *Rev*, 1076. Beale incorrectly cites Ezek 42:20, a passage that neither describes the measuring of height, nor, as explained in an earlier chapter, does it describe the wall of the temple. Eichrodt, *Ezekiel*, 543, argues that the temple wall here is more modest than John's city wall. While true that it is "more"

Block argues for a discrepancy here between Revelation and Ezekiel in that Ezekiel's city is square, while Rev 21:16 says the city is a cube, but the slight discrepancy shows a typological feature.[210] If a type points to an eschatological heightening, John's vision truly "heightens" the measurement of the structure by listing its height.[211] In addition, only one wall surrounds the entire new Jerusalem, whereas the previous temples had an outer wall and inner wall. Beale writes, "This is a hint of the escalation inherent in consummate fulfillment of OT prophetic types..."[212] Ezekiel's enormous extra wall in Ezek 42:15–20 may show a typological escalation of previous temples, providing an impetus for John to escalate the final fulfillment to an even greater degree. So, John's differences show antitypical fulfillment. John mentions one wall instead of two, and his one wall is far bigger than Ezekiel's already huge temple wall.[213]

In the final portion of this section, John describes the materials of the new walls and city (Rev 21:18–21). As stated earlier, the precious stones symbolize the luminous glory of YHWH (see Rev 4:3; Ezek 1).[214] The text repeats words like "pure" and "clear," meaning that the city is able to reflect perfectly YHWH's glory.[215] However, John probably does not merely intend to include jewels to reflect God's glory, but also to link

---

modest, Eichrodt seems to downplay the temple wall's size, which actually is quite big.

210. Block, *Ezekiel 25–48*, 503. The discrepancy is slight because a cube is square.

211. Beale, *Revelation*, 1073. Duguid, *Ezekiel*, 482, uses this point to underscore the concern for purity, which Ezekiel's temple reflects. Per Beale, *Revelation*, 1076, and Mounce, *Revelation*, 392, perhaps in the background is the description of the most holy place in Solomon's temple as a cube (1 Kgs 6:20). However, Beale, *Temple and Church's Mission*, 348; Robinson, *Temple of Presence*, 150, also argues that Rev 21:16 uses "four-square" to reflect Ezekiel, a term not used in 1 Kgs 6:20. Mathewson, *New Heaven and New Earth*, 106–7, comments, "What no-one appears to have noticed, however, is that John may have been attracted to the description of the holy of holies in 1 Kgs 6.20 through the reference to the holy of holies ... present in Ezek 41.4."

212. Beale, *Revelation*, 1078.

213. Robinson, *Temple of Presence*, 143, concludes that the allusion of Revelation to Ezekiel is only "probable," and bases her judgment on the similar purpose of walls to delimit holy space. Robinson neglects, however, the above arguments regarding the exaggerated sizes of the walls, which strengthens a link between Ezekiel and Revelation.

214. Caird, *Revelation*, 274; Mounce, *Revelation*, 393. The particular order and inclusion/exclusion of particular stones, Mounce, *Revelation*, 394, explains, "... has been the subject of an extended, yet rather fruitless, debate."

215. Beale, *Revelation*, 1079. Mathewson, *New Heaven and New Earth*, 148, appropriately argues for a pastiche of OT allusions and he concludes, "[The stones] are primarily meant to symbolize the perfected community itself."

temple imagery of costly building materials to the new city.[216] The jewels may also demonstrate symbolism of the cosmic mountain. The jewels lie on the four points of the compass (Rev 21:13–14) and *Targ Neof* Exod 28:17 describes four rows of gems representing the four regions of the world.[217] Ezek 28's Edenic cosmic mountain also contains many of these jewels.[218] Thus, John provides a picture of the new city as the fulfillment of the temple's cosmic mountain ideology, fulfilling the description in Ezekiel.[219] The city is also pure gold, probably a reflection of Solomon's temple completely overlaid in gold (1 Kgs 6:20–22).[220]

Block contends that Revelation cannot describe the fulfillment of Ezekiel's vision, and one reason he gives is that Ezekiel's city is made of ordinary stones while Revelation's is made of precious stones (Rev 21:11, 18–21).[221] However, the link in Rev 21:11 with Ezekiel's description of the glory of God explains the differences between the gates' materials. The precious stones, reflecting the language of Ezek 43:2, demonstrate the presence of YHWH's glory.[222] Revelation and Ezekiel need not correspond exactly, since the "city" is a metaphor for the bride, so the precious stones have a symbolic meaning of God's glory. Moreover, one need not expect a complete, one-to-one escalation of Ezekiel's temple at every point because John depends on other OT prophecies as well, such as Isa 54. Other NT texts combine various prophecies and typology in unexpected ways. For example, Matthew presents Jesus as the new Moses

216. Fekkes, *Isaiah and Prophetic Traditions*, 96–97. Ezekiel does not list building materials, but the previous dwelling places do.

217. Cited in Beale, *Revelation*, 1082; Mathewson, *New Heaven and New Earth*, 134.

218. Mathewson, *New Heaven and New Earth*, 131. Isa 54 and the high priest's breastplate in Exod 28 also provide important background for the jewels mentioned.

219. Caird, *Revelation*, 277, is generally correct when he says, "With the list of foundation-stones John has for the time being deserted his primary Old Testament source, Ezekiel xl–xlviii." Ezek 40–48 does not mention precious stones. He overstates the situation, however, for as noted above, links to cosmic mountain ideology provide links to Ezek 40–48.

220. Beale, *Revelation*, 1079; Caird, *Revelation*, 273; Mathewson, *New Heaven and New Earth*, 153–54. Ezekiel's temple is made of stones, or at least no other materials are described.

221. Block, *Ezekiel 25–48*, 503. In a similar manner, Alexander, "Ezekiel," 923, sees them as different because of the different city gates and their names. He concludes that the cities are not identical but show the similarities between the millennium and eternal state.

222. Beale, *Revelation*, 1067.

(Matt 5–7) and messianic king (Matt 2:6, etc.). The OT never portrays Moses as a king, but Jesus fulfills both prophetic types at the same time. In a similar way, John may creatively show how the new Jerusalem fulfills both Ezek 40–48 and other OT prophecies. The new city may reflect Ezekiel's temple in some ways and Isaiah's prophecies in other ways.

The New "Temple" (Revelation 21:22–27)

The following passage is a *crux interpretum* for understanding the relationship of Ezek 40–48 and Rev 21–22. The argument against typology seems obvious on the surface. John says there is no temple in the new Jerusalem (Rev 21:22), so how can the new heavens and new earth fulfill the typology of Ezekiel's temple? Block states that a clear discrepancy manifests itself here, since Ezekiel's vision places the temple at the center of all cultic life, while in Rev 21–22 no temple exists.[223] This section will examine the text to show that even here Ezek 40–48 influences John's writing. Thus, interpreters should not assume that John suddenly departs from Ezekiel's influence to completely contradict the words of the OT prophet.[224]

John states, "And I saw no temple in it [the city], for the Lord God the Almighty is its temple, as well as the Lamb" (Rev 21:22). Strictly speaking, John does not state that he sees no temple at all. John views no physical building, but he does describe a temple, that temple being God and the Lamb.[225] Thus, the claim that John contradicts Ezekiel misses the mark.

---

223. Block, *Ezekiel 25–48*, 503. Robinson, *Temple of Presence*, 158, states, "The omission of a temple in Rev 21:22 is unexpected, if not shocking." As Stevenson, *Power and Place*, 2–3, notes, the importance of the temple in Revelation itself leads to the reader being startled at the mention of no temple at the end.

224. For example, Mounce, *Revelation*, 395, writes, "At this point John demonstrates his independence from the prophet Ezekiel, whose imagery plays a prominent role in the Seer's vision." Vogelgesang, "Interpretation of Ezekiel," 77, says, "This is a deliberate and radical reinterpretation of his *Vorlage*." Similarly, Mathewson, *New Heaven and New Earth*, 159. Instead, Töniste, *Ending of the Canon*, 172, correctly states, "There is no radical departure from Ezekiel if we understand that both are merely using architectural rhetoric to communicate a new pattern of relationships with God and between [sic] humans using temple as a model."

225. Beale, *Revelation*, 1090, writes, "It is not that John saw no temple, but only that he saw no physical temple." So also Beale, *Temple and Church's Mission*, 348; McKelvey, "Temple," 810. Additionally, Beale, *Revelation*, 1092–93, points out that the term ναός is anarthrous only in the first occurrence in Rev 21:22a (he argues for a *lectio difficillior* reading of the presence of an article in the second occurrence, as attested in

Instead, John describes the very fulfillment of Ezekiel's temple, the greater temple of God's presence.[226] Stewart writes, "John thus does not develop many of the temple details of Ezekiel because for him they are fulfilled in the divine presence with his people."[227] Since God and the Lamb dwell in the city, in this sense one can also say the city is the temple.[228]

The context of the usage of the temple term ναός in the book of Revelation also points to a heightened fulfillment rather than a physical temple structure. Beale makes a compelling case, saying,

> Without exception 'sanctuary' (ναός) elsewhere in Revelation refers to the heavenly temple of the present ([Rev] 7:15 [though there the consummation is included]; 14:15, 17; 15:5–6, 8; 16:1, 17). In [Rev] 11:1–2 the same word is used of the people of God as members of God's temple in heaven though they still live on earth. 'Sanctuary' is also used of the temple of God's presence dominating the new age of the future ([Rev] 3:12; 7:15; 11:19). Indeed, the only other use of the phrase 'temple of God' outside 11:1 is in 11:19, where it refers to the end-time *heavenly* temple ... In this light, Christ's earlier promise in [Rev] 3:12 that he will make each overcomer 'a pillar in the temple of my God' might better be translated 'a pillar in the temple *that is* my God' (appositional genitive)."[229]

As seen above, even earlier in Revelation John points to a future temple, and he cannot be contradicting himself when he later says there

---

Codex A). Thus, in the only place in Revelation where the term refers to a material temple, there is no article. This points to a distinction between material and spiritual in John's concept of the temple.

226. Beale, *Revelation*, 1090, adds that this text fulfills the prophecies of Hag 2:9 and Jer 3:16–17, which both foresee a more extensive glory.

227. Stewart, "Future of Israel," 574. John does add discuss many details, but applies them to his city. Stewart is correct if he means the details such as building measurements and sacrificial legislation.

228. Deutsch, "Transformation of Symbols," 113, writes, "The New Jerusalem is identified with the temple. John indicates this by referring to the city as God's dwelling place ... with people ... and by describing the city in such a way as to leave no doubt that he has identified the entire city as apocalyptic Temple."

229. Beale, *Revelation*, 1091. For a similar conclusion, see Tabb, *All Things New*, 174; Stevenson, *Power and Place*, 4. On Rev 3:12, Tabb, *All Things New*, 203, writes, "Victorious believers will never be excluded from God's presence but will permanently dwell in the temple city ..." On Rev 11:1–2, Bauckham, *Climax of Prophecy*, 272, says, "It is highly unlikely that ... John intends to speak literally of the temple which had been destroyed in A.D. 70 ..., in which he nowhere else shows any interest. He understands the temple and the city as symbols of the people of God."

is no temple. Instead, the earlier uses of "temple" speak symbolically of being in the presence of God. Thus, Mounce incorrectly argues, "It is unimportant that in [Rev] 7:15 it was said that the tribulation martyrs serve God day and night 'in his temple.' The purpose of the statement is not to describe the architecture of heaven but to speak meaningfully to a people for whom the temple was supremely the place of God's presence."[230] If so, then why does John not do the same (speak of a temple using Israel's terminology) at the end of his book? Or why does he not explain in Rev 7:15 that actually there is no temple? Instead, the previous uses in Revelation of the temple, and especially their influence from Ezek 40–48, show that John purposefully uses Ezekiel language in Rev 21–22, all the while acknowledging there is no future physical temple.[231] Revelation presents the "temple" as the heavenly temple, i.e., God's dwelling place, which is ultimately the new city where God's glory dwells forever.

Rather than contradicting Ezekiel, this passage (Rev 21:22) shows the new "temple" as the heightened, eschatological fulfillment of Ezekiel's prophecy. As Stevenson says, "When temple gives way to city and throne, it is precisely because the full meaning of what a temple is and what it does has been realized in the direct and immediate presence of God that the covenant people enjoy the fullness of divine blessing."[232] Just as in Ezekiel, John's city of new Jerusalem makes the "temple" its focal point. God's presence defines the new city, which is exactly what Ezek 48:35 points forward to.[233] "YHWH Shammah" is so named because of the temple's (YHWH's) presence within it, not as a sign pointing *to* the temple.[234]

The argument grows stronger when one considers the conclusion that Ezekiel's temple and city are on the same mountain, showing an even closer relationship between the two. So, as Morales further explains, "In the new earth there is no temple in the sense that *God* through Jesus is humanity's temple; there is no temple in the sense that *humanity* is God's dwelling place; and there is no temple also because the *cosmos*, cleansed and consecrated, is finally the house of God, the context and stage for

230. Mounce, *Revelation*, 395.

231. Vogelgesang, "Interpretation of Ezekiel," 80–100.

232. Stevenson, *Power and Place*, 306. Similarly, see Caird, *Revelation*, 278–79.

233. Tabb, *All Things New*, 203.

234. Ellison, *Ezekiel*, 143, says, "The Shekinah glory has moved from temple to city (cf. Jer. 3:17), and if so, where is the need of a temple any longer? So in Rev. 21 the temple has vanished and we see only the city." One minor quibble, though, is that YHWH's glory extends from temple to city in Ezek 40–48, rather than moving entirely.

humanity's endless engagement with God. The end is life with God in Eden."²³⁵ Why, then, does John's vision include details that initially seem so different from Ezekiel's temple? Beale says, "The primary reason that John throughout [Rev] 21:9—22:5 excludes most of the detailed descriptions of the Ezekiel 40–48 temple and its ordinances is because he understands it as fulfilled in God and Christ's presence and not in a physical structure."²³⁶ John uses enough details to show a resemblance between the visions, but because the fulfillment is not physical, the descriptions of the structure need not be as fully detailed.

Additionally, John shows that now the "temple" expands to take over the entire land. The enormous size of the city, which John now tells us is completely filled with God's glory, reveals this. So as Beale says, "Another feature of escalation is that, whereas the original paradise was only a small geographical part of the earthly creation, now it would appear that the paradisal temple encompasses the entire geography of the new Creation . . ."²³⁷ The entire city is now the most holy place.²³⁸ Furthermore, the new Jerusalem equates to the new heavens and new earth (Rev 21:1–2), which is the cosmic Eden. Ezekiel's prophecy, though, already pointed in this direction. First, Ezekiel's temple is far larger than any predecessor. YHWH's glory filled the enormous temple (Ezek 43:5).²³⁹ Moreover, the identification of the city with YHWH's presence shows that his glory is not limited to the temple (Ezek 48:35). Finally, the river of life miraculously expanding throughout the land shows YHWH's life-giving presence spreading.²⁴⁰ Like the word τύπος implies, then, John's new city is different, but in the same "mold."

---

235. Morales, *Who Shall Ascend?*, 304.

236. Beale, *Revelation*, 1091.

237. Beale, *Revelation*, 1106; Caird, *Revelation*, 278–79. See also Beale, *Revelation*, 1091, where he says, "The perimeters of the new temple will be able to encompass the entirety of the new cosmos."

238. Duguid, *Ezekiel*, 483. So also Robinson, *Temple of Presence*, 161–63, though her lexical study is unconvincing.

239. As Cook, *Ezekiel 38–48*, 21, writes, "I argue for understanding the holiness of the Presence to seep out of the temple and spread widely, transforming and sanctifying both the people and the land of Israel . . . The utopia's *unwalled* inner court and *unwalled* temple building signify the vision's aim of opening up to all Israel the life-giving power of a resident God." Such an "unwalled" temple vision actually fits with John's description of no temple.

240. Levenson, *Program of Restoration*, 13, writes, "When the presence of God has returned to the navel of the world, the Land is transfigured through the life-giving

Finally, as it concerns Rev 21:22, this verse appears to show a difference between Ezekiel and Revelation by virtue of an absence of the sacrificial system. In Block's words, "Sacrifices are at the heart of worship [in Ezek 40–48] . . . ," while Rev 21:22 shows the sacrificed Lamb at the center of worship.[241] This study previously dealt with the question of Ezekiel's sacrificial system, arguing for a theological reading that underscores YHWH's holiness and the need for purity to approach YHWH. Such a picture fits with John's presentation in Rev 21:27 that the unclean will not enter the new city.[242] Just as one could say that there *is* a temple in the new Jerusalem, God and the Lamb, one could also say that there *is* a sacrificial system, the Lamb slain (see Rev 5:6, 12). Revelation certainly excludes the detailed regulations of Ezekiel, but Ezekiel's legislation points forward to the need for sacrificial cleansing to approach YHWH's holiness. Revelation provides the fulfillment of the once-for-all sacrifice at the center of the worship of God's covenant people.[243]

As John proceeds in the passage, he adds that the city has no need of sun or moon because the glory of God provides light (Rev 21:23). Isa 60:19–20 influences John's presentation here.[244] However, just as in Rev 21:11, Ezek 43 probably provides a background here as well.[245] According to the OT prophet, YHWH's glory emanated from the temple and filled it (Ezek 43:5). Likewise, God's glory/light emanates from the new "temple," God and the Lamb, and fills the whole city/land. Moreover, Ezek 43:2 says that the earth (אֶרֶץ) shone with YHWH's glory. Perhaps in a creative way John sees the prophecy "literally" fulfilled in the sense that YHWH's glory fills *all* the earth, not just the land that Ezekiel sees, as Ezekiel's text might imply.[246]

---

stream thus renewed. Logically, all the Land of Israel should be healed through the mysterious waters, not only the land to the east."

241. Block, *Ezekiel 25–48*, 503.

242. Duguid, *Ezekiel*, 482, "There is still the same radical separation between the holy and the unholy on which Ezekiel insisted. The wall around Paradise has not been knocked down but has been raised even higher and made even thicker (Rev. 21:17) . . . The final separation has taken place between the righteous and the unrighteous."

243. Duguid, *Ezekiel*, 483.

244. Mounce, *Revelation*, 395; Beale, *Revelation*, 1093.

245. Beale, *Revelation*, 1094; Beale, *Revelation*, 1092, writes that some Jews appealed to Ezek 43:2 as prooftext that the light of creation was created from a primordial temple (*Midr. Rab.* Gen 3:1; *Midr. Rab.* Lev 31:7).

246. Also, here in Rev 21:22 another connection with creation appears (Gen 1:3, 14–18). As Beale, *Revelation*, 1092, argues, probably the reason John links temple

This section of the text ends with a description of kings bringing their glory into the new Jerusalem, while the unclean are excluded (Rev 21:24–27).[247] Once again, John alludes to Isaiah's prophecy (Isa 60). Mounce says that here John takes over from prophets like Isaiah the language of Gentiles on earth after the establishment of God's kingdom. This does not necessarily mean that they are unregenerate, for the text simply says that Gentiles come into the kingdom.[248] Perhaps John describes what actually happens in the new heavens and new earth, but the words may be symbolic.[249] The latter conclusion fits with an interpretation of the city as the bride, not a physical city. In this respect, the description fits with Ezek 40–48. Ezekiel's vision describes a "real life" of coming and going through the land (Ezek 47:23), of fishing and salt mining (Ezek 47:10–11). However, Ezekiel's imagery may simply describe a vision of utopia, the good life, without necessarily requiring a literal fulfillment.

More saliently, John's description accords with Ezek 40–48's concept of purity. One doubts that these kings in Rev 21:24–26 are pagans, but rather have been cleansed, since Rev 22:27 says, "But nothing unclean will ever enter it." This reflects Ezekiel's concern that idolaters not encroach upon the temple (Ezek 44:9).[250] One can read Ezekiel's concern typologically. In other words, Ezekiel does not mean that all Gentiles are excluded from YHWH's presence, but that Ezekiel excludes the "uncircumcised of heart," i.e., rebellious against God.[251] Reading the temple vision in the

---

themes along with creation themes in his new creation is that, throughout the OT, writers link the temples with creation (Eden).

247. Mounce, *Revelation*, 396–97, summarizes different views on the interpretation of this verse concerning whether these kings are pagans or converted saints.

248. Mounce, *Revelation*, 397, is generally correct on this point, but he incorrectly says, "As John utilized aspects of their visions in portraying the eternal scene he inadvertently retained certain elements that were not entirely appropriate to the new setting. This is certainly the answer to the presence of nations 'outside the new Jerusalem' throughout eternity." Considering the complexity of the book of Revelation, one doubts the author inadvertently included something. Instead, John uses one aspect of the prophecy (the inclusion of Gentiles) without importing the meaning of unregenerate people in the new heavens and new earth.

249. Beale, *Revelation*, 1096–97, interprets the verses as a symbolic description of kings bringing their obedience to God, not literal riches.

250. Robinson, *Temple of Presence*, 157–58. Mounce, *Revelation*, 397; Beale, *Revelation*, 1102; Mathewson, *New Heaven and New Earth*, 178, also cite Isa 52:1.

251. Mathewson, *New Heaven and New Earth*, 178, appropriately clarifies that Ezekiel adds a moral element when he addresses the condition of the heart. Block, *Ezekiel 25–48*, 503, says Ezekiel's vision is "parochially Israelite," but John's is universal

context of Ezek 36, YHWH will ensure that those who approach him are cleansed (Ezek 36:25, 29). Ezekiel's ultimate concern is for the purity of God's people, and John reflects the same concern.[252]

Block sees this issue as evidence that John's vision does not fulfill Ezekiel's temple, saying that in Ezekiel a need exists to distinguish between pure and impure people, while Revelation assumes the absolute purity of all (Rev 21:26-27).[253] However, John simply says that the unclean will not enter, and so does Ezekiel. Neither of them describes what happens to the unclean.[254] Ezekiel provides regulations for purity, but this is Ezekiel speaking typologically, in his own terms, of the need for purity to approach YHWH.[255] However, Ezekiel does not describe impure people as present in the new temple or what their place will be in the new society. Both Ezekiel and John assume that impurity is dealt with somehow. Moreover, Ezekiel emphasizes the glory of YHWH emanating

---

in Rev 21:24-27. Along these same lines see Deutsch, "Transformation of Symbols," 114. The claim misunderstands Ezekiel's vision, which even includes sojourners (Ezek 47:22-23). So also Beale, *Temple and Church's Mission*, 349. Additionally, the purpose of the cosmic mountain of YHWH's presence was that all peoples would stream to it (Isa 2:1-5). So, as Vanhoye, "L'utilisation du livre d'Ezéchiel," 467, says, "Symétriquement, la nouvelle ville, loin d'être réservée aux cir- concis comme en Ez. 44,9, est présentée comme la demeure de Dieu . . . ," translated as, "Strictly speaking, the new city, far from being reserved for the circumcised as in Ez. 44.9, is presented as the abode of God . . ."

252. Vogelgesang, "Interpretation of Ezekiel," 39, states, "A concern for the purity of the New Jerusalem is found in both Revelation and Ezekiel." Mathewson, *New Heaven and New Earth*, 110, points out that the walls have basically the same function in both visions, which is to separate clean from unclean.

253. Block, *Ezekiel 25-48*, 503. Vogelgesang, "Interpretation of Ezekiel," 107, writes, "The nature of the New Jerusalem is diametrically opposite that of the Ezekielian city." He argues for a universalism in that all who enter the city are transformed and become God's people.

254. In the context of Revelation, one can assume that God throws the unclean into the lake of fire (Rev 19:11-15). However, John could have said this at Rev 21:27 but does not. Why does he repeat that the unclean will not enter, if one assumes that at this point the unclean are destroyed already? Another option per Beale, *Revelation*, 1104, is that that the "bright as crystal" river of life serves to purify the uncleanness and sins of the people. However, the text never states this, and the point remains that John seems to assume uncleanness has been dealt with already. In conclusion, either John is emphasizing a point about uncleanness by repeating it, or deliberately echoing a text like Ezek 40-48.

255. Beale, *Temple and Church's Mission*, 349, explains this as inaugurated but not consummated eschatology in Ezekiel. Still, the context of Ezekiel assumes that YHWH removes uncleanness by this point (Ezek 36:25).

from the temple, which has a transforming, purifying effect.[256] Also, most notably in regards to purity emanating to all the land, Ezek 47:1–12 shows God's life-giving presence emanating from the temple to bless the entire land.[257] At the same time, the thick walls in Ezekiel's temple fit with John's emphasis that the unclean may not enter (Rev 21:27).[258] So, in both Ezekiel and Revelation, the texts hint that YHWH's purity emanates from his being and sanctifies the impurities of the people in the land. They both also have guards against impurity, even while assuming impurity is dealt with. So, then, John actually uses multiple aspects of Ezekiel's typology to describe the new Jerusalem.

The River of Life (Revelation 22:1–5)

The end of Revelation reveals an *inclusio* with the beginning of Scripture, the creation account in Genesis.[259] Just as prominent as the Eden imagery, though, is imagery from Ezekiel's temple.[260] In fact, as Tabb says, "These allusions to Eden are filtered through Ezekiel's temple vision."[261] That is, Rev 22:1–5 describes details Ezekiel lists but Genesis does not, such as a river flowing from the throne, tree(s) of life on both sides of the river, healing leaves, and monthly-renewed fruit.[262] "Καὶ ἔδειξέν μοι" (Rev 22:1) shows the writer's intention to start a new section and to refer back to the

---

256. Cook, *Ezekiel 38–48*, 21.

257. Cook, *Ezekiel 38–48*, 22.

258. Robinson, *Temple of Presence*, 138, writes, "In both Revelation and Ezekiel, the walls serve a similar function [to keep out the unclean]."

259. Tabb, *All Things New*, 189; Mounce, *Revelation*, 398; Beale, *Revelation*, 1103. See especially the helpful chart by Töniste, *Ending of the Canon*, 135.

260. Robinson, *Temple of Presence*, 175, says, "Based on similar terminology, strong contextual affinities, and a clear allusion with respect to the water imagery, the allusion will be categorized as clear." Zimmerli, *Ezekiel 2*, 515, writes, "In the NT the most obvious use of Ezekiel 47 is to be found in Rev 22:1ff."

261. Tabb, *All Things New*, 190. Similarly, Eichrodt, *Ezekiel*, 584; Vogelgesang, "Interpretation of Ezekiel," 108; Mathewson, *New Heaven and New Earth*, 186; Vanhoye, "L'utilisation du livre d'Ezéchiel," 471–72. Contra Caird, *Revelation*, 280, who says, "In John's vision the river becomes the river of Eden . . ."

262. Tabb, *All Things New*, 190. Beale, *Revelation*, 1104, also claims a possible background in Ezekiel if one assumes that the nations walk down the street wading in the water. Such a picture reflects the prophet Ezekiel wading in Ezek 47:3–5.

vision before Rev 21:22, resuming the more prominent background of Ezek 40–48.²⁶³

Furthermore, John expands Ezekiel's prophecy numerous times.²⁶⁴ Revelation uses the term "river *of life*," linking to Ezek 47:9, where the river vivifies every creature in contact with it, though the body of water is simply called "a river."²⁶⁵ Ezekiel's river gives life to the dead, transforming the land as it flows, whereas John's river eternally maintains life.²⁶⁶ Also, John's river flows from the throne, not the sanctuary, since no physical temple building exists (Rev 21:22). The detail may appear to contradict Ezekiel, but Ezekiel's text also describes the river flowing from the throne room of the temple.²⁶⁷ Thus, John probably just reflects Ezekiel here, rather than expanding on his text.²⁶⁸ Regarding the river texts, another expansion occurs. In Ezekiel's river, the water begins as a trickle, but grows as it flows toward the Dead Sea, whereas John's river is full at every part.²⁶⁹

Revelation expands Ezekiel's prophecy in a few more ways. John mentions specifically that the tree yields twelve kinds of fruit, the number twelve serving as a common trope in Revelation, adding a detail not in Ezek 47.²⁷⁰ Next, John adds that the leaves are "... for the healing *of the*

---

263. Mathewson, *New Heaven and New Earth*, 187. Although Ezek 40–48 provides important background for Rev 21:22–27, as seen above, that passage does focus on Isaiah with its description of kings entering the city.

264. The section on expansion largely depends on Tabb, *All Things New*, 190–91, who notes these in an especially clear manner. These expansions pertain even though, as Robinson, *Temple of Presence*, 165, notes, John condenses Ezekiel's twelve-verse vision into two verses.

265. The text also echoes Zech 14:8. See Block, *Ezekiel 25–48*, 694–95; Mathewson, *New Heaven and New Earth*, 188. Beale, *Revelation*, 1103–4, takes ποταμὸν ὕδατος ζωῆς as an adjectival genitive, i.e., "living waters" rather than appositional, i.e., "waters, those that are life."

266. Duguid, *Ezekiel*, 542; Vogelgesang, "Interpretation of Ezekiel," 109.

267. So also Beale, *Revelation*, 1106–7.

268. So also Robinson, *Temple of Presence*, 165, claiming, "John's indication ... may reproduce Ezekiel's imagery even more closely than first imagined." Nonetheless, Tabb, *All Things New*, 190, is correct if he means that the river does not flow from a physical building. Alexander, "Ezekiel," 918, notes the point as the major difference between the river visions, leading to his insistence that this river must begin in the millennium and change later in the eternal state.

269. Duguid, *Ezekiel*, 532. Tabb, *All Things New*, 190–91, does not mention this expansion.

270. Though Robinson, *Temple of Presence*, 173, points out the logical transition

nations," which Ezek 47:1–12 does not specify.[271] Interestingly, at this point death is already abolished (Rev 21:4), so the leaves do not actually eternally heal.[272] Likely, then, John includes the "leaves for healing" to even more clearly reflect Ezekiel. Moreover, by mentioning the nations here, John heightens the Ezekiel type in a more explicit way.[273] Finally, another possible link Tabb does not mention is the claim in Rev 22:5, "And they will not need light of lamp or sunlight, for the Lord God will be their light . . ." The statement may refer to the absence of the temple with its lampstand.[274] If so, the text may show another connection with Ezekiel's temple, which mentions no lampstand. As explored before, the lack of lampstand may have its fulfillment in the trees for healing, which would fit with the presentation in Rev 22:1–5.

Besides expansions, John reflects Ezekiel's text with a number of other features. Both texts describe many life-giving trees on the river's shores (Rev 22:2; Ezek 47:7). Tabb argues here for expansion on John's part, but it is better to see John reflecting on Ezekiel here.[275] John, ac-

---

from "monthly" fruit (Ezek 47:12) to twelve kinds (Rev 22:2).

271. Also Mathewson, *New Heaven and New Earth*, 190; Moyise, *Old Testament in Revelation*, 81. Recall previous chapters, however, that examined the presence of the sojourner as inheriting land and becoming fully part of YHWH's people (Ezek 47:22–23). Allen, *Ezekiel 20–48*, 285, writes, "For [John] the leaves were for the healing of the nations (Rev 22:2). Ezekiel does not go that far: he makes a necessary pastoral start in the healing of the people of God, disoriented by trauma and exile." John's passage fits with Ezekiel, for John simply expands the people of God (Rev 21:3) as people in Christ from all nations. Eichrodt, *Ezekiel*, 585, argues for universal effects present in Ezekiel's description of the river scene. This contrasts with Mathewson, *New Heaven and New Earth*, 118–19, who sees John as international and Ezekiel as only national.

272. Beale, *Revelation*, 1108. Robinson, *Temple of Presence*, 173, summarizes other views on the function of the leaves.

273. Bauckham, *Climax of Prophecy*, 316, contends for a link with the previous description of the city (Rev 21:12–14) where the number twelve, representing Israel, merges with an international focus (the names of the apostles signifying the church). In the river vision, the twelve kinds of fruit represent Israel, but the healing is for the nations.

274. Beale, *Revelation*, 1117. On Rev 21:23, Mathewson, *New Heaven and New Earth*, 135, writes, "The introduction of a 'lamp' at this point is perhaps significant due to the important role the lamp played in the Old Testament sanctuary and temple to light the holy of holies. Its presence here to depict the light given by the Lamb coheres with the depiction of the city as a holy of holies (21.16) and with the fact that the Lamb replaces the temple (21.22), accentuating the nature of the city as God's dwelling place."

275. Tabb, *All Things New*, 191. So too Mathewson, *New Heaven and New Earth*, 189.

cording to Tabb, describes one tree of life to reflect the garden of Eden, while Ezekiel describes many life-giving trees. Rev 22:1–2 contains some ambiguity on this matter, however.[276] While "tree" is singular (ξύλον), the text indicates that the tree is on either side of the river (καὶ τοῦ ποταμοῦ ἐντεῦθεν καὶ ἐκεῖθεν ξύλον ζωῆς . . .). If so, the tree is either large enough to bridge both banks or ξύλον represents many trees as a collective singular.[277] Tabb's conclusion that John transforms Ezekiel's vision into a single tree is less probable than the simpler alternative that the text uses the collective singular, and thus many trees dot the riverside, marking a closer connection to Ezekiel's vision.[278] Therefore, John's vision shows closer connection to Ezekiel here than to Eden.[279] The move also demonstrates an escalation of the Eden type, a move Ezekiel already made.[280]

Rev 22:1–5 shows, then, the heightened and eschatological fulfillment of Ezek 47:1–12. Against those who insist on woodenly "literal" interpretation, John need not harmonize the geographic details of his vision with Ezekiel's vision.[281] As Mathewson argues, Revelation does not

276. Tabb, *All Things New*, 191. Duguid, *Ezekiel*, 532, also sees a singular tree.

277. Beale, *Revelation*, 1106. Arguing for a single tree are Tabb, *All Things New*, 191; Mathewson, *New Heaven and New Earth*, 189; Mounce, *Revelation*, 387; Vogelgesang, "Interpretation of Ezekiel," 108. Beasley-Murray, *Revelation*, 331, provides another option, which is that the river diverges into two branches on either side of the one tree. Another issue is the punctuation after ἀρνίου at the end of Rev 22:1. The Textus Receptus places a full stop after ἀρνίου, while NA28 does not. In the TR reading, the river flows from the throne (destination unspecified), so the tree of life goes through the middle of the street. In the latter NA28 reading, the river flows from the throne through the middle of the street. Caird, *Revelation*, 280, argues based on Ps 46:4 that the one river has many streams, and each stream goes down the middle of each street in the city. The conclusion does not substantially affect interpretation, however (Mounce, *Revelation*, 399; Beale, *Revelation*, 1104–5). The important question for this study is about how many trees there are, for that affects the conclusion of whether Ezekiel or Eden provides a more prominent background.

278. So Beale, *Revelation*, 1104; Alexander, "Ezekiel," 918; Töniste, *Ending of the Canon*, 180. Cook, *Ezekiel 38–48*, 265, notes, "Rev 22:1–2, like Ezekiel, speaks of a group of trees representing the one archetypal tree." This is more likely than the conclusion of Vogelgesang, "Interpretation of Ezekiel," 112, that John alludes to Babylon, which had a river flowing through its center and trees on the sides of the main street.

279. Contra Deutsch, "Transformation of Symbols," 117, who argues based on the conclusion of a singular tree, and its name as "tree of life," that John reflects Eden more than Ezekiel.

280. Beale, *Revelation*, 1106; Osborne, *Revelation*, 776.

281. So Ironside, *Ezekiel*, 323–25, though he sees many aspects of the temple being fulfilled in the millennium. He claims agnosticism on whether there will be a physical river. Feinberg, *Ezekiel*, 271, simply dismisses the similarities by saying, "But the

intend to present "... a geographically consistent visualization ... [but] meanings conveyed by symbols."²⁸² Throughout the OT, imagery of the eschatological kingdom (Zion) also includes water as a figure for life (Isa 35:6–9; 41:17–20; 43:18–20; Joel 3:18).²⁸³ So, Beale concludes, ""[I]t is abundantly clear that Rev. 22:2 interprets the Ezekiel picture in this manner [as figurative]."²⁸⁴ John uses the meaning of Ezekiel's symbols and adjusts them as appropriate. Most often he reflects Ezekiel directly, and sometimes he expands on Ezekiel's details.²⁸⁵ In doing so, John connects paradise with temple, yet expands the temple to a cosmic temple-city.²⁸⁶ Moreover, both John and Ezekiel heighten the earlier Eden type. As Beale writes, "Both Ezekiel and Revelation thus envision an escalated re-establishment of the garden of the first creation in which God's presence openly dwelled."²⁸⁷ Typology explains how Ezekiel develops a previous OT type (Eden) and escalates it, which John escalates even more.²⁸⁸

Revelation text is not speaking of the same time as that of Ezekiel." Alexander, "Ezekiel," 871, notices the similarities, but the differences lead him to conclude that Ezekiel prophesies a river that begins in the millennium and exists in modified form in the eternal state. In contrast, Ellison, *Ezekiel*, 140, says, "To me it seems indubitable that the river of Ezek. 47 is the river of Rev. 22:1f ... Even so Ezekiel saw the river of water of life against the background of the parched and thirsty Wilderness of Judea, while John saw it in the new earth, but it is the same river ... For me the fact that both the setting of the vision [Ezek 40:2] and one of its most important parts are symbolic is sufficient to show that the whole is to be taken as so symbolic."

282. Mathewson, *New Heaven and New Earth*, 191.

283. Beale, *Revelation*, 1107.

284. Beale, *Revelation*, 1107.

285. For example, Duguid, *Ezekiel*, 533, points out that Ezek 47:1–12 shows both the emanating presence of YHWH to give life, while restricting it to the land of Israel. John appears to combine both lessons, heightening the vision to apply it to the cosmos and not just Israel. Similarly, Robinson, *Temple of* Presence, 171. Alexander, "Ezekiel," 869, sees what he calls "... the full circle of God's redemptive program ..." prophesied in Ezek 47:1–12 and completed in Rev 22:1–5.

286. Mathewson, *New Heaven and New Earth*, 195, 197.

287. Beale, *Revelation*, 1106. Beale, *Revelation*, 1107, though, incorrectly argues that John sees Ezek 47:12 as describing the "... reestablishment of an eternal Eden." Better to use typology to say that Ezekiel uses Eden's type and escalates it. Ezekiel does not intend to establish an exact replica of Eden, else he would have included many more details of similarity.

288. Vogelgesang, "Interpretation of Ezekiel," 110, uses language of typology saying, "This interpretation also creates an *Endzeit als Urzeit* motif, common to apocalyptic also, which universalizes the Ezekielian reference, since the tree of life in Gen 2:9 was part of the Garden of Eden, and associated with the creation of all human beings rather than the restoration of just Israel." See also Mathewson, *New Heaven and New*

Typology of Ezekiel 40–48 in Revelation 21–22

A careful study of Rev 21:1—22:5 shows that John describes remarkable similarities with Ezek 40–48 as well as important differences.[289] Typology explains both sets of circumstances. First, the differences between the visions show that the new Jerusalem typologically *fulfills* Ezek 40–48 rather than exactly describing the same structure.[290] For example, Beale, rightly noting the many similarities, concludes too much when he sees Ezekiel's temple and John's new city as both visions of the same reality, the heavenly temple descending to earth. As he says, "The two prophets' visions prophesy the same reality of the final, permanent establishment of God's presence with his people."[291] Beale accurately notes that the two visions ultimately have the same meaning, showing God's eternal dwelling with his people. However, he seems to mean they prophesy exactly the same thing. In another work (later than his Revelation commentary), Beale writes, "Ezekiel 40–48 foresees an ideal heavenly temple that already has existence and that will descend to earth at the end of history."[292] He also writes, "John's temple is like Ezekiel's because *it is*, in fact, what Ezekiel prophesied."[293] These conclusions, however, do not adequately account for the differences between the prophecies.[294]

Earth, 195.

289. Duguid, *Ezekiel*, 482, says, "These similarities and differences find striking focus in the new Jerusalem... That the visionary 'Holy City' is modeled on the temple of Ezekiel 40–48 is indisputable... Yet the differences from Ezekiel's vision are equally striking."

290. So Ellison, *Ezekiel*, 139. Also, without using the term typology, Duguid, *Ezekiel*, 482, writes, "[John] has shown how the same themes [of Ezekiel 40–48] (separation of the holy from profane and sacrifice) look when they are viewed through the lens of fulfillment in Christ." Presser, "Escatología Apocalíptica," 130–31 argues that typology explains the same in Ezek 38–39's use in Rev 20.

291. Beale, *Revelation*, 1065.

292. Beale, *Temple and Church's Mission*, 335.

293. Beale, *Temple and Church's Mission*, 351. In several places such as Beale, *Temple and Church's Mission*, 348, 351, Beale uses the term "fulfill." This study argues for typological fulfillment, but by his usage in the context of this quoted statement that Revelation is what Ezekiel prophesied, Beale seems to indicate one-to-one fulfillment. Similarly, Robinson, *Temple of Presence*, 125, argues, "The cities in both Ezekiel and Revelation are relational rather than spatial entities." Robinson's work is valuable in many respects, but she does not adequately examine Ezek 40–48 to determine how to properly interpret the vision. Like Beale, she appears to equate Ezekiel's and John's visions too much.

294. For example, responding to the objection that Ezekiel's temple is made of

Typology, though, explains these differences by providing the concept of eschatological heightening. As seen above, John heightens Ezekiel's prophecy in many ways.[295] Typology, for example, understands the theological meaning of the holiness of the temple and the detailed sacrifices, while yet providing an explanation for their absence in the new city.[296] Revelation heightens Ezekiel's temple and sacrificial system by showing the presence of God and the sacrificial Lamb filling the cosmos. The heightening, on one hand, shows a place for the importance of Ezekiel's vision, while, on the other hand, seeing Ezekiel's prophecy in its canonical context as not the ultimate fulfillment. As Duguid says, "The new Jerusalem is not a literal fulfillment of Ezekiel's vision but a creative appropriation of its central themes for the different situation of the early church."[297] Typology provides a textual rubric for understanding the fulfillment.[298]

---

regular stones, while the new city has precious stones, Beale, *Temple and Church's Mission*, 348, claims that Ezekiel's temple could actually be made of precious stones. Thus, he stretches his argument to make a one-to-one correspondence. Moyise, *Old Testament in Revelation*, 78–81, similarly overreaches when he claims that John takes on the "persona" of the prophet Ezekiel. The claim is difficult to prove but also neglects the differences of the visions.

295. Mathewson, *New Heaven and New Earth*, 112–19, calls the distinctions "transformations of symbols" and attributes them to a "... *heilsgeschichtliche* shift in ages, where the new situation brought about by Christ entails the abrogation of the temple and its cultic functions" (*New Heaven and New Earth*, 15). Furthermore, the new city heightens the typology of other OT texts as well. As Osborne, *Revelation*, 776, claims, "The New Jerusalem will not only be the final holy of Holies (21:9–27) but also the final Eden (22:1–5)."

296. Duguid, *Ezekiel*, 483, though he refrains from the terminology of typology. Robinson, *Temple of Presence*, 179, also uses language of fulfillment. Dumbrell, *End of the Beginning*, 38, writes, "The New Jerusalem thus not only fulfills the political ... but includes sacral functions as well ..." Vogelgesang, "Interpretation of Ezekiel," 116, notes that John does not use all of Ezekiel's details but emphasizes the main aspects, thus his use of Ezekiel is intentional.

297. Duguid, *Ezekiel*, 549. Similarly, Stewart, "Future of Israel," 574, writes, "When John read Ezekiel 40–48 he was not uncertain about when and how the vision would be fulfilled; he clearly under- stood it as referring to the final state of salvation for all of God's people (Jew and Gentile) in God's new creation." Vogelgesang, "Interpretation of Ezekiel," 116, argues that John focuses on the main features of Ezekiel's vision. Thus, though John does not go into all the details, he clearly writes on the fulfillment of Ezek 40–48. This contrasts with Moyise, *Old Testament in Revelation*, 83–84, who denies the appropriateness of typology, opting instead for intertextuality that requires the reader to solve a "hermeneutical challenge." The method of this study, though, argues that typology lies in the text and not in the reader's correspondence.

298. Mathewson, *New Heaven and New Earth*, 116, says, "The transformation of Ezek. 40–48 could be described as 'typological', in that what the temple anticipated has

On the other hand, instead of equating the visions, others say the two visions have little to do with each other, and thus the later vision cannot fulfill the earlier. If one expects a literal, physical fulfillment in both cases (an actual temple/land as Ezekiel prophesies and an actual city as John describes), the differences must indicate contradiction, and therefore the texts must refer to two different future fulfillments. This view fails to account for the significant amount of similarities.[299]

The differences between the texts lead some to conclude that Ezekiel's temple will only exist in the millennium, or that Rev 21:9—22:5 describes some aspects that begin in the millennium (namely, the river) but lead into the eternal state.[300] Feinberg writes, "Details must be taken into consideration, and it is precisely the Jewish elements used by Ezekiel that reveal he had something different in mind than the message of John."[301] Alexander lists some of these details, such as the differing dimensions of the respective cities, the different sources for the river, the presence or absence of a temple, and the presence or absence of a sea. He concludes, "The dissimilarities . . . indicate that Ezekiel's vision is more concerned with millennial concepts than the eternal state, whereas the vision in Revelation is focused on the eternal state."[302] Nevertheless, Alexander

---

now been fulfilled in God and Christ's immediate presence with the people in a far greater way." He cites Davidson's criteria for typology.

299. Feinberg, *Ezekiel*, 235, errs in arguing that similarities are only general and the details show great dissimilarity. The above study shows the great detail in the similarities. As Robinson, *Temple of Presence*, 179, puts it, "Consider the pervasive use of Ezekiel 40–48 throughout Rev 21–22, the omission of the temple cannot be accidental. John intentionally generated the dissonance . . . to draw attention to essential points."

300. Ellison, *Ezekiel*, 12, writes, "I have applied the term Millennium to this period [Ezek 40–48], but I must not be taken to be saying Amen to much of the gross materialism that is postulated of this period in so much popular literature. For me the Millennium is essentially the time in which the limitations of the earthly are prepared for the eternal state." Later, Ellison, *Ezekiel*, 142, further explains, "The Millennium is the antechamber of and the preparation for the eternal state. Its glories are less than those of eternity, but they are of the same nature." Even so, Ellison takes the fulfillment to be symbolic. Scofield, *New Scofield Reference Bible*, 1375, in his only comment on Rev 21:1—22:5, says the new Jerusalem is the eternal heavenly dwelling for the saints of all time. Thus, unfortunately he does not discuss similarities and differences with Ezekiel's vision.

301. Feinberg, *Ezekiel*, 235. Strangely, Feinberg, *Ezekiel*, 252, mentions several texts where the book of Ezekiel influences the book of Rev, but fails to mention any influence upon Rev 21–22.

302. Alexander, "Ezekiel," 870.

explains the similarities as result of the millennial state being a beginning or "microcosm" of the eternal state.[303]

Typology, though, explains how Ezek 40–48 (not to mention other prophetic texts) influences John's presentation of the new heavens and earth. The similarities do not reflect a microcosm in the millennium, because neither Ezekiel nor Revelation speaks of Ezekiel's temple existing *in the millennium*.[304] Instead, the similarities between Ezekiel's temple and the new Jerusalem concern the eternal state.[305] It appears that millennial interpreters use a different hermeneutical presupposition, which influences their exegesis. Alexander argues that to "change" the grammatical-historical hermeneutic to mean that one should interpret the vision symbolically results in subjective interpretation.[306] He adds, "There are no governing interpretive principles except the interpreter's mind, though appeal is often made to the 'NT's understanding of the OT.'"[307] However, he admits the prophets do not distinguish between the millennium and eternal state, but that this comes as a result of progressive revelation.[308] In other words, Alexander too uses a NT reading of the OT, and thus dismisses the approach too speedily. This study does not seek to use subjective interpretation, but it simply examines how the book of Revelation itself understands Ezekiel's vision.[309]

---

303. Alexander, "Ezekiel," 871.

304. Stewart, "Future of Israel," 574, "He did not connect its fulfillment to the millennial kingdom or a period of time before Jesus's parousia in any literal fashion. Ezekiel's original vision focused on the ethnic and national restoration of Israel, but this is expanded in John's interpreting vision to include the salvation of all God's people in God's new creation."

305. Dumbrell, *End of the Beginning*, 25, based on the location of Ezek 40–48 after Ezek 38–39, argues, "[The 'city of God'] is thus a concept to be associated with the final indwelling of God and not with any prospect of an intermediate reign."

306. Alexander, "Ezekiel," 868. Another example is Feinberg, *Ezekiel*, 238, who writes, "His [the one who opposes the "literal" view] basic theological error is that he believes that from the destruction of Jerusalem in the first century A.D., there has been no longer a congregation of the Lord in Israel outside the church of the Lord." The claim is puzzling but, regardless, shows a presupposition of Feinberg's.

307. Alexander, "Ezekiel," 868.

308. Alexander, "Ezekiel," 870.

309. This point holds regardless of one's conclusion regarding Ezek 40–48 itself and the conclusions of previous chapters in this study. However, this study's argument that Ezekiel's temple vision presents itself as typological buttresses the point even further. Rather than subjective eisegesis, this study pursues appropriate exegesis of the text according to its own clues.

The conclusion of this chapter is that, rather than positing a hypothetical millennium, Revelation uses Ezek 40–48 to show the ultimate fulfillment of YHWH's covenant promise in the eternal dwelling, new Jerusalem. Töniste argues, "While asserting the fulfilment of visions such as Isa. 54 and Ezek. 40–48 Revelation affirms consistently with the rest of the NT tradition . . . that the physical temple has become obsolete ([Rev] 21.22) . . . The author of Revelation equates his own faith community as the spiritual new Jerusalem."[310] The similarities between the visions indicate that a typological relationship exists, rather than two separate fulfillments, while the differences show a fulfillment rather than one-to-one correspondence.[311]

Conclusion: Ezekiel 40–48 Typology in the New Testament

While previous chapters argued that Ezek 40–48 includes clues of typology, this chapter demonstrates that (at least two) NT books successfully detect those clues. The author of the Fourth Gospel uses not just temple theology, but specifically Ezek 40–48, to develop a major theme of his book, Jesus the Christ as the temple. Specifically, John presents Jesus as the fulfillment of YHWH's covenant promise to dwell with his people, and as an eschatological, non-structural temple from whom rivers of living water flow. Likewise, the writer of Revelation uses Ezek 40–48 as a major source of influence in his presentation of the new heavens and new earth, the new Jerusalem. While John says there is no structural temple (Rev 21:22), he describes God's dwelling place as the fulfillment of the temple. God's covenant dwelling culminates in a new city, which remarkably describes many aspects of Ezekiel's final vision. Notably, Rev 21–22 ends the canon, and uses Ezek 40–48 to do so, signifying that Rev 21–22 is a rubric through which to read the entire Scriptures.[312]

---

310. Töniste, *Ending of the Canon*, 152.

311. Deutsch, "Transformation of Symbols," 108–9. Moyise, *Old Testament in Revelation*, 135–36, argues for an intertextual reading that involves interplay between Ezekiel and Revelation, even to the extent that eventually one could read the former text as if it is based on the latter. Such intertextual theory contains philosophical assumptions that cannot be addressed here. Suffice to say the method of typology roots the text in history. Thus, the study argues that John reads clues in Ezek 40–48.

312. Töniste, *Ending of the Canon*, 132, "This location attributes to Revelation a special significance that other eschatological writings do not have. This significance

This study argues that typology explains both the similarities and the differences between OT and NT, promise and fulfillment, type and antitype. Neither the Fourth Gospel nor Revelation present "temples" as new buildings made up of physical materials. Both present non-structural yet very real fulfillments. To do so, both appropriately use indicators of typology. John and Revelation both evidence the criteria set forth by the "prefiguration school." They develop a historical institution, the temple, develop previous OT prophecies (Ezek 40–48), present a heightened eschatological fulfillment, and clearly show a christological-soteriological fulfillment (John 2:19–21; Rev 21:22). In addition, they develop the three added criteria.[313] John and Revelation both develop ambiguity in Ezekiel. For example, Revelation equates the temple and city (Rev 21:9–27), just as Ezekiel appears to do. Also, in Ezekiel, YHWH's glory fills not just the temple but extends outward. John presents Jesus as the "mobile" dwelling place of God while Revelation shows God's glory filling the cosmos. John and Revelation both also develop an epochal institution. Notably, the coming of Jesus the Christ, and the coming of the final eternal state are also epochal institutions, so one would expect antitypical fulfillment in both cases. Finally, both John and Revelation develop previous OT texts along with Ezekiel. Both writers use Eden and tabernacle images especially in developing temple theology through the lens of Ezekiel.

Significantly, the Fourth Gospel and Revelation display a unity with each other as they develop the type of Ezek 40–48. Both works appear to have a shared context in the destruction of Herod's temple, just as Ezekiel addresses exiles after the first temple's destruction.[314] Peterson writes, "John seems to intimate [in John 2:19] what the author of Revelation [21:22] comes out and says clearly."[315] For both, the ultimate fulfillment of Ezekiel's temple is not a physical building. Or, as Hoskins writes, "In the book of Revelation one finds the consummation of God's promise to dwell among his people. As the Fourth Gospel anticipated, the union between

---

comes from recognizing that endings have special importance due to their literary function." See the discussion on the importance of the canon's ending in Tõniste, *Ending of the Canon*, 132–38.

313. Note these three criteria are intended to be indicators within the OT text.

314. On the importance of the temple's destruction for Revelation, see Stevenson, *Power and Place*, 18–19. On the Fourth Gospel, see Köstenberger, "Composition of the Fourth Gospel," 69–108. On the similar contexts of Ezekiel and Revelation, see Robinson, *Temple of Presence*, 112.

315. Peterson, *John's Use of Ezekiel*, 109. Like Ezekiel, Jesus indicts the temple and points forward to the eschatological "temple."

Christ and the people of God comes to fruition in the New Jerusalem when God's people are finally with God in the city of God ([Rev] 21:3). In that city, they are able to behold Father and Son who are its temple."[316] Since both John and Revelation are consistent in their understanding of Ezek 40–48, this buttresses the hypothesis that Ezekiel's vision inherently contains clues towards a non-structural, typological fulfillment.

---

316. Hoskins, *Jesus as Fulfillment*, 201. Similarly, Oren Martin, *Bound for the Promised Land*, 112–13, discusses the trajectory from Ezek 40–48 to Jesus the temple, concluding with the new city in Rev 21–22.

6

Summary and Conclusion

Summary

THE THESIS OF THIS study is that Ezek 40–48 presents the temple as a type, pointing forward in the NT to Jesus and the new heavens and new earth. Thus, the study argues that the purpose of the writer of Ezek 40–48 is not to describe a temple so that it would be physically constructed, either after the exile or in an eschatological future. Instead, clues within the text indicate typological features, such that the author intends a heightened, non-structural fulfillment. The inherently typological nature of the vision possibly explains why no community in history attempted to build the structure. At the very least, the typological features explain why later authors in the NT use Ezek 40–48 as a type to describe antitypical fulfillments. In particular, the writer of the Fourth Gospel uses Ezek 40–48 to illuminate how Jesus fulfills the OT institution of the temple. The author of Rev 21–22 uses Ezek 40–48 comprehensively to describe the ultimate fulfillment of the temple, the new Jerusalem. Ezek 40–48 provides a transition in the canon from YHWH's presence in a building (the tabernacle and Solomonic temple) to a more extensive presence. While using the historical institution of a physical temple, Ezekiel presents a temple with typological features that point towards a non-physical fulfillment.

Implications of the Study

Interpreting Ezekiel's Temple Vision

Modern scholars do not present Ezek 40–48 as typological. Instead, three general views prevail. Some scholars argue that Ezekiel presents a blueprint, a description of a physical temple that the prophet expects a community to build at some point in the future. Among this group, some hold that the prophet intended for the temple be built in Ezekiel's near future, that is, after the exile, while others more specifically claim that the temple should be built in the millennium described in Rev 20:1–6. The second interpretation of the vision is the symbolic view. These scholars claim that Ezekiel's vision is not for physical construction, but that the text makes theological claims for Ezekiel's audience to live out. Beale provides a third view, that Ezekiel sees a real heavenly temple in non-structural form, the same temple that will one day come down from heaven in Rev 21.

Those arguing for a physical construction view do not adequately account for symbolic aspects of the vision. On the other end of the spectrum, those who argue for a symbolic view present a good deal of important evidence, but do not account for all the details in the vision, such as those that present a very realistic situation. Beale's view also has much to commend it, but he unnecessarily flattens out Ezekiel's vision and inadequately addresses the features of realism. Thus, the thesis of the work is that typology appropriately combines the realistic features of the vision, rooting the vision in history, while the "symbolic" aspects point forward to a heightened, eschatological fulfillment.

The main implication of this study is a fresh understanding of Ezekiel's temple vision (Ezek 40–48) by interpreting the passage through the lens of typology. The study makes sense of the text presented holistically. Thus, the study presents another example of how to read Ezek 40–48 without dissecting the text into a multitude of strata and redactions. In addition, the work inspects Ezek 40–48 in light of the whole book's context, showing an intentional composition of the book to show unity, and even an artistic beauty, in the book's message.

The study also addresses a particular exegetical conclusion that the temple will be built in the millennium. One's conclusion on the arguments in this work need not necessarily influence one's interpretation of Rev 20:1–6 or other positions on eschatology. After all, Rev 20:1–6 says nothing of a temple built, and Ezek 40–48 says nothing of a millennium. In other words, one could hold that Ezekiel's temple will be built physically while not holding a premillennial view. Likewise, one can conclude that Ezekiel's temple is typological and still hold a premillennial view without necessitating that Ezekiel's temple will be built at that time. Nonetheless, the two conclusions generally go together in the history of interpretation. Premillennial interpreters are some of the strongest proponents for the physical temple view. At the very least, the present work could lead to a fresh understanding of the events surrounding the millennium. Broader doctrines of eschatology are not the concern of this study, but, due to the history of interpretation of Ezek 40–48, this study could have some implications for eschatology. The purpose of the study, however, is to recover the OT meaning without presupposing a view carried over from interpretation of the NT.

As to the interpretation of Ezek 40–48, this work also shows the disadvantages of the view that Ezekiel describes a heavenly temple, a view that Beale most prominently propounds.[1] Beale appropriately sees the temple as real, yet does not conclude that a physical building will be constructed. Thus, his argument has much to commend it, and this work depends on his scholarship at many points. Beale's view, however, assumes too many one-to-one correspondences in Ezekiel's vision. For example, Ezekiel does actually describe a building made of stones, yet Beale claims that Ezekiel describes the same heavenly temple that John describes coming down out of heaven in Rev 21–22. The structures described are very different, though. Thus, typology provides a better rubric for understanding the vision. Typology explains how Ezekiel can see a real structure, a building made of stone and an actual land in Israel, yet typology does not limit Ezekiel's fulfillment to a physical building and land. The features that Beale explains as showing a heavenly temple are, in reality, features of typology.

Advancing Biblical Theology

The main significance of the study is that it advances discussion of biblical theology, especially in regards to the temple. The study shows the unity of Ezek 40–48 with the rest of the canon, yet, perhaps due to its complexity, scholars encounter difficulty in explaining the vision's role in the canon. As chapter 1 of this study shows, in works of biblical theology, even works

---

1. Beale, *Temple and Church's Mission*.

that explore the temple, Ezekiel's vision is not given its due attention. Gratefully, some scholars are emphasizing the importance of the temple for OT theology.[2] Still, works on biblical theology of the temple generally follow Beale's line of argumentation that Ezekiel reveals a heavenly temple.[3] The "heavenly temple" view neglects to show the magnitude of the role of Ezekiel's vision in the canon, for Ezekiel presents a major shift away from a physical temple presence.[4]

These recent works, such as those by Alexander and Beale, emphasize the garden of Eden and its fulfillment in the new heavens and new earth. Ezek 40–48 thus becomes a checkpoint in that understanding, since he uses Eden imagery, but the works do not develop how Ezekiel provides a major transition in understanding YHWH's dwelling place. In contrast, the rubric of typology best explains the historical situation of Ezekiel while pointing forward to an escalated fulfillment. In the view of Ezek 40–48 as typology, God's perfect dwelling presence begins in Eden. From there, the canon shows God's progressive revelation of how he will dwell amongst sinful people, including the important stages of the tabernacle and first temple. Upon the temple's destruction, however, Ezekiel reveals a massive shift in how YHWH will dwell with his covenant people. While speaking in terms that Israel understands, that is, a physical temple, Ezekiel shows how YHWH's dwelling would not be restricted to a physical building. Taylor writes, "[Ezekiel] removes every vestige that God's dwelling would be in a physical temple."[5]

This perspective explains the treatment of the temple at the end of the canon. Chronicles, ending the Hebrew canon, closes the canon mostly with a description of the temple's destruction. The text ends with Cyrus's

---

2. Clements, *God and Temple*; Clowney, "Final Temple;" Levenson, *Sinai and Zion*; Levenson, "Temple and the World;" Taylor, "Temple in Ezekiel," 67–71; Beale, *Temple and Church's Mission*; Morales, ed., *Cult and Cosmos*; Hays, *Temple and the Tabernacle*; Duvall and Hays, *God's Relational Presence*; Alexander, *Eden to New Jerusalem*; Alexander, *City of God*. See also the dictionary entries in McKelvey, "Temple," 806–11; Meyers, "Temple, Jerusalem," 350–68; Jenson, "Temple," 767–75.

3. Martin, *Bound for the Promised Land*, 110–13. Alexander, *Eden to New Jerusalem*; Alexander, *City of God*, bases his arguments on Taylor, "Temple in Ezekiel," that Ezekiel's temple is symbolic, but generally uses the same theme as Beale that the temple progresses from Eden to New Jerusalem, with Ezekiel being a symbol of such a trajectory.

4. Other helpful works simply do not provide an adequately detailed look at Ezek 40–48, such as Carson, "Lord Is There," 43–62; Hays, *Temple and Tabernacle*, 180–82; Duvall and Hays, *God's Relational Presence*, 145–47.

5. Taylor, "Temple in Ezekiel," 70.

decree for return (2 Chr 36:22–23), but with no mention of the second temple or its rebuilding. When the second temple is rebuilt, those who had known the first temple wept (Ezra 3:12), presumably because the latter temple paled in comparison. Notably, unlike with the tabernacle and Solomon's temple, no mention is made of YHWH's glory returning to dwell in the second temple. Moreover, God proclaims through Haggai that the glory of the coming temple would be greater than the glory of the first temple (Hag 2:7–9). Surely, if such had taken place in Ezra 6, the text would have mentioned it. The OT canon concludes, then, with an expectation of a coming greater glory in the temple. YHWH's glory departed east from the temple (Ezek 11:23) and had yet to return. Ezekiel's temple vision points forward to the moment when YHWH's glory would, in fact, return to dwell with his people.

Ezekiel's vision thus prepares the way for the Fourth Gospel to present YHWH's temple dwelling in the incarnate Word, Jesus (John 2:19–21), and then for Revelation to present YHWH's covenant dwelling in a temple-city where, in fact, no physical temple exists, for the temple is the Lord God Almighty and the Lamb (Rev 21:22). As Dumbrell says, "All aspects of the temple symbolism have come together in this pattern of expectation of the last two chapters of the Bible."[6] Ezek 40–48 develops an important typological trajectory from Eden to New Jerusalem. Future works of biblical theology do well to give greater attention to this important transition stage in the canon's presentation of the temple.

Future Research

This study provides an extensive examination of Ezek 40–48 through the lens of typology. Even with such narrowed focus, not every text of the vision could be examined. Future study can probe further into Ezekiel's vision, discussing more particular aspects in the text, including specific features of the building or the calendrical feasts.

Another major area for future research concerns other NT antitypical fulfillments of Ezek 40–48. This study only focuses on the Gospel of John and Rev 21–22. Many more avenues can be explored to discern whether or not Ezek 40–48 provides special insight into the NT's development of the temple theme.[7] Though John emphasizes Jesus as the

---

6. Dumbrell, *End of the Beginning*, 38.
7. Clowney, "Final Temple," 156–89; Alexander and Gathercole, eds., *Heaven*

temple, the Synoptic Gospels also contain critique of Israel's temple and in a more subdued way present Jesus as the fulfillment of the institution.[8] The book of Acts also demonstrates how the NT church moved away from the institution of the temple and towards an understanding of the church as the temple.

The Epistles further develop temple theology by presenting the church as the temple, so discerning thematic and lexical connections particularly with Ezek 40–48 as a background would be a fruitful study.[9] The letters of Paul develop the spiritual understanding of the temple. For example, 1 Cor 3:9–17 presents the church as the temple and 2 Cor 6:14–18 states that the believer's body is a temple (see also 2 Cor 5:1). In Ephesians, Paul describes Jesus as the cornerstone of the "building" (temple) that is the church (Eph 2:20), a building built in love (Eph 4:12, 16). Are these concepts of a non-physical temple related to Ezekiel's vision?

Other non-Pauline letters present the church as the fulfillment of Israel's temple. In 1 Pet 2:4–10, the writer describes the church as living stones built up into a spiritual house. The description of the church throughout the NT as a οἶκος ("house"), imagery Peter capitalizes on, reflects temple imagery. The Letter to the Hebrews also presents the temple as typological, only the typology is vertical, rather than horizontal. In other words, the true temple in heaven provides the original type, of which the tabernacle/temple on earth is the antitype ("they serve as a copy and shadow of the heavenly things . . . ;" Heb 8:5).[10] Heb 11:10 says Abraham looked forward to ". . . the city that has foundations, whose designer and builder is God." Heb 12:18–29 says the church comes to the true Mount Zion in heaven and the heavenly Jerusalem, while Heb 13:14 says NT believers seek after the heavenly city. While Hebrews mostly focuses on the Mosaic legislation and the tabernacle as typological, a few of these texts also capitalize on Zion theology. Once again, future study should explore if Ezek 40–48 provides any background or influence on these texts from the non-Pauline epistles.

---

on Earth, trace the temple theme throughout the NT but only occasionally touch on Ezek 40–48.

8. Clowney, "Final Temple," 166–81.

9. Clowney, "Final Temple," 182–89.

10. Caneday, "SBJT Forum," 97. See also Heb 9:9 ("which is symbolic for the present age," ESV); Heb 10:1 ("the law has a shadow of the good things to come, instead of the true form of these things").

As to other aspects of further research, chapter 5 of this study could only examine Rev 21–22 and briefly touch on other texts in Revelation that speak of a temple. Although Ezek 40–48 most clearly stands as a background in Rev 21–22, the temple vision probably impacts other texts in Revelation as well. In general, Revelation uses ναός to portray a heavenly temple. Perhaps the description of the heavenly temple throughout Revelation also reflects Ezek 40–48, similar to how the Qumran community used the OT prophet's vision.

A secondary contribution this study makes is to the scholarship on typology. This study, in particular, notes three additional criteria that other scholars do not use, at least explicitly (ambiguity, epochal institution, OT development). In this study, however, these criteria could only be applied to Ezek 40–48. A few examples are noted in the first chapter, such as Melchizedek and Ishmael/Isaac. Future studies should explore these criteria to see how they apply. Perhaps some texts that many consider a type may not fit the criteria (such as the example given of Gen 22), and others that people do not often consider a type actually do fit the criteria (such as Ezek 40–48). The study of typology appears to be gaining in prominence for those who read Scripture canonically. Christian biblical theology seeks to understand how to responsibly see Christ in all the Scriptures. Various schools understand typology in different ways. This study argues that typology should attempt to remain rooted in the OT text rather than the correspondences of a reader. Instead of "reading backwards" in light of the NT, typology studies should begin with the OT. A properly defined method for discerning types will prevent fanciful interpretations akin to allegory. Future explorations of typology, therefore, may use the criteria set forth here, and perhaps add even further criteria.

Conclusion

Ezek 40–48 is a vision in which the prophet takes a temple tour guided by an angelic figure. Yet, after wading through the life-giving river (Ezek 47:1–12), without explanation, the prophet and his guide disappear. There is no conclusion to Ezekiel's narrative regarding the vision or his life. From Ezek 47:13—48:35, YHWH simply speaks. The book, and temple vision, end not with Ezekiel's words, but YHWH's. He states concisely and powerfully, "YHWH Is There." Fittingly, the book of Ezekiel ends not with the prophet but with YHWH. A book full of judgment ends not with final condemnation but with a word of hope. In the new city, with a new temple, in a restored land, YHWH Is There. Herein lies the meaning of the vision. Here is the destiny of redeemed humanity. YHWH will bring his people to his holy mountain.

> Jesus shall reign where'er the sun,
> Does its successive journeys run;
> His kingdom spread from shore to shore,
> Till moon shall wax and wane no more.
> To Him shall endless prayer be made,
> And endless praises crown His head;
> His name like sweet perfume shall rise
> With ev'ry morning sacrifice.[11]

---

11. Isaac Watts, "Jesus Shall Reign."

Bibliography

Abba, Raymond. "Priests and Levites in Deuteronomy." *Vetus Testamentum* 27 (1977) 257–67.
———. "Priests and Levites in Ezekiel." *Vetus Testamentum* 28 (1978) 1–9.
Albright, W. F. *From the Stone Age to Christianity: Monotheism and the Historical Process*. 2nd ed. New York: Doubleday, 1957.
Alexander, Ralph H. *Ezekiel*. Everyman's Bible Commentary. Chicago: Moody, 1976.
———. "Ezekiel." In *Jeremiah-Ezekiel*, vol. 7 of *Expositor's Bible Commentary*, edited by Tremper Longman III and David E. Garland, 641–925. Rev ed. Grand Rapids: Zondervan, 2010.
Alexander, T. Desmond. *The City of God and the Goal of Creation*. Short Studies in Biblical Theology. Wheaton, IL: Crossway, 2018.
———. *From Eden to the New Jerusalem: An Introduction to Biblical Theology*. Grand Rapids: Kregel, 2009.
Alexander, T. Desmond, and Simon Gathercole, eds. *Heaven on Earth: The Temple in Biblical Theology*. Carlisle, UK: Paternoster, 2004.
Allen, Leslie C. *Ezekiel 1–19*. Word Biblical Commentary 28. Dallas: Thomas Nelson, 1994.
———. *Ezekiel 20–48*. Word Biblical Commentary 29. Dallas: Thomas Nelson, 1990.
Allison, Jr., Dale C. "The Living Water (John 4:10–14, 6:35c, 7:37–39)." *St. Vladimir's Theological Quarterly* 30 (1986) 143–57.
Andiñach, Pablo R. *El Dios que Está: Teología del Antiguo Testamento*. Estudios Bíblicos. Navarre. Spain: Verbo Divino, 2014.
Apóstolo, Silvio Sergio Scatolini. "Imagining Ezekiel." *Journal of Hebrew Scriptures* 8.13 (2008) 1–30.
Awabdy, Mark A. "YHWH Exegetes Torah: How Ezekiel 44:7–9 Bars Foreigners from the Sanctuary." *Journal of Biblical Literature* 131 (2012) 685–703.
Baker, David L. *Two Testaments, One Bible: The Theological Relationship Between the Old and New Testaments*. 3rd ed. Downers Grove, IL: InterVarsity, 2010.
———. "Typology and the Christian Use of the Old Testament." *Scottish Journal of Theology* 29 (1976) 137–57.
Barker, Margaret. *King of the Jews: Temple Theology in John's Gospel*. New York: SPCK, 2014.
Barr, James. "Allegory and Typology." In *Westminster Dictionary of the Bible*, edited by John D. Davis and Henry Snyder Gehman, 11–15. Philadelphia: Westminster, 1944.
———. *Old and New in Interpretation: A Study of the Two Testaments*. London: SCM, 1966.

Bauckham, Richard A. *The Climax of Prophecy: Studies on the Book of Revelation.* New York: T. & T. Clark, 1993.
Baumgärtel, Friedrich. "The Hermeneutical Problem of the Old Testament." Translated by Murray Newman. In *Essays on Old Testament Hermeneutics*, edited by Claus Westermann and James Luther Mays, 134–59. Richmond, VA: John Knox, 1963.
Beale, G. K. *The Book of Revelation.* New International Greek Testament Commentary. Grand Rapids: Eerdmans, 1999.
———. *Handbook on the New Testament Use of the Old Testament: Exegesis and Interpretation.* Grand Rapids: Baker, 2012.
———. *John's Use of the Old Testament in Revelation.* Library of New Testament Studies 166. New York: Sheffield Academic, 1998.
———. *A New Testament Biblical Theology: The Unfolding of the Old Testament in the New.* Grand Rapids: Baker, 2011.
———. "Positive Answer to the Question." In *The Right Doctrine from the Wrong Texts?: Essays on the Use of the Old Testament in the New*, edited by G. K. Beale, 387–404. Grand Rapids: Baker, 1994.
———. *The Temple and the Church's Mission: A Biblical Theology of the Dwelling Place of God.* New Studies in Biblical Theology 17. Downers Grove, IL: Intervarsity, 2004.
Beasley-Murray, George R. *The Book of Revelation.* Rev. ed. Eugene, OR: Wipf & Stock, 2010.
———. *John.* 2nd ed. Word Biblical Commentary 36. Nashville: Thomas Nelson, 1999.
Bechtel, Christopher. "Ezekiel and the Politics of Yahweh: A Study in the Kingship of God." PhD diss., University of Edinburgh, 2012.
Bergsma, John S. "The Restored Temple as 'Built Jubilee' in Ezekiel 40–48." *Proceedings* 24 (2004) 75–85.
Berry, G. R. "The Authorship of Ezekiel 40–48." *Journal of Biblical Literature* 34 (1915) 17–40.
Bertholet, Alfred. *Das Buch Hesekiel.* Abteilung 12. Kurzer Hand-Commentar zum Alten Testament. Tübingen: Mohr/Siebeck, 1897.
———. *Hesekiel.* Handbuch zum Alten Testament 13. Tübingen: Mohr/Siebeck, 1936.
Betts, Terry J. *Ezekiel the Priest: Custodian of Tôrâ.* Studies in Biblical Literature 74. New York: Peter Lang, 2005.
Biggs, Charles R. "The Role of the Nasi in the Programme for Restoration in Ezekiel 40–48." *Colloquium* 16 (1983) 46–57.
Blenkinsopp, Joseph. *Ezekiel.* Interpretation. Louisville: Westminster John Knox, 1990.
Block, Daniel I. *Beyond the River Chebar: Studies in Kingship and Eschatology in the Book of Ezekiel.* Eugene, OR: Cascade, 2013.
———. *The Book of Ezekiel: Chapters 1–24.* New International Commentary on the Old Testament. Grand Rapids: Eerdmans, 1997.
———. *The Book of Ezekiel: Chapters 25–48.* New International Commentary on the Old Testament. Grand Rapids: Eerdmans, 1998.
———. *By the River Chebar: Historical, Literary, and Theological Studies in the Book of Ezekiel.* Eugene, OR: Cascade, 2013.
Bodi, Daniel. "The Double Current and the Tree of Healing in Ezekiel 47:1–12 in Light of Babylonian Iconography and Texts." *Die Welt Des Orients* 45.1 (2015) 22–37.
Borchert, Gerald L. *John 1–11.* New American Commentary 25A. Nashville: B&H, 1996.
———. *John 12–21.* New American Commentary 25B. Nashville: B&H, 2002.
Boustian, Ra'anan S. "Hekhalot Literature." In *DEJ*, 719–21.

Brettler, Marc Zvi. *How to Read the Bible*. Philadelphia: Jewish Publication Society, 2005.

Brodsky, Harold. "The Utopian Map in Ezekiel (48:1–35)." *Jewish Bible Quarterly* 34 (2006) 20–26.

Brooke, George J. *The Dead Sea Scrolls and the New Testament*. Minneapolis: Fortress, 2005.

Brown, Raymond E. *The Gospel According to John: I–XII*. Anchor Bible Commentary 29. New York: Doubleday, 1966.

———. *The Gospel According to John: XIII–XXI*. Anchor Bible Commentary 29A. Garden City, NY: Doubleday, 1970.

Brownlee, William H. "The Aftermath of the Fall of Judah According to Ezekiel." *Journal of Biblical Literature* 4 (1970) 393–404.

———. *Ezekiel 1–19*. Word Biblical Commentary 28. Waco, TX: Word, 1986.

Bruce, F. F. *Commentary on Galatians*. New International Greek Testament Commentary. Grand Rapids: Eerdmans, 1982.

Bryan, Steven M. "The Eschatological Temple in John 14." *Bulletin for Biblical Research* 15 (2005) 187–98.

Caird, G. B. *A Commentary on the Revelation of St. John the Divine*. Harper's New Testament Commentaries. New York: Harper & Row, 1966.

Caneday, Ardel B. "Covenant Lineage Allegorically Prefigured: 'Which Things Are Written Allegorically' (Galatians 4:21–31)." *Southern Baptist Journal of Theology* 14.3 (2010) 50–77.

———. "The SBJT Forum: Biblical Theology for the Church." *Southern Baptist Journal of Theology* 10.2 (2006) 96–98.

Carson, D. A. *The Gospel According to John*. Pillar New Testament Commentary. Grand Rapids: Eerdmans, 1991.

———. "The Lord Is There: Ezekiel 40–48." In *Coming Home: Essays on the New Heaven and New Earth*, edited by D. A. Carson and Jeff Robinson Sr., 43–62. Wheaton, IL: Crossway, 2017.

———. "Mystery and Fulfillment: Toward a More Comprehensive Paradigm of Paul's Understanding of the Old and the New." In *Justification and Variegated Nomism: The Paradoxes of Paul*, edited by D. A. Carson, Peter T. O'Brien, and Mark A. Seifrid, 2:393–436. Tübingen: Mohr/Siebeck, 2004.

———. "Systematic Theology and Biblical Theology." In *NDBT*, 89–104.

Chanikuzhy, Jacob. *Jesus, the Eschatological Temple: An Exegetical Study of Jn 2,13–22 in the Light of the Pre-70 C.E. Eschatological Temple Hopes and the Synoptic Temple Action*. Contributions to Biblical Exegesis and Theology 58. Leuven: Peeters, 2012.

Childs, Brevard. *Old Testament Theology in a Canonical Context*. Philadelphia: Fortress, 1985.

Clark, Terry Ray. "'I Will Be King over You': The Rhetoric of Divine Kingship in the Book of Ezekiel." PhD diss., University of Denver, 2008.

Clements, R. E. *God and Temple*. Philadelphia: Fortress, 1965.

Clifford, Richard J. *The Cosmic Mountain in Canaan and the Old Testament*. Harvard Semitic Monographs 4. Cambridge, MA: Harvard University Press, 1972.

Clowney, Edmund P. "The Final Temple." *Westminster Theological Journal* 35 (1972) 156–89.

———. *Preaching and Biblical Theology*. Grand Rapids: Eerdmans, 1961.

Cogan, Mordechai. "Into Exile." *The Oxford Dictionary of the Biblical World*, edited by Michael D. Coogan. Oxford: Oxford University Press, 1998.

Collins, John J. *The Apocalyptic Imagination*. 3rd ed. Grand Rapids: Eerdmans, 2016.

Collins, Terrence. *The Mantle of Elijah: The Redaction Criticism of the Prophetical Books*. Biblical Studies 20. Sheffield, UK: JSOT Press, 1993.

Coloe, Mary L. *God Dwells with Us: Temple Symbolism in the Fourth Gospel*. Collegeville, MN: Liturgical, 2001.

Cook, Stephen L. *Ezekiel 38–48: A New Translation with Introduction and Commentary*. Anchor Bible Commentary 22B. New Haven, CT: Yale University Press, 2018.

———. "Innerbiblical Interpretation in Ezekiel 44 and the History of Israel's Priesthood." *Journal of Biblical Literature* 114 (1995) 193–208.

Cook, Stephen L. and Corrine L. Patton, eds. *Ezekiel's Hierarchical World: Wrestling with a Tiered Reality*. Society of Biblical Literature Symposium Series 31. Atlanta: Society of Biblical Literature, 2004.

Cooke, George A. *A Critical Commentary on the Book of Ezekiel*. International Critical Commentary 1. Edinburgh: T. & T. Clark, 1936.

Crane, Ashley S. *Israel's Restoration: A Textual-Comparative Exploration of Ezekiel 36–39*. Vetus Testamentum Supplement Series 122. Leiden: Brill, 2008.

Darr, Katheryn Pfisterer. "Ezekiel." In *Isaiah–Ezekiel*, vol. 6 of *The New Interpreter's Bible*, edited by Leander Keck. Nashville: Abingdon, 2001.

———. "The Wall around Paradise: Ezekielian Ideas about the Future." *Vetus Testamentum* 37 (1987) 271–79.

Davidson, Richard M. *Typology in Scripture: A Study of Hermeneutical Typos Structures*. Andrews University Seminary Doctoral Dissertations Series 2. Berrien Springs, MI: Andrews University Press, 1981.

Davila, James R. "The Macrocosmic Temple, Scriptural Exegesis, and the Songs of the Sabbath Sacrifice." *Dead Sea Discoveries* 9.1 (2002) 1–19.

Davis, Ellen F. *Swallowing the Scroll: Textuality and the Dynamics of Discourse in Ezekiel's Prophecy*. Journal for the Study of the Old Testament Supplement Series 78. Decatur, GA: Almond, 1989.

Day, John, ed. *Temple and Worship in Biblical Israel*. Library of Hebrew Bible/Old Testament Studies 422. New York: T. & T. Clark, 2005.

De Boer, E. A. *John Calvin on the Visions of Ezekiel: Historical and Hermeneutical Studies in John Calvin's Sermons Inédits, Especially on Ezek. 36–48*. Kerkhistorische Bijdragen 21. Leiden: Brill, 2004.

DeHaan, Martin R. *The Tabernacle*. Grand Rapids: Zondervan, 1955.

De Jonge, Henk Jan, and Johannes Tromp, eds. *The Book of Ezekiel and Its Influence*. Aldershot, UK: Ashgate, 2007.

Dempster, Stephen G. *Dominion and Dynasty: A Theology of the Hebrew Bible*. New Studies in Biblical Theology 15. Downers Grove, IL: IVP Academic, 2014.

Deutsch, Celia. "Transformation of Symbols: The New Jerusalem in Rv 21:1—22:5." *Zeitschrift für die Neutestamentliche Wissenschaft und die Kunde der Älteren Kirche* 78.1–2 (1987) 106–26.

Dodd, C. H. *The Interpretation of the Fourth Gospel*. Cambridge: Cambridge University Press, 1958.

Draper, J. A. "Temple, Tabernacle and Mystical Experience in John." *Neotestamentica* 31 (1997) 263–88.

Duguid, Iain M. *Ezekiel*. NIV Application Commentary. Grand Rapids: Zondervan, 1999.

———. *Ezekiel and the Leaders of Israel*. Supplements to Vetus Testamentum 56. Leiden: Brill, 1994.

———. "Putting Priests in Their Place." In *Ezekiel's Hierarchical World: Wrestling with a Tiered Reality*, edited by Stephen L. Cook and Corrine L. Patton, 43–60. Society of Biblical Literature Seminar Series. Atlanta: SBL, 2004.

Duke, Rodney K. "Punishment or Restoration? Another Look at the Levites of Ezekiel." *Journal for the Study of the Old Testament* 40 (1988) 61–81.

Dumbrell, William J. *Covenant and Creation: An Old Testament Covenantal Theology*. Exeter, UK: Paternoster, 1984.

———. *The End of the Beginning: Revelation 21–22 and the Old Testament*. Moore Theological College Lectures. Eugene, OR: Wipf & Stock, 1985.

Duvall, J. Scott, and J. Daniel Hays. *God's Relational Presence: The Cohesive Center of Biblical Theology*. Grand Rapids: Baker, 2019.

Eichrodt, Walther. *Ezekiel*. Translated by Cosslett Quin. Old Testament Library. Philadelphia: Westminster, 1970.

———. *Theology of the Old Testament*. Translated by J. A. Baker. Old Testament Library. Louisville: Westminster John Knox, 1961.

———. "Is Typological Exegesis an Appropriate Method?" Translated by James Barr. In *Essays on Old Testament Hermeneutics*, edited by Claus Westermann and James Luther Mays, 224–45. Richmond, VA: John Knox, 1963.

Ellison, H. L. *Ezekiel: The Man and His Message*. London: Paternoster, 1956.

Emerson, Matthew Y. "Arbitrary Allegory, Typical Typology, or Intertextual Interpretation?" *Biblical Theology Bulletin* 43.1 (2013) 14–22.

Emerton, J. A. "Priests and Levites in Deuteronomy." *Vetus Testamentum* 12 (1962) 129–38.

Evans, Craig A. "Jesus' Action in the Temple: Cleansing or Portent of Destruction?" *Catholic Biblical Quarterly* 51 (1989) 237–70.

———. *Word and Glory: On the Exegetical and Theological Background of John's Prologue*. Journal for the Study of the New Testament Supplement Series 89. Sheffield, UK: Sheffield Academic, 1993.

Ewald, Heinrich. "Hezeqiel, 'Yesaya' XL–LXVI." *Commentary on the Prophets of the Old Testament*. Vol. 4. Translated by J. Frederick Smith. Edinburgh: Williams and Norgate, 1880.

Fairbairn, Patrick. *Ezekiel and the Book of His Prophecy*. 4th ed. Edinburgh: T. & T. Clark, 1876.

———. *The Typology of Scripture: Viewed in Connection with the Whole Series of the Divine Dispensations*. Vol. 1. New York: Funk & Wagnalis, 1900.

Fechter, Friedrich. "Priesthood in Exile According to the Book of Ezekiel." In *Ezekiel's Hierarchical World: Wrestling with a Tiered Reality*, edited by Stephen L. Cook and Corrine L. Patton, 27–41. Society of Biblical Literature Symposium Series 31. Atlanta: SBL, 2004.

Fekkes, Jan. *Isaiah and Prophetic Traditions in the Book of Revelation: Visionary Antecedents and Their Development*. Journal for the Study of the New Testament Supplement Series 93. Sheffield, UK: JSOT Press, 1994.

Fishbane, Michael. *Biblical Interpretation in Ancient Israel*. New York: Oxford University Press, 1985.

Fohrer, Georg and Kurt Galling. *Ezechiel*. Handbuch zum Alten Testament 13. Tübingen: Mohr/Siebeck, 1955.

Foulkes, Francis. *The Acts of God: A Study of the Basis of Typology in the Old Testament*. London: Tyndale, 1958.

Fowler, William Glenn. ""The Influence of Ezekiel in the Fourth Gospel: Intertextuality and Interpretation." PhD diss., Golden Gate Baptist Theological Seminary, 1995.
France, R. T. *Jesus and the Old Testament: His Application of Old Testament Passages to Himself and His Mission.* Downers Grove, IL: InterVarsity, 1971.
Frei, Hans W. *The Eclipse of Biblical Narrative: A Study in Eighteenth and Nineteenth Century Hermeneutics.* New Haven, CT: Yale University Press, 1974.
Gaebelein, Arno C. *The Prophet Ezekiel: An Analytical Exposition.* New York: Our Hope, 1918.
Ganzel, Tova. "The Defilement and Desecration of the Temple in Ezekiel," *Biblica* 89 (2008), 369–79.
———. "The Descriptions of the Restoration of Israel in Ezekiel." *Vetus Testamentum* 60 (2010) 197–211.
———. "The Shattered Dream: The Prophecies of Joel, a Bridge between Ezekiel and Haggai?" *Journal of Hebrew Scriptures* 11.6 (2011) 1–22.
Ganzel, Tova, and Shalom E. Holtz. "Ezekiel's Temple in Babylonian Context." *Vetus Testamentum* 64 (2014) 211–26.
Garrett, Duane A. *Rethinking Genesis: The Sources and Authorship of the First Book of the Pentateuch.* Grand Rapids: Baker, 1991.
Garscha, Jörg. *Studien zum Ezechielbuch: Eine redaktionscritische Untersuchung von Ez 1–39.* Europäische Hochschul Studien 23. Frankfurt: Peter Lang, 1974.
Gentry, Peter J., and Stephen J. Wellum. *Kingdom Through Covenant: A Biblical-Theological Understanding of the Covenants.* Wheaton, IL: Crossway, 2012.
Gese, Hartmut. *Der Verfassungsentwurf des Ezechiel (Kap 40.48): Traditionsgeschichtlich untersucht.* Tübingen: Mohr/Siebeck, 1957.
Gile, Jason. "Deuteronomic Influence in the Book of Ezekiel." PhD diss., Wheaton College, 2013.
Goldingay, John. *Old Testament Theology: Israel's Gospel.* Vol. 1. Downers Grove, IL: IVP Academic, 2003.
Goldsworthy, Graeme. *Christ-Centered Biblical Theology: Hermeneutical Foundations and Principles.* Downers Grove, IL: IVP Academic, 2012.
———. *Gospel-Centered Hermeneutics.* Downers Grove, IL: InterVarsity, 2006.
Goppelt, Leonhard. *Typos: Die Typologische Deutung des Alten Testaments im Neuen.* Munich: C. Bertelsmann, 1939.
———. *Typos: The Typological Interpretation of the Old Testament in the New.* Translated by Donald H. Madvig. Grand Rapids: Eerdmans, 1982.
———. "Τυπος, Κτλ." In *TDNT*, 246–59.
Greenberg, Moshe. "The Design and Themes of Ezekiel's Program of Restoration." *Interpretation* 38.2 (1984) 181–208.
———. *Ezekiel 1–20: A New Translation with Introduction and Commentary.* Anchor Bible Commentary 22. Garden City, NY: Doubleday, 1983.
———. *Ezekiel 21–37: A New Translation with Introduction and Commentary.* Anchor Bible Commentary 22A. Garden City, NY: Doubleday, 1997.
———. "Idealism and Practicality in Numbers 35:4–5 and Ezekiel 48." *Journal of Ancient Oriental Studies* 88 (1968) 59–65.
———. "What Are Valid Criteria for Determining Inauthentic Matter in Ezekiel?" In *Ezekiel and His Book: Textual and Literary Criticism and their Interrelations*, edited by Johan Lust, 123–35. Leuven: Leuven University Press, 1986.

Gundry, Robert H. "In My Father's House Are Many Monai (John 14:2)." *Zeitschrift für die Neutestamentliche Wissenschaft und die Kunde der Älteren Kirche* 58 (1967) 68–72.

Gunneweg, Antonius H. J. *Leviten und Priester: Hauptlinien der Traditionsbildung und Geschichte des Israelitisch-Jüdischen Kultpersonals*. Forschungen zur Religion und Literatur des Alten und Neuen Testaments 89. Göttingen: Vandenhoeck & Ruprecht, 1965.

Gurtner, D. M., and N. Perrin. "Temple." In *DJG*, 939–47.

Haenchen, Ernst. *John 1: A Commentary on the Gospel of John, Chapters 1–6*. Translated by Robert W. Funk. Hermeneia. Philadelphia: Fortress, 1984.

———. *John 2: A Commentary on the Gospel of John, Chapters 7–21*. Translated by Robert W. Funk. Hermeneia. Philadelphia: Fortress, 1984.

Hals, Ronald M. *Ezekiel*. The Forms of the Old Testament Literature 19. Grand Rapids: Eerdmans, 1989.

Hamid-Khani, Saeed. *Revelation and Concealment of Christ: A Theological Inquiry into the Elusive Language of the Fourth Gospel*. Wissenschaftliche Untersuchungen zum Neuen Testament 2, 120. Reihe. Tübingen: Mohr/Siebeck, 2000.

Hamilton, James M. *God's Glory in Salvation through Judgment: A Biblical Theology*. Wheaton, IL: Crossway, 2010.

Hanson, Anthony T. *The Prophetic Gospel: A Study of John and the Old Testament*. Scholar's Editions in Biblical Studies. New York: T. & T. Clark, 2006.

Hanson, Paul D. *The Dawn of Apocalyptic: The Historical and Sociological Roots of Jewish Apocalyptic Eschatology*. Philadelphia: Fortress, 1975.

Haran, Menahem. "Ezekiel, P, and the Priestly School." *Vetus Testamentum* 58 (2008) 211–18.

———. "The Law-Code of Ezekiel XL–XLVIII and Its Relation to the Priestly School." *Hebrew Union College Annual* 50 (1979) 45–71.

———. *Temples and Temple-Service in Ancient Israel: An Inquiry into Biblical Cult Phenomena and the Historical Setting of the Priestly School*. Winona Lake, IN: Eisenbrauns, 1985.

Hays, J. Daniel. *The Temple and the Tabernacle: A Study of God's Dwelling Places from Genesis to Revelation*. Grand Rapids: Baker, 2016.

Hays, Richard B. *Reading Backwards: Figural Christology and the Fourfold Gospel Witness*. Waco, TX: Baylor University Press, 2014.

Herrmann, Johannes. *Ezechielstudien*. Leipzig: J. C. Heinrichs, 1908.

Hiebel, Janina Maria. *Ezekiel's Vision Accounts as Interrelated Narratives: A Redaction-Critical and Theological Study*. Beihefte zur Zeitschrift für die alttestamentliche Wissenschaft 475. Berlin: De Gruyter, 2015.

Himmelfarb, Martha. "The Temple and the Garden of Eden in Ezekiel, the Book of the Watchers, and the Wisdom of Ben Sira." In *Sacred Places and Profane Spaces: Essays in the Geographics of Judaism, Christianity, and Islam*, edited by J. S. Scott and P. Simpson-Horsley, 63–78. Westport, CT: Greenwood, 1991.

Hölscher, Gustav. *Hezekiel: Der Dicther and das Buch*. Beihefte zur Zeitschrift für die alttestamentliche Wissenschaft 39. Giessen: A. Töpelmann, 1924.

Hoskins, Paul M. *Jesus as the Fulfillment of the Temple in the Gospel of John*. Paternoster Biblical Monographs. Eugene, OR: Wipf & Stock, 2007.

House, Paul R. *Old Testament Theology*. Downers Grove, IL: IVP Academic, 2018.

Hullinger, Jerry M. "The Function of the Millennial Sacrifices in Ezekiel's Temple, Part 1." *Bibliotheca Sacra* 167 (2010) 40–57.

———. "The Function of the Millennial Sacrifices in Ezekiel's Temple, Part 2." *Bibliotheca Sacra* 167 (2010) 166–79.

Hunt, Alice. *Missing Priests: The Zadokites in Tradition and History*. Library of Hebrew Bible/Old Testament Studies 452. New York: T. & T. Clark, 2006.

Hurowitz, Victor. *I Have Built You an Exalted House: Temple Building in the Bible in Light of Mesopotamian and Northwest Semitic Writings*. Library of Hebrew Bible/Old Testament Studies 115. Sheffield, UK: Sheffield Academic, 1992.

Hwang, Sunwoo. "איש in Ezekiel 40–48." *Scandinavian Journal of the Old Testament* 23 (2009) 183–94.

Ironside, H. A. *Expository Notes on Ezekiel the Prophet*. Neptune, NJ: Loizeaux Brothers, 1949.

Jenson, Philip P. "Temple." In *DOTP*, 767–75.

Joyce, Paul M. "Dislocation and Adaptation in the Exilic Age and After." In *After the Exile: Essays in Honour of Rex Mason*, edited by John Barton and David J. Reimer, 45–58. Macon, GA: Mercer University Press, 1996.

———. *Divine Initiative and Human Response in Ezekiel*. Journal for the Study of the Old Testament Supplement Series 51. Sheffield, UK: JSOT Press, 1989.

———. *Ezekiel: A Commentary*. Library of Hebrew Bible/Old Testament Studies 482. New York: T. & T. Clark, 2007.

———. "Ezekiel 40–42: The Earliest 'Heavenly Ascent' Narrative?" In *The Book of Ezekiel and Its Influence*, edited by Henk de Jonge and Johannes Tromp, 17–42. Aldershot, UK: Ashgate, 2007.

———. "The Prophets and Psychological Interpretation." In *Prophecy and the Prophets in Ancient Israel: Proceedings of the Oxford Old Testament Seminar*, edited by John Day, 133–48. Library of Hebrew Bible/Old Testament Studies 531. New York: T. & T. Clark, 2010.

———. "Temple and Worship in Ezekiel 40–48." In *Temple and Worship in Biblical Israel*, edited by John Day, 145–63. Library of Hebrew Bible/Old Testament Studies 422. New York: T. & T. Clark, 2005.

Joyce, Paul M., and Dalit Rom-Shiloni, eds. *The God Ezekiel Creates*. Library of Hebrew Bible/Old Testament Studies 607. New York: T. & T.z Clark, 2015.

Kaiser, Walter C. *Toward an Old Testament Theology*. Grand Rapids: Zondervan, 1991.

Kasher, Rimon. "Anthropomorphism, Holiness and Cult." *Zeitschrift für die alttestamentliche Wissenschaft* 110 (1998) 192–208.

Keener, Craig S. *The Spirit in the Gospels and Acts: Divine Purity and Power*. Peabody, MA: Hendrickson, 1997.

Keil, Carl Friedrich. *Biblical Commentary on the Prophecies of Ezekiel*. Vol. 2 Translated by James Martin. Edinburgh: T. & T. Clark, 1876.

Keil, Carl Friedrich, and Franz Delitzsch. *Ezekiel, Daniel*. Vol. 9 of *Commentary on the Old Testament*. Translated by James Martin and M. G. Easton. Peabody, MA: Hendrickson, 1996.

Kerr, Alan R. *The Temple of Jesus' Body: The Temple Theme in the Gospel of John*. Journal for the Study of the New Testament Supplement Series 220. New York: Sheffield Academic, 2002.

Kim, Soo J. "YHWH Shammah: The City as Gateway to the Presence of YHWH. *Journal for the Study of the Old Testament* 39 (2014) 187–207.

Kinzer, Mark. "Temple Christology in the Gospel of John." In *Society of Biblical Literature 1998 Seminar Papers: Part One*, 447–64. Society of Biblical Literature Seminar Papers Series 37. Atlanta: Scholars, 1998.

Klein, Ralph W. *Ezekiel: The Prophet and His Message*. Columbia, SC: University of South Carolina Press, 1988.

Klostermann, August. "Ezechiel: Ein Beitrag zu Besserer Würdigung seiner Person und seiner Schrift." *Theologische Studien und Kritiken* 50 (1877) 391–439.

Koester, Craig R. *The Dwelling of God: The Tabernacle in the Old Testament, Intertestamental Jewish Literature, and the New Testament*. Catholic Biblical Quarterly Monograph Series 22. Washington, DC: Catholic Biblical Association of America, 1989.

———. *Revelation: A New Translation with Introduction and Commentary*. Anchor Bible 38A. New Haven, CT: Yale University Press, 2014.

Konkel, Michael. *Architektonik des Heiligen: Studien zur zweiten Tempelvision Ezechiels (Ez 40–48)*. Bonner Biblische Beiträge 129. Berlin: Philo, 2001.

———. "Das Datum der Zweiten Tempelvision Ezechiels (Ez 40,1)." *Biblische Notizen* 92 (1998) 55–70.

Köstenberger, Andreas J. "'The Destruction of the Second Temple and the Composition of the Fourth Gospel." In *Historical and Literary Studies in John: Challenges to Prevailing Paradigms*, edited by Peter Head and John Lierman, 69–108. Wissenschaftliche Untersuchungen zum Neuen Testament 2, 219. Tübingen: Mohr/Siebeck, 2006.

———. *John*. Baker Exegetical Commentary on the New Testament. Grand Rapids: Baker Academic, 2004.

———. "John." In *Commentary on the New Testament Use of the Old Testament*, edited by D. A. Carson and G. K. Beale, 415–512. Grand Rapids: Baker, 2007.

Kunz, Marivete Zanoni. "O Espaço Divino no Discurso de Ezequiel nos Capítulos 8 a 11 e 43 a 48." ThD diss., Escola Superior de Teologia, 2012.

Kutsko, John F. *Between Heaven and Earth: Divine Presence and Absence in the Book of Ezekiel*. Biblical and Judaic Studies 7. Winona Lake, IN: Eisenbrauns, 2000.

Lampe, G. W. H. "The Reasonableness of Typology." In *Essays on Typology*, 9–38. Studies in Biblical Theology 22. Naperville, IL: Allenson, 1957.

Latto, Anti. *Josiah and David Redivivus*. Coniectanea Biblica Old Testament 33. Stockholm: Almqvist & Wiksell, 1992.

Leithart, Peter J. *Deep Exegesis: The Mystery of Reading Scripture*. Waco, TX: Baylor University Press, 2009.

Levenson, Jon D. "Ezekiel in the Perspective of Two Commentaries." *Interpretation* 38 (1984) 210–17.

———. *Sinai and Zion: An Entry into the Jewish Bible*. Minneapolis: Winston, 1985.

———. "The Temple and the World." *Journal of Religion* 64 (1984) 275–98.

———. *Theology of the Program of Restoration of Ezekiel 40–48*. Harvard Semitic Monograph Series 10. Missoula, MT: Scholars, 1976.

Levine, Baruch. "The Temple Scroll: Aspects of Its Historical Provenance and Literary Character." *Bulletin of the American Schools of Oriental Research* 232 (1978) 5–23.

Levine, Lee I. *The Ancient Synagogue: The First Thousand Years*. New Haven, CT: Yale University Press, 2000.

Levoratti, Armando J. *Comentario Bíblico Latinoamericano, Antiguo Testamento: Libros Proféticos y Sapienciales*. Vol. 2. Navarre, Spain: Verbo Divino, 2007.

Lilly, Ingrid E. *Two Books of Ezekiel: Papyrus 967 and the Masoretic Text as Variant Literary Editions*. Vetus Testamentum Supplement Series 150. Leiden: Brill, 2012.

Lindars, Barnabas. *The Gospel of John*. New Century Bible Commentary. Grand Rapids: Eerdmans, 1982.

Liss, Hanna. "'Describe the Temple to the House of Israel': Preliminary Remarks on the Temple Vision in the Book of Ezekiel and the Question of Fictionality in Priestly Literatures." In *Utopia and Dystopia in Prophetic Literature*, edited by Ehud Ben Zvi, 122–45. Publications of the Finnish Exegetical Society 92. Göttingen: Vandenhoeck & Ruprecht, 2006.

Lockett, Darian R., and Edward Klink III. *Understanding Biblical Theology: A Comparison of Theory and Practice*. Grand Rapids: Zondervan, 2012.

Lohfink, Norbert. "The Song of Victory at the Red Sea." In *The Christian Meaning of the Old Testament*, translated by R. A. Wilson, 67–86. Milwaukee: Bruce, 1968.

Longman, Tremper R., III. *Psalms*. Tyndale Old Testament Commentaries 15–16. Downers Grove, IL: InterVarsity, 2014.

Ludwig, Alan. "Ezekiel 43:9: Prescription or Promise?" In *Hear the Word of Yahweh: Essays on Scripture and Archaeology in Honor of Horace D. Hummel*, edited by Dean O. Wenthe, Paul L. Schrieber, and Lee A. Maxwell, 67–78. St. Louis: Concordia, 2002.

Lust, Johan. "Ezekiel 36–40 in the Oldest Greek Manuscript." *Catholic Biblical Quarterly* 43 (1981) 517–33.

———. "Ezekiel Salutes Isaiah: Ezekiel 20:32–44." In *Studies in the Book of Isaiah: Festschrift Willem A.M. Beuken*, edited by J. van Ruiten and M. Vervenne, 367–82. Bibliotheca Ephemeridum Theologicarum Lovaniensium 132. Leuven: Peeters, 1997.

———. "Ezekiel's Utopian Expectations." In *Flores Florentino: Dead Sea Scrolls and Other Early Jewish Studies in Honour of Florentino Garcia Martinez*, edited by A. Hilhorst, E. Puech, and E. Tigchelaar, 403–20. Leiden: Brill, 2007.

———. "The Use of Textual Witnesses for the Establishment of the Text: The Shorter and Longer Texts of Ezekiel." In *Ezekiel and His Book: Textual and Literary Criticism and Their Interrelations*, edited by Johan Lust, 7–20. Leuven: Leuven University Press, 1986.

Lyons, Michael A. *From Law to Prophecy: Ezekiel's Use of the Holiness Code*. Library of Hebrew Bible/Old Testament Studies 507. New York: T. & T. Clark, 2009.

MacDonald, Nathan. *Priestly Rule: Polemic and Biblical Interpretation in Ezekiel 44*. Beihefte zur Zeitschrift für die alttestamentliche Wissenschaft 476. Berlin: De Gruyter, 2015.

Mackay, Cameron M. "Ezekiel's Division of Palestine among the Tribes." *Princeton Theological Review* 22.1 (1924) 27–45.

Maier, Johann. "The Architectural History of the Temple in Jerusalem in Light of the Temple Scroll." In *Temple Scroll Studies: Papers Presented at the International Symposium on the Temple Scroll*, edited by George J. Brooke, 23–62. Sheffield: JSOT Press, 1989.

Manning, Gary T., Jr. *Echoes of a Prophet: The Use of Ezekiel in the Gospel of John and in the Literature of the Second Temple Period*. Journal for the Study of the New Testament Supplement Series 270. New York: T. & T. Clark, 2004.

Martin, Oren. *Bound for the Promised Land*. New Studies in Biblical Theology 34. Downers Grove, IL: InterVarsity, 2015.

Martínez, Florentino García. "L'Interprétation de la Torah D'Ézéchiel Dans les MSS. de Qumran." *Revue de Qumran* 13 (1988), 441–52.

Mathewson, David. *A New Heaven and a New Earth: The Meaning and Function of the Old Testament in Revelation 21.1–22.5*. Journal for the Study of the New Testament Supplement Series 238. New York: Sheffield Academic, 2003.

———. "Assessing Old Testament Allusions in the Book of Revelation." *Evangelical Quarterly* 75.4 (2003) 311–25.
Mayfield, Tyler D. *Literary Structure and Setting in Ezekiel*. Tübingen: Mohr/Siebeck, 2010.
McCaffrey, James. *The House with Many Rooms: The Temple Theme of Jn. 14,2–3*. Analecta Biblica 114. Rome: Pontifical Biblical Institute, 1988.
McConville, J. Gordon. "Priests and Levites in Ezekiel: A Crux in the Interpretation of Israel's History." *Tyndale Bulletin* 34 (1983) 3–31.
McKelvey, R. J. *The New Temple: The Church in the New Testament*. London: Oxford University Press, 1969.
———. "Temple." In *NDBT*, 806–11.
McNamara, Martin. "'To Prepare a Resting-Place for You.' A Targumic Expression and John 14:2f." *Milltown Studies* 3 (1979) 100–108.
Mein, Andrew, and Paul M. Joyce, eds. *After Ezekiel: Essays on the Reception of a Difficult Prophet*. Library of Hebrew Bible/Old Testament Studies 535. New York: T. & T. Clark, 2011.
Merrill, Eugene H. *Everlasting Dominion: A Theology of the Old Testament*. Nashville: Broadman & Holman, 2006.
Meyers, Carol. "Temple, Jerusalem." In *ABD*, 6:350–68.
Michaels, J. Ramsey. *The Gospel of John*. New International Commentary on the New Testament. Grand Rapids: Eerdmans, 2010.
Milgrom, Jacob. *Studies in Levitical Terminology, I: The Encroacher and the Levite, the Term 'Aboda*. Near Eastern Studies 14. Berkeley, CA: University of California Press, 1970.
Milgrom, Jacob, with Daniel I. Block. *Ezekiel's Hope: A Commentary on Ezekiel 38–48*. Eugene, OR: Cascade, 2012.
Moo, Douglas J. "The Problem of Sensus Plenior." In *Hermeneutics, Authority, and Canon*, edited by D. A. Carson and John D. Woodbridge, 175–213. Grand Rapids: Baker, 1995.
Morales, L. Michael, ed. *Cult and Cosmos: Tilting Toward a Temple-Centered Theology*. Biblical Tools and Studies 18. Leuven: Peeters, 2014.
———. *The Tabernacle Pre-Figured: Cosmic Mountain Ideology in Genesis and Exodus*. Biblical Tools and Studies 15. Leuven: Peeters, 2012.
———. *Who Shall Ascend the Mountain of the Lord?: A Biblical Theology of the Book of Leviticus*. New Studies in Biblical Theology 37. Downers Grove, IL: InterVarsity, 2015.
Morris, Leon. *The Gospel According to John*. New International Commentary on the New Testament. Grand Rapids: Eerdmans, 1971.
Mounce, Robert H. *The Book of Revelation*. 2nd ed. New International Commentary on the New Testament. Grand Rapids: Eerdmans, 1998.
Moyise, Steve. "Ezekiel and the Book of Revelation." In *After Ezekiel: Essays on the Reception of a Difficult Prophet*, edited by Andrew Mein and Paul M. Joyce, 45–57. New York: T. & T. Clark, 2011.
———. "Intertextuality and Historical Approaches to the Use of Scripture in the New Testament." In *Reading the Bible Intertextually*, edited by Richard B. Hays, Stefan Alkier, and Leroy Andrew Huizenga, 23–34. Waco, TX: Baylor University Press, 2009.
———. *The Old Testament in the Book of Revelation*. Journal for the Study of the New Testament Supplement Series 115. Sheffield, UK: Sheffield, 1995.

Murray, David P. *Jesus on Every Page: 10 Simple Ways to Seek and Find Christ in the Old Testament*. Nashville: Thomas Nelson, 2013.

Nevader, Madhavi. "Exile and Institution: Monarchy in the Books of Deuteronomy and Ezekiel." DPhil thesis, Oxford University, 2009.

———. *YHWH versus David*. Oxford Theological Monographs. Oxford: Oxford University Press, forthcoming.

Newsom, Carol. "Merkabah Exegesis in the Qumran Sabbath Shirot." *Journal of Jewish Studies* 38 (1987) 11–30.

Ng, Wai-Yee. *Water Symbolism in John: An Eschatological Interpretation*. Studies in Biblical Literature 115. New York: Peter Lang, 2001.

Nicholson, Ernest W. *God and His People: Covenant and Theology in the Old Testament*. New York: Oxford University Press, 1986.

———. *The Pentateuch in the Twentieth Century: The Legacy of Julius Wellhausen*. Oxford: Oxford University Press, 1998.

Nickelsburg, George W. E. "The Temple According to 1 Enoch." *BYU Studies Quarterly* 53.1 (2018) 7–24.

Niditch, Susan. "Ezekiel 40–48 in a Visionary Context." *Catholic Biblical Quarterly* 48 (1986) 208–24.

Nielsen, Kirsten. "Ezekiel's Visionary Call as Prologue: From Complexity and Changeability to Order and Stability?" *Journal for the Study of the Old Testament* 33.1 (2008) 99–114.

Ninow, Friedbert. *Indicators of Typology within the Old Testament: The Exodus Motif*. Friedensauer Schriftenreihe, Reihe A: Theologie 4. Frankfurt: Peter Lang, 2001.

Nobile, Marco. "Ez 38–39 Ed Ez 40–48: I Due Aspetti Complementari del Culmine di Uno Schema Cultuale di Fondazione." *Antonianum* 62.2–3 (1987) 141–71.

Oded, B. "'Yet I Have Been to Them *Lemikdash Meat* in the Countries Where They Have Gone' (Ezekiel 11:16)." In *Sefer Moshe: The Moshe Weinfeld Jubilee Volume: Studies in the Bible and the Ancient Near East, Qumran, and Post-Biblical Judaism*, edited by Chaim Cohen, Avi Hurvitz, and Shalom M. Paul, 103–14. Winona Lake, IN: Eisenbrauns, 2004.

O'Day, Gail R. "John." In *Luke–John*. vol. 9 of *The New Interpreter's Bible*, edited by Leander Keck, 490–875. Nashville: Abingdon, 1995.

Odell, Margaret S. *Ezekiel*. Smith & Helwys Bible Commentary. Macon, GA: Smith & Helwys, 2005.

———. "'The Wall Is No More': Temple Reform in Ezekiel 43:7–9." In *From the Foundations to the Crenellations: Essays on Temple Building in the Ancient Near East and Hebrew Bible*, edited by Mark J. Boda and J. Novotny, 339–55. Alter Orient und Altest Testament 366. Münster: Ugarit, 2010.

Odell, Margaret S., and John T. Strong, eds. *The Book of Ezekiel: Theological and Anthropological Perspectives*. Atlanta: Scholars, 2000.

O'Hare, Daniel M. *Have You Seen, Son of Man? A Study in the Translation and Vorlage of Ezekiel 40–48*. Septuagint and Cognate Studies Series 57. Leiden: Brill, 2011.

Osborne, Grant R. *Revelation*. Baker Exegetical Commentary on the New Testament. Grand Rapids: Baker, 2002.

Parker, Brent E. "Typology and Allegory: Is There a Distinction? A Brief Examination of Figural Reading." *Southern Baptist Journal of Theology* 21.1 (2017) 57–83.

Patton, Corrine L. "Ezekiel's Blueprint for the Temple of Jerusalem." PhD diss., Yale University, 1991.

Paul, M. J. "The Order of Melchizedek (Ps 110:4 and Heb 7:3)." *Westminster Theological Journal* 49 (1987) 195–211.

Paulien, Jon. "Criteria and the Assessment of Allusions to the Old Testament in the Book of Revelation." In *Studies in the Book of Revelation*, edited by Steve Moyise, 113–29. New York: T. & T. Clark, 2001.

Peterson, Brian Neil. *Ezekiel in Context: Ezekiel's Message Understood in its Historical Setting of Covenant Curses and Ancient Near Eastern Mythological Motifs*. Princeton Theological Monograph Series 182. Eugene, OR: Pickwick, 2012.

———. *John's Use of Ezekiel: Understanding the Unique Perspective of the Fourth Gospel*. Minneapolis: Fortress, 2015.

Petter, Donna Lee. "The Book of Ezekiel: Patterned after a Mesopotamian City Lament?" PhD diss., University of Toronto, 2009.

Pohlmann, Karl-Friedrich. *Das Buch des Propheten Hesekiel*. 2 vols. Göttingen: Vandenhoeck & Ruprecht, 1996, 2001.

———. *Ezechiel: Der Stand der theologischen Diskussion*. Darmstadt, Germany: Wissenschaftliche Buchgesellschaft, 2008.

———. *Ezechielstudien: Zur Redaktionsgeschichte des Buches und zur Frage nach den ältesten Texten*. Berlin: De Gruyter, 1992.

———."Forschung am Ezechielbuch 1969–2004." *Theologische Rundschau* 71 (2006) 265–309.

Pohlmann, Karl-Friedrich, with Thilo Rudnig. *Der Prophet Hesekiel/Ezechiel Kapitel 20–48*. Das Alte Testament Deutsch 22.2. Göttingen: Vandenhoeck & Ruprecht, 2001.

Poythress, Vern K. *Understanding Dispensationalists*. 2nd ed. Phillipsburg, NJ: P&R, 1994.

Presser, Nicolás. "La Escatología Apocalíptica de Ezequiel En La Revelación de Juan." *DavarLogos* 12 (2013) 129–46.

Procksch, Otto. "Fürst und Priester bei Hesekiel." *Zeitschrift für die Alttestamentliche Wissenschaft* 58.1–2 (1940) 99–133.

Provan, Iain. *The Reformation and the Right Reading of Scripture*. Waco, TX: Baylor University Press, 2017.

Ragavan, Deena, ed. *Heaven on Earth: Temples, Ritual and Cosmic Symbolism in the Ancient World*. Oriental Institute Seminars 9. Chicago: University of Chicago Press, 2013.

Rashi. *Ezekiel: Volume Two*. Translated by A. J. Rosenberg. Mikraoth Gedoloth. New York: Judaica, 1991.

Rendtorff, Rolf. *The Canonical Hebrew Bible: A Theology of the Old Testament*. Translated by David Orton. Tools for Biblical Studies 7. Leiden: Deo, 2005.

Renz, Thomas. *The Rhetorical Function of the Book of Ezekiel*. Vetus Testamentum Supplement Series 76. Leiden: Brill, 1999.

Ribbens, Benjamin J. "Levitical Sacrifice and Heavenly Cult in Hebrews." PhD diss., Wheaton College, 2013.

———. "Typology of Types: Typology in Dialogue." *Journal of Theological Interpretation* 5.1 (2011) 81–95.

Ribera, Josep. "Relación Entre el Targum y las Versiones Antiguas: Los Targumes de Jeremías y Ezequiel Comparados con LXX, Peshitta y Vulgata." *Estudios Bíblicos* 52 (1994) 317–28.

Ridderbos, Herman. *The Gospel of John: A Theological Commentary*. Grand Rapids: Eerdmans, 1997.

Robinson, Andrea L. *Temple of Presence: The Christological Fulfillment of Ezekiel 40–48 in Revelation 21:1—22:5*. Euguene, OR: Wipf & Stock, 2019.

Rom-Shiloni, Dalit. "Ezekiel as the Voice of the Exiles and Constructor of Exilic Ideology." *Hebrew Union College Annual* 76 (2005) 1–45.

Rooke, Deborah W. *Zadok's Heirs: The Role and Development of the High Priesthood in Ancient Israel*. Oxford: Oxford University Press, 2012.

Rooker, Mark F. "Evidence from Ezekiel." In *The Coming Millennial Kingdom: A Case for Premillennial Interpretation*, edited by Donald K. Campbell and Jeffrey L. Townsend, 119–34. Grand Rapids: Kregel, 1997.

Rowley, H. H. "Melchizedek and Zadok (Gen. 14 and Ps. 110)." In *Festschrift für Alfred Bertholet*, edited by Walter Baumgartner et al., 461–72. Tübingen: J. C. B. Mohr, 1950.

Rudnig, Thilo. *Heilig und Profan: Redaktionskritische Studien zu Ez 40–48*. Beiheft zur Zeitschrift für die Alttestamentliche Wissenschaft 287. Berlin: De Gruyter, 2000.

Ruiz, Jean-Pierre. *Ezekiel in the Apocalypse: The Transformation of Prophetic Language in Revelation 16,17–19,10*. European University Studies 23.376. Frankfurt: Peter Lang, 1989.

Ryrie, Charles Caldwell, ed. *The Ryrie Study Bible: New American Standard Translation*. Chicago: Moody, 1978.

Salier, Bill. "The Temple in the Gospel According to John." In *Heaven on Earth: The Temple in Biblical Theology*, edited by T. Desmond Alexander and Simon Gathercole, 121–34. Carlisle, UK: Paternoster, 2004.

Schnackenburg, Rudolf. *The Gospel According to St John*. Vol. 1. Translated by Kevin Smyth. New York: Crossroad, 1987.

———. *The Gospel According to St John*. Vol. 2. Translated by Cecily Hastings et al. New York: Seabury, 1980.

Schrock, David. "From Beelines to Plotlines: Typology That Follows the Covenantal Topography of Scripture." *Southern Baptist Journal of Theology* 21.1 (2017) 35–56.

Schwartz, Baruch J. "Ezekiel's Dim View of Israel's Restoration." In *The Book of Ezekiel: Theological and Anthropological Perspectives*, edited by Margaret S. Odell and John T. Strong, 43–67. SBL Symposium Series 9. Atlanta: Society of Biblical Literature, 2000.

———. "'Term' or Metaphor—Biblical *nasa' 'awon*." *Tarbits* 63 (1994) 149–71.

Schweitzer, Steven James. "Utopia and Utopian Theory." In *Utopia and Dystopia*, edited by Ehud Ben Zvi, 13–26. Publications of the Finnish Exegetical Society 92. Göttingen: Vandenhoeck & Ruprecht, 2006.

Scofield, C. I., ed. *The New Scofield Reference Bible*. New York: Oxford University Press, 1967.

Seitz, Christopher R. *The Character of Christian Scripture: The Significance of a Two-Testament Bible*. Grand Rapids: Baker, 2011.

———. *Figured Out: Typology and Providence in Christian Scripture*. Louisville: Westminster John Knox, 2001.

Semler, Johann S. *Versuch Einer Freiern Theologischen Lehrart*. Halle, Germany: Hemmerde, 1777.

Sequeira, Aubrey, and Samuel C. Emadi. "Biblical-Theological Exegesis and the Nature of Typology." *Southern Baptist Journal of Theology* 21.1 (2017) 11–34.

Sharon, Diane M. "A Biblical Parallel to a Sumerian Temple Hymn? Ezekiel 40–48 and Gudea." *Journal of the Ancient Near Eastern Society* 24 (1996) 99–109.

Shidemantle, C. Scott. "The Use of the Old Testament in John 7:37–39: An Examination of the Freed-Carson Proposal." PhD diss., Trinity Evangelical Divinity School, 2001.

Sicre, José Luis. *"Con los Pobres de la Tierra": La Justicia Social en los Profetas de Israel.* Madrid: Ediciones Cristiandad, 1984.

———. *Los Dioses Olvidados: Poder y Riqueza en los Profetas Preexílicos.* Estudios de Antiguo Testamento. Madrid: Ediciones Cristiandad, 1979.

———. *Introducción al Profetismo Bíblico.* 2nd ed. Navarre: Verbo Divino, 2011.

Simon, Bennett. "Ezekiel's Geometric Vision of the Restored Temple: From the Rod of His Wrath to the Reed of His Measuring." *Harvard Theological Review* 102 (2009) 411–38.

Smith, Jonathan Z. *To Take Place: Toward Theory in Ritual.* Chicago: Chicago University Press, 1987.

Speiser, E. A. "Background and function of the Biblical nāśīʾ." *Catholic Biblical Quarterly* 25 (1963) 111–17.

Spottorno Díaz-Caro, Ma Victoria. "El Papiro 967 como Testimonio Prehexaplar de Ezequiel." In *Simposio Biblico Español*, edited by N. Fernández Marcos, 245–53. Madrid: Universidad Complutense, 1984.

Stevenson, Gregory. *Power and Place: Temple and Identity in the Book of Revelation.* Beihefte zur Zeitschrift für die Alttestamentliche Wissenschaft 107. Berlin: De Gruyter, 2001.

Stevenson, Kalinda R. *The Vision of Transformation: The Territorial Rhetoric of Ezekiel 40–48.* Society of Biblical Literature Dissertation Series 154. Atlanta: Scholars, 1996.

Stewart, Alexander. "The Future of Israel, Early Christian Hermeneutics, and the Apocalypse of John." *Journal of the Evangelical Theological Society* 61.3 (2018) 563–75.

Strawn, Brent A. *The Old Testament Is Dying: A Diagnosis and Recommended Treatment.* Grand Rapids: Baker, 2017.

Strine, C. A. "The Role of Repentance in the Book of Ezekiel." *Journal of Theological Studies* 63.2 (2012) 467–91.

Strong, John T. "Grounding Ezekiel's Heavenly Ascent." *Scandinavian Journal of the Old Testament* 26 (2012) 192–211.

Sweeney, Marvin A. *Form and Intertextuality in Prophetic and Apocalyptic Literature.* Forschungen zum Alten Testament 45. Tübingen: Mohr/Siebeck, 2005.

———. *Reading Ezekiel: A Literary and Theological Commentary.* Reading the Old Testament. Macon, GA: Smyth & Helwys, 2013.

Tabb, Brian J. *All Things New: Revelation as Canonical Capstone.* New Studies in Biblical Theology 48. Downers Grove, IL: InterVarsity, 2019.

Talmon, Shemaryahu, and Michael Fishbane. "The Structuring of Biblical Books: Studies in the Book of Ezekiel." *Annual of the Swedish Theological Institute* 10 (1976) 129–53.

Taylor, John B. "The Temple in Ezekiel." In *Heaven on Earth: The Temple in Biblical Theology*, edited by T. Desmond Alexander and Simon Gathercole, 59–70. Carlisle, UK: Paternoster, 2004.

Töniste, Külli. *The Ending of the Canon: A Canonical and Intertextual Reading of Revelation 21–22.* Library of New Testament Studies 526. London: Bloomsbury, 2016.

———. "Measuring the Holy City: Architectural Rhetoric in Revelation 21:9–21." *Conversations with the Biblical World* 34 (2014) 269–93.

Tooman, William A., and Penelope Barter, eds. *Ezekiel: Current Debates and Future Directions*. Forschungen zum Alten Testament 112. Tübingen: Mohr/Siebeck, 2017.

Toy, Crawford H. "On the General Interpretation of Ezek. 40–48." *Journal of Biblical Literature* 50 (1931) xliv–xlvii.

Treier, Daniel J. "Typology." In *DTIB*, 823–27.

Tuell, Steven Shawn. "Divine Presence and Absence in Ezekiel's Prophecy." In *The Book of Ezekiel: Theological and Anthropological Perspectives*, edited by Margaret S. Odell and John T. Strong, 97–116. SBL Symposium Series 9. Atlanta: Society of Biblical Literature, 2000.

———. *Ezekiel*. New International Bible Commentary 16. Peabody, MA: Hendrickson, 2009.

———. "Ezekiel 40–42 as a Verbal Icon." *Catholic Biblical Quarterly* 58 (1996) 649–64.

———. *The Law of the Temple in Ezekiel 40–48*. Harvard Semitic Monographs 49. Atlanta: Scholars, 1992.

———. "The Priesthood of the 'Foreigner': Evidence of Competing Polities in Ezekiel 44:1–14 and Isaiah 56:1–8." In *Constituting the Community: Studies on the Polity of Ancient Israel in Honor of S. Dean McBride, Jr.*, edited by Steven Shawn Tuell, John T. Strong, and S. Dean McBride, 183–204. Winona Lake, IN: Eisenbrauns, 2005.

———. "The Rivers of Paradise: Ezekiel 47.1–12 and Genesis 2.10–14." In *God Who Creates: Essays in Honor of W. Sibley Towner*, edited by William P. Brown and S. Dean McBride Jr., 171–89. Grand Rapids: Eerdmans, 2000.

Um, Stephen. *The Theme of Temple Christology in John's Gospel*. Library of New Testament Studies 312. New York: T. & T. Clark, 2006.

Van Dyke Parunak, Henry. "The Literary Architecture of Ezekiel's *Mar'ot Elohim*." *Journal of Biblical Literature* 99 (1980) 61–74.

———. "Structural Studies in Ezekiel." PhD diss., Harvard University, 1978.

Van Goudoever, Jan. "Ezekiel Sees in Exile a New Temple-City at the Beginning of a Jobel Year." In *Ezekiel and His Book: Textual and Literary Criticism and Their Interrelation*, edited by Johan Lust, 344–49. Leuven: Leuven University Press, 1986.

Vanhoye, Albert. "L'utilisation du Livre d'Ezéchiel dans l'Apocalypse." *Biblica* 43.3 (1962) 436–76.

Vawter, Bruce. "Ezekiel and John." *Catholic Biblical Quarterly* 26 (1964) 450–58.

Vermes, Geza. *The Complete Dead Sea Scrolls in English*. 7th rev. ed. New York: Penguin, 2011.

Vogelgesang, Jeffrey M. "The Interpretation of Ezekiel in the Book of Revelation." PhD diss., Harvard University, 1985.

Von Rad, Gerhard. "Typological Interpretation of the Old Testament." Translated by John Bright. *Interpretation* 15.2 (1961) 174–92.

Walker, Christopher, and Michael B. Dick. *The Induction of the Cult Image in Ancient Mesopotamia: The Mesopotamian Mis Pi Ritual. Transliteration, Translation, and Commentary*. State Archives of Assyria Literary Texts 1. Helsinki: Neo-Assyrian Text Corpus Project, 2001.

Walker, Peter W. L. *Jesus and the Holy City: New Testament Perspectives on Jerusalem*. Grand Rapids: Eerdmans, 1996.

Waltke, Bruce K., with Charles Yu. *An Old Testament Theology: An Exegetical, Canonical, and Thematic Approach*. Grand Rapids: Zondervan, 2007.

Waltke, Bruce K., and Michael O'Connor. *Biblical Hebrew Syntax*. Winona Lake, IN: Eisenbrauns, 1990.

Bibliography

Weinfeld, Moshe. "The Covenant of Grant in the Old Testament and in the Ancient Near East." *The Journal for Ancient and Oriental Studies* 90 (1970) 184–205.

Wellhausen, Julius. *Prolegomena to the History of Ancient Israel*. New York: Meridian, 1957.

———. *Prolegomena zur Geschichte Israels*. 2nd ed. Berlin: George Reimer, 1905.

Wevers, John William. *Ezekiel*. New Century Bible Commentary. Grand Rapids: Eerdmans, 1982.

Whybray, R. N. *Thanksgiving for a Liberated Prophet: An Interpretation of Isaiah 53*. Journal for the Study of the Old Testament Supplement Series 4. Sheffield, UK: Sheffield, 1978.

Woollcombe, K. J. "The Biblical Origins and Patristic Development of Typology." In *Essays on Typology*, 39–75. Studies in Biblical Theology 22. Naperville, IL: Allenson, 1957.

Wu, Daniel Y. *Honor, Shame, and Guilt: Social-Scientific Approaches to the Book of Ezekiel*. Bulletin for Biblical Research Supplements. Winona Lake, IN: Eisenbrauns, 2016.

Yadin, Yigael. *The Temple Scroll*. Vol. 1. Jerusalem: Israel Exploration Society, 1983.

Zimmerli, Walther. "Das 'Gnadenjahr des Herrn.'" In *Archäologie und Altes Testament: Festschrift Kurt Galling*, edited by Arnulf Kuschke and Ernst Kutsch, 321–32. Tübingen: Mohr/Siebeck, 1970.

———. *Erkenntnis Gottes nach dem Buch Ezechiel, eine theologische Studie*. Abhandlungen zur Theologie des Alten und Neuen Testaments 27. Zürich: Zwingli-Verlag, 1954.

———. *Ezekiel 1: A Commentary on the Book of the Prophet Ezekiel, Chapters 1–23*. Translated by Ronald E. Clements. Hermeneia. Philadelphia: Fortress, 1979.

———. *Ezekiel 2: A Commentary on the Book of the Prophet Ezekiel, Chapters 24–48*. Translated by James D. Martin. Hermeneia. Philadelphia: Fortress, 1988.

———. *I Am Yahweh*. Translated by Douglas W. Stott. Atlanta: John Knox, 1982.